LIBRARY OF HEBREW BIBLE/
OLD TESTAMENT STUDIES

717

Formerly Journal for the Study of the Old Testament Supplement Series

Editors
Laura Quick, Oxford University, UK
Jacqueline Vayntrub, Yale University, USA

Founding Editors
David J. A. Clines, Philip R. Davies and David M. Gunn

Editorial Board
Sonja Ammann, Alan Cooper, Steed Davidson, Susan Gillingham,
Rachelle Gilmour, John Goldingay, Rhiannon Graybill, Anne Katrine Gudme,
Norman K. Gottwald, James E. Harding, John Jarick, Tracy Lemos,
Carol Meyers, Eva Mroczek, Daniel L. Smith-Christopher,
Francesca Stavrakopoulou, James W. Watts

CHARACTERS AND CHARACTERIZATION IN THE BOOK OF JUDGES

Edited by
Keith Bodner
and
Benjamin J.M. Johnson

LONDON • NEW YORK • OXFORD • NEW DELHI • SYDNEY

T&T CLARK

Bloomsbury Publishing Plc, 50 Bedford Square, London, WC1B 3DP, UK
Bloomsbury Publishing Inc, 1385 Broadway, New York, NY 10018, USA
Bloomsbury Publishing Ireland, 29 Earlsfort Terrace, Dublin 2, D02 AY28, Ireland

BLOOMSBURY, T&T CLARK and the T&T Clark logo are trademarks
of Bloomsbury Publishing Plc

First published in Great Britain 2024
Paperback edition published 2025

Copyright © Keith Bodner, Benjamin J.M. Johnson and contributors, 2024

Keith Bodner and Benjamin J.M. Johnson have asserted their right under the
Copyright, Designs and Patents Act, 1988, to be identified as Editors of this work.

All rights reserved. No part of this publication may be: i) reproduced or transmitted in
any form, electronic or mechanical, including photocopying, recording or by means of any
information storage or retrieval system without prior permission in writing from the publishers;
or ii) used or reproduced in any way for the training, development or operation of artificial
intelligence (AI) technologies, including generative AI technologies. The rights holders expressly
reserve this publication from the text and data mining exception as per Article 4(3) of the
Digital Single Market Directive (EU) 2019/790.

Unless otherwise indicated, the Scripture quotations contained herein are from The New
Revised Standard Version of the Bible, Anglicized Edition, copyright © 1989, 1995 by the
Division of Christian Education of the National Council of the Churches of Christ in the
United States of America, and are used by permission. All rights reserved.

Bloomsbury Publishing Plc does not have any control over, or responsibility for,
any third-party websites referred to or in this book. All internet addresses given in
this book were correct at the time of going to press. The author and publisher
regret any inconvenience caused if addresses have changed or sites have ceased
to exist, but can accept no responsibility for any such changes.

A catalogue record for this book is available from the British Library.

Library of Congress Cataloging-in-Publication Data

Names: Bodner, Keith, 1967– editor. | Johnson, Benjamin J. M., 1982– editor.
Title: Characters and characterization in the Book of Judges / edited by Keith Bodner
and Benjamin J.M. Johnson.
Description: New York, NY : Continuum International Publishing Group, Inc, 2023. |
Series: The library of Hebrew Bible/Old Testament studies |
Includes bibliographical references. | Summary: "Fills a gap in Hebrew
Bible scholarship by examining the characters and their characterization
in the Book of Judges, particularly focusing on their effect on
storytelling"— Provided by publisher.
Identifiers: LCCN 2023018510 (print) | LCCN 2023018511 (ebook) |
ISBN 9780567700506 (hardback) | ISBN 9780567700537 (paperback) |
ISBN 9780567700513 (ebook)
Subjects: LCSH: Bible. Judges. | Characters and characteristics. | Storytelling.
Classification: LCC BS1302.3 .C537 2023 (print) | LCC BS1302.3 (ebook) |
DDC 222/.3207—dc23/eng/20230831
LC record available at https://lccn.loc.gov/2023018510
LC ebook record available at https://lccn.loc.gov/2023018511

ISBN:	HB:	978-0-5677-0050-6
	PB:	978-0-5677-0053-7
	ePDF:	978-0-5677-0051-3

Series: Library of Hebrew Bible/ Old Testament Studies, volume 717

Typeset by RefineCatch Limited, Bungay, Suffolk

For product safety related questions contact productsafety@bloomsbury.com.

To find out more about our authors and books visit
www.bloomsbury.com and sign up for our newsletters.

CONTENTS

List of Contributors	vii
List of Abbreviations	ix

TIME WOULD FAIL ME TO TELL: AN INTRODUCTION TO
CHARACTER STUDY IN THE BOOK OF JUDGES 1
 Benjamin J.M. Johnson

Chapter 1
HUMOUR, CHARACTERIZATION AND THE THEOLOGY OF JUDGES 11
 Joel Kaminsky

Chapter 2
EHUD AND EGLON: CUNNING BEHAVIOUR IN THE BIBLE 27
 Greger Andersson

Chapter 3
DEBORAH – IF NOT A DELIVERER, WHAT KIND OF LEADER WAS SHE? 41
 Yairah Amit

Chapter 4
BLESSED DESTROYER: THE CHARACTERIZATION OF JAEL AS A
WARRIOR IN COMMAND AND AN INSTRUMENT OF YHWH 55
 Elizabeth H. P. Backfish

Chapter 5
GIDEON: EPIC HERO, BIBLICAL JUDGE AND POLITICAL SUBVERSIVE 75
 Susan Niditch

Chapter 6
THE MAN WHO WOULD BE KING 89
 Benjamin J. M. Johnson

Chapter 7
A GILEADITE RESPONDER: VERBING THE CHARACTER OF JEPHTHAH 105
 Tammi J. Schneider

Chapter 8
JEPHTHAH'S DAUGHTERS, ETHICAL AND UNETHICAL:
CHARACTERIZATION AND ETHICS   119
    David Janzen

Chapter 9
DOMESTICATING SAMSON   133
    Robert S. Kawashima

Chapter 10
DELILAH'S MYSTERIOUS ROLE IN SAMSON'S DESTINY:
THE DYNAMICS OF POWER, KNOWLEDGE AND MYSTERY   147
    Athena E. Gorospe

Chapter 11
SAMSON AS EVERYMAN IN ISRAEL   163
    Gregory T. K. Wong

Chapter 12
MOTHER'S LITTLE HELPER: MICAH AND HIS BIG IDEA   189
    Robin Baker

Chapter 13
A MOTHER, A SON, A LEVITE AND A TRIBE (JUDG. 17–18)   205
    Susanne Gillmayr-Bucher

Chapter 14
"OF ALL THE CHARACTERS IN SCRIPTURE, SHE IS THE LEAST":
THE LEVITE'S CONCUBINE AND THE DISCOURSE OF SILENCE   221
    Francis Landy

Chapter 15
SIX CHARACTERS IN SEARCH OF A DEITY: TALKING ABOUT
GOD IN THE BOOK OF JUDGES   239
    Keith Bodner

AFTERWORD   251
    J. Cheryl Exum

Bibliography   261

CONTRIBUTORS

Yairah Amit, Professor of Bible, Tel-Aviv University

Greger Andersson, Professor of Comparative Literature, Örebro University

Elizabeth H. P. Backfish, Associate Professor, School of Theology & Leadership, William Jessup University

Robin Baker, Emeritus Professor of Old Testament and Ancient Near Eastern Studies, University of Winchester

Keith Bodner, Stuart E. Murray Professor of Religious Studies, Crandall University

J. Cheryl Exum, Professor Emeritus, Sheffield University

Susanne Gillmayr-Bucher, Professor of Biblical Studies/Old Testament, Catholic Private University of Linz

Athena Gorospe, Professor of Biblical Studies, Asian Theological Seminary

David Janzen, Professor of Hebrew Bible/Old Testament, Durham University

Benjamin J. M. Johnson, Associate Professor of Bible, LeTourneau University

Joel Kaminsky, Morningstar Professor of Jewish Studies and Professor of Religion, Smith College

Robert S. Kawashima, Professor of Religion, University of Florida

Francis Landy, Professor Emeritus, University of Alberta

Susan Niditch, Samuel Green Professor of Religion, Amherst College

Tammi J. Schneider, Danforth Professor of Religion, Claremont Graduate University

Gregory T. K. Wong, Associate Professor of Biblical Studies, Evangel Seminary

ABBREVIATIONS

AB	The Anchor Bible
ABD	Freedman, David Noel, ed. *The Anchor Bible Dictionary*. 6 Vols. Garden City, NY: Doubleday, 1992.
ABRL	Anchor Bible Reference Library
AJSLL	*American Journal of Semitic Languages and Literature*
AOAT	Alter Orient und Altes Testament
ATD	Das Alte Testament Deutsch
ATSAT	Arbeiten zu Text und Sprache im Alten Testament
BAR	*Biblical Archaeology Review*
BASOR	*Bulletin of the American Schools of Oriental Research*
BCT	*The Bible and Critical Theory*
BDB	Brown, F., S. R. Driver, and C. A. Briggs. A Hebrew and English Lexicon of the Old Testament. Oxford, 1907.
Bib	*Biblica*
BibInt	*Biblical Interpretation*
BibSac	*Bibliotheca Sacra*
BIS	Biblical Interpretation Series
BMW	Bible in the Modern World
BO	Berit Olam
BSOAS	*Bulletin of the School of Oriental and African Studies*
BTB	Biblical Theology Bulletin
BZ	Biblische Zeitschrift
CBQ	Catholic Biblical Quarterly
CBR	Currents in Biblical Research
CSHJ	Chicago Studies in the History of Judaism
DCH	*Dictionary of Classical Hebrew*. Edited by D. J. A. Clines. Vols. 1–5, Sheffield: Sheffield Academic. Vols. 6–9, Sheffield: Sheffield Phoenix, 1993–2016.
DDD	*Dictionary of Deities and Demons in the Bible*. Edited by Karel van der Toorn, Bob Becking, and Pieter W. van der Horst. Leiden: Brill, 1995. 2nd rev. ed. Grand Rapids: Eerdmans, 1999.
EDB	*Eerdmans Dictionary of the Bible*. Edited by David Noel Freedman. Grand Rapids: Eerdmans, 2000
ETR	*Etudes théologiques et religieuses*
FCB	Feminist Companion to the Bible
HALOT	Koehler, L., W. Baumgartner, and J. J. Stamm, *The Hebrew and Aramaic Lexicon of the Old Testament*. Translated and edited under the supervision of M. E. J. Richardson. 4 vols. Leiden, 1994–1999.
HBM	Hebrew Bible Monographs
HBT	*Horizons of Biblical Theology*
HS	*Hebrew Scriptures*

HSM	Harvard Semitic Monographs
ICC	International Critical Commentary
IEJ	*Israel Exploration Journal*
Int	*Interpretation*
JAAR	*Journal of the American Academy of Religion*
JBL	*Journal of Biblical Literature*
JFSR	*Journal of Feminist Studies in Religion*
JHS	*Journal of Hebrew Scriptures*
JNES	*Journal of Near Eastern Studies*
JSJSup	Journal for the Study of Judaism in the Persian, Hellenistic, and Roman Periods Supplement Series
JSOTSup	Journal for the Study of the Old Testament Supplement Series
KEL	Kregel Exegetical Library
LHBOTS	Library of Hebrew Bible and Old Testament Studies
NAC	New American Commentary
NCBC	New Cambridge Bible Commentary
NICOT	New International Commentary on the Old Testament
NIDOTTE	*New International Dictionary of Old Testament Theology and Exegesis*. Edited by W. A. VanGemeren. 5 vols. Grand Rapids, 1997.
NIVAC	The NIV Application Commentary
OBT	Overtures to Biblical Theology
OTL	Old Testament Library
RTR	*Reformed Theological Review*
SBLDS	Society of Biblical Literature Dissertation Series
SJOT	*Scandinavian Journal of the Old Testament*
TDOT	*Theological Dictionary of the Old Testament*. Edited by G. J. Botterweck and H. Ringgren. Translated by J. T. Willis, G. W. Bromiley, and D. E. Green. 8 vols. Grand Rapids: MI: Eerdmans, 1974–2006.
TLOT	*Theological Lexicon of the Old Testament*. Edited by E. Jenni, with assistance from C. Westermann. Translated by M. E. Biddle. 2 Vols. Peabody, MA: Hendrickson, 1997.
TynBul	*Tyndale Bulletin*
UF	*Ugarit-Forschungen*
VT	*Vetus Testamentum*
VTSup	Vetus Testamentum Supplement Series
WBC	Word Biblical Commentary
ZAW	*Zeitschrift für die alttestamentliche Wissenschaft*

Time Would Fail Me to Tell: An Introduction to Character Study in the Book of Judges

Benjamin J.M. Johnson

Perhaps no book of the Hebrew Bible is so full of memorable and outlandish characters as the book of Judges. From Ehud, the left-handed assassin, to Jael, the household warrior, to Gideon, the idol-hacking, trumpet-blowing, timid warrior, to the villainy of Abimelech, to the sacrificial vows of Jephthah, to the wild adventures of Samson, the book of Judges is replete with unbelievable characters and their stories. Furthermore, as I will suggest in this introductory essay, perhaps no book of the Hebrew Bible is as dependent upon character analysis for understanding its rhetorical thrust as the book of Judges. An example of this can be seen by the two most recent surveys of scholarship.[1] Both of these surveys group the majority of their study by the various characters in Judges (Ehud, Deborah, Gideon etc.). While the literary make-up of the book makes this an obvious way to survey the scholarship on the book, it nevertheless makes the point that the study of the book of Judges is dominated by a study of its characters. We will further see the importance of character study of Judges below, but this point will suffice for now.

Much scholarship on the book of Judges has been fueled by Martin Noth's thesis of the Deuteronomistic History.[2] The interest in Judges from this perspective tended toward the atomistic: the parts are more interesting than the whole. Questions are asked about where individual texts fit within the various theories of redaction and less how the work of Judges fits together as a whole. As Mark O'Brien notes, 'advocates of the Deuteronomistic History hypothesis have tended to

---

1. Kenneth M. Craig, Jr., 'Judges in Recent Research,' *CBR* 1.2 (2003): 159–85; and Kelly J. Murphy, 'Judges in Recent Research,' *CBR* 15.2 (2017): 179–213.

2. Martin Noth, *The Deuteronomistic History* (JSOTSup 15; Sheffield: JSOT Press, 1981). For a survey of research on Judges in light of the Deuteronomistic History hypothesis, see Mark A. O'Brien, 'Judges and the Deuteronomistic History,' in *The History of Israel's Traditions: The Heritage of Martin Noth* (S. L. McKenzie and M. P. Graham, eds; JSOTSup 182; Sheffield: Sheffield Academic Press, 1994), 235–59.

become preoccupied with the nature and extent of the deuteronomistic redaction to the neglect of the stories and their relationship to this redaction.'[3]

Recent scholarship, however, has had a much greater interest in Judges as a literary whole. The work of J. P. U. Lilley represents an early example of study along this vein.[4] Lilley argued that the book as a whole had a 'general theme ... of increasing failure and depression.'[5] Numerous studies along this line have followed. Barry Webb's analysis argued that the literary framework of the book of Judges showed the 'progressive deterioration in Israel's condition, in relation to Yahweh, in relation to Israel's enemies, and in relation to Israel's own internal stability.'[6] Lillian Klein has argued that Judges as a whole is laced with irony and that irony is significant for understanding the rhetorical purpose of the book. This observation is based on the movement from the relatively non-ironic start to the book under Joshua and Othniel, through the more ironic left-handed assassin, the female warriors of Jael and Deborah, to the increased irony in Gideon's story, to the tragic irony of the conclusion.[7] Robert O'Connell argued that the narrative structuring and characterizing of the various deliverers serve the purpose of the book which is to uphold a vision for a Judahite king against other non-Judahite or foreign kings.[8] Others have seen the decline pictured in Judges as less of a political one and more of a spiritual one. Daniel Block has argued that the theme of the book is the 'Canaanization of Israelite society during the period of the settlement.'[9]

Not all, however, have held to the literary coherence of the book or the argument that the narrative portrays a progressive decline in Israel as signified by progressively negative characterization of the various judges. In a recent commentary, R. J. Ryan

---

3. O'Brien, 'Judges and the Deuteronomistic History,' 248. O'Brien is here summarizing an argument of Baruch Halpern, *The First Historians: The Hebrew Bible and History* (San Francisco: Harper & Row, 1988).

4. J. P. U. Lilley, 'A Literary Appreciation of the Book of Judges,' *TynBul* 18 (1967): 94–102.

5. Ibid., 102.

6. Barry G. Webb, *The Book of Judges: An Integrated Reading* (JSOTSup 46; Sheffield: JSOT Press, 1987), 176.

7. Lillian R. Klein, *The Triumph of Irony in the Book of Judges* (JSOTSup 68; Sheffield: Almond Press, 1988), esp. 17–21. Klein notes that in these stories we see 'ironic inversions of leaders, of judges' (p. 21).

8. Robert H. O'Connell, *The Rhetoric of the Book of Judges* (Leiden: Brill, 1996), 1. Numerous other studies have seen a pro-Davidic or anti-Saulide thread in the book of Judges. For example, Marc Brettler, 'The Book of Judges: Literature as Politics,' *JBL* 108 (1989): 395–418; Gale A. Yee, 'Ideological Criticism: Judges 17–21 and the Dismembered Body,' in *Judges and Method* (ed. Gale A. Yee; Minneapolis, MN: Fortress Press, 1995), 138–60; and Marvin A. Sweeney, 'Davidic Polemic in the Book of Judges,' *VT* 47 (1997): 517–29.

9. Daniel I. Block, *Judges, Ruth* (NAC 6; Nashville, TN: B&H, 1999), 58. See further Daniel I. Block, 'The Period of the Judges: Religious Disintegration under Tribal Rule,' in *Israel's Apostasy and Restoration: Essays in Honor of R. K. Harrison* (ed. A. Gileadi; Grand Rapids, MI: Baker, 1988), 39–58.

has argued that the narrator is explicitly critical of Israel as is seen in the repeated refrain that 'Israel did evil in the sight of the Lord' (Judg. 2:11; 3:7, 12; 4:1; 6:1; 10:6; 13:1). However, the narrator is not explicitly critical of the judge-deliverer characters. Instead, he argues that Judges 'uniquely presents the view that the characters who are raised up to deliver Israel from oppressors neither participate in, nor contribute to, what scholars refer to as Israel's moral and religious decline'.[10]

Another reading that is at least sympathetic to the characterization of the judges is Gregory Mobley's *The Empty Men*.[11] In this study Mobley recontextualizes the Judges narrative away from 'a religious history by Exilic theologians to that of an early Iron Age martial practice and heroic storytelling'.[12] By doing that, Mobley offers a more sympathetic reading of characters like Ehud, Gideon and Samson.

In a different vein, Greger Andersson has argued against the synchronic literary interpretation of the Book of Judges that we surveyed above on narratological grounds.[13] He argues that the autonomous nature of the individual stories within the book of Judges resists the kind of overarching narrative theme that is often suggested by those he calls 'synchronists' who interpret the book as a whole. Thus, for example, those who read the book of Judges as a whole frequently see Samson as a failure. Whereas, according to Andersson, if Samson's story is read in its own right it 'could therefore be described as a classic adventure story; and Samson, like Jacob (Gen. 25–33), can be compared to the hero figure of adventure stories'.[14]

What is significant about the various views of the book of Judges surveyed above is how dependent they are upon analysis of the characterization of the judges. On the one hand, the case for seeing a coherent narrative that depicts the progressive downward spiral of Israel is partially based on the characterization of the judges. It requires seeing Othniel as a paradigmatic judge who does no more or less than what is required of these judge figures. It sees Gideon as a judge who marks a turning point, who has a promising start but questionable finish to his career and whose son is the most negatively portrayed character in the book.

---

10. R. J. Ryan, *Judges* (Readings: A New Biblical Commentary; Sheffield: Sheffield Phoenix Press, 2007), 234. For a succinct critique of his position see, David J. H. Beldman, *The Completion of Judges: Strategies of Ending in Judges 17–21* (Siphrut; 21; Winona Lake, IN: Eisenbrauns, 2017), 42–45.

11. Gregory Mobley, *The Empty Men: The Heroic Tradition of Ancient Israel* (New York: Doubleday, 2005).

12. Ibid., 9.

13. Greger Andersson, *The Book and Its Narratives: A Critical Examination of Some Synchronic Studies of the Book of Judges* (Örebro Studies in Literary History and Criticism 1; Örebro: Universitetsbiblioteket, 2001). For a critique of Andersson's perspective see Gregory T. K. Wong, 'Narratives and Their Contexts: A Critique of Gregor Andersson With Respect to Narrative Autonomy,' *SJOT* 20.2 (2006): 216–30. For Andersson's response, see his 'A Narratologist's Critical Reflections on Synchronic Studies of the Bible: A Response to Gregory T. K. Wong,' *SJOT* 21.2 (2007): 261–74.

14. Andersson, *The Book and Its Narratives*, 175.

After Gideon, the judges appear more and more questionable.[15] Finally, the character of Samson is seen as something like the polar opposite of Othniel[16] or at least a climactic failure of the office of judgeship.[17] On the other hand, the case that resists this reading is largely based on characterization as well. Ryan's point that the narrative is clearly condemnatory of the Israelite idolatry but not of the judges' behaviour is one of characterization. Mobley's decision to read the narrative in the context of ancient heroic tradition is also an issue of characterization. Finally, Andersson's claim that the individual narratives resist the kind of coherent synchronic reading suggested by many scholars is a claim that the individual characters resist the theory-laden readings that are put on them.

It seems, then, that how one reads the book of Judges is very dependent upon how one sees this varied, provocative, and outlandish cast of characters.

In addition to being particularly significant for the study of Judges, the study of characterization is of vital significance for the study of biblical narrative generally. I have argued elsewhere that how one views a particular character is often an interpretive crux for how one interprets the biblical narrative,[18] or may even impact the very perceived genre of a text.[19] As we have seen in the above survey, that case can also be made for the book of Judges. How one perceives the characterization of the various judges greatly affects how one sees the story and its purpose. As Mieke Bal has noted, '[c]haracter is intuitively the most crucial category of narrative, and also most subject to projection and fallacies'.[20] Thus, we would do well to attend closely to characters and characterization in biblical narrative.

I will offer two examples that substantiate the importance of character study in the narrative of the Hebrew Bible. The first is April Westbrook's study of the place

---

15. This point was made by D. W. Gooding, 'The Composition of the Book of Judges,' *Eretz-Israel* 16 (1982): 70–79; but has been followed by numerous scholars since then. E.g., Webb, *Book of Judges*, 157–58; J. Cheryl Exum, 'The Centre Cannot Hold: Thematic and Textual Instabilities in Judges,' *CBQ* 52.3 (1990): 412; and J. Paul Tanner, 'The Gideon Narrative as the Focal Point of Judges,' *BibSac* 149 (1992): 146–61.

16. So Webb, *The Book of Judges*, 170–71.

17. E.g. O'Connell, *Rhetoric of Judges*, 224; Yairah Amit, *The Book of Judges: The Art of Editing* (BIS 38; Leiden: Brill, 1999), 267; Tammi J. Schneider, *Judges* (BO; Collegeville, MN: Liturgical Press, 1999), 193.

18. Benjamin J. M. Johnson, 'Character as Interpretive Crux in the Book of Samuel,' in *Characters and Characterization in the Book of Samuel* (LHBOTS 669; ed. Keith Bodner and Benjamin J. M. Johnson; London: Bloomsbury T&T Clark, 2020), 1–13.

19. Benjamin J. M. Johnson, 'An Unapologetic Apology: The David Story as a Complex Response to Monarchy,' in *The Book of Samuel and Its Response to Monarchy* (ed. Sara Kipfer, and Jeremy Hutton; Stuttgart: W. Kohlhammer, 2021), 225–42.

20. Mieke Bal, *Narratology: Introduction to the Theory of Narrative* (3rd ed.; Toronto: University of Toronto Press, 2009), 113.

of female characters in the story of David in Samuel and Kings.[21] Westbrook analyses what she calls a 'woman story pattern' in the Book of Samuel, which is the placement of women stories 'at strategic points within the unfolding political progression of David's life'.[22] In her analysis she argues that inclusion of these female characters, 'provides vital information that is often disconcerting in nature, but completely necessary for a balanced view of this charismatic and easily idealized king whose story might have convinced someone that monarchy is a great idea, without their constant reminders concerning the darker side of this all too human ruler'.[23] In other words, attending to the stories of these women and their characterization is essential for understanding the characterization of David, the narrative significance of 1–2 Samuel, and the view of monarchy in this story.[24]

Another recent example of the significance of characterization in biblical literature is John Barton's essay, 'Characterization and Ethics'.[25] In this essay Barton argues for the importance of narrative for ethical formation and the significance characters play in that engagement with narrative. 'The characters in biblical narrative,' he argues, 'illustrate moral truths. They may serve as terrible warnings ... but they may also show us what a really well-lived life would be like.'[26] But Barton pushes beyond this simple classification of positive or negative characterization. He argues that, 'in presenting ... characters as round, the biblical authors themselves challenge us to read them in a more complex way' and that the 'moral complexity of the round characters needs to be taken into account.'[27] An example of dealing with this complexity is Gordon Wenham's work on the ethical significance of biblical narrative.[28] In one instance Wenham engages with the disagreement between Meir Sternberg and David Gunn and Danna Fewell on the

---

21. April D. Westbrook, *'And He Will Take Your Daughters. . .' Woman Story and the Ethical Evaluation of Monarchy in the David Narrative* (LHBOTS 610; London: Bloomsbury T&T Clark, 2015).

22. Ibid., 21.

23. Ibid., 230.

24. Although there is no attempt to argue for a sort of 'woman story pattern' in Judges, the contributions on the various female characters in this volume from Yairah Amit's chapter on Deborah, to Elizabeth Backfish's contribution on Jael, to David Janzen's chapter on Jephthah's daughters, to Athena Gorospe's chapter on Delilah, and Francis Landy's chapter on the Levite's concubine all highlight the significance of the female characters in the Book of Judges.

25. John Barton, 'Characterization and Ethics,' in *Characters and Characterization in the Book of Kings* (LHBOTS 670; ed. Keith Bodner and Benjamin J. M. Johnson; London: Bloomsbury T&T Clark, 2020), 1–16.

26. Barton, 'Characterization and Ethics,' 3.

27. Ibid., 4.

28. Gordon J. Wenham, *Story as Torah: Reading Old Testament Ethically* (London: T&T Clark, 2000), 109–19.

interpretation of the rape of Dinah in Genesis 34.²⁹ As Wenham points out, Sternberg argues that the narrative characterizes the actions of Simeon and Levi as justifiable and the inaction of Jacob as problematic.³⁰ On the other side, is the reading of Fewell and Gunn, who counter Sternberg's reading point-by-point, not seeing Simeon and Levi as any sort of heroes and seeing at least 'a measure of sympathy' for Jacob, Hamor and Shechem.³¹ Wenham uses the differing interpretations of Sternberg on the one hand and Fewell and Gunn on the other to highlight the complexity of engaging with biblical narrative ethically. He concludes from this exchange and from his own reading of the rape of Dinah that 'no one comes out of this episode very creditably on the Israelite side'.³² Thus, for Wenham, the characterization of the various actors in this story is resistant to a simple moralistic reading. To return to Barton's point, we see here the issue of engaging with the complex characterization that can be found in biblical narrative. As Barton concludes his essay:

> The more highly developed biblical characters are far from being simple or obvious, and in thinking about their lives and deeds we can reflect on morality in a three-dimensional way, not resting content with a simple moralism but going on to think about the ways in which ethics is concerned with grey areas.³³

---

29. Meir Sternberg's initial reading can be found in his, *The Poetics of Biblical Narrative: Ideological Literature and the Drama of Reading* (Bloomington, IN: Indiana University Press, 1985), 445-75. Danna N. Fewell and David M. Gunn respond to Sternberg's reading in 'Tipping the Balance: Sternberg's Reader and the Rape of Dinah,' *JBL* 110 (1991): 193-211. Sternberg responded in another article, 'Biblical Poetics and Sexual Politics: From Reading to Counterreading,' *JBL* 111 (1992): 463-88. For an attempt to adjudicate between the two, see Paul Noble, 'A "Balanced" Reading of the Rape of Dinah: Some Exegetical and Methodological Observations,' *BibInt* 4 (1996): 173-203.

30. Sternberg, *Poetics of Biblical Narrative*, calls Jacob, on the one hand, 'the tale's least sympathetic character' while calling Simeon and Levi, 'the most intricate, colorful, and attractive characters in the story' (p. 473). Though, Sternberg's final analysis sees the story as more open ended, arguing that, 'The dilemma raised by the story is so complex and each choice so problematic that [the reader] cannot fully identify with any of the positions taken' (p. 475).

31. See their conclusion, 'Tipping the Balance,' 211.

32. Wenham, *Story as Torah*, 119.

33. Barton, 'Characterization and Ethics,' 16. For a sustained example of the kind of reading Barton is suggesting, see S. Min Chun, 'To Reform or Not to Reform: Characterization and Ethical Reading of Josiah in Kings,' in *Characters and Characterization in the Book of Kings* (LHBOTS 670; ed. Keith Bodner and Benjamin J. M. Johnson; London: Bloomsbury T&T Clark, 2020), 250-68. David Janzen's chapter, 'Jephthah's Daughters, Ethical and Unethical: Characterization and Ethics' in the present volume also follows the call for the kind of ethical reading that Barton describes.

Attending to characters and their characterization is thus an essential task in understanding biblical narrative. We have seen its significance in the arguments about the nature of the book of Judges. We have also seen how characters and characterization can affect biblical narrative generally. We have seen how the presence and significance of female characters and their characterization can shape a narrative. We have seen how significant characterization is for ethical engagement with biblical narratives. What remains now for the present volume is to engage in studies of the various characters to be found in the book of Judges.

To that end, Joel Kaminsky, opens this volume with a study of humour that can be found throughout the stories in the book of Judges. As he notes, there is an ever growing attention to the humour that can be found in biblical narrative. Kaminsky argues that not only does the humour of these stories entertain but that it 'highlights the limited human perspective we generally occupy and reveals how God's transcendent perspective can shatter our worldview'.[34] Greger Andersson analyses the story of Ehud and argues that if it is allowed to stand as a coherent and meaningful narrative on its own, without outside interpretive frameworks imposed upon it, then Ehud is characterized as 'a hero who deceives and defeats his mightier opponent and delivers his own people'.[35] His reading contrasts with some who see Ehud's actions as unethical.[36]

Yairah Amit offers an analysis of Deborah. She notes that it is easy to make more of Deborah than the text may allow. Nevertheless, she argues that though she 'was not a deliverer, she was a highly gifted leader, charismatic, wise, and functioning as both a prophetess and a judge in the judicial sense'.[37] She was, in Amit's words, 'sufficiently wise to decide what to do, when to do it, and how to do it'.[38] Following Amit's study of Deborah, Elizabeth Backfish offers a study of the other major female character in Judges 4–5, the tent-peg-wielding Jael. She notes that not only is Jael depicted as a warrior, as others have noted, she is also depicted as an instrument of the God of Israel, making the final note about her in Deborah's song that she is both 'blessed' and a 'destroyer' (Judg 5:24a, 27c) particularly on point.

The next two chapters offer readings of the stories of Gideon and his son Abimelech. Susan Niditch offers an analysis of Gideon that sees him in the context of epic heroes. As we noted above, there is a tendency to read Gideon as a largely negative character who is a turning point in the book of Judges. But like Gregory Mobley, who reads Judges in the context of heroic literature, Niditch sees Gideon as a 'traditional typological figure who might be compared to swashbuckling heroes in culture-reinforcing and self-defining epic accounts world-wide'.[39] Niditch

---

34. Kaminsky, 'Humor Characterization, and Theology in Judges,' 26.
35. Andersson, 'Ehud and Eglon: Cunning Behavior in the Bible,' 39.
36. Andersson, cites E. T. A. Davidson, *Intricacy, Design and Cunning in the Book of Judges* (Philadelphia: Xlibris, 2008), 109, and Lillian Klein, *The Triumph of Iron*, 46, as examples.
37. Amit, 'Deborah – Savior or Leader?' 41.
38. Ibid., 53.
39. Niditch, 'Epic Hero, Biblical Judge,' 75.

thus argues that Gideon can be read in this epic tradition rather than the moralism that some readers may force on him. In a different vein, however, Benjamin Johnson offers an analysis of Gideon's son, Abimelech, that is not so sympathetic. He sees Abimelech as an antagonist of Israel who takes the place in the narrative of foreign oppressors. Furthermore, as Israel's first experiment with kingship, the negative characterization of Abimelech cannot help but sound a warning note for Israel's future monarchy; not least in the fact that Jotham's parable further criticizes those who are looking for a king as well.

Turning to the Jephthah episode, Tammi Schneider offers an analysis of Jephthah that attends to what she calls '"verbing the character" where the character is examined by how they are described; instances where they are the subject of a verb; the object of a verb or a clause.'[40] Though much scholarship on Jephthah is focused on the horrible instance of his vow and sacrifice of his daughter, Schneider argues that the bulk of narrative material focuses on his work of negotiation. David Janzen, then offers an analysis of Jephthah's daughter. He offers two different portrayals of the character of Jephthah's daughter. One is the reading in which Jephthah's daughter recognizes the tragedy of her situation but sees the ethical thing to do as submitting to her father's vow. Janzen finds this reading ethically problematic. He offers another reading, however, 'in which she is aware of the ethical shortcomings of her father and other powerful social figures and dedicates her life to a protest of an unjust social system'.[41]

Three essays focus on the Samson cycle. Robert Kawashima analyzes Samson as an ambiguous and liminal character who 'is not so much a hero as an anti-hero ... who achieves certain "heroic" deeds by accident, or even in spite of himself'.[42] Athena Gorospe offers an analysis of the character of Delilah. She argues that Delilah functions as something like a 'counterpart of the mysterious divine visitor at Samson's birth'.[43] She functions, according to Gorospe, as an 'instrument of God's discipline and correction to a servant who has missed his calling'.[44] Finally, Gregory Wong studies the characterization of Samson and his relationship to other aspects of the book of Judges. Samson is seen as a flat character for Wong, which allows him to view Samson typologically as standing in for Israel. He shows how Samson's story breaks some aspects of the Judges cycle. This fact and a rhetorical link 'that shows Samson going for what was right in his own eyes'[45] allows Samson's story to act as a bridge between the main section of Judges (chapters 3–16) and the conclusion (chapters 17–21).

The final section of the book of Judges is the infamous set of stories that sit outside the cycle of judges that dominated the book in chapters 3–16. The first

---

40. Schneider, 'Jephthah: A Gileadite Responder,' 105.
41. Janzen, 'Jephthah's Daughters,' 127.
42. Kawashima, 'Domesticating Samson,' 133.
43. Gorospe, 'Delilah's Mysterious Role,' 147.
44. Ibid., 161.
45. Wong, 'Samson as Everyman,' 187.

chapter is Robin Baker's study of the character of Micah. As Baker notes, this section of Judges has probably received less attention than much of the book. However, Baker argues, 'in the mind of the Judges writer, Micah and his circle do not merit their relative obscurity. What they do deserve just as much as other unsavory characters he parades before us is infamy.'[46] Micah's story, Baker suggests, further makes the point 'that we are no different from him: ordinary persons whose impact will be determined by the choices we make and by the standards we adhere to.'[47] Susanne Gilmayr-Bucher follows up Baker's study of Micah by attending to the way that Micah, his mother, the Levite, and the Danites are intertwined in their characterization.[48] Finally, Francis Landy turns to examine the character of the nameless *pilegesh* in Judges 19. Landy follows Rhiannon Graybill in offering an 'unhappy' reading of the story,[49] highlighting the kind of story that 'sticks with the details of the story however horrible so as *not* to leave it behind'.[50] Landy gives focus to this character who is otherwise 'so entirely eclipsed by the narrative'.[51]

The final essay in this volume is Keith Bodner's study of God-talk. He looks at the characterization of God through the way that various characters speak of him. In this contribution he gives a concise review of much of the narrative material that has already been surveyed but with a specific focus on how God is characterized through others' speech. In the strictest definition of the word, therefore, Bodner offers a preliminary *theology* of Judges.

The present volume is concluded by Cheryl Exum's reflections on the studies offered here. She notes some of the tendencies that can be found in the various studies. Most of all, she recognizes that more work needs to be done. She especially calls us to go beyond the kinds of readings offered in this volume and offer resistant or critical readings. Having surveyed the various studies of the characterization of these various figures in the book of Judges, Exum challenges us to go further and to dare to take issue with the ideology of the book of Judges, to raise questions about the problem of 'othering' that this book raises. Her final words are a call for readers not to be satisfied with describing the biblical text but to go beyond and engage with it.

We have now reached a point where I sympathize with the writer of Hebrews. For I agree that 'time would fail me to tell of Gideon, Barak, Samson, Jephthah' (Heb. 11:32). I will, therefore, let the contributors to this volume take up that call.

---

46. Baker, 'Mother's Little Helper,' 191.

47. Ibid., 203.

48. Cf. my comments on what I have called 'character contingency' ('Character as Interpretive Crux,' esp. 5).

49. Rhiannon Graybill, *Texts after Terror: Rape, Sexual Violence, & the Hebrew Bible* (Oxford: Oxford University Press, 2021).

50. Landy, 'Of All the Characters in Scripture,' 222.

51. Ibid., 221.

Chapter 1

HUMOUR, CHARACTERIZATION AND THE
THEOLOGY OF JUDGES[1]

Joel S. Kaminsky

There are a host of humorous elements in the book of Judges, a number of which serve more than just an aesthetic function. These include the use of irony, satire, witty repartee and gender and ethnic humour among others.[2] One of the difficulties in exploring humour in an ancient text is attempting to distinguish between what we find amusing today and situations/narrative elements that actually might have been humorous to the ancient audience addressed by the text.[3] For example, the NRSV translates Judg. 14:6 as follows:

---

1. I would like to thank this volume's editors Ben Johnson and Keith Bodner along with Allison Hurst at Harvard University and my student assistant Caterina Baffa for their helpful comments and critiques on earlier drafts of this essay, even if at times I chose to ignore their sage advice.

2. My intention here is to explore various types and instances of humour found Judges and when relevant show how they affected the characterization of specific actors or the narrative structure of certain stories in Judges. I have not found arguments that the whole book is controlled by a single ideological or narrative outlook on the whole persuasive. Similarly, I am sceptical of those seeking to read the whole book through a particular genre of humour. Thus, while Adrian Bledstein's, 'Is Judges a Woman's Satire of Men who play God,' in *A Feminist Companion to Judges* (ed. Athalya Brenner; Sheffield: JSOT Press, 1993), 34–54, makes several excellent points, her attempt to read each narrative including short snippets relating to the so-called minor judges as satiric is quite forced and unconvincing.

3. There is growing interest in exploring humour in the Bible. For some broader surveys of this topic the reader might look at the following books: Mark E. Biddle, *A Time to Laugh: Humor in the Bible* (Macon, GA: Smyth & Helwys, 2013); Melissa A. Jackson, *Comedy and Feminist Interpretation of the Hebrew Bible: A Subversive Collaboration* (Oxford: Oxford University Press, 2012); *On Humour and the Comic in the Hebrew Bible* (JSOTSup 92; ed. Yehuda T. Radday and Athalya Brenner; Sheffield: Almond, 1990); J. William Whedbee, *The Bible and the Comic Vision* (Cambridge: Cambridge University Press, 1998).

The spirit of the LORD rushed on him, and he tore the lion apart barehanded as one might tear apart a kid. But he did not tell his father or his mother what he had done.

A contemporary audience might well laugh at the comparison this verse makes (assuming the NRSV translation is the most accurate rendering, a point that could be contested) because today few modern readers tear apart butchered livestock with their own two hands. Inasmuch as the humour found here is created by the distance between our setting and the biblical one, one can likely rule out this as an instance of the intentional deployment of humour by the biblical authors.

Humour in the Ehud/Eglon Narrative

However, Judges is filled with instances that many scholars believe the ancient authors intended to be humorous. A fairly straightforward example is the Ehud story. First, there are certain surface features of this passage that are humorous. In particular, one thinks of the narrator's repetition of Ehud's announcement that he has a secret message, or as he says the second time, a message from God for Eglon (Judg. 3:19-20). This message comes in the form of a dagger slyly delivered into Eglon's belly by Ehud's left hand.

But a closer reading of the Hebrew text suggests a number of other possible humorous elements including forms of humour tied up in the way the text depicts certain characters. Thus, it seems highly probable that the name given to the Moabite king, Eglon, is intended to call to mind the Hebrew word for a calf. In fact, in Judg. 3:17 we are told that Eglon was a very fat or perhaps a well-fed man. If so, then Eglon may be depicted as a fatted calf prepared for the slaughter in a manner that would have been viewed as humorous by the ancient Israelite audience.[4] It is true that in the ancient Near East sometimes warriors had or took on animal names. Thus Caleb, an Israelite figure involved in several military accounts, has a name that means 'dog'. However, the probability that Eglon's name and the way the text characterizes him were designed to evoke humour is bolstered by the fact that several other words that often occur in the context of ritual sacrifice are employed in the description of Ehud's bringing of the Israelite tribute to Eglon. In particular,

---

4. James K. Aitken, 'Fat Eglon,' in *Studies on the Text and Versions of the Hebrew Bible in Honour of Robert Gordon* (ed. Geoffrey Khan and Diana Lipton; Leiden: Brill, 2012), 141-53, notes that we cannot presume that the ancient audience had the equivalent of contemporary humour about fat people. However, Aitken acknowledges that the text is likely depicting the humour of Eglon as well fed on Israelite tribute and thus a fitting sacrificial offering, which is in line with the reading pursued here. Aitken also notes a possible connection between Eglon and Eli in 1 Sam. 4:18, which might be further reinforced by noting that Eli's sons regularly took the fat portions of Israelite sacrifices that belonged to God for their own dinner tables (see 1 Sam. 2:12-17).

the causative form of the verb קרב used to describe Ehud's delivery of the tribute is somewhat unusual in this context. The Hebrew phrasing found at the beginning of verse 17 and again repeated in similar form in verse 18 could carry a secondary meaning one might render into English as 'He [Ehud] offered/finished offering the vegetable offering' since the Hebrew word for tribute (מנחה) is identical to the word for the vegetable offering that frequently accompanied an animal sacrifice. Thus, the author may be implying that Eglon is the animal offering that accompanied the vegetable one. This is a role he is well suited to fulfil inasmuch as the text characterizes him as a very fat (or perhaps a well-fed) man by using the Hebrew word בריא, a word used in Gen. 41:2 to describe the seven 'sleek and fat' cows that Pharaoh saw in his dream. Equally possible is that the text is implying that Israel's tribute was fattening up Eglon, the calf-named king, who was about to be sacrificed to Israel's deity.

The narrative contains additional more subtle allusions to bodily humour surrounding eating, being overweight, and probably bathroom humour as well. For example, earlier in 3:16 the Hebrew describing Ehud's double-edged sword can be rendered more literally as it had 'two mouths' evoking a scene of reversal in which the enemy who was eating the wealth of the Israelites is to be consumed by Ehud's weapon. Several other elements in this story suggest that the text is mocking both Eglon and other Moabites for being fat. When Ehud stabs Eglon, the text reports that the fat closed over the blade and the hilt of the knife. While the meaning of the final Hebrew word used in 3:22 is unclear, many believe that it refers to faeces seeping out from the wounded Eglon's intestines or from the release of his anal sphincter upon his demise. Note that in the following verses his servants wait outside his locked chamber door because they think he is relieving himself due to the fact that his door was locked and quite possibly because the smell indicated that he was defecating.[5] In addition, 3:29 describes the defeated Moabite warriors with a somewhat unusual usage of the word שמן, usually translated as 'stout' in this instance but more commonly meaning 'fat'. This description of the Moabite warriors echoes the text's earlier emphasis of Eglon's corpulent or well-fed state (Judg. 3:17, 22). Thus, one axis of the humour in this narrative involves the following three themes: latent sacrificial language, an ethnic stereotype of Moabites as fat or well fed on Israelite tribute and somewhat mentally dense, and the use of some bathroom humour.[6] Clearly, humorous stereotypes play an important part in

---

5. Baruch Halpern has revealed the fuller extent of possible bathroom humour in this story although his claim that Ehud escaped through a second-floor toilet is somewhat speculative. Baruch Halpern, *The First Historians* (San Francisco: Harper & Row, 1988), 39–75, esp. 58.

6. One can see a connection between fatness and being imperceptive in other texts such as Isa. 6:10. On the ethnic dimensions of the humour deployed in the Ehud narrative see Lowell K. Handy, 'Uneasy laughter: Ehud and Eglon as ethnic humor,' *SJOT*, 6.2 (1992): 233–46. Handy points to yet additional more ethnic humorous touches such as the fact that the Moabite soldiers not only allow Ehud to escape by waiting so long to unlock Eglon's private room door (Judg. 3:23-26), but that they also let the Israelites capture the Moabite side of the Jordan river and kill all the fleeing Moabite soldiers (Judg. 3:28).

how Eglon, the Moabites who attend to him, and the Moabite warriors who fight for him are characterized within Judges 3. In fact, Handy argues that not only is it possible that 'the name Eglon should be taken as an invention of the author' but the whole story is by genre an 'ethnic joke' which was designed to be 'insulting to the Moabites while simultaneously being an example of the cleverness of the Israelites'.[7]

There is evidence of yet an even more subtle sexual form of humour in this account. There are a number of overlapping phrases and verbal cues shared between the Ehud story and Judges 19–20, the latter narrating the rape and murder of the Levite's concubine. These include both the Ehud and the Levite's concubine stories describe acts of penetration that shortly eventuate in the death of the victim, involve a closed doorway, and relate a discovery of a dead or dying person once a door is opened.[8] In Hebrew the linkage is more noticeable yet, in that the plural construct דלתות 'doors' occurs only four times in Judges, thrice in the Eglon story (3:23, 24, 25) and once in Judg. 19:27. Furthermore, both stories utilize three quickly echoing forms of words built out of the root פתח 'to open' (Judges 3 contains all three in verse 24, and Judges 19 has one in verse 26 and two more in verse 27). In some ways the two stories are inversions of each other. In both stories the person called master or lord is locked in a house, but in one instance he is murdered in a way that metaphorically calls to mind being raped, in the other this character avoids a rape that results in a murder by providing an alternative victim who is raped and murdered (though he claims the position of the victim in Judg. 20). These verbal cues provide support for the notion that Ehud's penetration and murder of Eglon with a dagger is intended to emasculate and humiliate Eglon in the process, deepening the mocking scorn heaped upon the Moabites in Judges 3.[9]

Further support of the notion that Ehud unmanned Eglon can be found in the immediately adjacent Deborah story in Judges 4. Here, the same verbal action used to describe Ehud's thrusting his dagger in Eglon's belly in Judg. 3:21 (תקע) is also used to describe Jael's murder of Sisera in Judg. 4:21, a murder scene that several

---

7. Handy, 'Uneasy Laughter', pp. 237 and 233. Handy notes that the Israelite authors of this story may have viewed the Moabites as stupid and culturally backward, a contention reinforced by other stories related to the Moabites such as Gen. 19:30-38, which suggests that the Moabite nation grew out of a drunken incestuous encounter. I am less certain that Gen. 19:30-38 is a negative ethnic comment on the Moabites and Ammonites as Lot's daughters' actions are somewhat analogous to those of Tamar in Gen. 38, and the text seems to frame Tamar heroically for the very unconventional actions that she takes in order to preserve Judah's lineage.

8. It is not certain from the Hebrew of Judg. 19 if the concubine expired upon the doorstep, or afterwards on the journey home, or only when the Levite cuts her into pieces after arriving back home.

9. For a fuller analysis of the many verbal and thematic connections between Judg. 3 and Judg. 19, see Joel S. Kaminsky, 'Reflections on Associative Word Links in Judges,' *JSOT* 36.4 (2012): 411–34, especially 425–28.

scholars suggest contains latent sexual imagery in which a woman takes on the manly role and emasculates the enemy general.[10]

Now I would contend that these many humorous elements in the Ehud story serve not just an aesthetic function but a theological one as well. Aesthetically speaking, the ancient audience would not only have found the use of humour highly pleasing and entertaining, but certain forms of ethnic humour would help to create an immediate solidarity among those Israelites hearing this tale. This is not all that different from the way in which Jackie Mason's depictions of gentiles create an immediate bond among Jews in his audience or Chris Rock's stereotypes of White people resonate with African Americans. While the various sophisticated wordplays may not have been caught by all audience members, one suspects that a culture like ancient Israel's, in which texts were typically read aloud and often memorized, included many a listener who would indeed have picked up on such wordplays. Yet, many scholars seem hesitant to acknowledge that the Bible contains any humour while others who acknowledge the Bible has many humorous touches deny the possibility that it might utilize baser forms of bodily humour. Thus even Yehuda Radday, a Jewish interpreter who takes others to task for missing so much of the humour of the Bible, proclaims that 'biblical humour is never scatological or frivolous, but intelligent, subtle, and implicit rather than explicit'.[11] One wonders how Radday could make such a statement when it is clear that the Eglon narrative in Judges 3:12-30 utilizes scatological humour as well as making fun of the corpulent Moabites whose king is unmanned by Ehud.

10. On the evidence that the Jael account contains sexual imagery, see Pamela Tamarkin Reis, 'Uncovering Jael and Sisera: A New Reading,' *SJOT* 19.1 (2005): 24–47. On the potential sexual imagery in the Ehud account, see Marc Tzvi Brettler, *The Book of Judges* (Old Testament Readings; London: Routledge, 2002), 31–32, which brings out a number of these sexual connections in particular noting a link to open and locked doors in Song of Songs 4:12 and 5:5. Other recent scholars such as Lawson Stone, 'Eglon's Belly and Ehud's Blade: A Reconsideration,' *JBL* 128.4 (2009): 649–63, esp. 654 and Jack M. Sasson, 'Ethically Cultured Interpretations: The Case of Eglon's Murder (Judges 3),' in *Homeland and Exile: Biblical and Ancient Near Eastern Studies in Honour of Bustanay Oded* (ed. Gershon Galil et al; Leiden: Brill, 2009), 571–95, esp. 590 have argued against such interpretations seeing them as a case of over-reading. However, once one notices the striking set of connections between Judg. 3 and 19 it becomes much more likely that the Ehud account does indeed make use of sexual innuendoes and inverted gender imagery to characterize Eglon's ignominious death.

11. Y. Radday, 'On Missing the Humour in the Bible: An Introduction,' in *On Humour and the Comic in The Hebrew Bible*, 21–38, at 38. Equally questionable is the following claim made by Ullendorff in his otherwise excellent article on bawdy language in the Hebrew Bible: 'The Old Testament may at times be bawdy in both substance and expression; it never is lascivious, salacious or sly.' Edward Ullendorff, 'The Bawdy Bible,' *BSOAS* 42:3 (1979): 425–56, here at 433.

Theologically speaking, some have recently argued that base ethnic humour, such as that found in the Ehud-Eglon story should be 'called out' and censured.[12] While recognizing that many uses of humour, not to mention ethnic humour more specifically, can be deployed in problematic ways, I am less certain that Judges 3 grew out of or reflects a culture that was dominating another weaker group as some other commentators seem to think. Rather, humour of the type found in the Ehud episode is often employed within the Bible in instances in which Israel's current situation seems hopeless. A somewhat analogous usage can be detected in Exodus when the two midwives, Moses' mother and his sister, not to mention Pharaoh's own daughter, end up making an utter mockery of Pharaoh's plan to kill all male Israelite infants. Not only is this genocidal plan foiled, but Moses' mother ends up nursing the redeemer baby while serving temporarily as part of Pharaoh's daughter's paid staff.[13] In short, Pharaoh's pretence of being in charge is shown to be a lie and as in Judges 3 the enemy bent on oppressing Israel is undermined in a reversal of events that mocks human claims to royal and in Pharaoh's case to divine power as well.[14] Both stories articulate the humour expressed by the oppressed against their oppressors, at a minimum within the thought world of these narratives, but also potentially representing the historical reality that ancient Israel was often dominated by other external powers.

Humour utilized in oppressive circumstances accomplishes several significant interrelated theological goals: it fractures and thus creates openings in our current limited view of the world and the possibilities it might offer, it points to God's higher transcendent order by mocking the pretensions of an Eglon or a Pharaoh, and finally it provides hope by demonstrating the transience of the current world order. While not often noticed, there is a structural affinity as well as a direct connection between humour and hope in that each proclaims that the reality of everyday life does not necessarily have the final word. As Peter Berger notes in the following quotation, humour challenges the dominant tragic worldview that confines humans to a stoic acceptance of the current conditions of existence.

> At least for the duration of the comic perception, the tragedy of man is bracketed. By laughing at the imprisonment of the human spirit, humour implies that this imprisonment is not final but will be overcome, and by this implication provides

---

12. See Handy, 'Uneasy Laughter' or more recently Johnny Miles, '"Who are you calling 'Stupid?'": Ethnocentric Humour and Identity Construct in the Colonial discourse of Judges 3:12-30,' *The Bible and Critical Theory* 4.1 (2008): 1–16.

13. For a fuller exploration of the use of humour and its theological significance in oppressive circumstances such as the Exodus account, see Joel Kaminsky, 'Humor and Hope from Passover to Purim,' *Marginalia* (12 April 2019): https://marginalia.lareviewofbooks.org/humor-hope-passover-purim/

14. Similar types of humour are operative in the Ark narrative in 1 Samuel 4–6 in which the Philistines and their God Dagon are mocked. See Benjamin J. M. Johnson, 'Humor in the Midst of Tragedy: The Comic Vision of 1 Samuel 4–6,' *JBL* 141.1 (2022): 65–82.

yet another signal of transcendence – in this instance in the form of an intimation of redemption.[15]

Hope presents a similar challenge to the status quo and also provides, in Berger's words, a 'signal of transcendence'.[16]

Humour and Gender

Closely related to ethnic humour is the use of gender-oriented humour in Judges, which I noted may have been deployed within the Ehud-Eglon story discussed above. There is some evidence to suggest that the biblical audience would have found role reversals in which women usurp the active role, or men are done in or symbolically castrated by active feminine wiliness, humorous. As Melissa Jackson rightly notes in her chapter on Deborah and Jael, 'while sexual situations do not inherently imbue a narrative with humour, gender-based components, when paired with the incongruity that is inherent in comedy, do bring humour to the story'.[17] Upsetting common expectations is a prominent feature of many forms of humour. Thus, in cultures with clearly demarcated gender roles, inversions of gender norms frequently provide fertile ground for humorists, as demonstrated by popular movies like *Tootsie, Victor Victoria,* and *Mrs. Doubtfire*. Judges contains a number of passages that play with gender stereotypes in humorous ways. To begin, within Judges 4–5 two quite active female characters, Deborah and Jael, seem to be set over against two rather passive male counterparts, Barak and Sisera. Interpreters remain divided over whether Barak is depicted as weak in relation to Deborah or is simply displaying pious obedience to God's prophet and the chosen leader of Israel. Whether one believes the text depicts Barak positively or negatively, Judg. 4:9 indicates that at a minimum Barak will be robbed of obtaining glory in battle because God 'will sell Sisera into the hand of a woman'.

In any case, it seems almost certain that the ancient audience hearing this text would have found the encounter between Jael and Sisera, in which a woman uses guile to lure in and then dispatch the fleeing and confused general, humorously entertaining. While the text describing Jael's interactions with Sisera is at times enigmatic, this encounter likely contains several allusions to a sexual liaison as well as depicting gender inversions in that Jael plays the role of the male while Sisera is

---

15. Peter Berger, *A Rumor of Angels,* Expanded edition (New York: Doubleday, 1990), 77–85, here at 79. Also see Berger's essay, 'Christian Faith and the Social Comedy,' in *Holy Laughter: Essays on Religion in the Comic Perspective,* edited by M. Conrad Hyers (New York: Seabury, 1969), 123–33.

16. Berger, *A Rumor of Angels,* 68–72. For further reflections on the deep connections between the Bible's use of humour and its theological linkage to hope, see my 'Humor and the Theology of Hope in Genesis: Isaac as a Humorous Figure.' *Interpretation* 54.4 (October 2000): 363–75.

17. Melissa A. Jackson, *Comedy and Feminist Interpretation of the Hebrew Bible,* 106.

unmanned and eventually killed.[18] The theme of gender reversal is highlighted in 4:20, in which Sisera tells Jael to stand outside the tent and instructs her that if anyone comes by and asks 'is there a man here?' Jael should respond negatively 'there is not'. In other words, when Sisera has Jael proclaim that no man is to be found in her tent it is telegraphing to the listening audience that a general hiding in a woman's tent is no longer a man. The narrator's mocking of the loss of Sisera's manhood as he hides in Jael's tent is surely a humorous touch that also portends Sisera's imminent death at the hands of a woman.

Sisera's emasculation is further underlined by the specific implement that Jael employs in 4:21, a מקבת translated as 'a hammer', but literally 'a hole puncher', or, more crudely, 'a female maker'. This word is from the root נקב which is the same root as the biblical Hebrew word for 'female', that is, 'the holed one', which the *BDB* dictionary (p. 666) in an attempt at modesty renders in Latin as *'perforata'*. Yet another aspect of Jael's and Sisera's encounter points to a narrative attempt to unman Sisera. Some of the imagery employed casts Jael as a mother figure and Sisera as an infant. Not only does she offer him some type of milk product (4:19; 5:25), but his death scene, in which he is depicted as falling between her knees, utilizes language that calls to mind a birthing scene (5:27). The mothering and birthing image is reinforced in the poetic version of the tale found in Judges 5 inasmuch as here Jael's killing of Sisera is immediately followed by the image of Sisera's actual mother awaiting his return from battle and musing about why he may have been delayed (Judg. 5:28). In fact, in Judg. 5:30 Sisera's mother and her ladies in waiting imagine that he must be delayed dividing up the spoils including the women prisoners her son will capture, here crudely spoken of as 'a womb, two wombs for each man' when translated literally.

A similar gender reversal story involves Delilah's conquest of Samson on behalf of the Philistines. Like Jael with Sisera, Delilah emasculates Samson, and he too appears to be restored to an infantile state. In Judg. 16:19 he is said to fall asleep on Delilah's knees, a sleep during which he has his locks shorn depriving him of his superhuman strength. The image of the baldheaded Samson on Delilah's knees likely evokes the notion of childbirth and the transformation of his love interest into a mother figure, or perhaps into a femme fatale of motherhood. Growing one's hair out is often associated with sexual power, while the removal of hair likely has associations with castration here as it does in other cultural contexts.[19]

At this point a few comments are in order on the connection between the theology of Judges and the various ways gender is inverted to create a humorous effect. First, the fact that several very macho men like Sisera and Samson are done in by women, or by seemingly submissive men in the case of Ehud's murder of Eglon, may be a critique of the notion that male aggressive power always triumphs or is the most effective way to accomplish things. It may also point to the theological

---

18. Pamela Tamarkin Reis, 'Uncovering Jael and Sisera'.

19. Gananath Obeyeskere, *Medusa's Hair* (Chicago: University of Chicago Press, 1981), 33-51.

truth that human pretensions are in greatest danger of being punctured when humans most believe that they can control events by the strength of their own hands (Deut. 8:17). These types of devastating reversals of human fortune may reveal some influence from wisdom thinking, which should not be utterly surprising in that scholars have detected strong wisdom themes in the Samson cycle's use of riddles and the prominence of dangerous foreign women (Judg. 14–16). Finally, the tendency of these texts to play with and at times invert gender expectations suggests that these biblical texts recognized that certain societal stereotypes concerning male and female roles might be or perhaps even should be called into question at times. It is also possible that these gender role inversions in Judges (and in other biblical texts like Genesis) might suggest that ancient Israel and Judah, two peoples often dominated for much of their histories by stronger Near Eastern nations, identified with female characters who exerted power in more covert and subversive ways.

Humour in Judges 6–11

Having explored the uses of humour in Judges 3–5, we will now survey the remainder of Judges with an eye toward various types and instances of humour exhibited elsewhere in the book. The next narrative cycle revolves around Gideon. The initial interactions between God and/or his angelic messenger (they seem to fade into each other) and Gideon evoke laughter, most especially in the scene where Gideon, reciting God's past deliverance of Israel, tells the angelic messenger that God has abandoned Israel. As is well known from contemporary movies and television, laughter is generated by characters who do not realize that the person they are complaining about is the person to whom they are complaining. This is all the more the case when that other party whom one fails to recognize is God. This extended scene is another instance in which humour opens up a theological horizon by allowing the reader/hearer to glimpse a broader transcendent reality that demonstrates how small-minded our quotidian perspective often is. Other humorous touches of particular note within the Gideon story include: the witty reply by Gideon's father Joash to the effect that if Gideon offended Baal and Baal is truly God it would be offensive to allow humans rather than Baal to punish Gideon (Judg. 6:31); Gideon's overhearing the Moabite soldier interpret his comrade's dream, an interpretation that assures Gideon of a decisive victory (7:14); and Gideon's witty reply to the Ephraimites that their efforts in capturing the two Midianite chieftains is more important than anything he has done, which he employs to ease their anger (Judg. 8:2-3). It is not that the Ephraimites are supposed to find this funny, it is that the audience can clearly recognize that Gideon somewhat facetiously strokes the egos of the offended tribe who are self-important enough to take Gideon's words at face value. Thus, the text lets the audience have a laugh at the pretensions of the Ephraimites.

Turning to the Abimelech story one finds heavy use of satire and parody. There is little doubt that Jotham's fable is spoken in a highly mocking tone.[20] In fact, Judges 9 as a whole is built around the mocking bravado of various macho male characters. Thus 9:27 employs the unusual word הלולים likely intended to evoke the notion of mockery along with the root קלל, 'to make light of' or 'curse'. In verse 38, in language that sounds strikingly contemporary, Zebul asks Gaal the son of Ebed where his loud mouth is now. The most darkly humorous scene occurs when a woman drops an upper-millstone on Abimelech, mortally wounding him in the head. He then requests that his armour-bearer run him through lest people say he was killed by a woman (Judg. 9:53-54). Readers of the Bible know from 2 Sam. 11:21 that Abimelech was done in by a woman, thus indicating that for later generations of Israelites Abimelech becomes a symbol not only of illegitimate rule but of stupidity and unmanliness. This last image is once more a gender reversal with the warrior slain by a woman. It also highlights the deep irony that just as Abimelech had slain his seventy half-siblings upon one stone (see 9:5) so he is killed by one stone.[21]

In terms of characterization, the likely intended meaning of Abimelech's given name stands in tension with his actions within the narrative suggesting a deep irony. Near the close of the Gideon narrative the Israelites approach Gideon and ask him to rule over them. But Gideon rejects this idea by indicating neither he nor his son will rule over the people, but rather God will rule over them (Judg. 8:22-23). With this in mind, Gideon's naming this one son Abimelech, a name meaning 'my father is king', was probably meant to highlight God's kingship over Israel. Yet in Judg. 9:1-6 Abimelech flouts his father's anti-monarchic sentiments that were expressed in his very name and has himself made king after murdering seventy of his half-siblings. Clearly, Judges 9 and the character of Abimelech is among the most ironic narratives in Judges as all of Abimelech's earlier actions come to redound literally on his head later in the narrative (Judg. 9:53-57). In particular, it shows that Abimelech's claim to kingship, a status that belongs to God and within the Hebrew Bible can only be conferred by God, when claimed illicitly produces utter social chaos and leads to the downfall of Abimelech. An additional irony is that Abimelech as king should be protecting the residents of Shechem. But in the end, he torches the fortified part of the city murdering about a thousand of its residents, in turn bringing to fruition Jotham's curse that fire should issue from Abimelech and destroy the Shechemites (Judg. 9:20).

Similarly, the humour found in the Jephthah account is also of a darker nature. It is generally used to highlight the self-destructive relationships between each of the major sets of actors. The narrative opens with the elders of Gilead, who, having driven Jephthah out due to his illegitimate birth status (11:1-2, 7), now seek to

---

20. For a full analysis of the satirical nature of Jotham's fable, see Ze'ev Weisman, *Political Satire in the Bible* (Semeia Studies; Atlanta: Scholars Press, 1998), 25–38.

21. As pointed out by T. A. Boogaart, 'Stone for Stone: Retribution in the Story of Abimelech and Shechem', *JSOT* 32 (1985), 45–56.

persuade him to return and fight their battles. The prolonged negotiations between Jephthah and these elders may also contain elements of humour. The elders open the conversation in 11:6 by telling Jephthah they seek to make him a commander (קצין) to fight the Ammonites. Only after Jephthah rebukes their initial approach do they return and tell Jephthah that he will serve as the head of all the inhabitants of Gilead (11:8). It is this title ראש 'head' that Jephthah accepts in his promissory statement contingent on his victory over the Ammonites. Mirroring this first set of negotiations is a much more elaborate set of exchanges between Jephthah and the Ammonite king conducted via messengers. Here Jephthah somewhat wittily points out that if the Israelites had indeed stolen the disputed piece of territory over which the Ammonites are now threatening to start a war, why did it take them 300 years to get upset about this possible infringement (Judg. 11:26)? It is possible that these drawn-out haggling scenes are employed to entertain the listener as he or she recognizes the art of negotiation as it has long been conducted in the Near East (see similarly Gen. 23).

In the following passage, Jephthah makes a vow stating that if he is successful in battle he will offer the first thing that comes out of the door of his house upon his safe return home as a sacrifice to YHWH. When he returns successful from battle, his virgin daughter and only child greets him with song and dance celebrating his victory. Jephthah openly admits his own mouth has gotten him in trouble (Judg. 11:35). While the text is somewhat ambiguous, it is possible to read the vow as unnecessary in that he receives God's spirit, a sure sign of his impending victory, before he utters his vow (Judg. 11:29-30). One wonders whether there is an ironic twist that the same brash male behaviour and verbal brinkmanship, which is Jephthah's strength as indicated by his negotiating prowess with the elders of Gilead and the Ammonite king, is also his fatal flaw as demonstrated by his bartering away his daughter's life and his hot-headed handling of the Ephraimites who challenge his authority (12:1-6). Inasmuch as Jephthah's name is related to the root 'to open' the text may be playfully utilizing various aspects of this root's meaning to flesh out the life of a character who opens his mouth early and often, a trait that at times serves him well and at others gets him into trouble, thus capturing the tragi-comic dimensions of his life. While the use of humorous wordplay and irony may entertain and draw the audience in, the outcome of Jehptah's rash vow may also have left the audience as troubled as Jephthah was when he was greeted by his only daughter upon his arrival home (see Judg. 11:35).

The final episode in the Jephthah cycle contains yet another form of humour, namely the recognition that speakers who share the same language often speak that common language in highly variant ways when they come from differing regions. While the presence of a distinctive accent is here employed to catch and kill the fleeing Ephraimites, it seems quite possible that this story makes use of an ancient joke concerning the variant regional pronunciations of the word Shibboleth. This would be analogous to how certain American jokes play on regional accents most prominently in either northerners telling jokes about southerners or vice versa. Such regional geographic humour resembles the ethnic humour found in the Ehud narrative as it may be mocking the intelligence of the

Ephraimites whose inability to pronounce a single Hebrew letter in the correct way leads to their demise.

Humour in the Samson Narratives

The Samson narratives contain a tremendous number of humorous elements. The opening sequence portrays Samson's father in a rather dense and derogatory fashion. He refuses to take his wife's word that an angelic being appeared to her with specific instructions and prays to God to send his messenger once more. When the messenger reappears to the woman, she runs to get Manoah who inquires what they are to do with the child who will be born. The divine being basically reiterates what he told the woman, who herself had already imparted this information to her husband (Judg. 13:7). Then, unlike his wife who seems to know she is dealing with a divine being early on (see 13:6), Manoah only realizes that the man they spoke with was the angel of God after the angel ascends in the sacrificial flames (13:21). Additionally, Manoah mistakenly deduces that he will die from having seen this divine being (13:22). His wife wisely rebukes him, explaining that if God wanted to kill them he would not have accepted their offering, appeared twice to them, and left detailed instructions concerning the impending birth of Samson (13:23). It is difficult not to see this story as making fun of male pretensions particularly of men thinking they are in control, a motif that recurs in the following chapters involving Samson. It is possible the humour may go deeper if, as argued by some scholars, the angelic visitor actually sired Samson, which would explain Samson's great strength (for a related tale, see Gen. 6:1-4).[22] If this latter possibility is assumed, then Manoah is depicted as even denser than he appears to be on the surface level of the narrative.

The sharp exchange of words at the beginning of Judges 14 between Samson and his parents concerning his taste in foreign women (portraying his concerned parents in ways that may have eventually given rise to the stereotype of the demanding Jewish mother), along with his rather terse self-centred reply 'Get her for me, because she pleases me' would likely have been found humorous by an ancient Israelite audience that was quite concerned about marrying within the group. Additionally, immediately after this exchange the narrator makes the reader privy to knowledge that none of the characters in the story possesses by telling us that Samson's desire for Philistine women stemmed from God who was seeking to break the Philistine hegemony over Israel (14:4). The technique of narrators sharing information with the audience that the characters in the story lack tends to create great potential for humour and thus is a staple of modern situation comedies.

---

22. The evidence for (and against) the angel actually fathering Samson is discussed in Adele Reinhartz, 'Samson's Mother: An Unnamed Protagonist,' *JSOT* 55 (1992): 25-37, especially pp. 33-36.

However, the deepest humour in the story comes from the interactions between Samson and various Philistines. The first centres around Samson's highly intelligent riddle and his verbal and physical responses to the Philistines who manage to get his wife to supply them with the answer. The scene describing Samson's wife nagging him day in and day out for a full week during the nuptial festivities inverts the celebratory marriage week into a living hell (14:16-17). He then replies with a witty, likely sexually tinged riposte to the Philistines who found the answer to his riddle by threatening Samson's new wife: 'If you had not ploughed with my heifer you would not have not have found out my riddle' (14:18b). To obtain the clothing items to pay off his bet with them he proceeds to murder thirty other Philistines (14:19). The use of carefully crafted sayings, the inversion of ritual scenes, and the fact that the Philistines only win the bet at such a high cost are all humorous. While these uses of humour play an aesthetic role, as noted earlier they also serve a theological purpose. The Philistines dominated Israel during the later period of Judges (Judg. 14:4; 15:11). Stories that mock the dominant power point to the limitations of any such power to control those under its dominion. Such humour hints at the transcendent dimensions of life and at God's coming redemption of his beleaguered people. In some sense, each bit of laughter is another chink in the armour of Philistine dominance.

Although the humour continues to escalate within the Samson narrative, the consequences that flow from it become ever darker. Thus, Samson's use of foxes to set fire to the Philistine's crops is in retaliation for the father of the woman who revealed the key to Samson's riddle marrying her off to another man during Samson's absence (15:1-5). This action in turn results in the Philistines murdering this woman and her father. Samson then replies that he will not stop until he has taken vengeance, which he does by killing yet more Philistines (15:6-8). The Philistines then encamp against Judah and tell the Judeans that they are warring against them to bind Samson and to do to him as he had done to them. When the Judeans ask Samson why he has put them in this compromising position, he replies that he has only done to the Philistines what they did to him (15:9-12). While the spiralling violence is disturbing, it also contains notes of humour at the absurdity of a self-perpetuating cycle of vengeance, whose beginning no one can quite remember. Samson allows the Judeans to bind him and bring him to the Philistines. But just as Samson reaches the Philistines the spirit of God rushes on him allowing him to break free of his bonds, reach for a fresh donkey's jawbone, and kill one thousand Philistines (15:14-15). Killing a thousand enemy soldiers with the jawbone of an ass is itself humorous if you are an Israelite. But the humour is substantially deepened when Samson comes up with a witty taunt playing on both the affinity between the location Lehi and the Biblical Hebrew word for jawbone as well as on the close association between the Hebrew word for heap (as in the heap of Philistine corpses) and that for donkey (15:16). Here humour, which is a verbal jab, is paired with actual physical aggression. Furthermore, it seems possible that the overstated violence in the Samson narratives is supposed to be entertaining and even humorous. This may be analogous to movies like *Pulp Fiction,* shows like *The Three Stooges,* or *Road Runner* cartoons that employ violence in such extreme and pervasive ways that it becomes funny and quite engaging.

Chapter 16 opens with a ribald celebration of Samson's masculinity. He visits a prostitute for the evening but learns an ambush is set to catch him in the morning. While most men would be physically exhausted after such a dalliance, Samson not only gets up in the middle of the night, but he pulls the entrance doors of the city gate out of their sockets and carries them on his shoulders approximately 35 miles up a steep ascent to a hill in front of Hebron.[23]

The manipulative scenes in which Samson and Delilah toy with each other concerning his revealing the source of his strength are playful in a humorous way. Of particular note, her nagging him daily until the text reports that he tells her the secret of his strength because 'he was tired to death' may well have evoked laughter at the poor state of their relationship and at how someone with Samson's great physical strength is so mentally weakened by the nagging of various women in his life (16:16; see similarly the scene in 14:16-17). That this results in Samson's capture by the Philistines who gouge out his eyes should not prevent one from recognizing the humour present here. Humour and tragedy are often close companions. In fact, the ending of the narrative is more suggestive of a comedy than a tragedy.[24] In 16:25, the Philistine audience asks that Samson come out and play/sport for them, likely meaning he should act as a type of jester. It is quite possible that the Hebrew here contains a pun on variant meanings of the Philistine's request to 'call Samson and let him entertain us' (16:25). The Hebrew roots שחק/צחק can imply both entertaining as in causing others to laugh but also possibly the sense of mocking others as in Genesis 39:14. Furthermore there is at least one usage in which it carries the idea of martial sporting (2 Sam. 2:14). Perhaps the Philistines here in some way get exactly what they requested. In support of this reading, the Philistines are depicted as a bit dim-witted in not noticing that Samson's hair, the purported source of his strength, had begun to grow again (16:22). In the memorable climactic scene Samson kills more Philistines in his suicide/death than during his lifetime (16:30), and by doing so fulfills his role as one who would begin the process of freeing Israel from Philistine oppression (Judg. 13:5).

While today some might label Samson's death a suicide and others might draw an equivalence between Samson and a contemporary suicide bomber/terrorist, the biblical text celebrates Samson's ultimate revenge and great victory over the Philistines. Samson is surely a character with fatal flaws at which the audience probably laughed. After all, God appears to exploit Samson's seemingly uncontrolled attraction to women, often in ways detrimental to Samson himself, to accomplish his purposes. Here it is worth noting that while laughing at Samson's foibles the Israelites might actually be indicting themselves inasmuch as Samson and his

---

23. See the note on 16:3 (p. 387) of *The New Oxford Annotated Bible* (5th edition; Michael D. Coogan, ed.; Oxford: OUP, 2018), which describes the approximate distance between Gaza and Hebron.

24. As argued by William Whedbee and Cheryl Exum, 'Isaac, Samson, and Saul: Reflections on the Comic and Tragic Visions,' *Semeia* 32 (1984): 5-40.

uncontrolled attraction to foreign women might be a kind of metaphor come alive, pointing to Israel's own tendency to 'whore' after other gods.[25] But Samson is also a character who wrought great destruction on the hated Philistine enemies in ways that no doubt left ancient Israelites laughing with him as well.

Irony in Judges 17–21

A number of authors have argued that many of the individual stories in Judges (as well as the book as a whole) are shaped and deeply pervaded by the notion of irony.[26] We have noted certain ironic twists earlier in the book such as those found in the Abimelech episode. But the use of irony is particularly heightened in the final chapters of the book where Israel's own internal problems pose a more serious threat than the host of external enemies so prevalent earlier in Judges. One need only note the manner in which religion is manipulated in ways that lead to idolatry, aggression and violence. Chapter 17 begins rather inauspiciously with an incident in which a man named Micah returns money he stole from his mother who, while twice invoking Israel's God, uses part of the returned silver to have a cast idol manufactured. The idol is set up in an illicit shrine that is overseen by an irregular clergy person. The chapter ends with the protagonist Micah, proclaiming 'now I know that the LORD will prosper me' (17:13a). In Judges 18 the idol and other cultic equipment are stolen by members of the tribe of Dan while on their way to slaughter the peaceful residents of Laish. The description of the Danites' behaviour against both Micah and the peaceful community of Laish strongly suggest that their use of religion is self-serving and speaks of a religious attitude that sees God as little more than a piety that is invoked while achieving one's personal gratification by any means necessary. The use of such ironic humour here provides a theological critique of the base ways that these Israelite characters use religion to justify their idolatrous and unethical actions.

Yet the deepest ironies in the whole book occur in the following episode of the Levite's concubine and the subsequent inter-tribal conflict that erupts in the wake of this crime. Particularly ironic is the manner in which the Israelite community solves the problem of providing wives for the Benjaminites. After warring against this tribe because of the rape and murder of the Levite's concubine by the citizens of a Benjaminite city, the eleven other tribes attack another community who failed to show up for battle in order to obtain virgin women as war brides for the surviving Benjaminite warriors. Still short 200 women, they instruct the spouseless Benjaminites to kidnap the remaining number of needed brides from an annual religious pilgrimage festival (Judg. 21:19-24). Thus, a crime analogous to the one that set off the civil war, the victimization of a woman, is now enacted on a mass

---

25. This idea is put forward by Edward L. Greenstein, 'The Riddle of Samson,' *Prooftexts* 1.3 (1981): 237–60.

26. Lillian Klein, *The Triumph of Irony in the Book of Judges* (JSOTSup 68; Sheffield: Almond, 1988).

scale with official sanction. The use of such irony may have allowed the authors or editors of this book to offer up a number of theological and political critiques in a subtle enough fashion that it could avoid being censored by those Israelite authorities who might find it offensive. While I think it is misguided to argue, as some other scholars have, that irony or satire shapes every story in Judges or that all the irony in Judges is directed toward a political goal (elevating Davidic kingship or deriding Saul's coming reign), many of the narratives in Judges employ irony and some certainly contain a political subtext.[27]

Concluding Reflections

This sketch of the many forms and instances of humour found in Judges indicates that humour is used not only for enhancing the aesthetic pleasure for those reading and listening to such stories but frequently serving various theological functions including: bolstering the spirit of those in the audience who might have come to believe God had abandoned Israel, or that the God of old was no longer operative in the same fashion; a way to mock Israel's enemies and/or the gods worshipped by Israel's enemies, which like much humour no doubt reinforced the audience's sense of belonging to a superior religious/ethnic group; an exploration and at times inversion of stereotypical gender roles, offering a critique of certain types of male bravado; a way to allow later Israelites to explore the strengths and foibles of their previous and current leaders; and several stories deliver pointedly ironic theological critiques of Israelite society. One could argue that the omniscient viewpoint of the narrator of Judges, who at times gives us a God's eye view of things, tends to create many potentially humorous situations by allowing the reader to see each of the characters in Judges with their strengths but also with their limitations, qualities of which the characters themselves, like most human beings, are inevitably not fully aware.[28] And Israel's own behaviour toward God and toward members of its own society is illuminated in a frequently unflattering way by deploying satire and irony. The humour in Judges, while serving many purposes, highlights the limited human perspective we generally occupy and reveals how God's transcendent perspective can shatter our worldview, allowing us to take stock of our shortcomings and improve upon our individual and societal behaviours.

---

27. Recent political readings of Judges that argue the book is ideologically aimed at deriding Saul's kingship and/or bolstering Judahite or Davidic claims to the throne include Yairah Amit, *The Book of Judges: The Art of Editing* (Biblical Interpretation 38; Leiden: Brill, 1999); Robert O'Connell, *The Rhetoric of the Book of Judges* (VTSup 63; Leiden: Brill, 1996); and Marvin Sweeney, 'Davidic Polemic in the Book of Judges,' *VT* 47 (1997): 517-29. For fuller bibliography and a comprehensive critique of this line of scholarship, see Gregory T. K. Wong, 'Is There a Direct Pro-Judah Polemic in Judges?,' *SJOT* 19.1 (2005): 84-110.

28. Robert Alter, *The Art of Biblical Narrative* (New York: Basic Books, 1981) 154-56 links biblical narrative techniques to ancient Israel's innovative religious outlook.

Chapter 2

EHUD AND EGLON: CUNNING BEHAVIOUR IN THE BIBLE

Greger Andersson

One of the first main characters (character in the sense of a motif or a figure in a story) in the book of Judges, Ehud (3:12-31), is presented as a cunning hero who fools and assassinates his mightier opponent Eglon, king of Moab, and then leads Israel in a successful war against its oppressors. Although the story[1] might appear easy to follow, it has often troubled readers, as well as professional interpreters. The reason for this is mainly that Ehud is one of several characters in the book of Judges, and the Hebrew Bible, whose acts are considered cunning and, by some readers, immoral. Moreover, it has been suggested that his acts deviate from the ethics presented in other texts in the Bible, and even from the moral order displayed in the narrative pattern that is presented in the frame of the book of Judges – a pattern that is repeated in the introduction to the individual narratives. This generates questions such as why stories like this one have been included in the Bible, how interpreters have tried to come to grips with such stories and how they affect the theology and ethics of the Hebrew Bible.

In my discussion of these issues, I will refer to the biblical text, commentaries,[2] the history of interpretation,[3] some studies in which scholars claim to have identified traces from the work of the redactors and/or literary device according to

---

1. I use 'story' in this chapter to denote a narrative configuration that functions as a literary unit built by motifs.

2. For example, Robert Boling, *Judges* (AB 6A; Garden City: Doubleday, 1975); J. Alberto Soggin, *Judges* (OTL; Philadelphia: Westminster, 1981); John Gray, *Joshua, Judges, Ruth* (NCBC; Grand Rapids MI: Eerdmans, 1986); and Trent C. Butler, *Judges* (WBC; Nashville, TN: Thomas Nelson, 2009).

3. For example, David M. Gunn, *Judges* (Malden, MA.: Blackwell, 2005).

which the individual stories of the book of Judges should be reinterpreted,[4] and to some literary studies concerned with biblical narrative.[5]

I begin by presenting the story of Ehud. I then discuss how it has been interpreted, primarily focusing on discussions relating to its moral and suggested reinterpretations. Finally, I reflect on what it would mean if we were to accept what I hold to be the most straightforward interpretation of the story, i.e., that Ehud is a hero whose cunning is supported by the structure of the narrative.

The Story of Ehud and Eglon[6]

The story of Ehud and Eglon begins with a series of causally connected acts: because of Israel's sin, the Lord strengthens the Moabites so they can oppress Israel, who then cries to the Lord, who sends a deliverer. In 3:15-16, Ehud is introduced. He is characterized in a nominal clause saying that his right hand is 'restricted', which might be an idiomatic expression for left-handedness or a literal description of a defect.[7] Lefthanded Benjaminites (sons of the right hand) appear also in Judg. 20:16. Taken as a motif in the story, the function of the phrase might be to depict Ehud as a trained warrior, or to explain why the guards and the king did not realize Ehud's potential lethalness. Regardless, the sentence provides more detail than most descriptions of a character in the Old Testament,[8] which implies that this information will be important in the ensuing story. Verse 16 is a portrayal of Ehud's weapon, a home-made sword. The expression that describes the sword is unique in the Bible and is therefore difficult to interpret; but it has been assumed to denote a thirty-centimetre-long sword.[9]

---

4. For example, Barry G. Webb, *The Book of Judges: An Integrated Reading* (Sheffield: JSOT Press, 1987); Lillian R. Klein, *The Triumph of Irony in the Book of Judges* (Sheffield, Almond Press, 1988); Yairah Amit, *The Book of Judges: The Art of Editing* (Leiden: Brill, 1999 [1992]); Robert H. O'Connell, *The Rhetoric of the Book of Judges* (Leiden: Brill, 1996); and E. T. A. Davidson, *Intricacy, Design and Cunning in the Book of Judges* (Philadelphia: Xlibris, 2008).

5. For example, Robert Alter, *The Art of Biblical Narrative* (New York: Basic Books, 1981); Meir Sternberg, *The Poetics of Biblical Narrative: Ideological Literature and the Drama of Reading* (Bloomington, IN: Indiana University Press, 1987); and Shimon Bar-Efrat, *Narrative Art in the Bible* (Sheffield: Almond Press, 1989).

6. This section is partly based on my chapter about Ehud in an earlier study of the book of Judges (Andersson, 2001).

7. Several commentators assume that Ehud was handicapped and hence yet another of the unexpected heroes in the Bible. O'Connell, however, claims that there is no reason for such an interpretation, *The Rhetoric of the Book of Judges*, p. 87 especially n. 45.

8. See Sternberg, *Poetics*, 326ff.

9. Gray, *Joshua, Judges, Ruth*, 250.

The story then recounts that Ehud delivers Israel's tribute to Eglon, the Moabite king, who is described as a very fat man, which some commentators hold is in line with his name, if it means 'calf'.[10] The motivation for this description might be that there is a connection between the gifts of Israel and the fatness of the king, or that Eglon is a fat calf, ready for slaughter or sacrifice.[11]

When Ehud has delivered the tribute, he returns home, but 'at the sculptured stones near Gilgal' he turns back to Eglon. According to commentators, it is difficult to determine what the 'sculptured stones' refer to. However, they do at least mark the border between Israel and Moab and hence function as an inclusion.[12] Ehud now says to Eglon, 'I have a secret message for you, O king.' The Hebrew word *dabar* might refer to a thing or a word. Ehud uses this phrase to engineer a situation where he is alone with the king, who interprets the term (the story presumes that the king knows Hebrew) as referring to a word, while readers know that it might refer to Ehud's sword. The flow of the narrative is then interrupted by descriptive clauses describing different rooms. These seem significant to the story but are difficult to translate. In any case, the point is that Ehud is able to enter the innermost room and be alone with the king.[13] In vv. 21-22, the assassination is described in detail. When Ehud has repeated his phrase, which brings Eglon to his feet, and has stabbed him with his sword, it is said that 'he did not draw the sword out of his belly' and that 'the fat closed over the blade'. The next line is difficult to translate. NRSV has: 'and the dirt came out', which seems to be a reasonable suggestion, since it would explain the reaction of the servants in verse 24. The locked doors and the smell from the room leads them to conclude that the king is relieving himself.[14]

Verse 24 begins with two clauses that describe simultaneous events: the servants enter the room at the same moment as the hero leaves it. Another effect of these lines is that the narrative now changes focus. In the next lines (vv. 24-25), the servants are the centre of interest. The story remains, so to speak, in the vestibule while Ehud escapes. The author uses dramatic irony – that is, the reader is more informed than the characters, and realizes that the characters misunderstand the situation. The irony is reinforced by the *hinneh* clause that marks a change to an internal point of view.[15]

---

10. Boling, *Judges*, 85; Soggin, *Judges*, 49.

11. Alter, *The Art of Biblical Narrative*, 39.

12. Boling, *Judges*, 86.

13. According to Alter, *The Art of Biblical Narrative*, p. 39, the narrative may imply a 'grotesque feminization' of the king.

14. See Butler, *Judges*, 71, while, for example, Boling instead holds that the phrase refers to Ehud's escape (*Judges*, 87).

15. See for example Bar-Efrat, *Narrative Art in the Bible,* 35 and Bruce K. Waltke & M. P. O'Connor, *An Introduction to Biblical Hebrew Syntax* (Winona Lake, IN.: Eisenbrauns, 1990).

In verse 26, the focus returns to Ehud. In the second phase of the liberation, he leads the Israelites in a successful war against the Moabites. The account of the war is, as usual in the Hebrew Bible, superficial, and it lacks the intense scenic atmosphere found in the foregoing episode. The final verse is a resolution that reports that equilibrium has been reinstated.

The Characters of the Story

The story is short and appears, as I said in the introduction, rather easy to follow. It is characterized by violence and a scabrous humour, and it assumes an implied reader who takes the perspective of Ehud and the Israelites. Even though the narrative includes two episodes, in which Ehud first assassinates Eglon and then leads Israel in a war against their oppressors, it is obvious that the slow pace of the narrative and its scenic character put the emphasis on the encounter between the protagonist and antagonist.[16] Although the narrative covers a time span of about 100 years, the focus is thus on a single episode. This concentration of attention on encounters between characters, as well as on the remarkable, characterizes all stories in Judges.

If we, with Gerald Prince, define a character as 'an existent endowed with anthropomorphic traits and engaged in anthropomorphic actions',[17] we could perhaps say that the Moabites, Amalekites, Ammonites and Israelites are all characters in the narrative. However, the story focuses on Ehud, Eglon and Eglon's servants.

Ehud, Eglon and the servants are characterized both directly and indirectly. Ehud is 'restricted', cunning and brave, while Eglon and the Moabites are fat and stupid. However, the narrative has no interest in the characters or their development.[18] They are rather functions in the story. If we refer to Algirdas J. Greimas' actantial model of narrative structure,[19] Ehud is the *subject*; the *object* is Israel's freedom from oppression; Ehud's *helpers* are his cunning and his sword; his *opponents* are the king, the guards etc.; the *sender* is God; and the *receiver* of the *object* is Israel. As a type in the book of Judges, Ehud is a judge, a deliverer and God's vehicle.

---

16. According to Alter, *The Art of Biblical Narrative*, p. 41f., the two episodes are in many respects analogous. He mentions, for example, that the same Hebrew word is used for the two 'blows' – the one with the sword and the one with the trumpet – and that both Eglon and the Moabites are said to be 'fat'.

17. Gerald Prince, *A Dictionary of Narratology: Revised Edition* (Lincoln: University of Nebraska Press, 2003), 12.

18. Just as in the story of Gideon, something changes when Ehud suddenly becomes a public leader, but the story does not focus on this transition.

19. Algirdas J. Greimas, *Structural Semantics: An Attempt at Method* (Lincoln: University of Nebraska Press, 1983).

In summary: Ehud is an 'underdog', who defeats his mightier opponent and delivers his people. He is the protagonist with whom readers sympathize, and they are thus prone to accept Ehud's claim when he says to his people that 'the LORD has given Moab, your enemy, into your hands" (3:28).

The Interpretation of the Story

My suggestion that the narrative is easy to follow, and that Ehud is a hero that readers are supposed to sympathize with, could, however, be put in question. Commentators have, for example, discussed issues that concern problems relating to translation, such as the length of the sword, Ehud's restrictedness, whether Eglon's dirt came out, and to reference, for example, what place 'the city of palms' denotes, and what 'the sculptured stones' refer to. A commonly discussed issue is why Eglon stands up when he hears that Ehud has a 'word' from God, and what it implies about his character and beliefs.

It is salient, when discussing issues like these, to distinguish between different approaches to the text. Are the questions directed to the world – a world that readers are supposedly informed about – or to the narrative as a story, i.e., as a meaningful configuration built up by motifs? In my summary of the story, presented above, I have taken the latter stance. This means, for instance, that the issue of why Eglon stands up concerns the meaning and function of the motif. We could thus answer, for example, that the author has Eglon stand up because he thereby becomes a possible target for Ehud's attack.[20] This would be in line with a tendency in the narrative according to which all details fall into place and makes Ehud's assassination possible and successful.

Another issue that can be used to illustrate the distinction between the two approaches is gap filling. If a narrative is considered to provide historical information, it could be assumed that the presented version is not *absolute* – it could be put into question and an interpreter could come up with better versions of the events the narrative refers to – and the world is *complete*, which means that the interpreter can consider all gaps as relevant. In fiction, on the other hand, the version is *absolute* and the world is not *complete*.[21] An interpreter thus has to consider whether or not gaps in a fictional narrative have a meaning and function in the story and if, in such a case, they have their meaning as gaps or if they are supposed to be filled out.[22] Biblical narratives, however, are often supposed to aspire to be historical at the same time as they are regarded as having been constructed like literary stories. A scholar like Meir Sternberg thus

---

20. It could also suggest to readers that Eglon respects Jahve.
21. I have these descriptions from Christer Johansson, 2008.
22. Kendall L. Walton, *Mimesis as Make-Belief: On the Foundations of the Representational Arts* (Cambridge, MA: Harvard University Press, 1990), 174–83.

holds that it is not relevant to fill all gaps in these narratives.[23] This indicates that the narratives have a purpose, a meaning, in relation to which a certain gap filling is considered as relevant or not. It also indicates that Sternberg assumes what I have described as a literary approach although he holds that the narratives aspire to be historical.

Yairah Amit suggests that there are several gaps in the story of Ehud and that they generally appear in the transitions between different episodes. She holds that this indicates that 'someone has taken care of the intervening stages, put the events in motion, and orchestrated their timing' and that 'this underlines the central role the author has assigned to God'.[24] Although this is an interesting suggestion that is in line with my reasoning concerning the fact that Eglon stands up, it could be argued that similar gaps are common in narratives and that they do not need to imply that God controls the events. Anyway, Amit's suggestion could be taken to imply a literary approach, since she holds that the gaps function as meaningful devices in the configuration, i.e., her purpose is not to fill out the world but to understand the meaning of the story.

A consequence of my reasoning is that one can determine interpreters' understanding of a narrative's aspirations and aim, from whether they direct their questions to the world the narrative is supposed to refer to, or to the story, and from their approach to, for example, gap filling.[25] In another study I have argued that some scholars who claim to read the biblical narratives as literature in fact approach them as historical accounts, assuming that the text is a version that it is not *absolute*, and that the world it refers to is *complete*.[26]

When I suggest that the narrative about Ehud is easy to understand, I assume a reading of the narrative as a story – in the sense of a meaningful construction built by motifs. Accordingly, I hold that readers have understood the function of its motifs in relation to the story.

The Moral of the Story

A study of the history of interpretation, such as David Gunn's *Judges*, makes clear that interpreters have also been concerned with the characters, their acts, and the evaluation of these acts. When it comes to God, interpreters have discussed

---

23. Sternberg, *Poetics,* 188.

24. Amit, *Reading Biblical Narratives*, 61.

25. Some scholars seem to put this distinction in question and to assume that we interpret fictional and non-fictional narratives in the same or a similar way. They can thus for example suggest that we should interpret and evaluate characters as we interpret and evaluate people we come across in our daily lives (see for example Gunn and Fewell, 1993: 50–51). I think this is a mistaken assumption.

26. Greger Andersson, *Untamable Texts: Literary Studies and Narrative Theory in the Books of Samuel* (London: T&T Clark, 2009).

questions such as how God can punish one sin (Israel's) through another sin (Moab's) and whether God really supports Ehud's deed.[27] The latter question relates to a particular concern among interpreters: 'Is Ehud's action morally defensible and a model for imitation?'[28] Gunn refers to several interpreters (such as John Milton) who think the story of Ehud can be taken to support regicide, and those (such as Voltaire) who condemn Ehud's act or try to explain it away as displaying an ancient and oriental moral.[29]

Interpreters can reason in two different ways when discussing the meanings and values of a story. First, they can suggest that the narrative should be reinterpreted and hence that it does not contain the values and meanings I have suggested. This can, as I have already suggested, be performed by scholars assuming a historical approach, according to which they can come up with new and better versions of the events the narrative is assumed to refer to, or by scholars advocating a literary approach, who suggest what they hold to be a better understanding of the literary configuration, the story. Secondly, one can accept that a story has certain values and meanings and then put these values and meanings in question.[30] It is obvious that the interpreters Gunn refers to reason according to the second option, i.e., they take the values and meanings of the story for granted but question whether these should be accepted and whether readers should apply them in their own lives. However, interpreters at times sway between the two approaches. Thus, when for example C. F. Keil and F. Delitzsch analyse the story of Ehud and the evaluation of Ehud and say that 'Ehud's conduct must be judged according to the spirit of those times,' they seem to take the values and meanings of the narrative for granted. Yet they also suggest that the narrative does not support Ehud's deeds since it is not said that the Spirit came upon Ehud. Their conclusion is that even though Ehud delivered his people, 'it by no means follows that the means which he selected were either commanded or approved by Jehova'.[31] This reasoning appears to presume that readers are inclined to regard Ehud's acts as supported by the story. Keil and Delitzsch question this evaluation, claiming on the one hand that the story is based on obsolete values and, on the other, that the narrative does not

---

27. It is, of course, important even here to make clear if the issue concerns God as a reality in the real world or as a motif in the text.

28. Gunn, *Judges*, 35.

29. Gunn quotes Milton: 'that Ehud's action provides scriptural authority for subjects sometimes needing to depose their rulers' (Gunn, 2005: 38), and Voltaire, who is one among many who advocate another position, when referring to Ehud: 'How many crimes have been committed in the name of the Lord' (Gunn, 2005: 44).

30. Greger Andersson, 'The problem of narratives in the Bible: moral issues and suggested reading strategies,' in *Narrative Ethics* (ed. Jakob Lothe, Jeremy Hawthorn; Amsterdam: Rodopi, 2013), 59–72.

31. C. F. Keil and F. Delitzsch, *Biblical Commentary on the Old Testament: Joshua, Judges, Ruth* (Grand Rapids, 1963), 298.

in fact say that God supported Ehud's acts. Thus, they simultaneously criticize the narrative and suggest that it should be reinterpreted. The suggested reinterpretation is based on the assumption that there are elements in the text that signal that the common interpretation is mistaken. That the text does not mention that the Spirit came upon Ehud would then be such a signal. This argument presumes in its turn that there are patterns in the book of Judges that indicate what certain elements, or the omission of certain elements, in the story of Ehud mean. This is an important issue that concerns the question of what context determines the values and meanings of a story. I will come back to this issue and to the suggestion that the individual stories in the book of Judges received a new and different meaning when the redactor(s) inserted them in the book. Scholars who advocate this reasoning hold that there are patterns in the book that affect how we should understand features in the stories and/or that the stories have lost their individuality and have become episodes in a larger narrative. But first I will address the question of why Ehud and similar characters in the Bible challenge readers.

Immoral Heroes in the Bible

It is not uncommon that in fictions such as fairy tales, movies and novels, readers sympathize with characters who behave in a way they would not accept in real life. The reason for this is probably both that readers are familiar with the genres and that the 'immoral' characters they sympathize with 'are standardly possessed of certain striking virtues'.[32] It could be added that these characters, so to speak, represent 'the right side'. David Chalcraft[33] has thus suggested that the value of an action in the book of Judges is judged according to who performs it and to whom. Yet if this reasoning were accepted, why then are cunning characters like Ehud in the biblical narratives considered problematic for readers as well as interpreters?

Consider this example:[34] When the Hebrew midwives, who spare the Hebrew children Pharaoh has commanded them to kill, lie to Pharaoh and say: 'Hebrew women are not like Egyptian women; they are vigorous and give birth before the midwives arrive' (Exod. 1:15), the author explains: 'God was kind to the midwives... And because the midwives feared God, he gave them families of their own" (Exod. 1:15-21). The biblical texts' evaluations of cunning acts are often indistinct or, as in the example with the midwives, even affirmative. However, the

---

32. Noël Carroll, *Beyond Aesthetics: Philosophical Essays* (Cambridge: Cambridge University Press, 2001), 261.

33. David J. Chalcraft, 'Deviance and Legitimate Action in the Book of Judges.' Pages 177-201 in *The Bible in Three Dimensions*. Edited by David J. A. Clines, Stephen E. Fowl and Stanley E. Porter (Sheffield: JSOT Press, 1990).

34. I discuss this example more thoroughly in an article (Andersson, 'The Problem of Narratives in the Bible').

narrative about the midwives is probably less provocative (since their aim was to protect innocent newborns) than the narratives about war heroes like Ehud, Jephthah, Samson and David, or about Jacob, who tricks his blind father (Gen. 25), or even virtuous characters who occasionally behave cunningly, such as when Abraham claims, in order to save his own life when he enters Egypt, that his wife is his sister (Gen. 12:10-20). Nevertheless, Tremper Longman III, who assumes that the Bible approves of the midwives' lying,[35] still feels obliged to explain, in another section in which he refers to the midwives, that readers must 'distinguish the behavior the text describes from what it approves or disapproves', because the narratives rarely pontificate 'about the actions of its characters, preferring to show rather than tell. Often we have to judge whether a character's actions are righteous or not by appeal to a didactic part of Scripture.'[36]

Keil and Delitzsch's reasoning about Ehud, as well as Longman's about the midwives, indicate, first, that they assume that readers are prone to expect that biblical narratives should give moral guidance and, secondly, that readers expect a certain ideological and moral consistency between different texts and text levels in the Bible. If this is related to my reasoning in the previous section, we can come up with the following putative explanations for readers' and interpreters' concern with the moral of the story of Ehud. First, interpreters can oscillate between a reading of the narrative as a story and as an account of real events (in the real world or in a story world), and therefore come to discuss and evaluate the events the narrative supposedly informs them about. Secondly, the interpreters' reactions might relate to their understanding of the character and intent of the narrative. They could, for example, assume that the intent of the narrative is to educate readers about God and God's ways with the world, and thus to display a biblical ethics.[37] Gunn even suggests when referring to the history of interpretation that 'The biblical character, chosen by God to be a "deliverer", is assumed to be a moral exemplar.'[38] Thirdly, interpreters might expect a certain consistency in the Bible, and thus hold that the moral that the story of Ehud conveys is countered by other texts, or layers in the text. This is the issue I will turn to next.

The Story of Ehud in the Book of Judges

Narratives with a plot are generally characterized by causality. This creates a pattern of meaning and cohesion in the lives of the characters in the narrative, and at times, even in the lives of the readers. But these patterns in the Bible are not unambiguous. For example, in the introductions to the narratives about judges

---

35. Tremper Longman, III, *How to Read Exodus* (Downers Grove, IL: IVP, 2009), 98.
36. Ibid. 25.
37. See Amit, *Reading Biblical Narratives*, 3.
38. Gunn, *Judges*, 46. Christopher J. H. Wright says in his *Old Testament Ethics for the People of God* (2004: 69-74) that the narratives are not principal but paradigmatic.

such as Ehud, the redactors display the religious and moral causality that governs the history of Israel according to Deuteronomy to 2 Kings.[39] According to this frame narrative, the Israelites forsook the Lord time and again and were punished by the Lord who gave them into the hands of raiders. When the people were in distress they prayed to the Lord, who then sent a judge who delivered them (see the pattern in 2:10-19, which is demonstrated in the short 'narrative' about Othniel 3:7-11). However, this pattern of causality does not appear to govern the events in the individual stories, and the judge is seldom presented as a 'moral exemplar'.[40] There is thus a tension between the moral and religious pattern displayed in the frame and in the individual stories in the book.

A recent scholarly approach, however, is to consider the book of Judges as a coherent work that, so to speak, functions as the context that determines the meaning and values of features in the individual stories. Accordingly, scholars can refer to traces of the work of the redactors and/or to putative literary devices and suggest that the individual narratives should be reinterpreted and be given a new meaning. The cover of E. T. A. Davidson's *Intricacy, Design and Cunning in the Book of Judges* says, for example: 'Each story in the book, she suddenly realized, was a gloss on every other story, and if one couldn't understand the whole book, and every word of it, one couldn't understand even one story,' and later on: 'The book was a puzzle waiting to be solved. The anomalies, it turns out, were not abnormalities to be disregarded, but "hidden objects", important clues to deciphering the text.'[41] Based on this approach, and the opinion that readers are invited to evaluate characters and their behaviour by both the moral standards of the wider text and the readers' own standards, Davidson condemns Ehud and his acts.[42] Lilian Klein regards the story of Othniel as a paradigm and examines closely how the other stories in the book of Judges conform to this paradigm. She holds that the narrative about Ehud diverges from the usual pattern in three ways: The Lord does not 'raise' Ehud as a deliverer but 'gives' him to Israel; the Spirit of the Lord does not come over him; and although he is a saviour, he does not judge the people. These observations lead Klein to the conclusion that YHWH does not participate in Ehud's deed, and that Ehud in his speeches uses the name of the Lord for his own purposes. Klein concludes: 'apparently unwilling to rely on Yahweh, Ehud practices

---

39. J. Alberto Soggin, *Introduction to the Old Testament: From Its Origins to the Closing of the Alexandrian Canon* (3rd ed.; London: SCM Press, 1989), 53–54.

40. Gunn, *Judges*, 46. The tension between the text levels can be exemplified by the fact that the equilibrium in the story is broken by Israel's sin, and then reinstated when the Israelites defeat the Moabites, not when they have stopped sinning (Robert Polzin, *Moses and the Deuteronomist: Deuteronomy, Joshua, Judges* [Bloomington, IN: Indiana University University Press, 1993], 155).

41. E. T. A. Davidson, *Intricacy, Design and Cunning in the Book of Judges* (Philadelphia: Xlibris, 2008).

42. Ibid., 109.

deception and trickery, achieving the Israelite goal of freedom from oppression but ironically negating the higher goal: contact with Yahweh'.[43] Thus, Ehud is regarded almost as an anti-hero who breaks the norm of the wider narrative, and the reader is supposed to see him as an ironic figure.

I am critical of this approach for several reasons.[44] Firstly, I hold that if the redactors really have tried to impose structures that should override the narrative structures that have governed the reading of these stories for centuries, they have simply failed. It is my contention that it is possible from a narratological and literary theoretical point of view to explain why this is so, and why narratives tend to keep their meaning even when inserted in a new context. The prime reason is simply that narratives are structural units (wholes). Hence, if one wants to change their meaning one must either adjust their form and content or prolong the stories and provide them with new endings. Accordingly, even if I cannot prove that the redactors have not tried to change the meaning of these narratives, I hold that I as a narratologist can explain why readers have not read them as critics like Davidson and Klein do.[45] Secondly, scholars who advocate the approach under consideration here come to very different conclusions regarding the interpretations of, for example, the story of Ehud.[46] Thirdly, I do not think that the author has constructed the story of Ehud with the intention that it should be a puzzle. The puzzle only occurs when readers or interpreters try to harmonize the different narratives and text levels into a single and unified text, or when they oscillate between interpretations of the narrative as historical information and as a story.

The Meaning of the Story of Ehud in its Context

It is interesting to ponder why the stories of the Book of Judges, for example the story about Ehud, have the form and content that they have. A first possible explanation can perhaps be termed historical since it says that the redactors for some reason did not rework the narratives into a single coherent text. A second and complementary explanation is that the stories have been formed to meet the test for 'tellability',[47] i.e., instead of only repeating a recurring didactic pattern they

---

43. Klein, *The Triumph of Iron*, 46.

44. See Greger Andersson, *The Book and Its Narratives: A Critical Examination of Some Synchronic Studies of the Book of Judges* (Örebro Studies in Literary History and Criticism 1; Örebro: Universitetsbiblioteket, 2001).

45. I develop this reasoning much more in *The Book and Its Narratives: A Critical Examination of Some Synchronic Studies of the Book of Judges*. Örebro Studies in Literary History and Criticism 1 (Örebro: Universitetsbiblioteket, 2001), which is an entire study about these issues.

46. See Webb, *Book of Judges: An Integrated Reading*; O'Connell, *The Rhetoric of the Book of Judges* and Amit, *The Book of Judges*.

47. William Labov, *Language in the Inner City: Studies in the Black English Vernacular* (Philadelphia: University of Pennsylvania Press, 1972).

emphasize the remarkable, the odd, and non-expected. It could even be suggested that they function as literature does.[48] They would then, just like literary narratives, according to Martha Nussbaum, 'emphasize the world's surprising variety, its complexity and mysteriousness, its flawed and imperfect beauty'.[49] A third possible explanation is that the stories reflect the authors' view of life, humanity and God and that this view either conflicts with or complements the views displayed in other texts or text levels. Scholars such as Meir Sternberg and Robert Alter argue that the content and form of the biblical narratives presume and display the writers' worldview and their view of humanity. For example, Alter says in a passage about biblical characters that tensions between divine election and moral character in the narratives, as well as the 'paradoxical double focus' on causation, can be explained by the authors' view on human nature: 'The very perception, on the other hand, of godlike depths, unsoundable capacities for good and evil, in human nature, also leads these writers to render their protagonists in ways that destabilize any monolithic system of causation'.[50] Narratives like those about Jacob, the Hebrew midwives and judges like Ehud would then display indirectly a view of God and a view of humanity and, if we refer to Sternberg, a poetic that attempts to form 'an art of indirection, a drama of reading, which "puts a premium on interpretation"'.[51] The stories would thus, in spite of the fact that they are not didactic, say something that their authors held was true about life.

Conclusion: The Theology and Ethics of the Story of Ehud

Finally, if we were to accept that the narrative of Ehud is a story, in the sense of a meaningful and artful composition, whose meaning and values are determined by its own content and structure – and the interpretation I hold follows from such an approach – how then does the story of Ehud relate to the book of Judges and the rest of the Old Testament? Robert Polzin, who reads Judges and the Deuteronomistic History as a cohesive text, thinks that it is dialogical.[52] Walter Brueggemann suggests in his *Old Testament Theology* that the Bible contains testimonies and counter-testimonies.[53] These are interesting suggestions that hold

---

48. See Andersson, *Untamable Texts*.

49. Martha Nussbaum, *Love's Knowledge: Essays of Philosophy and Literature* (New York: Oxford University Press, 1990), 3-4.

50. Alter, *Art of Biblical Narrative*, 117, 125–26 respectively.

51. Sternberg, *Poetics*, 44. I discuss this issue in Greger Andersson, 'Stories about Humans in a Complicated World: The Narratives of the Hebrew Bible,' in *God and Humans in the Hebrew Bible and Beyond: A Festschrift for Lennart Boström on his 67th Birthday* (ed. David Willgren. Sheffield: Sheffield Phoenix Press, 2019), 51–71.

52. Polzin, *Moses and the Deuteronomist*.

53. Walter Brueggemann, *Theology of the Old Testament: Testimony, Dispute, Advocacy* (Minneapolis, MN: Fortress Press, 1997).

that the task of interpreters is not to try to harmonize the texts but to give heed to the dialogue between texts and text levels.

I would thus argue that if the narrative of Ehud and Eglon is read as a story then Ehud is presented as a hero who deceives and defeats his mightier opponent and delivers his own people. I acknowledge that this reading has disturbed interpreters, who have suggested that Ehud and his acts should be evaluated negatively, referring to their own moral reaction, to the wider text, or to putative devices in the narrative itself. I hold that a better option is to regard the narrative as a story about a specific kind of hero, a kind that is not uncommon in the Bible; and that this implies that the writer's view of God and humanity as well as the moral of these stories, as it is displayed in the story, should be taken into account when trying to formulate systematic descriptions of the theology and ethics of the Bible. It is, I think, very interesting that the narratives of the Hebrew Bible time and again put the expected order in question, whether it is through heroes like Ehud, or stories in which God does not cover up for careless promises, as in Jephthah, or when Joseph suggests a teleological instead of a causal reading of his life story, or even in the book of Job, in which the very moral order is put in question.

Chapter 3

DEBORAH – IF NOT A DELIVERER, WHAT KIND OF LEADER WAS SHE?

Yairah Amit

Who was Deborah? Although we have a complete story of the war in which she participated (Judg. 4), and a long poem relating to her (Judg. 5, dealing with the same war), questions remain as to her figure as a judge in the days of the judges.[1] What kind of judge was she? According to the story's exposition, she was a prophetess who was also a judge in Israel at that time, and the Israelites came to her for judgement (4:4-5), but what kind of judgment did she deliver? Was she a juridical judge or perhaps the people of Israel came to her merely for advice? She may well have been a deliverer, as she played a meaningful role in the war against the Canaanite enemy.[2]

In this essay, I argue that according to the story despite the fact that Deborah was not a deliverer, she was a highly gifted leader, charismatic, wise, and functioning as both a prophetess and a judge in the judicial sense. I ignore historical and archaeological issues and focus on the task, status and character of Deborah, who never appears again in the entire Hebrew Bible, as the literary materials shows, and I avoid ideological goals as well.

---

1. Mark Brettler opens his chapter on 'Poetry and Prose in Judges 4–5' with the sentence: 'It is extremely difficult to say anything new about Judges 4–5' (Marc Brettler, *The Book of Judges* [London: Routledge, 2002]). Although he discusses primarily historical questions, I think that we can use the same sentence regarding questions of characterization in Judges 4–5.

2. These questions, and others, which I have not mentioned here, led me to analyse this story as a riddle story (Yairah Amit, *The Book of Judges: The Art of Editing* [Leiden: Brill, 1999], 198–220). See citation p. 199: 'In our story, the plot, the nature of the delivery, and the use of repeated formulae or summarizing accounts, all support the central means, namely, the riddle concerning the identity of the central hero or deliverer, or the one who shall smite Sisera.' Hence, actually there are two riddles: who is the deliverer, and who is the woman who will kill Sisera?

The essay is divided into three parts: the first is dedicated to Deborah according to the literal text; the second, to what the text does not say explicitly; and the third part is devoted to conclusions.

Deborah according to the Literal Text

The story about the victory in the era of Deborah (Judg. 4–5) raises the question of the deliverer's identity. The data throughout the story does not allow the reader to decide who the human figure was that saved Israel: Deborah, Barak or Jael. There are two reasons for this: first, the story's exposition does not mention that God raised Deborah as the deliverer of the Israelites; second, the partial participation of each of the human characters in the war against the Canaanites. In addition, the poem does not describe Deborah as the powerful heroine of the war.[3] Even in the song's editorial introductory verse (5:1), Deborah is mentioned with Barak at her side.[4] Afterwards, she appears as the initiator but not as a warrior (5:7).[5] The division of roles is unmistakable; she is the initiator and cheerleader, and he, the fighter: 'Awake, awake, Deborah! Awake, awake, utter a song! Arise, Barak. Lead away you captives, O son of Abinoam' (v. 12).[6] Later, Jael (5:24-27), the woman who kills Sisera appears, thus signifying the end of the battle. Olson assures us that 'All three contribute to saving Israel, but none of them can lay a sole claim to the title

---

3. Brenner underscores that the two chapters in Judg. 4 and 5 are 'one narrative which is narrated in two texts... Together, the two afford a unified picture of the narrative' (Athalya Brenner, 'A Triangle and a Rhombus in Narrative Structure: A Proposed Integrative Reading of Judges 4 and 5,' in *A Feminist Companion to Judges 4*; Sheffield: Sheffield Academic Press, 1993], 98-99).

4. Even the verb ותשר (she sang) in feminine singular does not show that she was the only singer, because biblical Hebrew allows the verb to follow the first subject in singular, even if afterwards there are more subjects, as for example Gen. 31:14; Num. 12: 1 and more (see GKC §146g). In addition, the speaker of the song is not Deborah, but the singer; see Burney's translation and interpretation of the verb 'שקמתי' in v. 7: 'Till thou didst arise' (Charles F. Burney, *The Book of Judges* [New York: Ktav Publishing House, 1970], 116). But for Niditch Deborah is the speaker: 'Until I arose' (Susan Niditch, *Judges: A Commentary* [OTL; Louisville: WJK, 2008], 68, 72). On the song as represented from the song's speaker, see Yairah Amit, *Judges: Introduction and Commentary* (Mikra Leyisra'el. Tel Aviv: Am Oved, Jerusalem: The Magness Press, The Hebrew University, 1999], 95, 98 (Hebrew).

5. For Ackerman 'Judges 5 is unambiguously and emphatic in its depiction of Deborah as Israel's chief military commander' and the fact that Barak's name is mentioned after Deborah's name in the song's editorial opening verse (5:1) is one of the proofs for the primacy of Deborah over Barak (Susan Ackerman. *Warrior, Dancer, Seductress, Queen: Women in Judges and Biblical Narrative* [New York: Doubleday, 1998], 31]).

6. The quotations are taken from the New Oxford Annotated Bible (NOAB).

of "judge" in this period. This shifting and inconclusive identity of the major judge in this story will contribute to a sense of suspense within the narrative plot as well as the theological significance of the story.[7]

Deborah in the Exposition

In the extensive and detailed story's exposition (4:1-5), there is no explicit mention of the fact that Deborah was raised as a deliverer. The exposition states that she was a prophetess,[8] wife of Lappidoth, and was a judge in Israel. According to Exum, 'Though the exact duties of the judges are not clear, some appear to have exercised legal function, while others were purely military leaders. Deborah combined these two important offices in addition to holding a third one, that of prophet' (4:4).[9] But the description that 'She used to sit under the Palm of Deborah between Ramah and Bethel in the hill country of Ephraim; and the Israelites would come to her for judgment' (4:5) explains that in this context judgment is merely the involvement in disputes and the offering of advice and recommendations. In other words, Deborah is not described as a warrior.[10] It seems that Deborah became famous and influential due to the way in which she solved the problems and resolved the disputes of those who came to her, and also because she was a prophetess and could mediate between the divine and the human.

The meaning of Deborah's name is 'bee', as it was customary to use animals' names for human beings.[11] Garsiel, who argues that biblical authors attributed significance to the names of people and places, connects the letters of Deborah's name with *dbry* ('utter song' in 5:12), and thus emphasizes the link between her

---

7. Dennis T. Olson, 'The Book of Judges,' in *The New Interpreter's Bible*. Volume Two (Nashville: Abingdon Press, 1994), 779; see also p. 783.

8. Conway emphasizes that 'the word נביאה is in the feminine form,' and in n. 8 she points out that in the many English versions that she checked, Deborah is called a prophet and not a prophetess, and thus the gender issue is ignored (Mary L. Conway, *Judging the Judges: A Narrative Appraisal Analysis* (Winona Lake, IN: Eisenbrauns, 2019), 110. See also Tammi J. Schneider, *Judges* (Collegeville, MN: Liturgical Press, 1999), 67.

9. J. Cheryl Exum, 'Deborah,' in *The HarperCollins Bible Dictionary* (3rd ed.; New York: HarperCollins, 2011), 189.

10. See Olson, 'Judges,' 779. On the double meaning of the root שׁפט (to judge) see Tomoo Ishida, 'The Leaders of the Tribal Leagues: Israel in the Pre-Monarchic Period,' *RevBib* 80 [1973]: 514–23); Amit, *Judges: Introduction and Commentary*, 9–10.

11. See Klass Spronk, *Judges* (Historical Commentary on the Old Testament; Leuven: Peeters, 2019), 146–47, who mentions this kind of names in the book of Judges, but there are more, as for example Shaphan and Huldah ('rabbit' and 'rat'; Kgs 22:14), Hamor ('donkey'; Gen. 34:2).

name and her song.¹² Following him, Shiran offers more options. Like the bee in Isa. 7:18-19, Deborah will sting and bring about victory.¹³ Moreover, Shiran stresses that as her name contains the root *d-b-r*, which can be interpreted as 'destroy, speak', and in Aramaic 'lead the herd', it alludes to her task as prophetess and leader, and even as a military leader.¹⁴ In addition, her femininity is underscored twice:¹⁵ by being a prophetess and by being the wife of Lappidoth.¹⁶ Unlike Othniel son of

12. Moshe Garsiel, *Biblical Names: A Literary Study of Midrashic Derivations and Puns* (Ramat-Gan: Bar Ilan University Press, 1991), 43–44. See also Elie Assis, 'Man, Woman and God in Judges 4,' *JSOT* 20 (2006): 124; Jack M. Sasson, *Judges 1–12: A New Translation with Introduction and Commentary* (AB; New Haven: Yale University Press, 2014), 254.

13. Tikva Frymer-Kensky notes: 'Like the queen bee, she raises up the swarm for battle, sending out the drones to protect the hive and conquer new territory' (*Reading the Women of the Bible* [New York: Schocken Books, 2002], 51).

14. R. Shiran, 'Deborah's Literary Character and the Portrayal of Her Leadership In Judges 4-5' (PhD thesis, Bar-Ilan University, Ramat-Gan, Israel, 2016), 32–33 (Hebrew).

15. Spronk (*Judges*, 147) adds: 'She is twice called אשה and twice referred to with the independent feminine pronoun היא.'

16. Interpreters have no accepted solution for the phrase 'wife of Lappidoth'. For the sages the name Lappidoth, meaning 'torches', points to the fact 'that she made wicks for the Temple' (b. Meg. 14a). According to Radak, Lapppidoth is her husband whose name is Barak (lightening), due to the similar meaning. Ralbag thinks that the name reflects a woman of valor, or an expression of power that indicates the level of prophecy. Modern exegetes also reflect on this name; see for example Burney (*Judges*, 85), Alonso-Schökel, 'Erzählkunst im Buche der Richter, *Biblica* 42 (1961): 160–61, and later Frymer-Kensky (*Reading*, 46). For Boling (*Judges*, 95) it is her husband's moniker. Niditch (*Judges*, 60, 62, 65) interprets 'Lappidoth' as an adjective for a fiery woman, and for Exum ('Deborah,' 189) she is spirited. Sasson's translation (*Judges*, 250) is 'wielder of flames' meaning divination using flames (see pp. 255–56). See also Spronk (*Judges*, 148–49). However, I prefer the interpretation according to which Lappidoth was the name of her husband, because it was accepted practice for women to be known by their husband's name, and see 2 Kgs 22:14, which deals with the prophetess Huldah. See, among others, J. Alberto Soggin, *Judges: A Commentary* (OTL; London: SCM Press, 1981), 72; Athalya Brenner, *The Israelite Woman: Social Role and Literary Type in Biblical Narrative* (Sheffield: JSOT Press, 1985), 62, 66; Garsiel, *Biblical Names*, 115; Schneider *Judges*, 66), and Butler *Judges*, 79–80, 92. Similarly, the phrase 'Jael wife of Heber the Kenite' (v. 17a) relates to Jael's husband, Heber, although the root and the context in vv. 11 and 17b indicate an ethnic group. This explanation disagrees with the one in my commentary; see Amit, *Judges: Introduction and Commentary*, 89. The occurrence of the same name used for people and ethnic groups is recognized, as for example Aram (2 Sam. 8:6; 1 Chr. 7:34), Ishmael (Gen. 25:13; 2 Kgs 25:25), Elam (Gen. 14:1; Ezra 2:7) and many others. However, Ora Brison interprets 'Heber' in its religious-magical connotation, meaning one who casts spells (see Deut. 18:11a); thus she offers an interesting explanation for the question of why Sisera wanted to come to her tent; see n. 18 below ('Between Biblical Heroines and the Divine Sphere: Female Heroics as Intermediaries between the Human and

Kenaz (3:9), or Ehud son of Gera (3:15), or even Shamgar son of Anath (3:31), who emerge as deliverers, according to the exposition Deborah was not appointed to deliver Israel.

Deborah throughout the Story and its Ending (vv. 6-24)

The continuation of the story's sequence complicates the situation. Deborah appoints Barak, and it appears that Barak is going to be the deliverer. But his refusal to accept an exclusive and independent role, following his condition that Deborah will accompany him, abrogates this possibility. However, Deborah's reaction to Barak's refusal reinstates the possibility that Deborah is going to be the deliverer, as she says: 'nevertheless, the road on which you are going will not lead to your glory, for the LORD will sell Sisera into the hand of a woman' (v. 9a). This reaction and the narrator's report that 'Barak summoned Zebulun and Naphtali to Kedesh; and ten thousand warriors went up behind him; and Deborah went up with him' (v. 10) reinforce the assumption that Deborah too will be the heroine of the battle, or at least a semi deliverer, as the deliverance will be shared by both. Furthermore, from the description of the battle (vv. 14-16), the reader understands that Deborah went up to Mount Tabor from Kedesh with Barak and even gave him the sign to set out to war, but she did not accompany him in the war itself: 'So Barak went down from Mount Tabor with ten thousand warriors following him' (v. 14). The reader gets the impression that Deborah herself did not go to the battlefield, where Barak and mainly God were active for the Israelites: 'And the LORD threw Sisera and all his chariots and all his army into a panic before Barak …while Barak pursued the chariots and the army' (vv. 15-16). The outcome of the battle was decided 'before Barak'.[17] Hence, Barak appears only as an instrument of God, who is the real deliverer of the war, and from this point until the end of the story Deborah disappears. Her last words to Barak were: 'Up! For this is the day on which the LORD has given Sisera into your hand. The LORD is indeed going out before you' (14a).

The surprise, which is the solution and fulfilment of Deborah's prophecy, is the last scene in the story (vv. 17-22), where we are told that the woman who killed Sisera is Jael and not Deborah. Thus, the prophecy uttered by Deborah in Barak's appointment scene (vv. 6-9) has been realized, and the reader has a solution to the riddle of the identity of the woman who will help affect the salvation of God, and into whose hand Sisera shall be given. This woman is not Deborah, who disappeared

---

the Divine;' [Doctoral Thesis Submitted to the Senate of Tel Aviv University, 2015], 95–97; and 'Jael, 'eshet heber the Kenite: A Diviner?' in *Joshua and Judges* [Texts@Contexts. Minneapolis: Fortress Press, 2013], 144–45.).

17. On the double meaning of 'before' (לפני), as an expression that could relate to both time and space – before his eyes and before he arrived. For a detailed analysis of vv. 14-16, see Amit *Book of Judges*, 208–11; See also Amit 'Judges,' in *The New Oxford Annotated Bible* (NRSV; New York: Oxford University Press, 2010), 363.

and was not part of the war itself, and not even an Israelite woman, but Jael the Kenite.[18]

Even in the concluding verses of the story (23-24), Deborah is not mentioned, but instead 'Then the hand of the Israelites bore harder and harder on King Jabin of Canaan, until they destroyed King Jabin of Canaan' (24). One learns from these verses that the battle over Kishon was only one issue in the overall complexity of the war intended to defeat and destroy the Canaanites along with Jabin, their king. Was Deborah a partner to the other battles? Was she the leader in the forty years of rest (5:31b)?[19] All this is a mystery; the gaps may be filled by imagination or by ideological interests.

Summary

After Jael killed Sisera, the limited contribution of each of the human deliverers is obvious. Deborah's task was to appoint Barak as deliverer, but since he hesitated to undertake this function, she was forced to support and encourage him, but still she did not accompany him to the battlefield. Barak's limited task was to pursue Sisera's army and their chariots, but not to capture Sisera. This was left to Jael, the third hero. Thus, Deborah is not a deliverer, God is the exclusive saviour in the story and the song, as he pulls the strings and the armies, and plans the fractional roles for each of the heroes, Deborah, Barak and Jael.[20] In fact, the task of the human heroes and Deborah among them is to highlight the divine salvation, as in the song: 'come to the help of the LORD against the mighty' (5:23b).

---

18. It is difficult to deduce Jael's motivation in killing Sisera, because on the one hand, v. 11 gives us information about the close ethnic connection between the Kenites and Israel, but v. 17b tells us that there was peace between Jabin, king of Hazor, and the house of Heber the Kenite, on the other. Moreover, the text does not refer to any personal motivation on the part of Jael. All this together with the earlier prophecy creates the impression that Jael acts according a predetermined plan of God, the God who acts behind the scenes. However, Brison ('Jael;' 'Between Biblical Heroines,' 89-115) relates to the motivation of Sisera, who knew that Yael's tent was a tent of a medium, and therefore he came to her to obtain more information regarding his future.

19. According to Pseudo-Philo's Antiquitatum Biblicarum XXXIII (1971: 179), Deborah Judged Israel for forty years.

20. See O'Connell *Rhetoric*, 112-13. In Butler's (*Judges*, 90) words: 'Yahweh, God of Israel, remains the main force behind what is happening.' This is why I claim, while using literary criteria, that God is the protagonist of this story and none of the human figures. See also Butler, *Judges*, 94. However, see Elie Assis ('The Hand of a Woman: Deborah and Yael (Judges 4),' *JHS* 5.19 [2005] 2) who on the one hand admits that 'God alone is responsible for victory'; but on the other, argues that Deborah is the heroine of the story (also Assis 'Man, Woman and God,' 113–14). Shiran ('Deborah's Literary Character,' 30–55), following him, dedicates the first chapter to proving that Deborah is the main hero of the story (Judg. 4), and of the song (Judg. 5).

Deborah According to the Things that the Text does not State Explicitly

We have seen that Deborah was a prophetess and a juridical judge, but what does this mean? What kind of prophet was she, and who gave her the authority to be a juridical judge?

What Kind of Prophetess was Deborah?

Deborah was not a prophet like Amos, Isaiah or Jeremiah, whom we call classical prophets, or rebuking prophets, or the writing prophets (whose prophecies were written and later became a book). These prophets' place in history spanned from the Assyrian occupation to the time after Malachi (from the eighth century BC to the fifth century BC). After that time it was a demand, 'From there on (Prov. 22:10) "bend your ear and listen to the words of the wise"' (seder olam raba 30:2). In other words, preference was given to the wise men, the interpreters of the Torah and the written prophecy.[21] Before the written prophets, during and after their time, different types of prophets were active, as seers, ecstatic prophets, prophets of other gods, those who had dreams, prophetesses and more. Essentially, Deborah was a seer, or a woman of God, meaning an emissary of God, analogous to 'a man of God'.[22] The editor in the story of Saul's anointment (1 Sam. 9:1–10:16) explains that 'Formerly in Israel, anyone who went to inquire of God would say, "Come, let us go to the seer"; for the one who is now called a prophet was formerly called a seer' (1 Sam. 9:9).[23] This story teaches us that when people went to the seer/prophet they had to pay money or give bread or different kinds of presents (9:7-8). People

---

21. E. E. Urbach, 'When did Prophecy Cease?' *Tarbiz* 17 (1946): 7–8 (Hebrew). See also Bava Batra 14b: 'Haggai, Zechariah, and Malachi were the last of the prophets'; 'As the Sages taught in a baraita (Tosefta 13:3): From the time when Haggai, Zechariah, and Malachi died the Divine Spirit departed from the Jewish people. As these three were considered the last prophets.' (Sotah 48b).

22. See Judg. 6:8; 1 Sam. 9:6, 8, 10; 1 Kgs 13:1; and more. It is not surprising that the term 'woman of God', which may create different associations regarding God, does not occur. Conway (*Judging the Judges*, 111; and see n. 10 there) suggests this translation: 'Deborah, a woman, a Prophetess, the wife of Lappidoth.' Ackerman (1975:10, 12) calls Deborah 'oracle-giver,' and uses the term 'oracular spokespersons' and argues that 'It is also possible that her title of prophetess is an anachronism.' He notes that 'There is insufficient evidence to claim that Deborah held an 'office' whose authority was recognized throughout the tribes.' Bal (1988:38) understands Deborah's activity as 'religious motivation.' Williamson argues that the passage which introduces Deborah as a prophetess (Judg. 4:4-5) is based on the introduction of Huldah (2 Kgs 22:14) and reflects the work of the deuteronomistic historian ('Prophetesses in the Hebrew Bible,' in *Prophecy and Prophets in Ancient Israel: Proceedings of the Oxford Old Testament Seminar* (ed. J. Day; New York/London: T&T Clark International, 2010, 68–72).

23. See also the dialogue between Amaziah the priest of Bethel and Amos, the first written prophet, who does not know that he is presenting the new phenomenon of classical prophets, and therefore denies his being a prophet (Amos 7:12-17).

went to those seers/prophets to ask, for example, about lost donkeys (9:6, 10) or a sick child (1 Kgs 14:1-18). Furthermore, these prophets also served leaders and kings, particularly in arduous situations, for example in times of famine or before war.[24] Seeligmann defines the seer as a free charismatic character, whose talents are the result of individual qualities that are unique to him.[25] It seems that Deborah was this type of prophet. Sasson adds: 'How Deborah practiced her art is beyond us to reconstruct, but all such techniques required an expert capacity to interpret the movement of flame or of smoke'.[26] It would be reasonable to assume that people came to her with their troubles, seeking her advice. Sasson stresses that 'Unlike prophets, diviners (and mantics) do not peddle unsolicited prognostications; they wait until a client, either personally or by proxy, comes to them with a specific query'.[27] We do not know about Deborah's struggle against idolatry or about her compassion for the poor, or her fight for moral issues. We have no clues regarding her preaching, reproofs or sermons, but we do know that she was a fortuneteller and could deliver the words of God.[28] Moreover, we may assume that she was a successful seer, a professional who commanded honour and a reputation, and similar to Samuel, things that she said came true; if not so, people would not have come to her.[29] The result was that when she delivered the divine message to Barak, he not only accepted it, but also demanded her presence beside him to ensure the existence of divine providence, in other words, success.

---

24. Most stories about these prophets in the Hebrew Bible are connected to situations of war. Just a few examples: 1 Sam. 22:5; 24:11, 19; 1 Chron. 21:19; 29:29; 1 Sam. 28:6; 1 Kgs 22:1-28; and there are many others, including the seer/prophetess Huldah (1 Kgs 22:14-20; 1 Chron. 34:22-28).

25. Isaac L. Seeligmann, 'On the Problems of Prophecy in Israel, its History and Nature.' Pages 170-88 in *Studies in Biblical Literature* (ed. A. Hurvitz et al;. Jerusalem, The Magnes Press, The Hebrew University, 1992), 173 (Hebrew). In this article, he argues that the prophecies of the ancient seers had a significant impact on the classical prophets.

26. Sasson, *Judges*, 256.

27. Sasson, *Judges*, 273.

28. Therefore, the tendency to compare Deborah to Samuel and even to Moses is always partial and mostly motivated by the desire to magnify Deborah. See Susanne Gillmayr-Bucher, 'Rollenspiel – Deborah und die Richter,' in *Ein Herz so weit wie der Sand am Ufer des Meeres, Festschrift für Georg Hentschel* (Erfurter Theologische Studien 90; Würzburg: Echter Verlag, 2006), 190; Bruce Herzberg, 'Deborah and Moses,' *JSOT* 38 (2013); Shiran, 'Deborah's Literary Character', 132–43). Williamson ('Prophetesses,' 69–73; see also n. 22 above) notes that the elements which align Deborah with Samuel and Moses and Huldah with Moses are the result of the deuteronomistic editorial work.

29. See the dialogue between Saul and the boy who accompanied him when tending to the donkeys. When Saul gave up looking for them and suggested they turn back, the boy said: 'There is a man of God in this town; he is a man held in honour. Whatever he says always comes true. Let us go there now; perhaps he will tell us about the journey on which we have set out' (1 Sam. 9:6).

Deborah as a Juridical Judge

Who appointed Deborah to have a role in the judiciary? Who were the judicial judges in the tribal period? Deuteronomy 16:18 tells us: 'You shall appoint judges and officials throughout your tribes, in all your towns that the LORD your God is giving you, and they shall render just decisions for the people.' There are laws in Deuteronomy, as for example the law in the case of a rebellious son (21:18-21), that mentions the elders of the town as the authority to decide.[30] It appears that the elders were the juridical authority not only in the tribal period, but in the monarchical period as well.[31] However, we do not know about women among the elders, and as the society was patriarchal, we do not expect women to be members of the elders' institution.[32] The elders would judge at the town gate (Deut. 21:19; 22:15; 25:7; Ruth 4:1-2, 11), but Deborah 'used to sit under the palm of Deborah[33] between Ramah and Bethel in the hill country of Ephraim; and the Israelites came up to her for judegment' (4:5). Conway's grammatical analysis leads her to the convincing conclusion that 'it is probable that Deborah has been judging

---

30. See also the laws regarding false accusations of the breach of marital contract (Deut. 22:13-23), the levirate marriage law (25:5-10), the place of the elders concerning the law of the cities of refuge (19:12) and the place of the ten elders in the case of Boaz (Ruth 4:1-11). These laws, although written in the monarchical period and later, represent the traditional judicial authority of the elders of the tribe and later of the elders of the town, see H. Reviv (*The Elders in Ancient Israel: A Study of Biblical Institution* [Jerusalem, The Magnes Press, The Hebrew University 1983], 48-64 [Hebrew]). McKenzie explains: 'The elders in the OT appear as a distinct social grade or collegiate body with certain political and religious functions and not merely as "old men"' ('The Elders in the Old Testament, *Biblica* 40 [1959], 522). Loewnstamm emphasizes that the elders belong to the secular judiciary, and they are mentioned in the early layer of the book of Deuteronomy ('Law, Biblical Law, in *Encyclopaedia Biblica*; Volume 5; Jerusalem: Bialik Institute], 629 [Hebrew]).

31. See 1 Kgs 21:8-14. For their status as advisors of the crown, see 1 Kgs 20:7-9; for their involvement in politics, see 2 Kgs 10:1-5. For a comprehensive discussion on the 'Elders' as institution, see Raviv, *The Elders in Ancient Israel*.

32. Matthews knows that 'Gender, once women have become postmenopausal, no longer disqualifies them from serving in an authoritative role' (*Judges & Ruth* [NCBC; Cambridge: Cambridge Unviersity Press, 2004], 64) However, he does not bring any example.

33. The tree was named after her. Soggin (*Judges*, 64) notes that 'palm tree does not normally grow on the highlands; it could therefore be regarded as a special palm, a sacred tree'. Boling (*Judges*, 95) learns from the fact that she had a tree named after her that she was responsible for Yahwist oracular inquiry. See also Sasson, *Judges*, 256. The sitting of a leader under a tree is mentioned also in the case of Saul: 1 Sam. 14:2; 22:6. This situation fits the days of the Judges and the early monarchy. Afterwards, we read about Solomon's Hall of Judgement in his palace complex (1 Kgs 7:7). Nevertheless, for Assis ('Man, Woman and God,' 119) a tree in mount Ephraim is a 'well established place of judgement'. The 'oak of Deborah' (Gen. 35:8), Rebecca's nurse, is also located in the Mountains of Ephraim, but below Bethel.

Israel for some time and that the Israelites habitually go to her for advice on various matters'.³⁴ Hence, it seems that Deborah became a legal judge because she was a successful seer, and wise enough to make the appropriate recommendations and decisions. The fact that she could intermediate between the divine and the human bore an impact on her role as judge. As Boda says: 'A prophetic figure would be dispensing justice (למשפט) because such a figure could seek the will of the deity and to offer the correct decision in difficult cases.'³⁵

Deborah – a Wise Woman

There is no explicit mention of Deborah being a wise woman, but in her case, we must trust the wisdom of the crowd.³⁶ If 'Israel came up to her for judgement,' it follows that people knew she was wise and they could rely on her judging. Wise women gained recognition and appreciation in ancient Israel, as we learn from the case of the woman from Tekoa, whom Joab brought to convince David – whose heart was yearning for Absalom – to bring Absalom back from Geshur (2 Sam. 14:2). We know also of the wise woman from Abel of Beth-maacah (2 Sam. 20:16-22), who saved her city by convincing the inhabitants to behead Sheba ben Bichri, who rebelled against David, and throw it to Joab, thus putting an end to the siege and saving the city.³⁷ It seems that these women did not have any official capacity, but people came to them because they were famous for their ability to resolve personal and political issues by making clever decisions. Those women, including Deborah, acted in public;³⁸ they had popular authority and were gifted with

---

34. Conway *Judging the Judges*, 114. G. F. Moore thinks that v. 5 is 'A circumstantial addition by a letter editor' (*A Critical and Exegetical Commentary on Judges* [ICC; Edinburg: T&T Clark, 1966], 113), but already Burney (*Judges* 85) objects.

35. Mark J. Boda, 'Recycling Heaven's Words: Receiving and Retrieving Divine Revelation in the Historiography of Judges,' in *Prophets, Prophecy, and Ancient Israelite Historiography* (Winona Lake, IN: Eisenbrauns, 2013), 51. See also Matthews, *Judges & Ruth*, 64–65.

36. We may compare the judgement of Deborah to the work of mediators or arbitrators today, who gain the trust of their surrounding; see Olson, 'Judges,' 778–79, 782; Sasson, *Judges*, 256; Shiran, 'Deborah's Literary Character,' 122–23.

37. Abigail, who married David, is also characterized as a wise woman (1 Sam. 25:3). She resolved a private dispute, in connection to her property, while the two wise women mentioned above gave service to the public and remained nameless. According to Goitein (1967:258), the wisdom of the wise woman is more than a natural talent, but the entire combination of qualifications with which women gain leadership in their communities ('Women's Literature in the Bible,' in *Bible Studies* [Tel Aviv: Yavneh Publishing House, 1967]). Brenner (*Israelite Women*, 35–44) argued that wise women were an ancient institution that disappeared. Frymer-Kensky (*Reading*, 58–63) thinks that their namelessness indicates a particular role. She uses the expression: 'Wise Womanhood'.

38. Frymer-Kensky (*Reading*, 45) stresses, 'Deborah was active in the public arena as part of her normal everyday life,' but I do not think she is right in depicting Deborah as a warrior. In order to define Deborah as a warrior, she creates the term 'warrior by word'.

rhetorical talent and psychological understanding. Therefore, I accept Shiran's conclusion that Deborah also functioned as a wise woman, although she was not titled as such.[39]

Deborah – a Charismatic Personality

'The term "Charisma" will be applied to a certain quality of an individual personality by virtue of which he is set apart from ordinary men and treated as endowed with supernatural, superhuman, or at least specifically exceptional powers or qualities... In primitive circumstances, this peculiar kind of deference is paid to prophets, to people with a reputation for therapeutic or legal wisdom, to leaders in the hunt, and heroes in war. It is very often thought of as resting on magical powers.'[40] According to Weber, prophets in general and the deliverers of the book of Judges in particular were charismatic figures.[41] Although Deborah was not a deliverer, she was unlike ordinary people, as she was blessed with prophetic powers and wisdom, all this indicating that she was a charismatic person. As a prophetess who received the words of God and as a judge who had gained the people's trust, she must have been charismatic. Moreover, the fact that she could convince Barak, who lived in the north, to collect the army and to go to war against a threatening enemy equipped with 900 iron chariots, indicates that her name as a reliable messenger of God was known even in the far north. All this confirms the fact that she was charismatic.

---

39. Shiran, 'Deborah's Literary Character,' 126. According to Goitein ('Women's Literature,' 259), the adjective 'wise' in the phrase 'wise woman' relates to all the qualifications that make a woman a public leader.

40. Max Weber, *The Theory of Social and Economic Organization* (trans. A. M. Henderson and Talcott Parsons; London, Edinburgh, Glasgow: William Hodge and Company, 1947), 329. See also Weber, *Ancient Judaism* (trans. and ed. H. H. Gerth and D. Martindale; Glencoe, IL: The Free Press, 1952), 85–86, 96–105. But according to Assis ('Man, Woman and God,' 118), 'the presentation of Deborah as a judge in the judicial sense is meant to present her as a publicly recognized institution than a charismatic character.' He even emphasizes that to be charismatic is 'to arise charismatically from anonymity' and uses the term 'anti-charismatic' (p. 110). However, he does not take into account the possibility that before Deborah was appointed prophet and became a judge, she was charismatic and this is why and how she reached this status.

41. See Ze'ev Weisman, *Saviours and Prophets: Two Aspects of Biblical Charisma* (Tel Aviv: Hakibbutz Hameuchad, Aviv Publishing House, 2003), 119, who followed Weber and dedicated a whole book to the subject of charismatic leaders in the Hebrew Bible. However, he does not mention not Deborah nor Barak as charismatic leaders, because it is not said that God raised them up as deliverers or that the spirit of God came upon them. On the other hand, he admits the existence of the sociological-anthropological function of prophecy as intermediary (pp. 137–38).

Conclusion

Deborah, who initiated the war against the Canaanites, was a reliable seer/prophetess and a charismatic leader, who enjoyed a high status and enormous influence, as Brenner says: 'Deborah conforms to the stereotype of the multi-talented Great Leader.'[42] As she was a prophetess and a juridical judge, she was involved in public life, and interested in the political arena. Her charismatic personality and professional status made it possible for her to become an influential factor, respected by her community. Thus, she gained the title 'a mother in Israel' (5:7), who cares about her children and protects them, in Exum's words: 'a mother in Israel is one who brings liberation from oppression, provides protection, and ensures the well-being and security of her people'.[43] On the other hand, Deborah, who was not a deliverer, does not appear on Samuel's list of military judges (1 Sam. 12:11), but Barak, according to some versions, is included.[44]

The question remains: what happened to Deborah's leadership after the battle? Nothing appears in the text, and we may ask, was she part of the extended war against Jabin king of Canaan, or was she the limited hero of one battle? Was she a leader only on Mount Ephraim, or was she the leader of several tribes? We should remember that Deborah was never a national leader. Even 'her' song does not relate to all the tribes of Israel.[45] Everything is open to our interest in filling in the gaps, or the goals of our interpretation. As, for example, Deborah's leadership that

---

42. Brenner, Israelite Women, 62. Gillmayr-Bucher depicts her multitudinous leadership thus: 'Deborah acts as judge, she is responsible for the people and is portrayed as a savior. In addition, she adds prophetic-charismatic aspects to the more common, material image of a judge, transporting the image of a judge from a military leader to a prophetic, charismatic, and strategic leader' ('Memories Laid to Rest: The Book of Judges in the Persian Period,' in *Deuteronomy-Kings as Emerging Authoritative Books: A Conversation* [Atlanta: Society of Biblical Literature, 2014], 125).

43. J. Cheryl Exum, "Mother in Israel': a familiar figure reconsidered,' in *Feminist Interpretation of the Bible* (Oxford: Basil Blackwell, 1985), 85. Frymer-Kensky (*Reading*, 50) adds: 'The motherhood of this 'mother in Israel' goes beyond biology. It describes her role as counselor during the days before the war, and it indicates her role in preserving the heritage of Israel, in her case by advising in battle.' According to Goitein ('Women's Literature', 259) 'mother in Israel' is a title that every woman may obtain if all the people listen to her like sons who obey the discipline of their mother.

44. In the Masoretic version Barak is not mentioned, but rather Bedan. However, according to some, Barak is mentioned together with Gideon, Samson, Jephthah, David and Samuel. For Conway (*Judging the Judges*, 114–18, 124–25) Barak is the typical judge of the days of the judges, but she sees in him the beginning of the decline of the excellency of the judges.

45. See Ze'ev Weisman, 'Did A National Leadership Exist in the Era of the Judges?' in *Studies in the History of the Jewish People and the Land of Israel*, Fifth Volume (Haifa: University of Haifa, 1980) and especially p. 21 there.

did not captivate some of our Sages, who said: 'Alas to the generation that has a woman for its leader' (Midrash Tehillim [Buber] on Ps. 22).[46] On the other hand, for Block she is 'without doubt the most honorable human figure in the Book of the Judges'.[47] Shiran is convinced that Deborah 'is a unique example of a charismatic female leader and has much in common with the two greatest leaders of the Israelites in the period before the monarchy – Moses and Samuel . . . As a leader, Deborah continues Moses' path'.[48] In other words, for some scholars, merely name a leader and Deborah outshines him. However, I think that Butler is right in stating 'Commentators easily make too much of Deborah … In fact, it shows how exceptional Deborah, the woman, is rather than how typical. Still, her qualifications do not make her the heroine of the narrative.'[49]

I do hope that 'my' Deborah remains in the limits of her place and time, i.e. a charismatic figure who was a successful seer and a wise woman, and thus received the trust of the people, serving as a legal judge as well. All these traits made it possible for her to initiate the war against Sisera, the commander of Jabin's army, and convince and encourage Barak to become the commander of this battle. She was not a deliverer, but she was sufficiently wise to decide what to do, when to do it, and how to do it.

46. Against this midrash, there are those who praise Deborah. For different approaches of the Sages regarding Deborah, see Shulamit Valler, 'Strong Women Confront Helpless Men: Deborah and Jephthah's Daughter in the Midrash,' in *Words, Ideas, Worlds: Biblical Essays in Honour of Yairah Amit* (Sheffield: Sheffield Phoenix Press, 2012).

47. Daniel I. Block, 'Deborah among the Judges: The Perspective of the Hebrew Historian,' in *Faith, Tradition, and History: Old Testament Historiography in Its Near Eastern Context* (Winona Lake, IN: Eisenbrauns, 1994), 246.

48. Shiran 'Deborah's Literary Character,' I. She dedicates a whole unit to this purpose and avoids mentioning the differences, see pp. 132–45. See also n. 28.

49. Butler, *Judges*, 91. For Matthews (*Judges & Ruth*, 64) she is 'a liminal figure.'

Chapter 4

BLESSED DESTROYER: THE CHARACTERIZATION OF JAEL AS A WARRIOR IN COMMAND AND AN INSTRUMENT OF YHWH

Elizabeth H.P. Backfish

J. P. Fokkelman describes the narrator of a story as a 'veritable ringmaster'.[1] Imagine a Cirque du Soleil performance. The audience comes to the circus to see the perfectly-choreographed performing arts and death-defying stunts, but it is the ringmaster who shapes how the audience sees the show. Each performer plays a pivotal role in the overall story of the circus, and everything the audience members know about these individuals is shaped by the way in which the ringmaster has designed the show and presented them.

So it is with the storytellers of Judges 4–5. Here we have character portrayals from two different ringmasters, a narrator and a poet. Each character in this cycle deserves close examination, but one is arguably the 'star performer'. She raises and subverts expectations from other characters and from readers. She does what other characters cannot, and she is lauded by the leaders of her time for her acts of courage. Her inner thoughts and motives are masked behind the artful reticence of the narrator and poet, but the reader cannot help but be drawn to her, just as an audience is drawn to the star performer in the circus's grand finale.

The following essay will argue that both narrator and poet characterize Jael as a warrior in command, a point that has not been missed in scholarship. However, they also characterize her as an instrument of God, and this point has perhaps been undervalued. In other words, she fully embodies the first and final words that describe her in chapter 5: she is 'blessed' as an instrument of divine warfare, and she is a 'destroyer' of God's enemies (Judg. 5:24a, 27c). After a brief word on methodology, this essay will examine how the narrator and poet have characterized Jael as a warrior in command and as an instrument of YHWH. The essay will conclude by comparing and contrasting other scholarly opinions of Jael's characterization and the rhetorical significance of the characterization argued for here.

---

1. J. P. Fokkelman, *Reading Biblical Narrative: An Introductory Guide* (trans. Ineke Smit; Louisville, KY: Westminster John Knox, 1999), 56.

Methodology

A few preliminary words are in order about the text, characterization in general and the place of ambiguity. As for the text, there has been much scholarly discussion on textual priority and dependence. Diachronic questions of which account came first are important, but less so for this present study, which is primarily synchronic. The concern of this essay is how the two accounts together, in their final form, shape the character of Jael.

The first issue of characterization pertains to the type of character our ringmasters have presented. Adele Berlin sees not just Forster's classical 'flat' and 'round' character types, but also a third type: the agent. Agents 'effect' the plot and contrast with other characters, often provoking their responses.[2] If round or 'full-fledged' characters involve change, development, or a clear window into the inner workings of a character, then Jael probably does not qualify as a round character. However, nor is she a flat character, which are typically 'types'[3] or have minimal impact on the plot. Jael subverts standard 'types' and her actions arguably constitute the climax of the plot. According to Berlin's classification, therefore, Jael is an agent.

The second matter is to determine which techniques our various ringmasters use to characterize Jael. Berlin identifies four techniques of characterization, the latter two of which are most employed in Judges 4–5: 1) description, 2) inner life, 3) speech and actions, and 4) contrast with other characters and expectations.[4] The accounts of Jael provide little direct description, save from her identification as the 'wife of Heber' (Judg. 4:17) and Deborah's description of Jael as 'most blessed' (Judg. 5:24). Similarly, the inner thoughts and motivations of Jael are left to the readers to infer based other factors in the story, such as speech, action, and contrast.[5]

---

2. Adele Berlin, *Poetics and Interpretation of Biblical Narrative* (Winona Lake, IN: Eisenbrauns, 1994), 32. Mieke Bal agrees that Forster's binary categories do not fit within the biblical narratives, which 'mock precisely such categories,' *Narratology: Introduction to the Theory of Narrative Account* (3rd ed.; Toronto: University of Toronto Press, 2009), 115.

3. J. Cheryl Exum is representative of scholars who view the female characters in Judges largely as types that reinforce the androcentric agenda of the narrator. She argues that Deborah is characterized as the 'good mother' whereas Jael is the 'death-dealing mother,' 'Feminist Criticism: Whose Interests Are Being Served?' in *Judges and Method: New Approaches in Biblical Studies* (ed. By Gale A. Yee; 2nd ed.; Minneapolis: Fortress, 2007), 71.

4. Berlin, *Poetics and Interpretation of Biblical Narrative*, 34–40.

5. Koen de Temmerman refers to these methods of indirect characterization as metonymic and metaphorical characterization. Metonymic characterization uses the characters actions and words to shape the character, and metaphorical characterization uses comparison and contrast to characterize them, *Crafting Characters: Heroes and Heroines in the Ancient Greek Novel*, (Oxford: Oxford University Press, 2014), 30–31.

These techniques of 'indirect shaping,' as Shimon Bar-Efrat calls them, make it difficult for readers to determine a character's motives.[6] Robert Alter describes 'the underlying biblical conception of character as often unpredictable, in some ways impenetrable, constantly emerging from and slipping back into a penumbra of ambiguity,'[7] and these features all describe the characterization of Jael. She is unpredictable, her inner life is in some ways impenetrable, and much of her motives are clouded in ambiguity. Such uncertainly might initially appear to be a problem for interpreters. However, David M. Gunn and Danna Nolan Fewell claim that this ambiguity and scarcity of direct description can actually be understood as assets to the story. They argue, 'Reticence does not necessarily mean emptiness. Simplicity may indicate openness to inference rather than closure.'[8] This 'openness' invites the readers to speculate about a character's motivations and inner life. Gunn and Fewell propose that such speculations are not only permissible in the interpretative process, but even inevitable.[9] In other words, it is not a question of *whether or not* readers will speculate about the inner worlds of characters, but rather *how well* they will do it.

If the openness of characterizations invites readers to make thoughtful inferences based on a close reading of the text and its various contexts, some methodological safeguards should guide the imaginative process.[10] These might include the following test questions: 1) Is this characterization in line with the overall purpose of the narrative (or book)? For our story, this will include the theme of divine deliverance from the consequences of idolatry through various instruments of deliverance. 2) Is this characterization in line with contributions from the social sciences? For our story, this will include how pre-monarchical Israelites viewed the realms of private and public life and the sociological roles of men and women. 3) Is this characterization in line with the historical and cultural contexts? For our story, this will include issues of hospitality and warfare.

With this invitation to explore, and with the methodological guardrails in place, let us turn now to the star attraction.

The Characterization of Jael as a Warrior in Command

Through her words, actions, and connections with other characters within and outside of this pericope, the ringmasters of Judges 4–5 characterize Jael as a warrior in command of those around her.

---

6. Shimon Bar-Efrat, *Narrative Art in the Bible* (London:T&T Clark International, 2004), 64–65, 77.

7. Robert Alter, *The Art of Biblical Narrative* (rev. ed.; New York: Basic Books, 2011), 129.

8. David M. Gunn and Danna Nolan Fewell, *Narrative in the Hebrew Bible* (The Oxford Bible Series; Oxford: Oxford University Press, 1993), 49.

9. Ibid.

10. What I am describing as safeguards, Bal describes as 'verification,' arguing that the speculation needed in character analysis must be followed up with verification in a constant 'dialectic' (*Narratology*, 127).

Commanding Words

Jael's words are few and restricted to the narrative account, but they are powerful. If Alter is correct when he proposes that a character's opening words have 'revelatory' importance,[11] then the weight afforded to Jael's first and only recorded words to Sisera and then Barak is particularly significant. Consider her parallel commands to each man, which form an *inclusio* around the climactic action of her assassination:

Verse 18a   And Jael went out to meet Sisera
        18b   And she said to him,
        18c   'Turn aside (סורה), my lord, turn aside (סורה) to me. Do not be afraid.'
        18d   And he turned aside (ויסר) to her, to the tent, and she covered him with a blanket.

Verse 22b   And Jael went out to meet him
        22c   And she said to him,
        22d   'Come (לך), and I will show you the man whom you are seeking.'
        22e   And he went (ויבא) to her, and behold, Sisera was fallen dead and a peg was in his temple.[12]

Both scenes begin with Jael coming out of her tent to meet a man whom she then invites or commands into her home. The narrator uses verbal repetition to frame the scene: each time, Jael 'goes out to meet' a man, each time she is the first to speak, and in each speech, she uses exactly three verbs. The verbal repetition heightens the correlation between these two interactions. Not only are the words themselves important, but also the way in which she uses them, and the responses they solicit.

With Sisera, Jael uses repetition to denote the urgency of her request, and she addresses Sisera with the respectful title of 'my lord' (אדני), even (and ironically!) exhorting the general not to be afraid (אל־תירא), when one would expect the lone woman to be the one afraid of this famously brutal commander.[13] In fact, according to Anne Létourneau, when used in contexts of warfare, this expression is most often used of a superior to someone inferior in rank.[14]

---

11. *Art of Biblical Narrative*, 74; See also Benjamin J. M. Johnson's careful study of David in 'Making a First Impression: The Characterization of David and his Opening Words in 1 Samuel 17:25-31,' *TynBul* 71/1 (2020): 75–93.

12. All translations are the author's unless otherwise indicated.

13. Johanna W. H. van Wijk-Bos notes the irony that 'the woman tells the warrior not to be afraid!' 'Out of the Shadows: Genesis 38; Judges 4:17-22; Ruth 3,' *Semeia* 42 (1988): 53, 56.

14. Anne Létourneau, 'Campy Murder in Judges 4: Is Yael a Geberèt (Heroine)?' In *Gender Agenda Matters: Papers of the 'Feminist Section' of the International Meetings of The Society of Biblical Literature* (ed. Irmtraud Fischer; Newcastle-upon-Tyne: Cambridge Scholars Publishing, 2015), 53.

With Barak, Jael's tone subtlety changes, and the narrator characterizes his response in a slightly different way. Jael again uses three verbs in her short exchange with her male counterpart, but the urgency and polite title are dropped. Here the imperative takes the force of a command, rather than a request, and echoes Deborah's authoritative word to Barak in Judg. 4:6. Also, rather than comforting Barak as a means of deception, she straightforwardly explains that she will show him the enemy he seeks. If Barak was hoping that Sisera were still alive within Jael's tent, that hope is soon dashed when the point of view shifts (signalled by the particle הנה) and readers view the dead Sisera through the surprised and disappointed eyes of Barak.

Another significant difference between the men is how the narrator characterizes their responses to Jael's imperatives. When Jael implores Sisera to 'turn aside' (סורה), he does exactly that, using the same exact verbiage (ויסר). When Jael commands Barak to 'come' (לך), he basically does so, but the narrator uses a different word with a similar meaning (ויבא). The verb בוא also has a sexual connotation, especially when combined with the prepositional phrase 'to her' (אליה).[15] Many scholars interpret this, and other images in the text, as clear indicators of seduction or rape. Either Jael is enticing the men into her tent so as to seduce them[16] or they are entering her tent as a means to (or a metaphor for) entering her sexually.[17]

However, it seems unlikely that this language is meant to describe actual sex between a woman who is later praised as 'most blessed' and men who are running exhausted for their lives. Much more likely, from a literary and sociological perspective, is that the narrator is using sexual imagery as one more layer of de-masculinizing Sisera and Barak. If any reverse-rape is happening between Jael and Sisera, it is a literary construct of a narrator who wants to highlight the irony that the would-be rapist (Judg. 5:30) is being figuratively defiled. Similarly, the sexual innuendos between Jael and Barak most likely serve to heighten the gender reversal between Jael and Barak, and to underscore Deborah's prophetic word that the honour of battle would go to a woman (Judg. 4:9).[18]

---

15. Gen. 29:23; 30:3, 4; 38:2, 8; Judg 16:1; Ruth 4:13; 2 Sam. 12:24.

16. Scholars make much of the seeming parallels between Jael's going out and inviting men to turn or come into her home with the adulterous woman of Prov. 7:10 and Lady Folly in Proverbs 9:13-18 (Elie Assis, "'The Hand of a Woman': Deborah and Yael [Judges 4]' *JHebS* 5/19 [2004–2005]: 9–10; Létourneau, 'Campy Murder in Judges 4: Is Yael a Gebèrèt [Heroine]?,' 46–49). However, such scholars seem to ignore the pious and non-sexual parallel invitations of Lady Wisdom (Prov. 9:1-12).

17. According to Fewell and Gunn, 'At least in biblical literature, a man seldom enters a woman's tent for purposes other than sexual intercourse. The woman's tent is symbolic of the woman's body,' 'Controlling Perspectives: Women, Men, and the Authority of Violence in Judges 4 & 5,' *JAAR* 58/3 (1990): 392; Victor H. Matthews and Don C. Benjamin, *Social World of Ancient Israel: 1250–587 BCE* (Grand Rapids, MI: Baker Academic, 1993), 94.

18. It could also be that Barak misinterpreted Jael's command as being a sexual invitation, which would correspond with his earlier inability to rightly size-up a situation (Judg. 4:8), but again, would not suggest that sex was actually a narrative action.

Commanding Actions

With every word recorded from her mouth, Jael is in control of those around her, wielding the upper hand with tact and courage. In fact, even at moments when she appears to be on the receiving end of the commands, her actions actually betray something very different from simple submission.

When Jael requested that Sisera turn aside to her, the narrator-ringmaster shows him doing so, using verbatim repetition. Alter calls this type of verbatim mirroring 'dialogue-bound narration.'[19] However, Jael's actions are never bound by Sisera's requests. Sisera makes two demands of her.[20] First, in Judges 4:19, he asks her for water. Jael responds by giving him milk instead of water. The milk might have been a soporific to lull him to sleep or an aphrodisiac (less likely), or it might have been a way of showing profuse hospitality.[21] Whatever the implication of 'milk' might potentially be, it is first and foremost *not* water. In other words, on a literary level, this break from dialogue-bound narration is a way of saying that Jael still holds the upper hand. She gave her request, and Sisera obeyed. He gave his request, and Jael deviates to show that she maintains power over the situation.

The narrator also shows Jael's control over the situation in that Sisera's two verbs (the request for water and the reason for his request) is met with three verbs describing Jael's response: she opens the milk, pours it, and then covers him. Opening the milk seems like an unnecessary detail, since naturally a skin of milk would need to be opened in order to pour it,[22] and covering or re-covering[23] him also seems redundant, unless the narrator is highlighting how her actions (three of them) move beyond Sisera's commands (two of them). Additionally, the poet in chapter 5 elaborates on the type of bowl in which Jael serves Sisera his milk. This 'bowl of majesty' (v. 25) is often understood to

---

19. Alter, *Art of Biblical Narrative*, 77.

20. Typically, the guest was not permitted to make requests of the host, Victor H. Matthews, 'Hospitality and Hostility in Judges 4,' *BTB* 21/1 (1991): 19.

21. However, this 'one-upmanship' was never between a request from a guest (which was not permitted) and what the host opted to give them. It was an escalation between what the host originally offered and what the host then delivers, Matthews, 'Hospitality and Hostility in Judges 4,' 15, 18.

22. Although milk could be stored in ceramic storage jars, the collocation ותפתח את־נאוד החלב is probably best rendered 'and she opened a skin of milk,' which is supported lexically (HALOT, 1:657) and ethnographically (Leann Pace, 'Tools and Utensils,' 189; David Ilan, 'Storage,' 253; both in *T&T Clark Handbook of Food in the Hebrew Bible and Ancient Israel* [ed. Janling Fu, Cynthia Shafer-Elliott and Carol Meyers; London: Bloomsbury, 2022]).

23. Some scholars, such as Matthews and Benjamin, interpret the first use of the phrase ותכסהו בשמיכה to refer to her covering the opening of the tent (*Social World of Ancient Israel*, 92), but the verbs used in both v. 18 and in v. 19 are identical (ותכסהו), suggesting that she covered him twice or that her covering of him is mentioned twice, possibly for emphasis, just as her request that Sisera 'turn aside' was repeated twice for emphasis.

characterize Jael's flattery of Sisera, treating him like a king so as to further gain his trust. However, according to Mieke Bal, the serving utensils denote the social status of the host, rather than the guest. Rather than flattering Sisera, Jael was subtly showing her sovereignty over him.[24]

Sisera's second demand is for Jael to guard the door and tell anyone who might approach that there is not 'a man' in her tent (v. 20). The tone of this second string of imperatives is much more commanding. In fact, Sisera even uses the masculine verbal form when commanding Jael to stand guard (עמד).[25] Nowhere else in the Hebrew Bible is this form used with a feminine object. Sisera seems to be treating Jael as one of his male soldiers through his use of words. Thus, the narrator even uses the inflection of Sisera's dialogue to further characterize Jael as a warrior.[26] However, Sisera's orders to his 'subordinate soldier' are not followed, because Jael is not in fact a subordinate soldier. This is her battlefield and she is about to reveal her own battle plan. Jael sneaks up to her victim in order to make his words literally come true, that indeed there is not 'a man' in her tent (v. 21)!

Sisera uses six verbs in his request in v. 20. The narrator matches those six verbs with six more verbs describing Jael's response in v. 21 (aside from the parenthetical explanation off the main line of narration), which has the effect of a well-matched combat:

Table 1 *Judg 4:20-21:*

ויאמר אליה עמד פתח האהל והיה אם־איש יבוא ושאלך ואמר היש־פה איש ואמרת אין:	And he said to her, '<u>Stand</u> at the entrance of the tent, and <u>it will be</u> if a man <u>comes</u> and <u>asks you</u>, <u>and he says</u>, 'Is there a man here?' Then <u>you shall say</u>, 'There is not.'
ותקח יעל אשת־חבר את־יתד האהל ותשם את־המקבת בידה ותבוא אליו בלאט ותתקע את־היתד ברקתו ותצנח בארץ והוא־נרדם ויעף וימת:	And Jael, the wife of Hever, <u>took</u> a tent peg and <u>she placed</u> the hammer in her hand, and <u>she went</u> to him in secrecy, and <u>she thrust</u> the peg in to his temple, and <u>it went down</u> on the ground (now he was sleeping and he was exhausted) and he died.

---

24. Bal, *Murder and Difference: Gender, Genre, and Scholarship on Sisera's Death* (Indiana Studies in Biblical Literature; Bloomington, IN: Indiana University Press, 1992), 129.

25. Gary Rendsburg's excellent study on *diglossia* identifies the tendency for spoken language to use 'gender neutralization' whereby expected feminine forms are often rendered with masculine ones (and occasionally vice versa); *Diglossia in Ancient Hebrew* (American Oriental Series, vol. 72; New Haven: CN: American Oriental Society, 1990), 35–67. However, this phenomenon seems to be restricted to plural grammatical forms, so it seems unlikely to be in play in Sisera's command to Jael. In other words, there is strong grammatical support for seeing Sisera's use of the masculine imperative as additional evidence that the narrator is characterizing Jael as a warrior.

26. Létourneau sees the masculine imperative as evidence of the gender ambiguity in this narrative, 'Campy Murder in Judges 4: Is Yael a Gebèrèt (Heroine)?,' 64.

This is further supported by the similar verbal parallel in the song between the string of Jael's actions (Judg. 5:25-26) and Sisera's downfall (Judg. 5:27). Both contain seven finite verbs:

Table 2 *Judg 5:25-27:*

מים שאל חלב <u>נתנה</u>	Water he asked for, milk <u>she gave</u>
בספל אדירים <u>הקריבה</u> חמאה:	In a bowl of majesty <u>she brought</u> curdled milk
ידה ליתד <u>תשלחנה</u>	Her hand <u>stretched out</u> to the peg
וימינה להלמות עמלים	And her right hand for the hammer of the workman
<u>והלמה</u> סיסרא <u>מחקה</u> ראשו	And <u>she smote</u> Sisera, <u>she annihilated</u> his head.
<u>ומחצה וחלפה</u> רקתו:	And <u>she shattered and pierced</u> his temple.
בין רגליה <u>כרע נפל שכב</u>	Between her feet, <u>he knelt, he fell, he lay down</u>
בין רגליה <u>כרע נפל</u>	Between her feet, <u>he knelt, he fell,</u>
באשר <u>כרע</u> שם <u>נפל</u> שדוד:	Where <u>he knelt</u>, there <u>he fell</u>, destroyed.

The poet also depicts Sisera as standing (or possibly sitting), which not only dramatically describes his figurative 'downfall' but also draws on combat imagery, encouraging readers to view Jael and Sisera both standing, well-matched, in hand-to-hand combat. The song also skips over the deception and goes straight to the assassination, further masculinizing the killing scene and downplaying Jael's need to use deception to compensate for her inferior physical strength.[27]

Whereas the deception in the narrative is heightened by the domestic objects Jael uses, her actions reflect warrior imagery. Each object she uses seems innocuous in her matriarchal role.[28] The cover (a blanket or rug) is something one would expect to find in a tent. A skin of milk is something clearly within the world of the household. Even the tent peg and hammer are common household tools, which might not raise a single eyebrow for an ancient reader. In Judg. 4:21c, however, those domestic items become weapons in the actions of a warrior.

At least two actions depict Jael as a warrior. First, the narrator describes her in Judg. 4:21 as sneaking up to Sisera 'in secret' (בלאט), using language similar to other covert military exploits, such as when David snuck up on Saul to cut off a portion of his robe (1 Sam. 24:4 [5]). Second, the narrator and poet emphasize that Jael wields her household 'weapon' in her 'hand' (Judg. 4:21; 5:26), a common image of military control and a fulfilment of Deborah's prophecy to Barak that Yaweh would sell Sisera into the hand of a woman (Judg. 4:9).

One might wonder if readers should interpret this use of deception negatively, or if the ringmaster is portraying his star performer as a deviant. Two reasons suggest not. First, Jael was naturally limited in her strength and her access to equally-matched weaponry. Sisera was a well-trained and presumably armed man. Jael would have to be resourceful in how she could fight her opponent. Second, deception was not viewed as unequivocally negative in ancient Israel. Victor H.

---

27. Fewell and Gunn, 'Controlling Perspectives,' 405.
28. Van Wijk-Bos, 'Out of the Shadows,' 54-55.

Matthews and Don C. Benjamin explain, 'Hebrew villagers lived on the margins of their social world. Like all marginalized people, they admired the clever who improved themselves at the expense of the establishment. Cleverness was the wisdom of the powerless.'[29] Jael's resourcefulness and courage to overcome the enemy, even as a woman and an outsider, invites other marginalized readers to identify with her and to be empowered by her example.

Sexual and maternal imagery also shape the characterization of Jael. In addition to the sexual undertone of the expression 'he came (in)to her' mentioned above, other sexual imagery includes the portrayal of men entering the tent of a woman alone (Judg. 4:18, 22), Jael penetrating a man's body[30] with a phallic-shaped tent peg (Judg. 4:21; 5:26), and the imagery of Sisera falling 'between her feet' (Judg. 5:27). This sexual imagery seems to serve the irony that the man who could have been defiling women (according to his mother and her ladies in 5:30) was himself figuratively defiled by a woman. The maternal imagery includes Jael's covering of Sisera and offering him milk. This maternal imagery serves to deceive Sisera and also to draw a comparison between Jael's figurative mothering and Deborah's mothering of Israel, as well as a contrast between the actual mother who brought Sisera life and the figurative mother who brings his death. Sexual and maternal imagery may also have been what Sisera, Barak and original readers might have expected, especially from a foreign woman.[31] In this way, the narrator raises and subverts our expectations, just as Jael raises and subverts the expectations of Sisera and Barak, who assume that she harbors safety, protection, and possibly even sexual pleasure.[32]

The matter of hospitality is often raised in scholarship because both Sisera and Jael break hospitality rules. This issue is important for understanding the

---

29. Matthews and Benjamin, 17. Michael Williams has also shown convincingly that, within the book of Genesis, The narrator views deception positively when the deceiver is righting a deception against him or herself. Michael James Williams, *Deception in Genesis: Investigation into the Morality of a Unique Biblical Phenomenon* (Studies in Biblical Literature, vol. 32; New York: Peter Lang, 2001).

30. While most scholars translate רקה as 'temple' in 4:21-22 and 5:26 Fewell and Gunn argue that the rare word means 'mouth,' which would convey even more sexual connotations, 'Controlling Perspectives,' 393.

31. Fewell and Gunn, 'Controlling Perspectives,' 406.

32. Fewell and Gunn add that both Deborah and Jael subvert the two primary expectations of women in ancient Israel: to produce heirs and to gratify men's sexual desires. Both women are described with wife and mother imagery, yet their sexuality and their motherhood are both used for the sake of delivering Israel (ibid., 397); for a summary review of scholars who view this narrative as (at least in part) an anti-rape narrative, see Charlene van der Walt, '"Is There a Man in Here?": The Iron Fist in the Velvet Glove in Judges 4,' in *Feminist Frameworks in the Bible: Power, Ambiguity, and Intersectionality* (ed. L. Juliana Claassens and Carolyn J. Sharp; London: Bloomsbury, 2017), 121–22.

characterization of Jael, but not for the reason most scholars suggest. First, it could be proposed that Sisera was out of line by going to Jael's tent, when instead he should have gone to the patriarch first.[33] However, the text could just as easily read, 'Sisera fled on his feet *towards* the tent of Jael' (4:17), i.e., in that direction. If Sisera were going directly to Jael's tent, there would be no need for her to come out and urgently invite him inside. It has also been argued that as a guest, he should not have asked for something before it was offered by the host.[34] Perhaps he broke a rule of hospitality on this count, but he was the commander of the king's army and represented Jabin himself. Moreover, he was fleeing for his life in the midst of an exhausting battle, so it is not a stretch to imagine that he could have asked for some desperately-needed water before Jael had a chance to offer it. Hospitality etiquette is often overridden in emergencies, especially during war. This is no less true for biblical times, as when David asks Nabal for food before it was offered to him during a time when he was being constantly hunted Saul and his army (1 Sam. 25:5-9). Abigail, too, not only fulfills Nabal's neglected hospitality, but also breaks hospitality and marriage norms when she offers David food behind her husband's back and against his wishes (1 Sam. 25:24-31).

Jael is most often accused of breaking hospitality norms, by usurping her husband's role in offering Sisera hospitality and obviously by killing Sisera rather than fulfilling the host's responsibility to protect the guests.[35] However, Jael's violation of hospitality norms for a more righteous cause stands in good company with others in the Hebrew Bible. In addition to Abigail, whose actions warrant the highest praises of YHWH's anointed (1 Sam. 25:32-33, 39-40) Judah's daughter-in-law Tamar is also an exemplar of convention-breaking for a higher good. Posing as a prostitute in order to seduce and deceive one's father-in-law clearly broke some cultural norms, and yet Judah lauded Tamar as 'more righteous' than he (Gen. 38:26) and she became a matriarch of the line of David.

Jael's violation of hospitality norms also fits within her pattern of overturning expectations, and not just as a means of deceiving Sisera, but also as a way of signalling to readers that Jael is in company with other military heroes who break norms of hospitality and social convention when in war and hostile situations, and in company with other righteous women who know when to buck the system for the greater good.

---

33. Matthews, 'Hospitality and Hostility in Judges 4,' 16; Anne Katrine de Hammer Gudme, 'Invitation to Murder: Hospitality and Violence in the Hebrew Bible,' *Studia Theologica – Nordic Journal of Theology* 73/1 (2019): 101.

34. Matthews and Benjamin, *Social World*, 92; Matthews, 'Hospitality and Hostility in Judges 4,' 15; Gudme, 'Invitation to Murder,' 91; Julian A. Pitt-Rivers, 'The Law of Hospitality,' in *From Hospitality to Grace: A Julian Pitt-Rivers Omnibus*,' (ed. Giovanni da Col and Andrew Shryock; Chicago: Hau Books, 2017), 179, 181.

35. Gudme, 'Invitation to Murder,' 99; Pitt-Rivers, 'The Law of Hospitality,' 182.

Comparisons and Contrasts with Other Commanding Characters

One final way that the ringmasters of Judg. 4–5 have characterized Jael as a commanding woman is by drawing clear connections of comparison and contrast between her and other commanding figures in the book of Judges.[36]

First and foremost, Jael's character is closely tied to Deborah. Jael validates Deborah's role as prophetess by fulfilling her prophetic word that YHWH would sell Sisera into the hand of a woman (Judg. 4:9). Both women are geographically identified by a tree (Judg. 4:5, 11). Both are identified by their husbands (Judg. 4:4, 17), neither of whom play any part in the story,[37] and they are also described as mothers or with maternal imagery. They even seem to upset cultural expectations of their roles as wives and mothers. Fewell and Gunn explain, 'And as for the mothers and lovers who, in patriarchy, are programmed to give life and pleasure, a new script is written. Objects of pleasure and procreation review themselves to be potential instruments of agony and death.'[38]

Both women also take command of those around them. Deborah directs and leads Barak to the battlefield at the beginning of the battle, and Jael uses the same imperative (לך) to direct and lead Barak into where the battle has ended, the floor of her tent (Judg. 4:22; cf. 4:6).[39] Deborah and Jael are the two essential commanders at the beginning and end of the Canaanite conflict.[40] Streets were abandoned and people refused to fight 'until' Deborah arose to lead them (Judg. 5:7c). Jael brought closure to the conflict by assassinating the commander of Jabin's army, after the majority of his army had fallen in battle.

Whereas the connections between Jael and Deborah highlight their similarities and their common objective of defeating the Canaanite threat to Israel, Jael's connections to Sisera and Barak involve both similarities and differences. Jael is similar to both men in her role as a warrior. Sisera commands her as though she is one of his soldiers (Judg. 4:20) and she courageously delivers the final blow of the battle both men had hoped to win.

Jael's contrast with Sisera also sheds light on her characterization as a commanding woman. The sexual imagery of the text serves to raise and subvert

---

36. As Fotis Jannidis persuasively argues, characters are not 'self-contained'. What they say and do not only reveals something about the character herself, but also something about the other characters, as well as the narrator, 'Character,' in *Handbook of Narratology*(ed. Peter Hühn, John Pier, Wolf Schmid, Jörg Schönert, vol. 19; Berlin: De Gruyter, 2009), 23.

37. Meir Sternberg, *The Poetics of Biblical Narrative: Ideological Literature and the Drama of Reading* (Bloomington, IN: Indiana University Press, 1987), 281.

38. Ibid., 405. Exum argues that the 'nurturing mother' image of Deborah and the 'dangerous mother' image of Jael cannot be separated, but must be viewed together. Both women are portrayed as nurturers and as deadly, with the implicit message (and warning) that all mothers contain both possibilities, and 'you can never be sure when the good mother will turn into the bad mother'. 'Feminist Criticism,' 72.

39. Matthews and Benjamin, *Social World*, 94.

40. Fewell and Gunn, 'Controlling Perspectives,' 402.

expectations, and it also serves to draw an ironic contrast between Sisera and Jael. Had Sisera been the victor, he would have been busy defiling women and collecting sexual plunder (Judg. 5:30); instead, he himself was being figuratively defiled between the feet of a woman.

There is even greater contrast between Jael and Barak. She is the woman who usurped his glory and, as Sternberg describes it, Barak finds himself at the end of the narrative with 'little to show for his trouble except a junior partnership in a female enterprise'.[41] Barak proves to be hesitant and insecure, whereas Jael is determined, cunning and independent. Deborah underscores this contrast by describing the dishonour of Barak (Judg. 4:9) and the honor and blessedness of Jael (Judg. 5:24).[42] The narrator offers no character evaluation, but according to Bar-Efrat, the word of a prophet 'carries particular weight, and it can be assumed that the author identifies fully with the prophet'.[43] Thus, the dishonour of Barak and the honour of Jael are made explicit in these prophetic declarations.

Connections to other deliver figures in the book of Judges further shed light on the characterization of Jael as a commanding warrior. She is paired with Shamgar in Judg. 5:6:

In the days of Shamgar, son of Anat
In the days of Jael, highways ceased.

This is similar to the way in which Deborah and Barak are paired later in the poem (Judg. 5:12), suggesting that Jael and Shamgar were viewed in a similar role, even though Jael did not serve in any official role as a שׁופט or מושׁיע, and the text does not explicitly state whether or not YHWH raised her for deliverance or if the Spirit was upon her. Jael is also similar to Shamgar (and Samson) in her use of an unconventional weapon. She shares Ehud's use of deception,[44] as well as the tactics of Delilah, who is also characterized as a female warrior fighting her enemies.[45]

---

41. Sternberg, *The Poetics of Biblical Narrative*, 283.

42. Bal offers an extensive analysis of the honour–dishonour relationship between Deborah, Barak, Jael and Sisera. As Barak and Sisera are characterized by shame, Deborah and Jael are characterized by honour, *Murder and Difference*, 118–21.

43. Bar-Efrat, *Narrative Art in the Bible*, 84.

44. Daniel I. Block (*Judges, Ruth* [NAC 6; Nashville: Broadman & Holman, 1999], 201) also notes the chiastic relationship between Jael's assassination of Sisera and Ehud's assassination of Eglon:

A Ehud assassinates enemy leader (3:15-25)
B (Moabite) enemy army is defeated (3:26-29)
B' (Canaanite) enemy army is defeated (4:4-16)
A' Jael defeats enemy leader (4:17-23)

45. Elizabeth H. P. Backfish, 'Nameless in the Nevi'im: Intertextuality between Female Characters in the Book of Judges,' in *Reading Gender in Judges: An Intertextual Approach* (ed. Paul Kim, Shelley Birdsong, and Cornelis de Vos; Atlanta, GA: SBL Press, 2023) 71–88.

Hopefully, the above analysis has shown that the ringmasters present their star performer as a commanding warrior through her words, her actions, and her connections with other characters. However, would the image of a seemingly ordinary wife functioning as a warrior even have been conceivable in early Iron Age Israel? Is such a characterization beyond imagination? According to Carol Meyers, the book of Judges might reflect what historians and anthropologists have found to be an overlap between public and private (or domestic and political) domains during this time.[46] Gale Yee concurs, explaining that there were no standing armies at the time and households would send out volunteers to fight battles, making war 'basically a domestic matter'.[47] Historians and anthropologists agree that women held domestic authority in ancient Israelite households, which suggests that they had considerable exposure to and influence over military decisions.[48] Women would have had the opportunity to watch, if not learn, the fighting tactics practised at home by their fathers, brothers, and husbands.

Not only is the warrior characterization feasible within its cultural context, but it might also invite readers to expand on this image. Yee argues that the 'woman warrior' metaphor used for Jael is an external metaphor, meaning that Jael shares the qualities within the semantic domain of the vehicle of 'warrior'.[49] This would mean that Jael's characterization as a warrior in command are not limited to the warrior-like features described in the text, but also warrior features not explicitly described in the text, including attributes such as prestige and honour (which are made more explicit in the song than in the prose account), as well as the status of protector and the element of danger.[50]

By drawing comparisons with other people in command, the ringmasters of Judg. 4–5 characterize Jael as a warrior in command, a woman who has the courage and determination to do what men more typically did, but what the men in these chapters failed to do. Too often, discussions on Jael's characterization end there. However, Jael is not just set up as a better military hero than the men in her story, nor is she characterized solely as a way to celebrate the victory of Israel over and against their enemies. She is specifically characterized as an instrument of YHWH, who is characterized throughout the book of Judges as the divine commander and warrior par excellence.

---

46. Meyers, *Rediscovering Eve: Ancient Israelite Women in Context* (Oxford: Oxford University Press, 2013), 123, 145.

47. Gale A. Yee, 'By the Hand of a Woman: The Metaphor of the Woman Warrior in Judges 4,' *Semeia* 61 (1993): 111.

48. Victor and Matthews, *Social World*, 25; Carol Meyers, *Rediscovering Eve*, 143–46.

49. Ibid., 103.

50. Ibid., 105.

The Characterization of Jael as an Instrument of YHWH

In the book of Judges, YHWH is characterized, among other ways, as the divine warrior who makes all other warriors rise or fall. Israel and their various deliverers are successful only in so far as YHWH grants them success. Out of his mercy, he chooses to use human instruments for his purposes, but the victory ultimately and always belongs to him. This is clear throughout Judges, and not least of all in chapters 4–5 (4:6-7, 23; 5:2-4, 8, 23). Jael too is characterized, not only as a warrior, but specifically as God's warrior. The ringmasters make this clear with the specific words they use to characterize Jael, as well as the literary framing of the text.

Specific Words

Jael's only recorded words spoken to Sisera include the exhortation, 'do not be afraid,' which we noted above was often spoken by a superior to an inferior, and in this case, it could also be serving to comfort and lure Sisera to his death. Additionally, in the Hebrew Bible, these words are most often spoken by YHWH, or by one of his angelic messengers or representatives (Moses or David, for example).[51] Indeed, there are only two other occurrences in the Hebrew Bible in which a woman is the subject, and each time she is a midwife speaking to another woman who is about to die in childbirth (Gen 35:17; 1 Sam 4:20). Consider the six times this expression (אל with ירא) is used in Joshua and Judges. Of the four expressions in Joshua, God is the subject in three instances (Josh. 8:1; 10:8; 11:6), and in the remaining instance (Josh. 10:25), Joshua is relaying language that YHWH has already told him ('Do not be afraid and do not be discouraged; be strong and be courageous'). In the other occurrence of this expression in Judges, YHWH is the subject (Judg. 6:23). By using this expression typically reserved for YHWH or his representatives, Jael too is characterized as one of his representatives.

The poem also uses key words to characterize Jael as an instrument of YHWH. The opening lines describing her call her 'most blessed' (תברך + a מן of comparison) forming an *inclusio* around the strophe with the repetition of the accolade:

<u>Most blessed</u> of women is Jael,
The wife of Heber the Kenite
Of women who dwell in tents, <u>most blessed</u> (5:24)!

There are two words used for 'blessed' in the Hebrew Bible. One is more secular, denoting a state of happiness more generally (אשרי), whereas the one used for Jael

---

51. In the wider corpus of the Deuteronomistic History, the expression is most often used with God or his representatives (prophets, kings) as the subject. Matthews and Benjamin, *Social World*, 90.

in this passage is more theological, often denoting the covenant relationship between YHWH and his people.⁵² Michael Brown explains, 'Whereas *šrê* can have a 'secular' meaning, all usages of *bārûk* presuppose God as either the ultimate author (of blessing) or receiver (of praise).'⁵³ The poet chose this word over and against the more secular option, suggesting that Jael's actions were done in conjunction with the divine Warrior.

A third word that characterizes Jael as a divine instrument is the last word in the stanza devoted to Jael (v. 27), and describes the fate of Sisera as שָׁדוּד ('destroyed'). Although this passive participle is foremost describing Sisera's state of destruction, it also characterizes Jael as the one who destroyed him. The word seems to function like an exclamation point, highlighting a fact that hardly needs to be spelled out. After seven finite verbs describing Jael's feigned hospitality and attack, and another seven finite verbs describing Sisera's downfall, it is quite clear that Sisera is in fact 'destroyed'. In addition to emphasis, however, the use of this word in particular portrays Jael as *YHWH*'s destroyer.

The root שדד occurs nowhere else in the Torah or Former Prophets. Its fifty-eight occurrences are exclusively in the Latter Prophets, with a handful of occurrences in Job, Psalms and Proverbs. It is typically used of specific enemy nations that YHWH either destroys directly (e.g., Jer. 6:26; 48:8) or through a non-Israelite instrument (Ezek. 32:12; Jer. 49:28; Isa. 33:1). If the majority of scholars are right to suggest that Jael, like her husband, was not a native Israelite, then the use of שדד to describe her destruction of Sisera falls in line with the word's association with non-Israelite destroyers and underscores her role as an instrument of YHWH's divine warfare.

A final way in which specific words characterize Jael as an instrument of YHWH occurs in the last couplet of the poem (Judg. 5:31). These parallel lines set up a binary contrast between YHWH's 'enemies' and 'those who love him', with no neutral ground:

So shall all of your enemies perish, O Yahweh,
But those who love him (will be) like the rising of the sun in its might
(Judg. 5:31).

From the perspective of this song (and in the theology of the book more broadly), there are only two groups of people: those opposed to YHWH and those loyal to YHWH. Regardless of Jael's motives, her actions align her with YHWH, putting her in the category of those who 'love' him, and further highlighting her characterization as an instrument of YHWH.

---

52. Michael L. Brown, 'ברך' *NIDOTTE* (ed. Willem A. VanGemeren; Grand Rapids, MI: Zondervan, 1997), 1:759.

53. Ibid., 763.

Literary framing

The way that the narrator and poet frame the story also characterize Jael as an instrument of YHWH, in at least two ways. First, Jael's heroism fulfils the prophetic words of Deborah, that 'Yahweh will sell Sisera into the hand of a woman' (Judg. 4:9). Again, regardless of Jael's motives, her actions worked into God's plan to deliver his people. Second, the narrative ends with this claim: 'And God subdued on that day Jabin, king of Canaan, before the children of Israel. And the hand of the children of Israel pressed harder and more severely against Jabin, king of Canaan, until they had destroyed Jabin, king of Canaan' (Judg. 4:23-24). These verses come immediately after the scene of Jael's assassination of Sisera, and they serve to give a broader view of the battle. This was not primarily a conflict between Barak and Sisera, or even between Jael and Sisera, but between YHWH and king Jabin. Sisera was an instrument of Jabin just as Jael was an instrument of YHWH. YHWH's instrument, of course, prevailed.

Conclusions

Before the circus draws to a close and performers leave the arena, we should consider how other interpreters have understood the characterization of Jael, and also what the characterization described in this essay offers the reader.

Other Interpretations

Many interpreters, past and present, have viewed Jael's deceit and violence negatively, thus characterizing her as lacking faith or morals. *The Woman's Bible*, published at the end of the nineteenth century as a critique of traditional biblical interpretation, claimed that Jael's assassination of Sisera 'seems more like the work of a fiend than of a woman'.[54] Similarly, Abraham Kuyper, Calvinist theologian and Prime Minister of the Netherlands, claimed in 1934 that Jael 'lacked faith' because she did not first pray to God for direction and did not confront Sisera honestly or with what he considered to be adequate courage.[55]

Some contemporary commentators continue to view Jael negatively. Daniel Block, for example, describes Sisera as 'innocently' entering Jael's tent and offering a 'polite request' for water, as though Sisera were being a perfect gentleman, and

---

54. Elizabeth Cady Stanton, *The Woman's Bible* (New York: European, 1895); cited in Yee, 'By the Hand of a Woman,' 123.

55. Abraham Kuyper, *Women of the Old Testament* (6th ed; trans. Henry Zylstra; Grand Rapids, MI: Zondervan, 1934), 77. Kuyper here is contrasting Jael with David, whom he claims fought Goliath without deception. However, 1 Sam. 17 nowhere states that David first prayed to God for direction. In fact, the first inquiry David makes, after asking his brothers how they are, is how the victor will be rewarded (1 Sam. 17:26).

not an enemy of God or in violation of hospitality customs.⁵⁶ Block also considers Deborah's prophetic praise of Jael as 'most blessed' (Judg. 5:24) to be qualified by the line 'of women who dwell in a tent,' i.e., non-Israelite women, since most Israelite women lived in houses.⁵⁷ Thus, Jael was indeed blessed – for a foreigner. Such a qualified and limited statement of praise hardly seems to fit the exuberant tone of the poem.

Lillian R. Klein likewise considers the narrator's view of Jael to be dubious. She argues that the female characters in this cycle (Deborah, Jael, and Sisera's mother) diminish in morality, mirroring the diminishing morality in the larger context of the book of Judges.⁵⁸ Rather than seeing Deborah and Jael working in conjunction (as argued here) she sees them in strong contrast. As for Jael's positive characterization in the song, Klein reflects, 'Ironically, the Israelites honor Jael's deceptive (and brutal) acts on her own initiative more than Deborah's honorable and ethical leadership under YHWH's guidance.'⁵⁹

The characterization of Jael has also been a focal point within the field of gender studies. Scholars in this field have shown that gender is a social construct. As such, the assumed roles and expectations of man and woman within ancient Israel are, according to Shawna Dolansky and Sarah Shectman, 'relational,' meaning that 'masculinity is performed and thereby defined in relation to femininity, and vice versa.'⁶⁰ Jael's usurpation of traditionally masculine roles and expectations strip Sisera and Barak of their own masculinity, creating character reversals. Some interpreters see this reversal as a means of shaming Israelite men or warning Israelite women, especially if chapter 4 is read apart from Jael's positive appraisal in chapter 5. Amy Kalmanofsky, for example, likens the narrative to Genesis 3, claiming, 'Judges 4, like Genesis 3, offers a lesson in submission. Both narratives use an unconventional gender dynamic to argue for a conventional one in which women submit to male authority, and men submit to God's authority.'⁶¹ However, reading chapters 4 and 5 together, the gender reversal expectations in the story of Jael are arguably much more positive. Jael's victory as a warrior empowers the marginalized and highlights God's sovereignty in the victory.

---

56. Block, *Judges, Ruth*, 206-7.

57. Ibid., 240.

58. Klein, *The Triumph of Irony in the Book of Judges* (JSOTSup, vol. 68; Bible and Literature Series, vol. 14; Sheffield: The Almond Press, 1989), 46.

59. Ibid., 47.

60. Dolansky and Shectman, eds, 'Gendered Historiography: Theoretical Considerations and Case Studies,' *JHebS* 19/4 (2019): 10. For more on gender as a social construct and gender asymmetry, see Peggy Day (ed.), *Gender and Difference in Ancient Israel* (Minneapolis, MN: Fortress, 2006).

61. Kalmanofsky, *Gender-Play in the Hebrew Bible: The Ways the Bible Challenges Its Gender Norms* (Routledge Interdisciplinary Perspectives on Biblical Criticism; New York: Routledge, 2016), 62.

The recent attention to intersectionality in gender studies supports this characterization of Jael as a representative for the marginalized, because she was not only marginalized as a woman in the battle, but also as a Kenite in Israelite land. L. Juliana Claassens and Carolyn J. Sharp explain, 'intersectional thinking helps us to understand that one cannot speak in simple binary categories of unilateral power relations that turn men into perpetrators and women into helpless victims'.[62] Jael's gender does not render her a victim or a model of 'bad' womanhood, and her ethnicity does not preclude her from being one of Israel's most celebrated heroes.

Yee argues that as a woman within the masculine thought domain of 'warrior', Jael becomes a 'liminal' character, neither fully masculine nor fully feminine, restricted to the 'margins of society'.[63] Many people find themselves in similar liminal spaces and can undoubtedly appreciate Jael's representation as a character unrestricted to the bounds of traditional gender norms. Even for those who do not relate to Jael's liminal quality, her sheer unconventionality might serve to intrigue and engage readers in ways that flat characters or 'types' do not.[64]

Speaking of conventions, much has been made about the hospitality conventions of ancient Israel and whether or not Jael and Sisera were breaking these norms. This has important implications for understanding the characterization of Jael, as discussed above. Matthews's view has been very influential. He argues that Sisera posed a physical threat to Jael and her household, violating 'every step in the customary ritual'.[65] Jael likewise broke hospitality rules by going out to him, inviting him into her tent, neglecting to wash his feet, and killing him. Instead of viewing Jael as a woman in control from start to finish, he views Sisera as the one commanding control when he responds to her request for him to 'turn aside' to her by instead turning *her* aside.[66] Matthews views Jael's breach of the hospitality code as more excusable than Sisera's because she was defending herself

---

62. L. Juliana Claassens and Carolyn J. Sharp, 'Introduction: Celebrating Intersectionality, Interrogating Power, and Embracing Ambiguity as Feminist Critical Practices', in *Feminist Frameworks and The Bible: Power, Ambiguity, and Intersectionality* (ed. L. Juliana Claassens and Carolyn J. Sharp; LHBOTS 630, London: Bloomsbury, 2017).

63. Yee, 'By the Hand of a Woman', 99; cf. Aysha W. Musa, who argues that Jael should not be interpreted within the traditional binary gender framework in her recent dissertation 'Jael's Gender Ambiguity in Judges 4 and 5' (PhD thesis, University of Sheffield, 2020); see also Létourneau's similar thesis and engagement with Judith Butler's 'dissonant juxtaposition of genders' in 'Campy Murder in Judges 4: Is Yael a Gebèrèt (Heroine)?'

64. Berlin notes how characteristics traditionally associated with females are given to Jonathan and characteristics traditionally associated with males are given to Mical, and in both cases the characters are full-fledged (round) characters who lose nothing in their divergent gender associations, *Poetics and Interpretation of Biblical Narrative*, 24.

65. Matthews, 'Hospitality and Hostility', 20.

66. Matthews and Benjamin, *Social World*, 90-92.

against his threats.⁶⁷ Matthews raises important issues of cultural context and hospitality, but his characterization does not take into account the many times in which traditional conventions of hospitality are set aside in emergencies, not least of all in matters of life and death. He also falls short of explaining the significance of such breaches in hospitality conventions. Jael broke hospitality norms, to be sure, but she did so for a particular purpose: to bring down an enemy of Israel.⁶⁸

Interpreters throughout the centuries have identified the sexual imagery in Judg. 4-5 as the primary feature of Jael's characterization. Pseudo-Philo expanded on her story, adding that Jael laid roses on her bed, so as to lure Sisera into her tent and heighten the reverse-rape imagery of the story.⁶⁹ Rabbinic tradition also embellished the story, describing Jael's unique beauty and claiming that Jael and Sisera had sex seven times and that he even drank milk from her breasts.⁷⁰ More recently, Pamela Tamarkin Reis has claimed that this story 'smolders with sex' and is 'feverish with sex'.⁷¹ She likens Jael's going out to invite Sisera into her tent with the similar invitation of the prostitute in Prov. 7, and counts at least three instances where Jael has sex with Sisera before killing him.⁷² However, as mentioned above, rather than denoting literal sexual relations, the narrator and poet's use of sexual imagery seems to function as a means of emasculating Sisera and Barak and highlighting the irony of the downfall of the would-be rapist. Moreover, both narrator and poet celebrate Jael as an instrument of God, someone to be praised, rather than a prostitute to be shunned.

Implications of the Commanding Instrument of YHWH Characterization

The ringmasters' characterization of Jael as a commanding warrior and an instrument of YHWH leads to at least three important implications for readers. These pertain to the roles of ambiguity, identification and theology.

Even if readers have been convinced that Jael is characterized as a commanding instrument of YHWH, much ambiguity remains, most notably her motive. Rather

---

67. Matthews claims that Jael's murder of Sisera was justifiable 'as the proper reaction to the violation of the code of hospitality,' 'Hospitality and Hostility,' 17.

68. Gudme argues that Jael's hospitality was obviously feigned, saying, 'It is almost as if the author suggests that if you are silly enough to expect and accept hospitality from another man's woman, and to mistake this for 'proper' hospitality, then you only have yourself to blame if you end up like Sisera with your head nailed to the floor.' Gudme also notes the contrast between the 'ideal' hospitality offered by Abraham and Lot in Genesis 18–19, which was marked by humility, and Jael's 'hospitality' that lacked any such humility. Thus, according to Gudme, 'in Judges 4 the code of hospitality is not violated by Sisera's murder, because the code of hospitality is never observed in the first place,' 103–4.

69. Yee, 'By the Hand of a Woman,' 122.

70. Megillah 15a; Yevamot 103a; Nazir 23b; Niddah 55b; cited in Geoffrey D. Miller, 'Canonicity and Gender Roles: Tobit and Judith as Test Cases,' *Bib* 97/2 (2016): 210.

71. Reis, 'Uncovering Jael and Sisera: A New Reading,' *SJOT* 19/1 (2005): 24, 43.

72. Ibid., 27-34.

than viewing this ambiguity as problematic, it is possible to see it as an asset of the text, and a gift from the ringmasters, inviting us into the very lives of the performers. Bar-Efrat explains, 'A great deal can be learned about people from the decisions they make. Because it involves choosing between alternatives, decisions reveal a person's scale of values.'[73] In other words, readers can deduce certain features of her character based on her choices. Jael had at least three options: 1) she could deceive and kill Sisera; 2) she could ignore him and probably remain safe; or 3) she could help him, but then possibly become a captive of the Israelites. As for this third option, it is unlikely that the Israelites would take captive any Kenite women, since the conflict was primarily against the Canaanites, and not those simply 'at peace' (Judg. 4:17) with the Canaanites. This makes it clear that, regardless of her motives, she chose the most dangerous and difficult option. She was courageous when she could have been timid, she was determined when she could have been paralyzed with indecision, and she chose the cause of the Israelites, even though her people were largely neutral in the conflict.

The remaining ambiguity of her motivation might be intentional on the part of the ringmasters. She is praised for her deeds and that is enough. She is an instrument of YHWH, whether she recognized it or not, and whether she did it for YHWH's glory or her own. This ambiguity provides space for people to enter into the story who might not feel as though they are 'on YHWH's side'. People who might feel like outsiders to the faith can be drawn in to the story of courage and deliverance from oppression. Of course, the Hebrew Bible does not allow anyone to stay in this space of motivational ambiguity. Those who enter the story through the characterization of Jael must eventually choose whether or not they will intentionally serve YHWH, but everyone is invited in.

The characterization of Jael also directly contributes to her representative role among readers. Susan Niditch explains, 'Jael has identification power for the early Israelite audience, for in a sense Israel is Jael; she becomes an archetype or symbol for the marginal's victory over the establishment.'[74] Like Jael, Israel was an outsider among their neighbours. They were disadvantaged by their inferior weaponry, number and military experience, just as Jael was disadvantaged in her fight against one of the most skilled and proven soldiers in her known world. Israelites could identify with and be inspired by this marginalized underdog.

Finally, the characterization of Jael as a commanding instrument of YHWH enables women to identify with the divine Warrior metaphor so commonly employed in the Hebrew Bible. When the Hebrew Bible describes YHWH as a divine warrior, readers should know that the thought domain of that metaphor also includes women warriors, making the metaphor at least a little more inclusive than it might initially appear.

---

73. Bar-Efrat, *Narrative Art in the Bible*, 81.

74. Niditch, *Judges: A Commentary* (OTL; Lousiville, KY: Westminster John Knox, 2008), 52.

Chapter 5

GIDEON: EPIC HERO, BIBLICAL JUDGE AND POLITICAL SUBVERSIVE

Susan Niditch

Tales of Gideon offer one of the fuller portraits of biblical heroes in the book of Judges. The character engages the listener or reader, ancient or contemporary, on various levels at once. With his daring, his martial prowess, his cleverness and his ability to attract devoted followers, he is a traditional typological figure who might be compared to swashbuckling heroes in culture- reinforcing and self-defining epic accounts worldwide.[1] He is moreover a typical biblical hero who exhibits devotion to his divine helper YHWH coupled with a charming self-doubt and insecurity about his chances for success, despite the deity's promised assistance. He is a biblical judge. Like other judges, his origins are modest, his leadership initially unexpected. He challenges oppressors for the benefit of the oppressed, and his power is decentralized and non-dynastic. He is meant to succeed, as various divinely sent signs indicate, and at the same time he relies on his own street-smarts and leadership skills. In thinking about the significance of Gideon's characterization for lasting messages and models, what perhaps most distinguishes him is the way he exemplifies a particular positive variety of political ethics, one which resists tyranny to liberate his people and which does not seek self-aggrandizing advancement for himself and his family. To examine these various threads, we will focus on the call narrative in Judges 6, the various 'signs' received by Gideon throughout the account, the interactions between Gideon and his followers and enemies in Judges 8, and scenes in Judges 6 and 8 that have special relevance to the nature of Gideon's leadership as it relates to his character or personal qualities. Along the way, we pay special attention to the traditional style in which the narrative is composed and Gideon's characterization takes shape.

The call or commission of Gideon reflects a shared set of motifs employed by ancient Israelite writers to introduce the careers of heroes. And like many epic

---

1. For a good description of the traditional epic hero see Richard M. Dorson, 'Introduction,' in *Heroic Saga and Epic: An Introduction to the World's Great Folk Epics* (ed. Felix J. Oinas; Bloomington, IN: Indiana University Press, 1978).

heroes who rescue a nation or people, Gideon is a 'mighty warrior' (6:12) endowed with a special spirit; he is chosen and protected by a divinity ('Yhwh is with you' 6:12). The background to the call in Judges 5 is subjugation by the Midianites and other easterners,[2] who are formulaically described in the Israelite medium to be as numerous as locusts (Judg. 6:5; 7:12; Isa. 7:18-19 for other insects). Like a massive locust infestation these enemies descend upon the land, destroying the Israelites' livelihood, their food resources, forcing Israelites to create hiding places in mountains and caves (6:2-6).

A theophany commences the story of Gideon. Israelite receivers of the opening scene know that the reference to a special tree where the figure first appears signals the presence of the potentially sacred and oracular, a zone where heaven meets earth and the human may encounter the divine. In this case, the tree is the oak in Ophrah that belonged to Joash the Abiezerite. There under this oak the visitor sits down. Lawrence Stager has discussed the role of sacred trees or groves in Levantine thought, for example the palm of the judge Deborah (see also Gen. 12:6).[3]

As the messenger arrives, Joash's son Gideon is beating out wheat in the winepress in order to hide it from the Midianites. The divine messenger of course appears as a human being, like the 'three men' in Genesis 18 who come to Abraham or the dangerous 'man' with whom Jacob wrestles at the River Jabbok (Gen. 34) or the 'man' who announces the birth of Samson in Judges 13. The Masoretic tradition calls the visitor Yhwh in vv. 14 and 16, setting aside the human cover, but again any reader versed in the tradition knows that the man is not just a human traveller, as the audience of the Odyssey knows that Mentor is Athena. The narrative requires, however, that the biblical hero be surprised and filled with dread by the visitor's true identity revealed in the dramatic immolation of the offered sacrifice in 6:21, for God is symbolized by the fire here as in Gen. 15:17, Exod. 3:2 and Judg. 13:19-20. The status of the being as messenger of the Lord and the Lord coalesces in the language of 6:22-23 as Gideon declares 'Alas, my Lord Yhwh, for I have seen the messenger of Yhwh face to face.' Yhwh urges him not to fear and says: 'Peace to you. Do not be afraid. You will not die.' A similar reveal concludes the annunciation to Samson's future parents in Judges 13 (cf. Gen. 32:30). Gideon's realization that he has been in God's presence, followed by the setting up of an altar to Yhwh and the naming of the place (6:24), equates Gideon with the patriarchs (e.g. Gen. 12:7, 8; 13:18; 26:23-25). Gideon's altar building, like theirs, serves to mark the place as

---

2. On the various attitudes to Midianites in the Hebrew Bible, some positive and some condemnatory, see Lawrence E. Stager's suggestion that the portrayal of 'benign relations' between the Midianites and Moses' group reflects the socio-historical situation before 1100 BC, whereas Judges 6 reflects a time 'when the camel-riding and -raiding Midianites had become archenemies of the Israelites' (Lawrence E. Stager, 'Forging an Identity: The Emergence of Ancient Israel,' *Oxford History of the Biblical World* [ed. Michael D. Coogan; New York: Oxford University Press, 1998], 143).

3. Lawrence E. Stager, 'The Shechem Temple: Where Abimelech Massacred a Thousand,' *BAR* 29 (2003): 26–35, 66–69, esp. 33–34.

belonging to Yhwh and his people, an important theme in this tale of political and territorial rivalry out of which emerges a special hero.

Additional formulaic motifs that characterize the narrative about Gideon include: the divine being's addresses to the hero with assurances of God's favour; the hero's attempt humbly to refuse the commission (cf. Exod. 3:11; Jer. 1:6; 1 Sam. 9:21); and his request for and receiving of a sign (cf. Gen. 15:8; Exod. 4:1; also 3:12-13). The content is thus fully traditional,[4] while the language is formulaic including references to the escape from Egypt (6:13; cf. 11:13, 16; 1 Sam. 8:8; 10:18; 15:2; 2 Sam. 7:6; Neh. 9:18), common commission language (v. 14 'Have I not sent you'; cf. Exod. 3:12; Ezek. 3:6), the expression of divine favour ('I will be with you' v. 16 and cf. Gen. 26:3; 31:3; 2 Sam. 7:9), and the nature of Gideon's response (v. 22; cf. the link with Moses in Num. 12:8). Language in this section is also internally repetitive (vv. 13, 15, 20, 21) and reveals significant parallelism in the style of traditional Israelite narration.

A scholar of comparative early and oral literatures, John Foley, coined a term for this formulaic aspect of traditional compositions: immanent referentiality. The content employed by traditional authors and the words they use to express content bring to bear on the composition the larger tradition that shares such narrative materiel.[5] This awareness of and familiarity with a shared story culture, in this case the way in which the hero is introduced and called upon to act on behalf of his people, in fact enriches the work, broadens it and makes it an expression of a group's worldview. For our purposes, however, one might well ask about the effect of this form of composition and reception on characterization itself. Does a composer endow Gideon with a unique and definable personality? The answer is that traditional authors, or as Albert B. Lord would have said, the best of them, do create interesting and special heroes within the contours of what is expected by audiences in language and content.[6] To bring individual characters to life with imagination and vitality is the challenge for the composer, and the author of the Gideon account exemplifies the capacity to work creatively to produce a specific hero within the traditional medium. Gideon's distinctive character, as developed by a particular composer, emerges in the opening call narrative in a number of ways.

Gideon's complaint that Yhwh is not acting as in the great days of the past when he rescued the Israelites from slavery in Egypt is evidenced elsewhere in the larger biblical tradition. Such critiques or doubts concerning the deity's loyalty and intentions is typical of Israel's national laments (cf. Ps. 74; 77:7-20). In Ps. 77 the poet recalls some of God's great acts on Israel's behalf, for example the redemption of Israel at the crossing of the sea, and he asks if the deity has now essentially

---

4. For a study of Gideon's 'appointment and investiture' that draws comparisons with tales of Moses see Hava Shalom-Guy 'The Call Narratives of Gideon and Moses: Literary Convention or More?' *JHS* 11 (2011): 1-19.

5. *Immanent Art: From Structure to Meaning in Traditional Oral Epic* (Bloomington, IN: Indiana University Press, 1991).

6. See his discussion in *The Singer of Tales* (New York: Atheneum, 1968): 13-29.

turned his back on his people (77:7-9). Similarly, the psalmist of Ps. 74 digs into ancient myth, the crushing of the heads of the sea monster Leviathan (74:14) and the creation of the cosmos (74:17). Both composers ask if God has now forgotten, given free rein to Israel's enemies (e. g. 74:11-12). The post-exilic author of Isa. 64 echoes such themes, recalling when Yhwh did awe-inspiring things (64:2[H] [64:3E]). Where is he now to rescue and relieve the suffering of his people? These examples from the psalms and Trito-Isaiah are expressions of writers dealing with the Babylonian invasions and destruction of the great temple in Jerusalem. This sacred space was supposed to be eternal, or so the eighth-century prophet Isaiah had expected and asserted. One also finds individual complaints as a biblical hero chastises the deity for not keeping promises. Similarly, the prophet Jeremiah calls his deity 'a disappointing stream/waters that do not flow true' (15:18). All of these biblical characters are portrayed as suffering from a kind of cognitive dissonance whereby their strongly held and self-defining beliefs are challenged, seeming to be false after all. As explored in sociologist Leon Festinger's well-known study of a twentieth-century mid-western millenarian group's beliefs and disappointments, the believer can either eventually give up hope and change his beliefs or double-down upon them, insisting that somehow the belief system has validity and that others should join him to validate the ultimate truth of his expectations.[7] Gideon's interaction with the divine messenger similarly suggests this deep dilemma involving long-held religious belief or faith. What is interesting here is that the interaction with the messenger is intimate and personal in a narrative setting, and contributes to the creation of Gideon's characterization, our sympathy for him, and an appreciation for his subsequent actions. A formulaic expression of alienation and doubt about the validity of long-held and shared cultural beliefs, found elsewhere in the tradition in biblical laments from the Psalms or the prophets, becomes in this way a mechanism of character development.

The way in which the Gideon takes issue with the messenger in Judges 6 is perhaps most reminiscent of Abraham's interaction with the deity in Gen. 15:2. The patriarch reminds the deity that he is still childless, implicitly making Yhwh's repeated promise of offspring that preceded this scene of covenant seem empty. 'Promises, promises,' the patriarch seems to say. So in Judges 6:13, Gideon responds to the divine being's confident greeting 'Yhwh is with you mighty man of valor,' in this way:

> With all due respect, my lord, if Yhwh is with us, why have we encountered all this? And where are all the wonderful acts that our ancestors told us about saying 'Has not Yhwh brought us up from Egypt?' But now Yhwh has forsaken us and he has given us into the hand of Midian.

Implicitly he asks whether the people-affirming myths of the ancestors about the Exodus are still true. Gideon points, significantly, to reasons why the oppressed

---

7. Leon Festinger, Henry W. Riecken, and Stanley Schacter, *When Prophecy Fails* (London: Pinter and Martin, 2008; first published in 1956 by the University of Minnesota Press).

people should not believe and join in the fight, and his response to the messenger beautifully captures a kind of cynicism or tendency to disbelieve a message about liberation in the face of severe oppression. Has God not cast off his people? Who is this God who claims to be able to free us from our dire situation? We will return to this theme in exploring Gideon's development as a leader of political resistance. This emphasis, the anxiety and insecurity it suggests, also beautifully intertwines with another recurring motif in the tale of Gideon critical to the characterization of the hero, the request for signs from the deity.

To be sure, requests for oracles, assurance in verbal or symbolic form that the deity is on the side of the petitioner is a common motif in Levantine literature and life. Kings will not go to battle without making such inquiry and receiving assurance of success as the pre-battle story concerning Ahab and Jehoshaphat's martial plans nicely reflects (1 Kgs 22:5-6, 15, 17-25). Similarly the description of the internecine war between Benjamin and the other tribes points to frequent requests for divine assurance through oracles (Judg. 20:18, 23, 27-28). Once again, however, this typical reflection of Israelite worldview and frequently found motif in traditional biblical battle accounts serve in the story of Gideon to frame his character and to see him as a person, one endowed with gifts but spectacularly insecure. This feature of his personality is part of his youthful charm at the beginning of his career, as the author presents an ancient traditional style Bildungsroman that traces the maturation and growing confidence of the hero.

The requested sign in Judges 6 is drawn from the hero's pastoral or rural daily life. He tells God that in order to be reassured that his campaign against the Midianites will succeed he needs to see that a fleece of wool he lays on the ground of the threshing floor in the evening is filled with water the next morning whereas the ground beneath it is dry. He checks the next morning and indeed the fleece is filled with water while the ground is dry. But then, he asks for another sign, the opposite, that the fleece be dry in the morning and the ground wet. God allows for this scenario as well. The double request not only engages the audience in the style of oral traditional performance and creates narrative tension, but also serves to underscore the hero's youthful uncertainty about his possibilities for success and the loyalty of his divine helper, God. The latter tolerantly responds to his charge, providing a sign. In fact, in Judges 7:9ff. the mentor deity himself anticipates Gideon's doubts.

The Lord commands him to attack the Midianite camp in the valley and assures him that that he God has given it into Gideon's hands, but the deity suggests that if the leader has some self-doubt, he should take his lad Puah, go down to the camp in a reconnaissance mission and 'listen to what they are saying'. Then his confidence will build and his 'hands will be strengthened'. Gideon and Puah do as God suggests and see the Midianites and Amalekites and all the easterners as numerous as locusts, their camels as plentiful as the sand on the shore of the sea – a formidable enemy to be sure.

At the encampment outpost Gideon and his mate experience a divinatory event. They overhear a man describing his dream to his friend. In the cultural milieu dreams are often regarded as symbolic messages about the future, a divinatory medium. A number of dream omen collections from the Levant have been preserved, and of course the Bible itself contains scenes of and references to dream interpretation, the story of Joseph the wise man being perhaps the richest resource.[8] Dreams are interpreted by means of idea association or word association in a kind of midrashic process, and as post-biblical reflections on dreams in the Talmud emphasize, the interpretation itself has the capacity to bring about that which is interpreted. It is this link between dream content, the way it is interpreted, and future events that make the overheard exchange in Judges 7:13-14, pertaining to himself no less, a divinatory medium, a kind of *kledon*. In ancient Greek divinatory belief the *kledon* is a random overhearing of a comment that can be interpreted to have relevance to the listener's life situation, a form of unintentional prophecy. And in this case the interpreter of his friend's dream actually mentions Gideon, the listener, by his name.

The dreamer describes his having seen a round barley bread turning over and over in the encampment of Midian. He says, 'It came to the tent and struck it so that it fell. It upturned it and the tent fell down' (Judg. 7:13). Now, the root for bread *lḥm* is also the triliteral found in words for war, warring etc. In this way via word-play, the aggressive barley bread is likened to a warring behaviour that attacks and collapses the enemy's tent and the listener interprets the dream to mean that God has given victory to Gideon and his allies: 'This is no other than the sword of Gideon, son of Joash, a man of Israel; into his hand God has given Midian and all the army' (Judg. 7:14). The narrator has us assume that already Gideon's name goes before him, even though he himself is as yet somewhat uncertain about his abilities and prospects, filled with a degree of fear as Yhwh knows, despite his bold and successfully executed night-time raid on the altar of Baal, ordered by Yhwh himself (6:25-32).

The raid that begins Gideon's career as a judge liberator of the Israelites allows his story to frame important issues in political ethics that in turn serve to complicate his characterization as protagonist of the tale. It is God's command that leads Gideon to tear down the altar of the Canaanite deity Baal and to cut down his *ăšērâ*, often translated 'sacred pole,' the iconic representation of Baal's female consort. He is a guerrilla warrior, a rebel, or in the language of social historian Eric Hobsbawm, a social bandit.[9] The altar and sacred pole are significantly said to belong to Gideon's own father, Joash (6:25). Gideon is commanded by God to use the wood of the pole as fuel for a sacrifice to YHWH. It is important to note that ethnic representation and in this case the identity of the oppressive overlords, the Midianites, and that of the oppressed, the Israelites, are connected to particular religious symbols and deities associated with them. Indeed this account seems to be the work of an aniconic writer such as the composer of Isaiah 40:18-20 and

---

8. On dream interpretation in the Bible and wider ancient Near East see Susan Niditch, *The Symbolic Vision in Biblical Tradition* (HSM 30; Chico, CA: Scholars Press, 1980), 1-19.

9. Eric J. Hobsbawm, *Primitive Rebels: Studies in Archaic Forms of Social Movement in the 19th and 20th Centuries* (New York: W. W. Norton, 1959), 13-28.

44:12-17 who insists that the icons are not infused with any power or symbolic inspirational value. Rather they are quotidian objects made of inert material. As the post-exilic author of Isaiah 44:16-17 states, these non-Yahwists use some of the wood to make a fire and roast meat, some of it to keep warm, and with the rest they make 'a god.' The wood that composes an *ăšērâ* serves Gideon good kindling and fuel for the sacrifice he offers on a new altar to Yhwh (Judg. 6:26, 28). Later in the tales of Gideon, issues arise concerning his own manufacture of an iconic representation of Yhwh, and we are able to see here as in the account of the golden calf in Exodus 32 echoes of an inner Israelite debate concerning the efficacy and validity of icons; in the written Israelite tradition the iconoclasts generally have the last word. What helps to make Gideon and his story special is the emphasis on his leadership of a resistance movement.

As is typical of some resistance movements, opposition or confrontation is not undertaken in the open by the light of day but involves subterfuge under the mask of darkness.[10] Gideon and ten of his men, those loyal to him, 'men from among his servants', go by cover of night and tear down the altar as God had commanded, for 'they feared his father's household and the men of the town' if they did such an act of subversion in the daylight (Judg. 6:27). Thus Gideon and his fellow rebels expect to incur the wrath not only of non-Israelites, in this case the oppressors, but also of his own kin, members of his ancestral household. The narrator does not state clearly whether the wrath of the townspeople the next morning is due to fear of their oppressors or fear of the deity Baal. In the ancient world, one hedged one's bets and monotheism is not a typical feature of worldview. As noted, this altar and its icon belong to Gideon's own father, an Israelite. One's own ancestral god or gods are those to whom one regularly sacrifices and upon whom one calls in distress but one might not want to anger other gods or dishonour them. Indeed, one might embrace them, depending upon the social setting in which one lives – rather like an immigrant family in the United States flying the largest American flag in the neighbourhood or placing a portrait of George Washington in the living room. Here the well-founded fear is no doubt also rooted in fear of the oppressors' reaction, fear of those for whom Baal is god, culturally, ethnically. Destroying his altar is no small thing. Like the Hebrew slaves of Egypt (Exod. 2:14; 5:20-21; 6:9), Gideon's neighbours thus do not initially support the leader or his act of subversion and indeed in the case of Gideon want to kill him, eliminating the trouble-maker in their midst.

---

10. Moving in an interpretative direction that differs from the one here offered, Lillian R. Klein approaches Gideon's actions under the cover of darkness as a means by which the narrator portrays Gideon's cowardice. Klein's negative assessment of Gideon applies to his construction of the ephod as well: *The Triumph of Irony in the Book of Judges* (Bible and Literature Series 14; Sheffield: Almond Press, 1989), 60, 66, 68. Similarly see Shalom-Guy, 'The Call Narrative,' 17, 19. See, however, a contrasting interpretation of the hero's demeanour and actions offered by erudite scholar Jack M. Sasson in *Judges 1–12: A New Translation with Introduction and Commentary* (AB; New Haven: Yale University Press, 2014) 341, 353–54, 367–68, 371–72.

An important theoretical framework that helps to elucidate the response to Gideon's first act of subversion is provided by political scientist Barrington Moore.[11] One might expect people who collectively experience systematic abuse and oppression to join forces and resist. More often than not, however, people in fact resist revolting. Moore thoughtfully explored this seeming paradox with reference to specific groups and historical moments, seeking to understand why oppressed people often prefer the status quo to resistance and what leads them finally to rise up. As Moore discusses, those who are oppressed tend not 'to counterattack' to respond to 'deprivation and injustice',[12] engaging in 'a process of self-repression';[13] nor, significantly, do they encourage others to resist on their behalf. Indeed, 'solidarity among the oppressed group forms readily against an individual protester or protector'.[14] Moore argues that this 'voluntary compliance' with their own subjugation is due to a variety of psycho-social factors.[15] Humans often seem to feel that the risk of rebellion is not worth it, that the situation, however bad, is better than total change and challenge to the status quo, better than bringing down upon oneself the wrath of those who have power and claim authority, and that somehow this authority is legitimate.

The response of the locals to Gideon's destruction of the altar of Baal suggests the contest motif in which God's power is tested against that of other gods. The strength of Baal's devotees and their power to control the Israelites' lives and livelihoods connote YHWH's weakness, and the Israelites' subversive and successful resistance connotes Yahwistic power.[16] In this account as in the foundational exodus and the confrontation with Egyptians, the Israelite deity is associated with the liberation of those who are enslaved or oppressed and it is in this power to resist and save the oppressed that he manifests his divinity. There is a profoundly religious and ethnic component to resistance in the tale of Gideon. Yahwism is the religion of liberation of Israel rather than one that supports an oppressive status quo. The quality of contest enshrined in Gideon's new name recalls Moses' confrontation with the Pharaoh's magicians (Exod. 7:11-12) and Elijah's confrontation with the priests of Baal (1 Kgs 18:20-40). The new name itself connotes an important passage point in the life of the hero.

Joash, the father of Gideon, comes to his defence when the townspeople seek to kill Gideon, whether in revenge for his sacrilege against Baal, a powerful deity after all, or in an effort to eliminate the subversive before the Midianites hear about

---

11. Barrington Moore Jr., *Injustice: The Social Bases of Obedience and Revolt* (White Plains, NY: M. E. Sharpe, 1978).

12. Ibid., 161.

13. Ibid., 77.

14. Ibid., 79.

15. Ibid., 34.

16. For thoughtful comments on the representation of the conflict between YHWH and Baal in this narrative see Mark S. Smith, *The Early History of God. Yahweh and Other Deities in Ancient Israel* (Grand Rapids, MI: Eerdmans, 2002), 143.

Gideon's actions and hold the town responsible. Again to reprise Moore, politically the goal may be to ruffle as few feathers as possible, to accept the status quo however unpalatable. Overt resistance, at least initially, may come with a high cost as other biblical characters such as Elijah and Moses both find out. Joash counters his neighbours by essentially declaring that if Baal is so powerful, let him take vengeance himself. Hence the new name for Gideon, Jerubbaal, 'Let Baal contend'. Such name changes in the life of a hero mark transformation and messages about a new identity (see Gen. 17:5; 15 concerning Abraham and Sarah; Gen. 32:28 concerning Jacob; Gen. 41:45 concerning Joseph).

The story of Gideon suggests authors thoughtfully grappling with issues that arise in resistance movements: the central importance of a particular kind of morally autonomous and charismatic leader; the reluctance of those he seeks to liberate to join him; their tendency indeed to turn against the leader himself. The ultimate message of these authors is that revolt can succeed and that Yhwh is a God of resistance and liberation, the deity of the oppressed. For our study of characterization in the tale of Gideon, attention to this issue in political ethics is especially important. Gideon shows himself, despite youthful self-doubts and insecurities, to be morally autonomous and charismatic in leadership, for ultimately he brings his father and his neighbours on board with his bold actions to free his people from fear, famine and oppression.

The author of the Gideon tale also deftly creates a story of maturation and personal growth. The leader is shown in interactions with allies and enemies in ways that underscore an earned wisdom and a much more confident leader, one who has learned from experience what leadership requires. The mature Gideon is shaped in part by the inclusion of a number of oral-traditional media.

A first scene in this category is found at Judg. 8:1-3 and involves a dispute between Ephraimites and Gideon. Tensions have arisen that ultimately concern access to war spoils. The men of Ephraim complain that they were not called up or included in the raid against the Midianites thereby implicitly losing an opportunity to achieve glory and goods. Such disputes are typical of bardic literatures and point to the imagined decentralized political and military structures in which the hero warriors operate. Gideon, displaying diplomatic skills, is able to diffuse tensions by means of a proverb in the typical pattern, 'better x than y' found, for example, in Prov. 22:1 and Eccl. 7:4 and in an international fund of folk wisdom.[17] The setting moreover is appropriate for the deploying of proverbs, drawing a comparison between a present situation and a metaphorically relevant motif or well-known event from traditional history in order to reduce tension between groups or individuals, jealous of their status. In other words, the proverb deflects anger, perhaps even introduces some humour into a potential confrontation. In this scene, the leader Gideon graciously compliments the Ephraimites for their superior accomplishments, saying obliquely that they have captured the greatest prize of

---

17. See Alan Dundes, *Interpreting Folklore* (Bloomington: Indiana University Press, 1980), 54.

battle, enemy leaders, the chieftains Oreb and Zeeb. His own victories pale in comparison. Their mere gleanings are more glorious than his vintage. Gideon's capacity to deal with allies in this way point to his qualities as a successful leader. He has come into his own.

Other confrontation with the 'chieftains of Succoth' and the 'men of Penuel', locations in the Jordan Valley, point to a different sort of leadership strength, the capacity to carry through on a threat against those who mock him and prove themselves unhelpful to his cause. Like other 'social bandits' in the bardic traditions of the Hebrew Bible, Gideon asks for material help from well-to-do local leaders or chieftains as he pursues his cause to defeat the Midianites and their allies. His weary troops are exhausted and hungry and need food. As in David's request to Abigail's husband Nabal (1 Sam. 25:8), and David's earlier request to the priests of Nob (1 Sam. 21:4), Gideon asks for food assistance ('round loaves of bread', Judg. 8:5). As in Nabal's response to David, the chieftains answer Gideon with sarcasm and derision. Requesting aid, he explains that he is in pursuit of the kings of Midian. The chieftains of Succoth respond, 'Is the palm of Zebah and Zalmunna now in your hands that we should give to your army bread?' (8:6) and Gideon says to them that once Yhwh gives these enemies into his hands he will return to 'thresh your flesh with the thorns of the wilderness and with briars.' The men of Penuel are similarly dismissive and he tells them that he will return victorious to 'break down this tower' (8:9). He is victorious in his mission, and fully carries out his threats. He is true to his word, capable, and self-assured.

His fully matured personality also emerges in his interaction with captured enemies, another scene rich in the nuances of bardic literatures and the particular war ideologies they present. Having captured the enemy leaders Zebah and Zalmunna, he interrogates them about the men, his allies, that they had killed in Tabor. The kings of Midian reply that these men were in effect noble, worthy enemies as is he: 'As you are, so were they. Each one had the form of the sons of a king' (8:18). Gideon informs them that these princely men were indeed his own maternal kin. Had the Midianites spared them, he would spare them now (8:19). This interaction is rich in the epic style interactions of a bardic war tradition, typical of an international fund of tales of heroes. As in the Song of Roland and the Iliad, enemies speak admiringly of their opponents in battle. Moreover an implicit code of war operates. Out of respect for his counterpart Joab, the general Abner hesitates to kill Asahel, Joab's younger brother, during the wars for control of the kingdom of Israel waged between the forces of Saul and the forces of David (2 Sam. 2:21-22). Mutual respect is implicit as are assumptions about when it is just to kill certain enemies. Gideon is shown to observe this code.

The execution scene points to an additional nuance in a kind of bardic ideology of war. The warrior who faces death would rather be killed by his equal in strength and status than a youthful underling. This is why Goliath so resents facing the young ruddy David in individual combat, a cameo scene in the battles between Philistines and Israelites. He asks, 'Am I a dog that you come to me with sticks?' (1 Sam.17:43). Similarly, in the scene between Asahel and Abner above, the latter, the mature warrior tells the young man, 'Turn aside on your right or on your left and seize for yourself one of the lads and take his plunder [lit. what is stripped off the enemy]', but zealous for glory, the lad will not turn aside and Abner kills him (2 Sam. 2:23). In the scene involving Gideon and the Midianite kings, Gideon tells his eldest son, a young warrior to execute the enemy, 'But the lad could not draw his sword because he was afraid because he was still a lad'. Now, Gideon's son takes the role of the ingenue, and Gideon is seen to be the leader, the famous warrior in a narrative that is a tale of maturation or Bildungsroman if we attend to matters of characterization in the development of the hero. The final words of the enemy kings emphasize this theme. They say to Gideon, 'You rise yourself and strike us down, for as the man, so his strength.' And he does so. The scene thus concludes with a proverb again appropriate to epic characters. In oblique speech the prisoners of war seem to negotiate their own deaths and speak to their executioner's worthiness as a hero.

A final area in the story of Gideon that points to matters of characterization has to do with his own political ambitions or lack thereof as described in Judges 8 and alluded to in Judges 9. This theme concerning kingship relates to issues in political ethics and moral autonomy and may serve as a guide in exploring the composers of tales of Gideon and their intended audiences.

The men of Israel ask Gideon to accept the mantle of kingship, to establish a dynasty so that he will rule and his sons after him (8:22), but Gideon flatly refuses. For the purposes of this essay we ask who might have portrayed this hero warrior to have such a negative view of dynastic kingship and how this aspect of his worldview relates to his characterization. First a close look at the interaction between Gideon and those who support his leadership and especially at his response.

The men of Israel say, 'Rule of over us, you and also your son, and also the son of your son, because you delivered us from the hand of Midian.' The repetitive emphasis on sons underscores the dynastic nature of the polity imagined, a serious change from the charismatic leadership of the judges whose rule is temporary and based in that particular leader's successes in protecting his people and defeating enemies. One is reminded of the scene in 1 Sam. 8:4-5 when the people ask Samuel to appoint for them 'a king to govern us like all the nations'. Samuel finally accedes to their wishes with God's permission (8:22) although the deity says to Samuel, 'Listen to the voice of the people, to all that they say to you, for it is not you that they have rejected, but me whom they have rejected from being king over them' (1 Sam. 8:7). In the scene of Judges 8, the human leader himself responds with antimonarchic sentiment that comports with the impression of the deity's own views expressed by the composer of 1 Samuel 8, an author whose political and theological ideologies reflect the same point of view found in the characterization of Gideon, who replies to his people, 'I will not rule over you and my son will not rule over you. Yhwh will rule over you' (Judg. 8:23).

Many scholars have suggested that the book of Judges is pro-monarchic and pro-Davidic in orientation. Marc Brettler concludes that 'Judges, a work narrating events of the pre-monarchic era, is really interested in issues arising from the monarchy, namely supporting David'.[18] He considers most of the judges to be portrayed as anti-heroes contrasting with the ideal leader David.[19] Similarly, Yairah Amit suggests that the 'subject of leadership' is 'an editorial guideline' for the book of Judges: 'the period of the judges is presented as a decisive stage towards a social-political change, whose significance lies in the transition from local and unstable government, intended to solve immediate problems, to a royal regime which encompassed all tribes'.[20] She underscores the judges' 'limitations as leaders and the need for a different type of leadership',[21] 'a fixed and powerful rule'.[22] Marvin A. Sweeney writes that 'Judges presents a polemical view of early Israelite history that promotes the interests of the tribe of Judah and the Davidic dynasty by pointing to inadequacies of the judges from the northern tribes of Israel'.[23] Gale Yee suggests that Judges 17–21 originates from a Deuteronomist layer and present 'the tribal period as anarchic and violent'. The Deuteronomist writer 'foreshadows the establishment of the Davidic monarchy' and 'paves the way for his ideal king Josiah'.[24] And yet even the clearly Deuteronomic writer of Deut. 17:14-20, who accepts the reality of monarchic rule, offers warnings about the shortcomings of kings, their potential excesses, problems that arise from weaknesses of character. He will be tempted to enrich himself, to acquire too many wives. That Judges even in its final redacted form is pro-monarchic propaganda is belied by the story of Gideon, the murderous actions of his would-be king son Abimelech and the response of a surviving son, the youngest, Jotham.

Gideon's very rejection of kingship is an indication of his strength of character and his moral autonomy. For him, Yhwh is the only king, and human rulership is temporary, a designation by the deity for particular settings and purposes. Abimelech is the exemplar of what can go wrong. He murders all but one of the sons of Gideon, seventy men, to secure his position. His is aided and surrounded by thugs, 'empty and wanton men'. Jotham stands on the top of Mt Gerizim and propounds a *māšāl*, a story about the trees setting out to select a king. A *māšāl* draws comparison between an actual situation and an imagined one, a communicative medium which like the proverbs discussed above, speaks obliquely, in this case offering critique of someone who holds power (Judg. 9:7-15). The connections drawn here between the tale and reality are indeed quite overt and

---

18. Marc Brettler, 'The Book of Judges: Literature as Politics,' *JBL* 108 (1989): 407.

19. Ibid., 407. See also Brettler, *The Book of Judges* (London/NY: Routledge, 2002), 111–16.

20. Yairah Amit, *The Book of Judges: The Art of Editing* (trans. Jonathan Chipman; BIS 38; Leiden: Brill, 1999), 61.

21. Ibid., 75.

22. Ibid., 117.

23. Marvin A. Sweeney, 'Davidic Polemic in the Book of Judges,' *VT* 47 (1997): 517.

24. Gale A. Yee, 'Ideological Criticism: Judges 17-21 and the Dismembered Body,' in *Judges and Method* (ed. Gale A. Yee; Minneapolis: Fortress, 1995), 158.

Jotham explains the meaning of his parable out loud, rather clearly at the end of his speech (Judg. 9:16-20). More widely, the parable asserts that only the worthless planting seeks to be a king, not the olive tree, nor the fig tree, nor the grape vine. Only the bramble agrees to be king among all the trees. This parable has resonances beyond the specific story of Abimelech and shines positive light back on Gideon who rejected kingship with all its trappings and power, since God is the only true king. Indeed Jotham mentions his father, how he had waged war for his people, risked his life to the limit, and saved them from the hand of Midian. He was a man of substance which Abimelech is not.

One final episode needs to be discussed which relates to questions about Gideon's characterization. After Gideon refuses to accept kingship, he asks his followers to contribute earrings of gold from the spoils of war and makes them into an ephod that he sets up in his town Ophrah. The ephod usually a special garment worn by the priest, elsewhere in the Hebrew Bible appears to be some sort of icon, statuary, sometimes a divinatory device (Judg. 17:5; 1 Sam. 23:6-11). Just as the Hebrew Bible admits of pro- and anti-monarchic voices, there are voices comfortable with the use of icons and other voices, probably a majority, harshly aniconic, associating such objects with foreign worship and idolatry. Frank Moore Cross has explored the golden calf incident involving Aaron's overseeing the manufacture of a golden calf with this clash of worldviews in mind. While some may have regarded the venerable Aaron as the originator of this ancient bull icon, employed by Northern kings at cult centres of Bethel and Dan, the dominant voices in Hebrew Bible condemn such iconic forms of worship.[25] In Judges 8 as well, an aniconic, Deuteronomistic writer describes the ephod negatively: 'and all of Israel whored after it, and it was to Gideon and his family a snare' (Judg. 8:27). It is interesting, however, that Judg. 8:28 continues with declaring that the land had rest during Gideon's judgeship for forty year, a good sign surely, that the leader went to his homestead, had seventy sons and many wives (also good) and died at a ripe old age. He is buried in his father's burial place, in peace, another positive sign. The overwhelming message of Judges 6–9 is that Gideon is heroic, successful and a worthy man filled with the spirit of Yhwh. The phrases about the ephod do offer evidence of the redactor of this material, the author who had the final word, but even this aniconic contributor treats the traditional biography with a light touch.

The study of characterization in the cycle of stories about the judge Gideon attunes us to the ways in which a traditional story teller creatively employs formulaic, culturally shared media and patterns in plot and expression to trace the career of a biblical hero and build a particular character. The composer shows us how the warrior matures from an insecure but talented lad, called by God, into a mature, wise, national leader. This epic cycle is particularly interesting in presenting key themes in ancient Israelite political ethics. A leader is one capable of encouraging the downtrodden to revolt, for it is human nature to accept things the

---

25. Frank Moore Cross, *Canaanite Myth and Hebrew Epic: Essays in the History of the Religion of Israel* (Cambridge, MA: Harvard University Press, 1973), 74.

way they are rather than to risk all to confront oppression. Gideon is a liberator, a subversive, and a social bandit, but above all has the capacity to inspire his people to take a risk and join him. Within an Israelite context, he is moreover dedicated to the deity's unique kingship and resists leaders' frequent desire for their own aggrandizement and that of their family. As such he expresses the worldview of a particular cultural thread in the Israelite ethical tradition.

Chapter 6

THE MAN WHO WOULD BE KING

Benjamin J. M. Johnson

Introduction

In Rudyard Kipling's short story 'The Man Who Would Be King', we are introduced to two roguish characters, Peachey Carnehan and Daniel Dravot. These two ne'er-do-wells launch a scheme to get one of them made king of Kafirstan. Their story does not end well. In an essay on Kipling's short story, literary critic, Jeffrey Meyers, writes, '*The man that would be king*, like Shakespeare's *Richard II*, considers the nature of kingship and kingly power, and both works, in different ways, emphasize the human qualities and fallibility of kings who are defeated by their own impetuosity and pride.'[1] The previous sentence could have been written about Abimelech's story in the book of Judges. In Abimelech we find a man who would be king. We see a story of political struggle, betrayal, and violence. We see the first experiment with kingship in Israel. Like Carnehan and Dravot's story, Abimelech's story does not end well. The purpose of this essay is to explore the character of Israel's first experiment with kingship. Along the way, we will see the way kingship itself is characterized.

Much has been written about Abimelech. Since Abimelech is the first Israelite king in the Hebrew Bible, much of the literature has focused on debate about whether or not Abimelech's story ought to be read as pro- or anti-monarchical.[2] Given Gideon's refusal of kingship and the overwhelmingly negative portrayal of Abimelech many scholars conclude that the stories of Gideon and Abimelech are clearly meant to portray an anti-monarchical ideology. Martin Buber's work is perhaps most famous in this category. He calls Jotham's fable, which is part of

---

1. Jeffrey Meyers, 'The Idea of Moral Authority in *The Man Who Would Be King*', *Studies in English Literature 1500–1900* 8.4 (1968): 711.

2. For a more detailed and recent survey of the literature on whether the Abimelech narrative reflects a pro- or anti-monarchical perspective see Sui Hung Albert Lee, *Dialogue on Monarchy in the Gideon-Abimelech Narrative: Ideological Reading in Light of Bakhtin's Dialogism* (BIS 187; Leiden: Brill, 2021), 10–32.

Abimelech's story, 'the strongest anti-monarchical poem of world literature'.[3] Others, however, have seen a positive portrayal of the idea of monarchy in Abimelech's story, despite a negative portrayal of Israel's first monarch. A recent study along these lines is Gordon Oeste's work.[4] Taking an interdisciplinary approach to the text, Oeste argues that the narrative portrays 'Abimelech and the Shechemites negatively and yet also serve[s] the interests of a centralized monarchy'.[5] Still others have argued that the text is inherently ambiguous. Sui Hung Albert Lee argues that there are pro- and anti-monarchical voices in the Abimelech narrative that are left unfinalized in the text, which presents 'a thorough understanding of the monarchy's twofold nature for further discussion and dialogue on the suitable polity form in Israel'.[6] The unfinalized nature of the Abimelech story allows for dialogue on the nature and necessity of monarchy from the Exile to the Persian period, Lee's proposed context for the Gideon-Abimelech narrative.[7] The strength of Lee's view is that it offers a way to engage with the tension in scholarship that sees differing ideologies on kingship present in the Gideon-Abimelech narrative.

Our approach in this study will be to analyse the character of Abimelech. Only after that analysis will we suggest what this might have to say by way of characterizing kingship in biblical narrative. As I have argued elsewhere, the analysis of character in biblical narrative often offers an interpretive crux for biblical narrative.[8] This is because biblical characters are often ambiguous or complex, which makes understanding their characterization crucial for understanding any sort of ideological claim within the narrative. Literary analysis must make space not just for the art of biblical narrative, or the description of the poetics of biblical narrative,[9]

---

3. Martin Buber, *Kingship of God* (3rd ed.; trans. Richard Scheiman; New York: Harper & Row, 1967), 75. For a further exploration of Buber's work on kingship in Judges, see Dennis T. Olson, 'Buber, Kingship, and the Book of Judges: A Study of Judges 6–9 and 17–21,' in *David and Zion: Biblical Studies in Honor of J. J. M. Roberts* (ed. Bernard F. Batto and Kathryn L. Roberts; Winona Lake, IN: Eisenbrauns, 2004), 199–218.

4. Gordon K. Oeste, *Legitimacy, Illegitimacy, and the Right to Rule: Window's on Abimelech's Rise and Demise in Judges 9* (LHBOTS 546; London: T&T Clark, 2011).

5. Oeste, *Legitimacy, illegitimacy, and the Right to Rule*, 232.

6. Lee, *Dialogue on Monarchy in the Gideon-Abimelech Narrative*, 148.

7. Ibid., 150–58.

8. Benjamin J.M. Johnson, 'Character as Interpretive Crux in the Book of Samuel,' in *Characters and Characterization in the Book of Samuel* (eds. Keith Bodner and Benjamin J. M. Johnson; London: Bloomsbury T&T Clark, 2020), 1–13.

9. I am, of course, alluding to the two seminal works: Robert Alter, *The Art of Biblical Narrative* (rev. ed.; New York: Basic Books, 2011); and Meir Sternberg, *The Poetics of Biblical Narrative: Ideological Literature and the Drama of Reading* (Bloomington, IN: Indiana University Press, 1985).

but for the '"the work of biblical narrative," namely what biblical stories accomplish cognitively, socially, and ethically, for good and ill.'[10] One of the ways that biblical narrative accomplishes this work is through characterization.

The Man Who Wouldn't Be King (and His Son)

The story and characterization of Abimelech actually starts with the story and characterization of his father, Gideon. The first key aspect of Gideon's characterization that influences Abimelech is his famous refusal of kingship. After his victories, the Israelites approach Gideon with a request that he and his progeny 'rule' (משל) over them (Judg. 8:22). Gideon refuses this offer and gives a theological rationale for it. He says, 'I will not rule (משל) over you, and my son will not rule (משל) over you; the Lord will rule (משל) over you' (Judg. 8:23).[11] Though the word 'rule' (משל) is used instead of the word 'reign' (מלך), there can be no doubt that what is offered is dynastic rulership, which we would otherwise describe as kingship.[12] Thus Gideon casts the first negative light on the concept of kingship as something that is meant for YHWH.[13] Ironically, Gideon refuses kingship by his words, but by his actions he appears at least to flirt with accepting something that looks substantially like kingship.[14] Whether or not he becomes a king or ruler subsequent to his rejection of the kingly offer, he at least entertains the idea of kingship.[15]

---

10. Danna Nolan, Fewell, 'The Work of Biblical Narrative,' in *The Oxford Handbook of Biblical Narrative* (ed. Danna Nolan Fewell; Oxford: Oxford University Press, 2016), 4.

11. Unless otherwise noted, all scriptural translations will be from the NRSV.

12. The commentaries regularly note this. E.g., Daniel I. Block, *Judges, Ruth* (NAC 6; Nashville, TN: B&H Publishing Group), 1999, 297; Barry G. Webb, *The Book of Judges* (NICOT; Grand Rapids, MI: Eerdmans, 2012), 262; Dennis T. Olson, 'The Book of Judges,' in *The New Interpreter's Bible Commentary, Volume II* (Nashville, TN: Abingdon Press, 2015), 203. However, because of the lack of use of מלך in this context, some commentators are hesitant to suggest that this is what the text is saying. E.g. Jack M. Sasson, *Judges 1–12* (AB 6D; New Haven, NJ: Yale University Press, 2014), 365.

13. There is an interesting resonance between the request for 'rulership' here and the request for 'kingship' (מלך) in 1 Samuel 8. In both instances the people approach the leader, who is a judge, and request a ruler/king which is then described as something God does (Judg. 8:23; 1 Sam. 8:7).

14. See, e.g., G. Henton Davies, 'Judges VIII 22–23,' *VT* 13.2 (1963): 151-57. As J. P. Fokkelman notes, 'Gideon firmly refused the offer to become ruler over his people (8:23), but it is doubtful whether he did so with all his heart; in 8:25-30 his behavior still gives the impression of a prince' ('Structural Remarks on Judges 9 and 19,' in *Sha'arei Talmon: Studies in the Bible, Qumran, and the Ancient Near East Presented to Shemaryahu Talmon.* [Winona Lake, IN: Eisenbrauns, 1992], 33).

15. For further reflection on Gideon's relationship with kingship and a positive assessment of Gideon's refusal, see Susan Niditch's contribution to the present volume.

This brings us to the part in Gideon's characterization that has bearing upon our primary interest, the characterization of Abimelech. Because perhaps the most interesting example of Gideon playing with the idea of kingship is in naming his son, Abimelech ('my father is king'). The name Abimelech, of course, has possible interpretations other than 'my father is king'.[16] However, the irony between Gideon's refusal of rulership, his acceptance of the trappings of kingship, and the naming of his son with a name that may suggest Gideon's own kingship is too ironic to avoid the idea that Abimelech's very name hints at the experiment with kingship among Gideon and his family.[17] This moment of characterization of Abimelech comes in a narrative context that appears to be critiquing his family's relationship to kingship. This is a dubious start to the characterization of Abimelech.

There is one more characterizing piece of information that we get about Abimelech before we ever meet him as a character. Abimelech is introduced to us, not just in the context of his father's relationship with kingship, but he is introduced to us through his mother. At the end of Gideon's life we are introduced to his sons. First, his seventy sons through his 'many wives' (Judg. 8:30). Then, we are then told that 'His concubine who was in Shechem also bore him a son, and he named him Abimelech' (Judg. 8:31). Two pieces of information are particularly important for our purposes. First, Abimelech's mother is identified as a 'concubine' (פילגש). Whatever the term *pilegesh* might mean specifically, it identifies a woman who is at least of secondary status to a primary wife.[18] In this context, Abimelech's mother is identified in a class outside of Gideon's 'many wives'. Thus, Abimelech's characterization is as something of an outsider, perhaps even a second-class member of Gideon's family.

Additionally, the narrative informs us that Abimelech's mother is a Shechemite. While we will shortly discuss the significance of the identity of the Shechemites, it does appear to suggest another factor that makes Abimelech an outsider to some degree, as his mother is the only member of Gideon's family labelled a Shechemite.

Thus, before we ever meet Abimelech, he is characterized by his father's problematic brush with kingship and the outsider status of his mother. The set-up is less-than-promising for the chance of Abimelech being a positively portrayed character.

---

16. Block, *Judges*, 303–04, lists three options: 'Melek is my father'; 'The [divine] king is my father'; and 'The king [Gideon] is my father'. For further discussion, see Wolfgang Bluedorn, *Yahweh Versus Baalism: A Theological Reading of the Gideon-Abimelech Narrative* (JSOTSup 329; Sheffield: Sheffield Academic Press, 2001), 191–94.

17. Cf. Webb, *Judges*, 268. Lillian R. Klein, *The Triumph of Irony in the Book of Judges* (JSOTSup 68; Sheffield: Sheffield Academic Press, 1989), 71, suggests that perhaps '[f]or Gideon, 'Abimelech' may have referred to Yahweh as father and king, but Abimelech bases his claim to kingship on the title offered his natural father, Gideon.'

18. For discussion of the meaning of the term פלגש, see Tammi J. Schneider, *Judges* (BO; Collegeville, MN: Liturgical Press, 1999), 128–30; *TDOT*; and the contribution by Francis Landy in the present volume, who suggests that the traditional term 'concubine' is probably not too far off (see pp. 000–00).

Abimelech's Rise to Power (9:1-6)

Abimelech's first act as a character is to go out to his mother's brothers in Shechem. We have already noted that he is at least partially characterized by otherness, but the narration of his initial actions here reinforce that perspective. It is important at this point to reflect on the identity of Shechem. As Tammi Schneider notes, '[t]he status of Shechem is necessary to understanding the context, though the text does not provide this information.'[19] On the one hand, numerous threads in Abimelech's story seem to treat the Shechemites as if they were Canaanite.[20] There is an emphasis on the presence of Baal worship there (Judg. 9:4; 9:46).[21] There is an emphasis in the text on their otherness, especially as Abimelech emphasizes his blood relationship with them (esp. 9:3). Gaal, at least, seems to assume that the Shechemites are the descendants of Hamor (Judg. 9:28), highlighting a Canaanite ethnicity.[22] On the other hand, Abimelech's kingship over Shechem clearly involves Israel (see 9:22; 55). Thus, the identity of the Shechemites is far from clear. As Robert Chisholm suggests, 'Perhaps the population was both Israelite and Canaanite; in fact it likely contained a racially mixed element (see 3:5-6).'[23] This ambiguity about the identity of Shechem will carry over into the characterization of Abimelech, who, in many ways, reflects something of a mixed identity of Canaanite and Israelite.

Upon going out to his Shechemite family, Abimelech offers his first words in the narrative. As has been noted, a character's first words in Hebrew narrative are often a 'defining moment of characterization.'[24] In Abimelech's first words we see a clever

---

19. Schneider, *Judges*, 135.

20. Cf. Victor H. Matthews, *Judges & Ruth* (NCBC; Cambridge: Cambridge University Press, 2004), 104.

21. Though 9:46 uses the term אל ברית, it is likely to be equated with the בעל ברית in 9:4. The rhetorical emphasis on Baal can probably also be seen by the repeated reference to the lords of the city as בעלים. Cf. Block, *Judges, Ruth*, 310. T. J. Lewis, 'The Identity and Function of El/Baal Berith,' *JBL* 115 (9916): 401–23, argues that בעל ברית likely functions as an epithet for אל ברית and thus does not refer to Baal. This may be possible, but the rhetorical emphasis on Baal throughout the Gideon/Abimelech narrative makes the use of בעל ברית suggestive of Baalism.

22. Gen. 34:2 identifies Hamor as a Hivite (MT) or Horite (LXX). On the overlap between Hivite and Horite, see Robert G. Boling, *Joshua* (AB 6; Garden City, NY: Doubleday, 1982), 264–65.

23. Robert B. Chisholm, Jr., *A Commentary on Judges and Ruth* (KEL; Grand Rapids, MI: Kregel, 2013), 313. For further discussion on the identity of Shechem, see Sasson, *Judges 1-12*, 389–90.

24. Robert Alter, *The David Story: A Translation with Commentary of 1 and 2 Samuel* (New York: W.W. Norton & Co., 1999), 105. For a fuller exploration of this narrative technique, see Benjamin J.M. Johnson, 'Making a First Impression: The Characterization of David and His Opening Words in 1 Samuel 17:25-31,' *TynBul* 71.1 (2020): 75–93.

plot to become king. But how do we characterize this opening speech? First, it is clever. By appealing to his kin and then having his kin appeal on his behalf, he has increased his chance of his appeal being heard. Second, however, it is in many ways a reversal of Gideon's refusal to rule.[25]

Gideon's Royal Refusal (8:23)	Abimelech's Royal Proposal (9:2)
'I will not rule over you, (משל + בכם) and my son will not rule over you; (משל + בכם) the LORD will rule over you.' (משל + בכם)	Which is better for you, that all seventy of the sons of Jerubbaal rule over you, (משל + בכם) or that one rule over you?' (משל + בכם)

Third, Abimelech's argument that it is better that one man rule rather than seventy men implies that his proposal is really a counter-proposal. For Abimelech's argument to work, it must have at least been thought that his brothers were attempting to enforce some kind of leadership role over Shechem.[26] Fourth, his appeal to his relationship with Shechem is, of course, ironic and absurd. He is appealing to bonds of brotherhood while he is plotting the death of his brothers.[27] His purported claim of loyalty is thus a farce.

Abimelech's royal proposal is accepted by the lords of Shechem. He is, after all, their brother (Judg. 9:3). And so they sponsor his royal aspirations with seventy pieces of silver from the temple of Baal-berith. This is the same Baal-berith with whom the Israelites prostituted themselves after Gideon had died (Judg. 8:33). Thus, Abimelech's royal plot is Baal-sponsored.[28] What he does with the money is hire some 'worthless and reckless fellows' (אנשים ריקים ופחזים, Judg. 9:4). What the NRSV translates as 'worthless' has been provocatively titled 'empty men' by Gregory Mobley, who suggests that this category is probably used for those who are lacking formal kinship groups or who are perhaps landless. He connects this category to the heroic tradition in ancient Israel.[29] He compares the description of the men who join David's band to this category of 'empty men.'[30] What is interesting about this category is that it encapsulates Abimelech in many ways. Though he is not without kinship groups, he eventually isolates himself from all kinship groups. Furthermore, the heroic tradition in ancient Israel will eventually be treated as 'empty' in the sense that the Hebrew Bible will move on from and downplay the

---

25. Cf. Fokkelman, 'Judges 9 and 19,' 34.

26. Cf. Chisholm, *Judges*, 311, n. 24; Schneider, *Judges*, 136.

27. T. A. Boogaart, 'Stone for Stone: Retribution in the Story of Abimelech and Shechem,' *JSOT* 32 (1985), 55, n. 8.

28. Cf. Webb, *Judges*, 271.

29. See Gregory Mobley, *The Empty Men: The Heroic Tradition of Ancient Israel* (ABRL; New York: Doubleday, 2005), especially 36–38.

30. Ibid., 36. Chisholm, *Judges*, 312, compares them to the *habiru* known from the Amarna letters.

heroic tradition,[31] Abimelech will turn out to be an 'empty' character in every sense of the word.

Abimelech takes his hired 'empty men,' goes to his father's house and he kills (הרג) his brothers (Judg. 9:5). It is significant that though Abimelech has hired a small army for the task, the verbal action is singular. It is Abimelech who is killing his seventy brothers. The singularity of verb form is matched by the singularity of the stone upon which the brothers are killed. Abimelech kills his brothers 'on one stone' (על־אבן אחת, Judg. 9:5). This seemingly strange detail will come up again at the end of his story. Abimelech's story begins and ends in violence and in both instances a single stone is involved.

As others have noted, Abimelech now most calls to mind Adoni-Bezek, the Canaanite king who cut off the thumbs and big toes of seventy rival kings (Judg. 1:6–7).[32] It is often said that one of the key themes of the book of Judges is the narrative of disintegration of the people of Israel and even their gradual Canaanization.[33] What we see in Abimelech is something of a personification of that process.

At the end of the account of Abimelech's bloody rise to power the narrator informs us that one brother, the youngest, Jotham, escaped and went into hiding (Judg. 9:5b). This younger brother offers a fable in a blistering critique of Abimelech and Shechem.

The Characterization of Abimelech in Jotham's Fable

Jotham's fable (Judg. 9:7-21) acts as something of a commentary on the narrative in which it is surrounded. As such, it offers an additional level of characterization of Abimelech. Interestingly, it nuances some of the characterization that we see of him. We will limit our comments to a few important aspects that impinge on our understanding of the characterization of Abimelech.[34]

---

31. On the idea of the fading warrior tradition in Israelite literature, see Mark S. Smith, *Poetic Heroes: Literary Commemorations of Warriors and Warrior Culture in the Early Biblical World* (Grand Rapids, MI: Eerdmans, 2014).

32. See, e.g., Gregory T. K. Wong, *Compositional Strategy in the Book of Judges: An Inductive, Rhetorical Study* (VTSup 111; Leiden: Brill, 2006), 204.

33. E.g., Daniel I. Block, 'The Period of the Judges: Religious Disintegration under Tribal Rule,' in *Israel's Apostasy and Restoration: Essays in Honor of R. K. Harrison* (ed. A. Gileadi; Grand Rapids, MI: Baker, 1988), 39–58; and Marvin A. Sweeney, 'Davidic Polemics in the Book of Judges,' *VT* 47.4 (1997): 517-529.

34. Recent examples of literature on Jotham's fable include: Karin Schöpflin, 'Jotham's Speech and Fable as Prophetic Comment on Abimelech's Story: The Genesis of Judges 9,' *SJOT* 18.1 (2004): 3–22; Silviu Tatu, 'Jotham's Fable and the Crux Interpretum in Judges IX,' *VT* 56.1 (2006): 105–24; David Janzen, 'Gideon's House as the אטד: A Proposal for Reading

First, it must be noted that the fable imagines that the idea of kingship is initiated by those who wish to be ruled by a king, not by the prospective king himself. After all, it is the trees that are seeking a king to rule over them. Whereas in the narrative, it appears that Abimelech is the one seeking kingship, not the Shechemites. This tension between the fable and the surrounding narrative is frequently noted. It has led commentators to note that the fable may have been secondarily inserted into this context.[35] Others, however, have argued that the function of the fable can still stand, even if it does not perfectly conform to the story.[36] Or, it has led some commentators to reinterpret the fable so that it fits the narrative context.[37] I propose that the parable allows us to fill in a gap in the narrative that we did not know was there.

We previously noted that Abimelech's proposal of kingship to the Shechemites implied that his brothers were already making a move for kingship. We assume that the instigators were Abimelech's brothers. However, if we allow the fable to interpret the narrative for us, we then assume that the Shechemites may have initiated the rulership of the sons of Jerubaal. The implication is that the Shechemites were looking for a king and Abimelech puts himself forward rather than his brothers. If this is the case, it offers a couple of nuances to our characterization of Abimelech. On the one hand, we may now see his move toward kingship as more reactionary than we did previously (although it was always seen as reactionary to some extent). On the other hand, however, the narrator has withheld this information until after Abimelech's bloody coup against his brothers, which has made the reader think that Abimelech is the instigator up until this point. So while we might gain some sympathies and see Abimelech more as an opportunist than an instigator, we have already spent the first part of the chapter thinking of him primarily as a bloody instigator. Why wait until now to reveal that the Shechemites were seeking a king, except to increase the negative characterization of Abimelech? We will see one other potential reason for this in a moment. But for now, we see that Abimelech's bid for kingship may be a little more complicated than was thought at first glance.

Jotham's Fable,' *CBQ* 74.3 (2012): 465–75; Francisco Martins, '"Faut-il que nous soyons gouvernés par un roi?": La fable des arbes (Jg 9,8–15) entre la satire et l'apologie,' *ETR* 93.2 (2018): 209–224; Zachary Margulies, 'Aesop and Jotham's Parable of the trees (Judges 9:8–15),' *VT* 69.1 (2019): 81–94.

    35. See, for example, Edgar Jans, *Abimelech und sein Königtum: Diachrone und synchrone Untersuchungen zu Ri 9*, ATSAT 66 (St. Ottilien: EOS-Verlag, 2001), 62–83; and Volkmar Fritz, 'Abimelech und Sichem in Jdc. IX,' *VT* 32 (1982): 129–44.

    36. E.g. Block, *Judges, Ruth*, 316–17; and Trent C. Butler, *Judges*, WBC 8 (Nashville, TN: Thomas Nelson, 2009), 240.

    37. David Janzen, 'Gideon's House as the אטד,' for example, has argued that the אטד (bramble) of the fable should be interpreted as Gideon's house not Abimelech. After all, the people of Israel did seek to make Gideon a king.

Second, the fable offers an implicit characterization of Abimelech via the metaphor of the bramble. If we pay attention to characterization in the fable itself, we see that it has interesting things to say about kingship in general, and Abimelech in particular. As the trees approach the various plants to offer kingship to them, each plant refuses on the basis of what it has to offer. The olive tree refuses to rule so that it can produce its oil which honours gods and men (Judg. 7:9). The fig tree refuses to rule so that it can produce its fruit (Judg. 9:11). The vine refuses to rule so that it can produce its wine which is the joy of gods and men (Judg. 7:13). There seems to be a twofold potential implication of this. First, the olive tree, the fig tree, and the vine are designed for good things, but they are not designed for rulership. Second, there is perhaps the implication that the good things that the olive tree, fig tree, and vine have to offer are better than rulership.[38] There is the old adage that those who cannot do, teach (quite unfair, in this teacher's estimation!). Perhaps the implication of this fable is that those who have nothing else to offer, rule.

In contrast, the bramble has nothing to offer. Or, if it has something to offer, it is only in the realm of violence as its thorny exterior implies.[39] How does this use of the thorn characterize Abimelech? As many have pointed out, it suggests that Abimelech is an objectively poor choice for ruler.[40]

The trees select their thorny king and the rest is history. Jotham appears to hold out the possibility that this relationship could work (Judg. 9:19). The reader, however, who has heard the fruitful and productive trees refuse to 'sway over the trees' (Judg. 9:9, 11, 13)[41] and has heard the choice of king described as a thorny tree, is probably not meant to be hopeful for a positive outcome to this royal venture.

The Fall of Abimelech (9:22-57)

After the interval of Jotham's fable (9:7-21), we are told that 'Abimelech ruled (שׂרר) over Israel three years' (Judg. 9:22). The use of the relatively rare word, שׂרר, instead of a more standard word for ruling, may show some reluctance by the narrator to

---

38. Cf. Schneider, *Judges*, 140. This is in contrast to Eugene Maly, 'The Jotham Fable – Anti-Monarchical?' *CBQ* 22 (1960): 303, who argued that the olive tree, fig tree, and vine, refused leadership for 'insufficient reasons.'

39. Silviu Tatu, 'Jotham's Fable and the Crux Interpretum,' has argued that the אטד of the fable should be understood as an impressive thorny tree and suggests the *Zizyphus spina-Christi* as the most likely referent. In this case it would offer something. Janzen, 'Gideon's House as the אטד,' similarly suggests that the fable may imply that the thorny tree is a good choice because it could offer a defense (see esp. pp. 468–71).

40. For example, see Chisholm, *Judges*, 315; Schneider, *Judges*, 140.

41. It must be said that the characterization of kingship as 'swaying over' (נוע) someone has to feel like an implicit critique of the institution to some extent.

describe Abimelech as reigning over Israel.[42] Furthermore, the description that Abimelech ruled for three years recalls the notice of the oppressive rules of foreign kings over Israel in the early portion of the book (e.g. 3:8, 14; 4:3; 6:1).[43] Abimelech, Israel's first experiment with kingship, is now characterized as the oppressor of Israel, akin to Israel's early oppressors in the book of Judges.

As elsewhere in the book of Judges, the notice of an oppressive ruler is followed by an act of YHWH. In the case of Othniel, for example, the spirit of YHWH (רוח־יהוה) immediately descends upon him that he might deliver the people of Israel (Judg. 3:10). In Abimelech's case God[44] does send a spirit, but instead of empowering a deliverer, God sends an evil spirit between Abimelech and the people of Shechem (Judg. 9:23). As Barry Webb notes, '[t]he 'evil spirit from God' (9:23), agent of retribution, is the dark counterpart of 'the Spirit of Yahweh' (6:34), agent of deliverance'.[45] The resultant discord between Abimelech and Shechem, where the Shechemites 'dealt treacherously' (בגד) with Abimelech, is in direct response to Abimelech and the Shechemites' treacherous dealing with the sons of Gideon/Jerubaal (Judg. 9:24). The theme of violent retribution is sounded.[46]

The tension between Abimelech and Shechem leads to the arrival of Gaal, who has much in common with Abimelech. T. A. Boogaart has noted the following commonalities, such that Abimelech is again most closely characterized with another non-Israelite:

1. a man comes to Shechem (9.1a; 9.26a);
2. the man is accompanied by his brothers/kinsmen (9.1b-3a; 9.26a);
3. the man conspires against the absent ruler of Shechem with a speech delivered at a gathering (9.2-3a; 9.28-29);
4. the speech emphasizes that the ties of the conspirator to Shechem are closer than those of the ruler (9.2b; 9.28);
5. the Shechemites put their trust in the conspirator (9.3b; 9.26b);
6. the conspirator encounters the ruler (9.5; 9.30–42).[47]

---

42. See Schneider, *Judges*, 142–43. Elie Assis, *Self-Interest or Communal Interest: An Ideology of Leadership in the Gideon, Abimelech and Jephthah Narratives (Judg 6–12)* (VTSup 106; Leiden: Brill, 2005), 153–54, even suggests that the use of this word may characterize Abimelech's reign like other ancient Near Eastern monarchies, thus adding to theme of Abimelech's paganization.

43. Heller, 'Abimelek,' 233.

44. It is perhaps worth noting that reference to YHWH (יהוה) disappears in the Abimelech account, and reference is only made to the generic God (אלהים).

45. Webb, *Judges*, 296. Cf. also, Klein, *Triumph of Irony*, 73, who sees the inversion of spirits in this action.

46. On this theme see Boogaart, 'Stone for Stone,' esp. 49.

47. Ibid. 50.

In the resulting conflict with Gaal a couple of insights can be made about Abimelech. First, he listens to the advice of the 'ruler of the city' (שׂר־העיר), Zebul (9:30-33). Unlike some of Israel's later ruler's, most notably David's rebellious son, Absalom (2 Sam. 17:1-14), Abimelech is capable of taking wise and practical advice. Second, Abimelech is a capable military leader. He not only takes the advice of Zebul, to lie in wait, but the text offers some insight into his tactics, showing Abimelech dividing up his men into four divisions (Judg. 9:34). His capability as a military leader is sometimes noted as a positive characteristic of Abimelech.[48] Gaal and his conspirators appear outmatched by Abimelech and Zebul. The narrative even offers a moment of beautiful schadenfreude on the part of Zebul as he turns to Gaal and says, 'Where is your boast now, you who said, 'Who is Abimelech, that we should serve him?' Are not these the troops you made light of? Go out now and fight with them' (9:38).

The next morning, after Abimelech's defeat of Gaal and his troops, the people go out into the field (9:42). The meaning of this action is a little vague. Presumably, these are the people of Shechem, but are they going out to resume their normal agricultural duties after the conflict or are they going out for war? The narrator reports that 'the people went out to the field', which probably implies an innocent activity of working the fields or assessing the damage.[49] However, in v. 43 we see the action from Abimelech's perspective (with the use of והנה) and it is only reported that 'the people were going out from the city' with no reference to the field. Perhaps then Abimelech sees the people coming out and all he can see is an enemy force. His response is one of extreme violence. '[H]e rose against them and killed them' (9:43). The narrative continues and gives some considerable detail about the massacre. Two of Abimelech's units attack the people in open while Abimelech's unit stands in the gate of the city, cutting off their retreat. Then Abimelech turns his attention on the city, and massacres the town (9:45). More than that, however, Abimelech additionally sows the area with salt, an act that is unprecedented in the Hebrew Bible. This act is likely symbolic, placing the area under a curse of infertility rather than a literal salting of the field to produce infertile ground.[50]

Abimelech is not through, however. As soon as he hears that the lords of the Tower of Shechem have fled to the stronghold of the house of El-berith, he goes up with his men and sets the stronghold on fire killing all the men and women seeking refuge there (9:48-49). Two things are perhaps significant for our understanding of Abimelech in this episode. First, this narrative of Abimelech burning down the stronghold with the lords of the tower of Shechem inside fulfills the now prophetic-looking fable of Jotham. Fire has gone forth from Abimelech and consumed the people of Shechem (see Judg. 9:19-20).

---

48. See Oeste, *Legitimacy, Illegitimacy, and the Right to Rule*, 109, 154–55.

49. Webb, *Judges*, 288; Chisholm, *Judges*, 318; Younger, *Judges*, 227. Though C.F. Burney, *Book of Judges*, 285, thinks that the people were coming out on 'one of the predatory excursions described in v. 25'.

50. See Sasson, *Judges*, 397–98. Cf. also, Webb, *Judges*, 289–90 and Chisholm, *Judges*, 319.

Second, the labelling of this stronghold at the house of El-berith (אל ברית) is quite provocative. Most scholars see this here as either a variant of Baal-berith (בעל ברית) that we know from 8:33 and 9:4[51] or an example of polemics against the Canaanite god El in addition to Baal.[52] However, given the identification of El with the God of Israel in the Hebrew Bible,[53] and the regular use of El with an epithet (El-elyon, El-olam, etc.[54]), may allow the reader to see an allusion to the God of Israel here. Thus Abimelech's father is known as one who contends with the Canaanite deity, Baal (Judg. 6:32), but Abimelech eventually slaughters a town that has a name that at least alludes to the God of Israel. The journey of relationship with the Israelite deity from father to son has not been a positive one.

The final episode of Abimelech's story sees him coming to Thebez and capturing it (9:50). Why Thebez? The text does not say. The absence of a textual rationale for this attack allows for the inference that there may be no rationale for this action outside Abimelech's own desire. Without wanting to psychoanalyze Abimelech too much, the move to attack Thebez without a rationale characterizes Abimelech as someone who decides on violence when there is no clear reason for it. Perhaps we are meant to see violence as Abimelech's default setting.

The scene starts as a repeat of the previous scene. There is a tower in the city and all the inhabitants flee to the tower. We are perhaps led to expect a similar fiery conclusion to this conflict. However, the difference between Abimelech's siege of Shechem and his siege of Thebez is 'one woman' (אשה אחת), who throws a millstone on Abimelech's head (9:53). The ironies of this action are extensive. First, Abimelech who pitched himself as the '*one* man' (איש אחד) who ought to rule Shechem (9:2), who kills his seventy brothers on '*one* stone' (אבן אחד, 9:5), is now killed by '*one* woman' (אשה אחת, 9:53). Second, Abimelech who, to use modern parlance, has put himself forward to be *the man* in Israel, is undone by a woman.[55] This ironic action interestingly both upholds and subverts a kind of patriarchy. It upholds a patriarchal perspective by the fact that it is ironic and unfitting in the text that a king would be killed by a woman. However, it also subverts that patriarchal perspective by that very fact. How can a male, even a king, be more significant than a woman when he is undone by a nameless 'certain woman'? Third, after Abimelech is struck by the woman of Thebez, he immediately asks his armor bearer to kill him, 'so people will

---

51. E.g., Day, *Yahweh and the Gods and Goddesses of Canaan*, 69–70; Webb, *Judges*, 291.

52. E.g. Block, *Judges*, 305–306; Chisholm, *Judges*, 320–21; etc.

53. On the identification of YHWH and El in the Hebrew Bible, see Smith, *The Early History of God*, 32–43.

54. For some of the various El compound names in the Hebrew Bible, see Rose, 'Names of God in the OT', *ABD* 4:1004–07.

55. This irony is regularly pointed out by scholars. For a recent and very helpful study highlighting the way that ideologies of masculinity come to play in Abimelech's story, see Jon-Michael Carman, 'Abimelech the Manly Man? Judges 9.1-57 and the Performance of Hegemonic Masculinity', *JSOT* 43.3 (2019): 301–16.

not say about me, "A woman killed him"' (9:54). The irony is, of course, that Abimelech is remembered precisely for being killed by a woman and becomes an object lesson in later biblical narrative (2 Sam. 11:20). Finally, the text offers an official narratorial interpretation of this event. Abimelech is killed for killing his seventy brothers, just as the people of Shechem were destroyed by Abimelech for their wickedness. The narrative thus concludes, 'on them came the curse of Jotham son of Jerubaal' (19:57). The self-destructive story of Abimelech's bid for kingship comes to a conclusion.

Conclusion: The Man Who Would Be King

In conclusion, then, how might we characterize Abimelech? It seems there is little doubt that Abimelech is characterized predominantly negatively in the narrative. Though he may show some positive qualities, he is without a doubt the villain of the story. However, his villainy contains some surprising elements. We have noted numerous aspects of his characterization along the way. While each of these is probably deserving of further study, we can do no more than sketch the characterization of Abimelech that we have seen.

First, we meet Abimelech as someone who is marked as an 'outsider' to some extent. He is a relative of the Shechemites and the son of a *pilegesh*. In a book that has a lot to say about insider/outsider dynamics and the dangers of Israel adopting foreign worship practices, this aspect of Abimelech's characterization carries extra weight. Related to this theme of otherness, we see in Abimelech a blurring of identities. For starters he is described as a king in Shechem, which we presume to be a non-Israelite polity. However, by the end of the story it has become clear that Abimelech is king over Israel as well (see 9:22, 55), making him Israel's first experiment with kingship. Second, from the first to the last, Abimelech is marked as someone for whom loyalty and kinship seem to be optional characteristics. From his betrayal of his brothers to his turning on the Shechemites (however justified), Abimelech is a character who embodies the breakdown of the ties that bind, rather than the building up of such relationships. In many ways, this is a characterization that will eventually mark Israel in the book of Judges (cf. chs. 17–21). Third, the characterization of Abimelech in Jotham's fable suggests that he is someone who has nothing to offer. He is ill-suited to rule. One wonders how many rulers are. The fable criticizes those who seek a ruler in spite of their qualifications for rulership. And it critiques a ruler who has no business ruling because they have nothing to offer. Fourth, Abimelech is characterized as someone for whom violence comes naturally and readily.

All four of these characterizations fall somewhat into the category of Mobley's 'empty men'. This warrior class that is perhaps marked by outsiderness, lack of kinship, and probably has nothing to offer but violence. Abimelech stands in for this tradition of the 'empty men' in the worst possible way.

Finally, and perhaps most importantly, he is in many ways characterized as being like a Canaanite king. He outdoes Adoni-bezek in his violence. His coup seems to be Baal sponsored. He is the oppressor of Israel in this story rather than a foreign king. The characterization of Abimelech is a litany of the worst things that Israel struggles with in the book of Judges. In this way, he embodies some of the worst of the characterization of Israel.

The Long Shadow of Abimelech's Characterization

As a thorny bramble, Abimelech may not have had an adequate shade to cast for the trees over whom he would rule. However, as a character, he has cast a long shadow over the biblical narrative. The characterization of Abimelech has far-reaching implications. We will only mention two.

First, the characterization of Abimelech has significance for the conclusion of the book of Judges. A number of factors put these two sections of the book in contact. (1) The only mentions of a concubine or secondary wife (פילגש) in the book are Abimelech's mother (Judg. 8:31) and the Levite's concubine (Judges 19–20). (2) Both Abimelech's story and the conclusion of Judges deal with the theme of kingship. Abimelech with his experiment with kingship and the conclusion with its refrain of the need for a king (Judg. 17:6; 18:1; 19:1; 21:25). (3) Both the Abimelech story and the conclusion to Judges feature stories of Israelites turning on each other.

So how does Abimelech's characterization effect the conclusion of the book? For Gregory Wong, for example, the negative characterization of Abimelech has caused him to interpret the refrain of 'there was no king in Israel' to suggest a longing not for a human king, but for a divine king.[56] After all, how could the conclusion of the book speak longingly for a king when Israel's first king was an unmitigated disaster? However, those who claim that the Abimelech narrative is primarily a critique of Abimelech and not the monarchy per se, are probably correct.[57] Nevertheless, that is only half the story. Gideon's refusal of monarchy and his theological rationale for it at least point us in the direction to read Abimelech's story as a critique of the idea of monarchy.

Thus, second, the characterization of Abimelech casts a long shadow that includes at least the first two kings of Israel. As Wong and others have noted, there are a number of textual links between the story of Abimelech and the story of Saul.[58] For example, both Abimelech and Saul attempt to remove their rivals to the throne, neither is fully successful (Judg. 9:5; 1 Sam. 18:11, 17, 25; 19:1, 10). Both

---

56. Wong, *Compositional Strategy*, 199–223, esp. 202–206.

57. E.g. Oeste, *Legitimacy, Illegitimacy, and the Right to Rule*, 81, 221, 232 and Gerald Eddie Gerbrandt, *Kingship according to the Deuteronomistic History* (SBLDS, 87; Atlanta: Scholars Press, 1986), 130–32.

58. See, for example, Wong, *Compositional Strategy*, 210–11, O'Connell, *Rhetoric of the Book of Judges*, 291–93; Ken Stone, "Gender Criticism: The Un-manning of Abimelech," in *Judges and Method: New Approaches in Biblical Studies*, ed. Gale A. Yee (2nd ed.; Minneapolis, MN: Fortress Press, 2007), 197–99.

Abimelech and Saul are the recipient of the attention of an 'evil spirit' (רוח רעה, Judg. 9:23; 1 Sam. 16:14). Both Abimelech and Saul are killed by their armour-bearers after being wounded in battle (Judg. 9:53–54; 1 Sam. 31:3–4). The story of Israel's first divinely anointed, Saul, recalls the story of the first king in Israel, Abimelech, in such a way that neither comes across very positively.

However, the characterization of Abimelech does not just reach out and touch Saul. David's story also recalls Abimelech, this time explicitly. After carrying out David's grisly command to have Uriah killed on the battlefield by having his troops go too close to the city of Rabbah where there were valiant warriors (2 Sam. 11:16-17), Joab sends a message to David confirming what has happened. Given the nature of Uriah's death, Joab gives the messenger instructions on what to do if David brings up the case of Abimelech, who has presumably become a by-word for the dangers of fighting too near a city wall. The ironic potential of this reference is significant, however. As Meir Sternberg has noted, Abimelech is a king whose inglorious downfall is due to a woman. David, in a different way, is also a king whose inglorious downfall is due to a woman.[59] Thus, Abimelech's characterization is carried forward to the very king who is described as a man after God's own heart (1 Sam. 13:14), who many would argue is the king anticipated by the final refrain in Judges 17–21.[60]

As Gregory Wong has articulated, 'Abimelech is perhaps the most negatively portrayed character among named Israelites in Judges.'[61] There are, of course, some pretty horrible unnamed characters! However, given that Abimelech is the first instance of kingship in the book of Judges and in Israel's primary history, we cannot help but see it as significant that he is characterized so negatively. Specifically, his characterization of one whose identity seems at least partially Canaanite, who does not seem to prioritize loyalty, and whose default mode is violence all speak to a character who functions as a strong negative example for the whole royal tradition in Israel. It may be true that the story of Abimelech is not an explicit critique on the monarchy per se. However, given Abimelech's connections to kingship in the book of Judges and beyond, his negative characterization is at least a warning about the kind of man who would be king.

---

59. See Sternberg, *Poetics of Biblical Narrative*, 219–22.

60. See, e.g., Andrew D.H. Mayes, 'Deuteronomistic Royal Ideology in Judges 17–21,' *BibInt* 9.3 (2001): 241–58.

61. Wong, *Compositional Strategies*, 203.

Chapter 7

A GILEADITE RESPONDER: VERBING THE CHARACTER OF JEPHTHAH

Tammi J. Schneider

Military hero,[1] horrible father,[2] or minor judge with expanded portfolio?[3] All of these are ways scholars have described the character of Jephthah in the book of Judges. The problem with Jephthah, as is the case with so many other biblical figures, is how one determines who and what components define a character. Should one characterize a biblical figure based on the theology of the book? The theology that scholars have imposed on the book? Translations that already interpret a character's personality for the reader? What characteristics matter?

Assessing Jephthah is difficult because he is one of the few characters who appears both in the Hebrew Bible (Judges 11–13, where there is no assessment of him) and in the New Testament, where he is listed as positive (Hebrews 11:32). He appears in the middle of the book of Judges, wins an important victory (Judg. 11:33), is loyal to the Israelite deity (Judg. 11:9), yet sacrifices his only daughter (Judg. 12:39) and oversees the slaughter of another tribe in Israel (Judg. 12).

This article will argue that Jephthah is depicted in the book of Judges as someone who responds to the actions of others. Despite his military reputation, both in the biblical text and in scholarship, the long text dedicated to Jephthah focuses on his negotiating. In these negotiations he presents history so that he is always blameless. He is also always devoted to the Israelite deity. His mother and daughter, the only women in his life, shape his character and how he is perceived by readers.

To assess Jephthah's character, I will apply an approach called 'verbing the character' where the character is examined by how they are described; instances where they are the subject of a verb; the object of a verb or a clause; and synthesis of the character by examining their relationships and how those relationships play out within the larger narrative of the book.[4] The approach was originally developed

---

1. Susan Niditch, *Judges: A Commentary* (OTL; Louisville: Westminster John Knox Press, 2008).

2. Carolyn Pressler, 'Jephthah's Daughter,' *EDB* 685.

3. Robert G. Boling, 'Jephthah,' *ABD* 3:680–62, here 680.

4. Tammi J. Schneider, *Mothers of Promise: Women in the Book of Genesis* (Grand Rapids: Baker Academic, 2008), 11–12.

as a means of trying to quantify qualitative data. The goal was that by counting and examining where a character is the subject or an object, and assessing the kinds of verbs applied to them, one could determine how active the character is. Included in the approach is an assessment of the terminology used to describe the character and an assessment of their relationships. The intent is that one could compare a character's description against the verbs associated with them, especially in comparison with their relationship with those around them to better understand the depiction of any actor in the text. The case of Jephthah reveals quite a gulf between one of his most prominent descriptions and his actions. This raises an interesting critique of the method: how are we to critique a character whose descriptions do not necessarily match their actions?

Jephthah's Description

The Hebrew language does not have many adjectives, and characters in the Hebrew Bible are often defined through nouns applied to them, especially kinship terms. Jephthah is described by seven terms, three of which are kinship terms (son, brother, father). In general, the terms describing Jephthah are complicated by lexical ambiguity. Thus, while one might assume that descriptions help understand a character, in Jephthah's case what they add about him is not always clear.

'Gileadite' is Jephthah's first and last description (Judg. 11:1; 12:7). This term can refer to a person, a subtribe of Manasseh, or a place, primarily the Transjordan, though the contours of what constitutes Gilead fluctuate.[5] Jephthah's relationship to the clan of Gilead evolves throughout his story. He is described as part of Gilead, rejected by Gilead, and when he is recruited by the elders of Gilead he is not located physically in Gilead. By the end of the story, he views himself as the representative of all things Gilead. Thus, Jephthah's first description toys with his relationship to Gilead.

Still in the first verse, Jephthah is described with an idiom often translated as 'a man of valor'.[6] Both *gibor* and *hayil* come from roots whose meanings are 'strong' or 'mighty'.[7] The term appears throughout the Deuteronomistic History with established fighters: Gideon (Judg. 6:12), Kish, the father of Saul (1 Sam. 9:1), David (1 Sam. 16:18), and Jeroboam (1 Kgs 11:28). Since the others on the list all are established men with property, some suggest the reference means Jephthah is exiled when he is already established.[8] Translators have trouble assessing what constitutes a person with such a title since the Hebrew phrase is identical for each of these characters yet most translations into English suggest different titles for

---

5. David Merling, 'Gilead (Place),' *EDB* 504.
6. Niditch, *Judges*, 124.
7. For *gibor* see 'גבור' *BDB* 150; for *hayil* see 'חול, חיל' *BDB* 298.
8. Mercedes L. Garcia Bachmann, *Judges* (Wisdom Commentary Series; Collegeville: Liturgical Press, 2018), 120.

each occurrence of the phrase.⁹ For example, the NJPS calls Jephthah an 'able warrior' but Saul's father Kish is a 'man of substance' and David is a 'stalwart fellow'. In the KJV, Jephthah is a 'mighty man of valor', Saul's father is a 'mighty man of power' and David is a 'mighty valiant man'. Later in the story, Jephthah is recruited by the elders of Gilead (Judg. 11:11) and at that point he may have an army (Judg. 11:3). The text provides Jephthah with a description with military connotations, though the actions supporting that are few and appear later in the story.

Still in the first verse introducing Jepthah, he is referred to as his mother's son. Her first label is an *isha zonah*. Most translations suggest the term means 'whore/prostitute' (NJPS, KJV, NRSV) which only references the second term in the phrase. Since Jephthah's mother must be female, it is not clear why the Hebrew includes 'woman' and 'prostitute' and why translators only translate one term. Like many stories in Judges, there is a woman involved in shaping the 'judge' and his place in the storyline, and where and how that impacts the story is significant.¹⁰

Here, the import of her being a 'prostitute' is complex and a major plot line. Traditionally, the term is translated as 'prostitute' suggesting a woman who accepts money in¹¹ exchange for sex yet no commentaries suggest actions by her and there are no examples in the Hebrew Bible of a woman doing so.¹² Instead, most commentaries suggest something like 'illegitimate parentage'. Later in the text, Jephthah is labelled the son of another woman (Judg. 11:2), suggesting the issue is not what his mother does for a living but her relationship to other females who have descendants in, or of, Gilead. Throughout the book of Judges, the verb, of which this is a nominal form, is what the Israelites have been doing against the Israelite deity (Judg. 2:17; 8:27). This reference is in the voice of the narrator and thus not an attack set in dialogue. Regardless of whether the term refers to his mother's occupation or that sex outside traditional Israelite marriage produced Jephthah, it seemingly establishes him as an outsider caused by the nature of his birth through his mother.

Jepthah's mother is described differently in the next verse. The sons of Gilead label him the son of another woman (Judg. 11:2). Contrary to the previous reference, this appears inside a quotation by his brothers in the context of ensuring he does not inherit with them. Though the term *isha* can mean woman or wife, no translation suggests she is another wife, likely because of the previous statement, even though it is a clear option. This point in the story would have been a great opportunity for Jephthah's brothers to use negative terminology towards Jephthah's

---

9. Consulted were: New Jewish Publication Society, New Revised Standard Version, and the King James Version.

10. Others include: Othniel (Judg. 1:12–15); Barak (Judg. 4:4–16); Abimelech (Judg. 9:1-55); Samson (Judg. 13–16).

11. Robert G. Boling, *Judges* (AB 6A; New Haven: Yale University Press, 2005), 190.

12. Many suggest that is precisely what Tamar is doing with Judah, though it is not supported by the text. See Schneider, *Mothers of Promise*, 161–60.

mother as they are explaining why they banish Jephthah. Instead, they use language that is seemingly less offensive to a modern ear and in the context to carry out a severe action against Jephthah. What both references suggest is that because of some characteristic of Jephthah's mother his brothers do not think him worthy of them or their father's wealth.

Jephthah's brothers are named as his brothers only in 11:3, where he flees from them. In the previous verse, where he is the child of another woman, the men are described as the sons of the woman, referring to the woman/wife of Gilead. Here, again in the voice of the narrator, these men are labelled 'his' brothers, presumably referring to Jephthah. One interpretation might be that the narrator views Jephthah's brothers as opposed to a relationship with him because of the role his mother plays within Gilead whereas the brothers, refusing to claim that relationship, suggest other reasons to justify their actions. The characterization of Jephthah as a brother raises issues concerning his mother, inheritance, and his relationship with Gilead.

Jephthah is described as a *katzin* twice, once in an offer (Judg. 11:6) and later as happening (Judg. 11:11). The term means 'chief/commander', even 'dictator'.[13] The term first appears in the mouth of the elders of Gilead, some group who entice Jephthah to return and help them after the Ammonites attack Gilead and no one from within the community steps up to the leadership role (Judg. 11:4-5). *Katzin* is not common within the biblical text and it is not clear if it is solely military or suggests some sort of political authority as well. In negotiations with these men, Jephthah is later made both head of Gilead and *katzin* (Judg. 11:11). While the impact of the word is unclear – is it a dictator and is that good or bad? – what is clear is that this is offered to Jephthah, he does not ask for it, and he receives this designation and more after negotiations.

Jephthah is also 'head' (*rosh*) as an offer in 11:8, theoretically in 9, and 11. As noted above, the title is presumably bigger than 'commander' as it follows Jephthah's discussion with the elders suggesting they are not interested in him until they need him. The reference to making him head over all the inhabitants of Gilead appears in the elders' counteroffer after Jephthah's response to their initial offer of commander. Jephthah notes if he wins, with the help of the Israelite deity, he will be their head (Judg. 11:9). Jephthah returns to Gilead and, before any battle occurs, is made both commander and head, though the second reference fails to clarify over whom he is head (Judg. 11:11).

Jephthah's final description is as a father. His daughter addresses him in direct speech employing this term after Jephthah tells her she has brought him low and become his troubler because of a vow he makes prior to his battle (Judg. 11:36). In the next verse, the narrator notes that she speaks again to her father, requesting that she go to the mountains with her friends before being sacrificed as a result of her father's vow (Judg. 11:37). While Jephthah is labelled a Gileadite upon his death, this is the last descriptor he receives, that is, 'father' to a child he will sacrifice.

---

13. 'קצין' *BDB* 298.

Jephthah's descriptions are bookended by the two major women in his life: his mother and daughter. The status of his mother is what defines his early story which has him banished from his home by his brothers. His relationship with his daughter is what turns a character who does more negotiating than battling into a problematic character by making a vow leading to her death. In between he is a strong military man who succeeds because of his military skill to become a commander, head of Gilead, who judges Israel (Judg. 12:7). The question here, especially through verbing the character, is how the reader is to understand a biblical character: through actions or descriptions?

Jephthah's Actions

Jephthah is the subject of twenty-six different verbs. He is only the subject more than one time for seven of those verbs. He is also the subject of verbs in the second person. These second-person verbs are usually in the mouth of another person who is explaining what Jephthah has or will do but technically, even though they are in the second person, they still have Jephthah as subject. Jephthah's actions are not those of a military man. He is usually responding to things others have done, except for his vow and sacrifice of his daughter, and he is seldom the subject of military action verbs.

Technically, Jephthah is first the subject of the verb 'to be' when noting that he is a Gileadite (Judg. 11:1). This reaffirms the importance of that aspect of Jephthah. He is again the subject of this verb in a different tense when he speaks with the Gileadites who offer to make him their commander and he repeats a form of their offer and ends by stating/asking/suggesting that if all the things happen, 'I will be your head' (Judg. 11:9). In this case, Jephthah has already started subtle negotiations because, as noted above, the elders first suggest making him their military commander and here Jephthah ups the ante as to what his role will be.

Jephthah next flees because of his brothers (Judg. 11:3). The brothers claim Jephthah will not inherit with them which does not fully explain why Jephthah must flee. There is a slight disconnect between the description of Jephthah as some sort of strong military man and fleeing because his brothers will not share an inheritance.

When Jephthah flees, he dwells in a place named 'Tob' (Judg. 11:3). Again, the terminology surrounding Jephthah does not correlate well with a mighty fighting man. Dwelling is not an aggressive action and suggests he moves on from Gilead. He moves to a place which, on the surface, means 'good'. Scholars have focused on where this place is, with most deciding that Tob is not far from Gilead.[14] The focus on these verses tends to be on the folks who gather around him, labelled 'empty men' (Judg. 11:3). They will not be discussed here because Jephthah is the object where they are concerned, not the subject. As far as Jephthah is concerned, this supposedly mighty military man flees his brothers and dwells in the 'good' place.

---

14. Boling, *Judges*, 197.

Jephthah is next the subject of the verb 'to say' *aleph-mem-resh*, a verb of which he is subject six times. He speaks to the elders of Gilead (Judg. 11:7, 9), the king of Amon (Judg. 11:15), the Israelite deity (Judg. 11:30), his daughter (Judg. 11:35), and the Ephraimites (Judg. 12:2). This is a fairly large range of characters. He does not initiate conversation with the elders of Gilead or the Ephraimites, but he does with the King of Amon, and the Israelite deity. The situation with his daughter is more complex as his speech to her is a response to her action. The numerous times Jephthah is the subject of this verb, and other verbs concerning speech, as well as his lengthy speeches, is a hallmark of his character.

Jephthah is the subject of another speaking verb *dalet-bet-resh*. In this case, Jephthah speaks to the Israelite deity. First, he says all the terms negotiated with the elders of Gilead (Judg. 11:11). Note here the text does not state categorically what the terms are that have been negotiated; the terms are simply summarized as 'the said things'. Thus, early in Jephthah's story is an example where the text does not explicitly recount what was previously said would happen, but it is simply summarized.

The second time Jephthah uses this verb is also with the Israelite deity but this time he says a 'vow' *nun-dalet-resh* (Judg. 11:30). The vow is one through which Jephthah's character often is evaluated: he will sacrifice whatever comes out of his house as a sacrifice (specialized kind including burning) to the deity upon his return from victory over the Ammonites. Unfortunately for Jephthah's daughter, she is the first thing that emerges from his house (Judg. 11:34). As above, when Jephthah carries out the action he had said, the text does not repeat the terms but simply summarizes that he did to her what he vowed he would do (Judg. 11:37).

Yet another unique feature highlighted by verbing the character is that the action for which much ink is spilled in commentaries, Jephthah's vow, receives little space in the Hebrew Bible. The reference appears, Jephthah will later follow it after his success, he will carry out the vow to great distress by readers but the text itself does not critique, comment, or spend much time on it: that is what interpreters do. The difficulty in assessing Jephthah is that this one action is lifted up as the major critique of him despite the fact that the text does not dwell upon it.

In Judges 11:11, Jephthah 'goes,' *hey-lamed-chaf*, here with the elders to Gilead. This verb appears in the same verse where the people make him their commander and head and he says/repeats all the terms before the deity. While Jephthah is the subject of an action verb here, he goes with them, after negotiations. He returns to Gilead victoriously and with a better title than had been offered originally (Judg. 11:6) but the elders too accomplish their mission to have Jephthah return and lead a military campaign that no one from Gilead is prepared to do.

Jephthah in his role as negotiator is the subject of the verb 'send,' *shin-lamed-chet*, three times, all to the king of Amon (Judg. 11:12, 14, 28). The military man begins his battle with the Ammonites in a battle of words. Jephthah sends a series of messages with messengers. His plan does not work but it is a noteworthy component of his character, and possibly of his daughter's, to begin any process with reviewing the history and restating a position so that he is the victim. He does this with the elders of Gilead, here, with his daughter, and with the Ephraimites.

Jephthah's next verb is in the negative: 'I have not sinned' *chet-tet-aleph* (Judg. 11:27). This claim is at the end of the long speech conveyed to the King of Ammon through messengers (Judg. 11:16-26). The sixteen-verse speech reviews the history between the Ammonites and the Israelites through the lens of the Israelites. At the end of the speech, Jephthah claims not to have sinned against the Ammonites and turns the blame to the Ammonites, also asking the Israelite deity to be the arbiter between them.

Jephthah is the subject of the verb 'to cross' *ayin-vet-resh* seven times, more than any other verb. He crosses three times alone in Judges 11:29 where the text names the places he visits before battling the Ammonites. In reference to crossing over to fight the Ammonites, again the verb appears in Judges 11:32. Jephthah is the subject of this verb when used by Ephraim asking Jephthah why he crossed over to fight the Ammonites without them (Judg. 12:1). Jephthah then speaks it when explaining his side of their conflict, suggesting he crossed to fight the Ammonites because Ephraim did not come to help (Judg. 12:1). This is an action verb that is not as action packed as one might expect from a military guy. It recounts movements, though not fighting, and later appears in more negotiations.

Jephthah is the subject of the verb 'to offer a burnt sacrifice' (hiphil of *ayin-lamed-hey*, Judg. 11:31). In this context it follows the spirit of the Israelite deity descending upon him, seemingly unbeknownst to Jephthah, and could show devotion to the deity or a continuation of Jephthah's attempt at negotiating. The wording of the offer is chilling. He states that he will offer whatever emerges from his house, *biti* which is also the same terminology for 'my daughter'. Thus, the text is playing with the problematic nature of Jephthah's vow from the moment he makes it.

Jephthah also 'smites,' *nun-chaf-hey* them, namely the Ammonites (Judg. 11:33). The whole point of recruiting Jephthah is to defeat the Ammonites (Judg. 11:6) and despite the lengthy episode focusing on Jephthah this is the only military verb used for him and he is only subject of it once. Despite the discussion about his military prowess, the biblical text rarely focuses on that aspect of Jephthah.

Following Jephthah's victory, he is the subject of a series of verbs which are connected to him only once. First, he 'comes', *bet-vav-aleph,* home (Judg. 11:34). This is when he sees his daughter coming out of the home, leading him to have to carry out his vow on her. Upon seeing her he carries out his next action: he tears *quf-resh-ayin* his clothes before telling her what seeing her means. In this same verse, he argues that he cannot 'return' *shin-vav-vet*, meaning go back on what he has vowed. Technically, here he is the subject of the verb 'to be able to' but the thing he cannot do is return or reverse what he has vowed.

In this same verse Jephthah uses another verb of which he is subject twice. First, he argues 'I opened' *pay-sade-hey* my mouth (Judg. 11:36), the thing from which he cannot return. Later, his daughter speaks to him agreeing that 'You opened your mouth,' telling him to do what came out of his mouth, continuing the play on words regarding his initial vow to sacrifice what came out of the opening of his house (Judg. 11:30). In this second case, Jephthah's daughter is speaking but she is speaking to her father, the second person 'you' of the sentence. making Jephthah the subject of the verb again.

Jephthah is the subject of the verb 'vow', *nun-dalet-resh*, once (Judg. 11:37). When he makes the vow, he is subject of the verb to speak, and it is directed towards the Israelite deity (Judg. 11:30). Only when he is doing it is he the subject of it. The text does not repeat the content of the vow when he does it (Judg. 11:39)

Following the sacrifice of Jephthah's daughter, he faces yet another issue, the Ephraimites. The next two verbs are in second person because the Ephraimites accuse Jephthah. First, they claim 'you' (Jephthah) did not '*call us*,' *quf-resh-aleph* (Judg. 12:1). Their claim cannot be confirmed or denied.

Jephthah responds to them by claiming he did call them using a different verb, *zayin-aleph-kuf* (Judg. 12:2). He further argues, 'I saw that you were not coming' (Judg. 12:3) using the verb 'to see' *resh-aleph-hey*. Both verbs are in the first person as they appear in Jephthah's direct quote of what he says to the Ephraimites. Finally, he argues, still in first person and in direct speech, that he put his soul in his hand (technically palm) and crossed over to the Ammonites (Judg. 12:3). Again, Jephthah, or his people, are threatened and he begins with negotiations. In this case, he contradicts the notion that he did not call the Ephraimites and argues it is their fault that he must act.

Despite Jephthah's attempts to avoid conflict through negotiation, all cases show him needing to fight. Here, Jepththah must gather the Gileadites (Judg. 12:4). It is also the only time he is subject of the verb 'battle,' *lamed-chet-mem*. Jephthah and the Gileadites fight the Ephraimites, another tribe in Israel, possibly a harbinger of the end of the book where the Benjaminites are almost destroyed (Judg. 20).

Jephthah is last the subject of three verbs, each appearing once, to sum up his life in Judges 12:27. Jephthah judges (*shin-pay-tet*)Israel, a phrase used as a summation for most of the judges in the book. He dies (*mem-vav-tav*), again common reference for the other judges. Finally, he is also buried (*quf-vav-resh*) in the cities of Gilead.

Despite the picture of Jephthah as a mighty warrior recruited by Gilead for his military prowess, Jephthah is only the subject of two military words, and each only appears once: 'smite' and 'battle'. Other terms with military significance could be 'gather' with the sense of 'summon', and 'cross-over'. Most of the verbs for which he is the subject have him responding to another situation. He speaks to the elders because they recruit him. He brings in the Israelite deity, but this is Jephthah's response to the elders' recruitment. Jephthah speaks with the king of Ammon but there too, the Ammonites, according to the text, start the conflict. So too, the Ephraimites initiated their conflict. The one thing Jephthah does not initiate is the sacrifice of what emerges from his house: his daughter. Even there, some of his actions are the result of her being the one coming out of his house first and her requesting something from him. Clearly the places where Jephthah is the subject of the verb do not completely align with the image of a mighty military man.

The disconnect between Jephthah's actions and his descriptions is another feature only revealed through verbing the character. The methodology is designed to highlight what the text states about a character versus what interpreters have suggested about them. Scholars have grappled with the complexity of Jephthah. This approach highlights, using the data from the text, how Jephthah is described does not match his actions. The issue for interpreters is what to do with this information? Does it mean that Jephthah is not a military man? Do we rely more on the characters actions versus their descriptions? This is particularly relevant in this case where his one action, namely his vow, carries significantly more weight in how scholars assess him than his other actions.

Jephthah as Object

Jephthah is often the object of either a verb or a phrase. In Hebrew, the phrase, 'my father' is often expressed as 'the father of me,' meaning simply because someone is an object does not mean they necessarily are passive. The places where Jephthah is an object reinforce the notion that Jephthah appears to respond to things rather than initiate them, except for sacrificing his daughter.

Jephthah is first an object when he is born. The text states Gilead bore Jephthah (Judg. 11:1). Because his mother is described as a prostitute, it is unclear if 'Gilead' here is the name of an individual named 'Gilead' or the entire city, tribe, or region of Gilead.

Some group 'banishes' (*gimmel-resh-shin*) Jephthah from Gilead (Judg. 11:2). The term means 'to drive out' and elsewhere in Judges is used when the deity describes ridding the land of Israel's oppressors (Judg. 6:9).[15] The group appears to be those identified as the sons whom the woman/wife of Gilead bore to him and who then grew older (Judg. 11:2). Here, either the citizens of Gilead do not want the son of the local prostitute sharing with the rest of the citizenry or Gilead is a specific individual who has sons through some more official/legitimate partner concerning inheritance. Regardless, some group, to which Jephthah is seemingly connected through his father but not his mother, do not want him around them.

Many characters speak to Jephthah using the verb *aleph-mem-resh*. First, the sons of Gilead speak to him, telling him he will have no share in their father's inheritance (Judg. 11:2). The elders of Gilead have a lengthy conversation to recruit Jephthah, repeatedly using this verb (Judg. 11:6, 8, 10). The King of Amon speaks to the messengers of Jephthah as his means of speaking to Jephthah (Judg. 11:13). His daughter speaks to him using this verb (Judg. 11:36, 37), as do the men of Ephraim (Judg. 12:1). Jephthah negotiates with all these people, except his daughter, who appears to negotiate with him.

Jephthah is next the object of the verb 'to gather,' *lamed-kuf-tet*. In this context, the verb is in the imperfect *hitpoel* meaning the subject of the verb are the worthless people and Jephthah is the object of the preposition 'to' meaning they self-gathered to him (Judg. 11:3). The next verb in the verse has these men 'going out,' *yod-tzade-aleph*, with him (Judg. 11:3). Contrary to the powerful military leader usually suggested about Jephthah, the text never claims Jephthah created this fighting force.

---

15. 'גרשׁ' *BDB* 176.

The intention of the elders of Gilead is stated to 'go to take' *lamed-kuf-chet* Jephthah from the good land (Judg. 11:5). While Jephthah negotiates and receives a promotion, they are successful.

Inside one of the many direct speeches of Jephthah he argues, 'you hated me' *sin-nun-aleph* (Judg. 11:7). In this case, Jephthah is speaking, the subject is second person plural, and Jephthah is the object. Whether this is true cannot be confirmed but from Jephthah's perspective, the brothers/elders of Gilead drove him out because of how they feel about him, not inheritance or his mother.

Again, using second person and indirect speech, Jephthah places words in people's mouths making him an object. In the first case, Jephthah, when speaking to the elders of Gilead notes they are the ones who hated him and drove him out and now they claim that they come to him (Judg. 11:7). So too in direct speech to the king of the sons of Ammon through a messenger, Jephthah claims that 'you' (the king of the Ammonites) have come to me to fight in my land (Judg. 11:12). As is the case above, the veracity of the claim is less important than Jephthah using the technique of making himself the object of actions he claims others have taken towards him.

Jephthah is next the object of the verb 'return' *shin-vav-vet*. First, following Jephthah's claim that they are the ones who banished him, the elders, sidestepping the comment, note they have returned to Jephthah (Judg. 11:8). In the next verse, in Jephthah's direct speech, he reiterates their claim that if 'you,' speaking to the elders of Gilead, return 'me,' referring to Jephthah, he will be promoted (Judg. 11:9). This is yet another odd place where Jephthah is the object in the middle of his own direct speech because he is reiterating what others have said to him previously.

Jephthah is four times the object of the verb 'to give,' *nun-tav-nun*, in a context where he is the speaker, and the subject of the verb is the Israelite deity. The first appears where Jephthah repeats what the elders of Gilead suggest and Jephthah notes that if the deity gives Ammon to his, here Jephthah, hand he will be promoted (Judg. 11:9). When Jephthah makes his vow, the first part is Jephthah's claim that if the deity gives the Ammonites into his, Jephthah, hand, he will sacrifice whatever first emerges from his house (Judg. 11:30). In this instance, Jephthah's vow is not in response to anything nor is he reiterating something another character has already articulated. Eventually, the deity gives the Ammonites into Jephthah's hand (Judg. 11:32). In direct speech, Jephthah references the deity giving the Ammonites into his hand when responding to the Ephraimites (Judg. 12:3).

Of the next eighteen terms making Jephthah an object, only two of them are used more than once. Many of them are inside direct speech from Jephthah where he either places actions or feelings in for others, making himself the object.

After returning to Gilead with the elders the people make him, Jephthah, their commander and chief (Judg. 11:11). The elders offer to make Jephthah their chief (Judg. 11:6), the elders then raise the offer to commander of all of Gilead (Judg. 11:8), which Jephthah reiterates (Judg. 11:9). When the various deals are offered by the elders of Gilead, the suggestion is Jephthah will receive the title when he returns with them to fight the Ammonites (Judg. 11:6, 8). In Jephthah's recitation of the events, he states he will receive the title when he returns to fight the

Ammonites and the deity delivers the Ammonites to his hand (Judg. 11:9). Jephthah's final position is more complex than the original offer, he must win. In Judges 11:11, Jephthah is made both chief and commander before fighting the battle. Also, the group making him so are the people, not the elders.

When Jephthah sends a note to the king of the Ammonites, he asks what the king has against him (Judg. 11:12). Technically this too is as though it was in direct speech and Jephthah asks what is between 'me and you.' Once again, Jephthah is speaking, he is the object of a situation he creates and, in this case, there is evidence he is playing with the facts. Thus far, the Ammonites attack Gilead which, until recently, rejected Jephthah. While the precise location of the 'good land' is unclear, it does not appear to be in what the elders or the people of Gilead consider Gilead. When the Ammonites attack Gilead, they are not attacking Jephthah, certainly not personally. Here, Jephthah makes himself the object of the Ammonite attack and a Gileadite.

Again, Jephthah in direct speech via his messenger to the king of the Ammonites, makes two statements in the same verse (Judg. 11:27). First, he argues he has not sinned against 'you', referring to the Ammonite king, and asks why stating 'you' referring to the king of the Ammonites, are doing bad to 'me.' He uses the term 'bad,' *resh-ayin-hey* which, with the definite article, appears throughout the book of Judges to refer to what the Israelites are doing to their deity.[16] Jephthah further unpacks the bad being done as 'fighting,' *lamed-chet-mem*, against him (Judg. 11:27). As in the above-mentioned situation, when the attack on Gilead first happens, Jephthah is not part of that group.

Despite fifteen verses of Jephthah attempting to talk the king of the Ammonites out of their conflict, the king of the Ammonites does not listen to the words of Jephthah (Judg. 11:28). In this case, Jephthah's appearance as an object is directly related to actions he initiates.

In the following verse the spirit of the deity is on Jephthah (Judg. 11:29). The 'spirit of the deity' is a phrase that occurs six times in the book of Judges (Judg. 6:34; 11:29; 13:25; 14:6, 19; 14:14). As this author argues elsewhere, many phrases begin as good concepts in Judges and by the end of the book carry horrific meanings.[17] This phrase may be one of them. Since the focus of this article is not on the book of Judges writ large, here it is not clear from the text if it is this spirit of the deity that provides Jephthah with the ability to defeat the Ammonites because in the next verse, he makes his vow that leads to the sacrifice of his daughter (Judg. 11:30). At most, the ramifications on Jephthah of the spirit of the deity are unclear.

The next few references show possession. Imbedded in Jephthah's vow is the reference that whatever comes out of the opening of 'my house'. Technically, it is the house that is the object, but it is the house of 'me', and Jephthah is the speaker (Judg. 11:31). So too, 'the one who greets me' and 'upon my return' highlight

---

16. Tammi J. Schneider, *Judges* (BO; Collegeville: Liturgical Press, 2000).
17. Schneider, *Judges*, 40–43, 49, 202, 211.

Jephthah in constructions where he is the object. In contrast to many places where Jephthah is the subject and it is in response to actions of others, here he is the subject but referencing things belonging to him.

When Jephthah returns home, his daughter greets him (Judg. 11:34). This is her undoing as it means she is the thing to be sacrificed (Judg. 11:35). It follows the pattern of Jephthah regularly responding to things other's initiate, but this is different because he is the one who makes the vow in the first place (Judg. 11:30).

Jephthah's daughter is also described as the 'daughter of him', making him the object. The wordplay with house is clear since the construct form of daughter and house are the same (Judg. 11:31). She is then described as his only child: there was not to him another either son or daughter, making him an object (Judg. 11:34).

Using direct speech and second person, Jephthah blames his daughter, 'you have brought me low' (Judg. 11:35). Jephthah is speaking to his daughter and her coming out to greet him upon his victory brings him low. In the same verse, he claims she troubles him. Note the pattern with Jephthah is he makes himself the object of events carried out by others, regardless of whether the actions are originally intended for him. Unlike the case with the elders of Gilead or the Ammonite king, in this case Jephthah is the one who initiated the vow. The episode finishes when Jephthah's daughter agrees that the deity makes for him, referring to Jephthah, vengeance (Judg. 11:36).

The last three cases all deal with second person. When the Ephraimites ask Jephthah why he did not ask them to join him in battle with the Ammonites, before receiving an answer, they claim they will burn his house over him (Judg. 12:1). This follows immediately upon his sacrificing his daughter, the kind that involves burning, for coming out of his house. Now the actual house itself is threatened with fire.

The last two cases concern direct dialogue with Jephthah speaking to the Ephraimites. He says, 'you did not save me' (Judg. 12:2). As noted, Jephthah's claim the Ephraimites were summoned cannot be confirmed. He then asks why 'you ... come up to me to war against me' (Judg. 12:3). In this case, it is possible Jephthah is the one in their crosshairs whereas with the Ammonite king it was less clear that Jephthah is his original target.

Jephthah is an object more often than he is a subject. There are many places where Jephthah claims to be the object of other's actions regardless of whether he is the original target. He places himself as the object meaning that he is never the aggressor nor the one in the wrong.

Jephthah's Relationships

Jephthah's relationships are odd. He seemingly makes peace with the Gileadites who banished him in the first place and yet sacrifices his daughter who appears to care about him. In all circumstances Jephthah is devoted to the Israelite deity, bringing the deity into all situations where Jephthah appears.

The text states nothing about Jephthah's relationship with his mother other than her title/occupation leads his brothers/elders of Gilead to banish him. While she is a defining character in his life, especially in terms of its trajectory, the text reveals nothing about their relationship.

Jephthah's 'brothers' are complicated. It is unclear if the text means biological brothers when referencing them, or if they are the people of Gilead or the elders of Gilead. These people have a problem with Jephthah since they banish him (Judg. 11:2, 3). When Jephthah negotiates with the elders, he claims they are the people who banish him from his father's house, suggesting the elders of Gilead are his brothers, or the elders of Gilead represent Gilead and his father could be anyone from Gilead (Judg. 11:1).

After discussing what his title will be and his position within Gilead if he returns, Jephthah returns with the elders (Judg. 11:11) and the people of Gilead place him in charge (Judg. 11:11). Throughout the rest of the story, when Jephthah speaks with the Ammonite king, talks to the Ephraimites, and is buried, he is labeled a Gileadite. In negotiations with the Ammonite king and the Ephraimites, all the things the narrator or Jephthah suggest happened to Gilead, Jephthah claims as having happened to him personally. Thus, Jephthah fully reclaims his Gileadite identity.

The text references empty men who gather around Jephthah and they have a relationship with him but there are no references he has one with them (Judg. 11:3). He goes to the 'good land' and they gather around him but nowhere is Jephthah a subject to anything with them, nor is he described connecting him to them. Once the elders of Gilead recruit Jephthah, they disappear from the story.

Jephthah has a relationship with the elders of Gilead who may or may not be biologically related to him. They initially recruit him (Judg. 11:4-6) and Jephthah is not impressed. Jephthah establishes his pattern by reminding them of their history. The history he recounts aligns with what the previous verses suggest about their relationship, if they are somehow his brothers. The elders do not respond to his critiques and continue offering him things. It does not take much for Jephthah to acquiesce (Judg. 11:11). Once the Gileadites place him in charge he accepts his Gileadite identity.

Jephthah has a strong connection with the Israelite deity. Jephthah brings the deity into negotiations with the elders of Gilead (Judg. 11:9). The Gileadites agree (Judg. 11:10). Jephthah repeats all of it in front of the deity at Mizpah (Judg. 11:11). Jephthah credits the Israelite deity with Israel's success in taking the land (Judg. 11:20, 21, 23). He likens the Ammonites relationship to their deity Chemosh with that of the Israelites (Judg. 11:24). He makes a vow, regardless of how smart it is, to the Israelite deity (Judg. 11:30) and his daughter does not question him adhering to it, even though it means losing her life (Judg. 11:36). Jephthah credits the deity with his victory over the Ammonites in his conversation with the Ephraimites (Judg. 12:3). Jephthah is a devotee of the Israelite deity.

The deity approves of Jephthah. The spirit of the deity infuses Jephthah (Judg. 11:29). According to the narrator, the deity gives the Ammonites to Jephthah's hand (Judg. 11:32). Neither the deity nor the narrator comments upon Jephthah's vow or sacrifice of his daughter.

Jephthah seemingly has a good relationship with his daughter and she with him, until he sacrifices her. She emerges from the house first, celebrating his victory.

In any other circumstance that would be expected and a sign of love and excitement for the accomplishment of a parent or returning hero. In Jephthah's classic fashion, he blames everyone for negative situations. By recounting to his daughter the circumstances of his vow (Judg. 11:35), as he does with the king of the Ammonites and the Ephraimites, he reviews history in a way that makes him blameless and then attacks. His daughter is respectful of her father, makes one small request of him, and submits to her death without fanfare (Judg. 11:36-39).

Clearly far less text is dedicated to Jephthah's vow, his relationship with his daughter, and what he does to her than Jephthah's account of the history of Ammon and Israel. Does this mean the text is suggesting this is not important in assessing Jephthah character? I would have a hard time arguing such is the case but what is distressing is that the text shows no negative critique of Jephthah because of this relationship. The same is true of Jephthah's daughter: she is not negatively evaluated. Clearly the text of Judges struggles with what to do with military men who are not perfect. Similar critiques could be made about Barak, Gideon/Jerubaal, and Samson and outside of the book of Judges, King David. It is quite possible that the Hebrew Bible does not make the assessment because that should be the job of the reader/interpreter.

Jephthah does not initiate the relationship with the Ephraimites. As with all situations concerning Jephthah, they threaten him, he recounts a history that leaves him innocent and appears as the victim, justifying his following actions. The Ephraimite case is problematic because 42,000 Ephraimites are killed in this context for reasons that appear excessive (Judg. 12:4-6), though by the end of Judges not for that book. Here, the text lists Jephthah as gathering and defeating the Ephraimites (Judg. 12:4) but in the specifics of killing people based on their word pronunciation, Jephthah's name is absent (Judg. 12:5). The text connects him to the victory over the Ephraimites but not with what is viewed, at least in modern times, as the uncomfortable aspects of the story.

Jephthah's relationship with the Gileadites begins and ends his story. At the beginning he is rejected by Gilead, because his father is either a person with another wife or, potentially, everyone in the town (Judg. 1:1). After the elders of Gilead make him an offer he cannot refuse (Judg. 11:8), he returns and from that point on he claims his Gileadite status whole heartedly from his negotiating with the Ammonites through to the conflict with the Ephraimites (Judg. 12:1-3). In the verse recounting his death, he is identified as Jephthah, the Gileadite (Judg. 12:7).

Conclusions

Jephthah is clearly a military figure but the bulk of the text focusing on him assumes that aspect and it is not a focus. His life is shaped by his mother's status in Gilead and the sacrifice of his daughter by his own words. Throughout the rest of his actions and those of others upon him, he responds rather than initiates. He tries to avoid all the conflicts in which he then participates and is successful. He is a devotee of the Israelite deity. The aspect of his life which he embraces most fully is his role as a Gileadite, the thing he is first denied in his story.

Chapter 8

JEPHTHAH'S DAUGHTERS, ETHICAL AND UNETHICAL: CHARACTERIZATION AND ETHICS

David Janzen

In an essay entitled 'Characterization and Ethics,' John Barton notes that characters in biblical texts are often rounder – they have more depth, we could say – than is sometimes recognized. The biblical authors created characters who were more than just exemplars of individual moral virtues, he writes, and so these writers hoped to push readers to do some complex ethical reflection as they encountered key figures in biblical narrative.[1] Barton notes that some characters seem relatively flat because they are minor players who are present in biblical stories only so that the plot can move along,[2] but in what I see as a kind of sequel to Barton's essay I want to show here that our exegetical attempts to deal with even a character as minor as Jephthah's daughter, who appears in only seven verses and whom the author did not even bother to provide with a proper name, can end up raising difficult ethical questions. To explain the motivation interpreters attribute to the action of any character in a narrative, they must have some sense as to why such a figure would act in the ways that he or she does; this demands reflection on the broader ethical worldview that readers think inform the character's actions, and the point of this essay is to show that such ethical reflection can become quite complex, even in the case of characters who exist only at the margins of biblical narratives.

Any character in any text is produced by readers through their interpretations; even when one is aiming to reconstruct authorial intention, one cannot know what a text means or who a character in a story is without using one's interpretive intelligence, and so *characterization* as I am using the term here is work performed by the reader.[3] And while space does not permit an investigation of the very

---

1. John Barton, 'Characterization and Ethics,' in *Characters and Characterization in Kings* (ed. Keith Bodner and Benjamin J. M. Johnson; LHBOTS 670; London: T&T Clark, 2020), 1–16 (1–4).

2. Barton, 'Characterization and Ethics,' 4.

3. The notion that only interpretation can produce meaning, that meaning is not somehow inherently present in the dots and lines we encounter on the page, is a hermeneutical presupposition I am relying on here, since we all have to rely on some set of

interesting question as to how one could judge the validity of these competing characterizations, insofar as Jephthah's daughter is the creation of our interpretations there is more than one of her, since there are so many conflicting characterizations. Arguably, one important reason why such a large volume of scholarly interpretations and literally hundreds of works of art have been devoted to the story of Jephthah's daughter[4] is because our constructions of her character raise important ethical questions that we interpreters feel compelled to solve. What kind of person acts as the daughter does in this story? Is she a willing martyr or an unwilling sacrifice?[5] Is she an unwitting stooge of a morally corrupt patriarchal culture or in rebellion against it?[6] Does she act to benefit her people or does she reject their cultural goods?[7] Different readers have adopted all of these positions, and others as well – they have created many different daughters, to put that another way – but all of them have had to confront the question as to whether or not the character they have constructed is ethical, for in every case the daughter makes decisions to act and speak in particular ways, and interpreters are thus forced to

them. Persuasive arguments that readers' interpretations are what produce textual meaning can be found in works such as Jacques Derrida's 'Structure, Sign and Play in the Discourse of the Human Sciences,' in *Writing and Difference* (tr. Alan Bass; London: Routledge, 2001), 351–70; Richard Rorty's *Consequences of Pragmatism (Essays: 1972–1980)* (Minneapolis: University of Minnesota Press, 1982), 90–109; and Stanley Fish's *Doing What Comes Naturally: Change, Rhetoric, and the Practice of Theory in Literary and Legal Studies*, PCI (Durham, NC: Duke University Press, 1989), 37–67.

4. Mikael Sjöberg refers to a mid-twentieth-century study that counted about five hundred artistic works that feature Jephthah's daughter (*Wrestling with Textual Violence: The Jephthah Narrative in Antiquity and Modernity*, BMW 4 [Sheffield: Sheffield Phoenix Press, 2006], 1).

5. For an example of the first position, see Lauren A. S. Monroe, 'Disembodied Women: Sacrificial Language and the Deaths of Bat-Jephthah, Cozbi, and the Bethlehemite Concubine,' *CBQ* 75 (2013): 32–52 (51–52); for an example of the second, see Elie Assis, *Self-Interest or Communal Interest: An Ideology of Leadership in the Gideon, Abimelech and Jephthah Narratives* (VTSup 106; Leiden: Brill, 2005), 215–16.

6. For an example of the first position, see J. Cheryl Exum, 'Judges: Encoded Messages to Women,' in *Feminist Biblical Interpretation: A Compendium of Critical Commentary on the Books of the Bible and Related Literature*, ed. Louise Schottroff and Marie-Theres Wacker (Grand Rapids, MI: William B. Eerdmans, 2012), 112–27 (119–20); for an example of the second, see Cristiana García-Alfonso, 'Judges: Subaltern Women,' in *Postcolonial Commentary and the Old Testament* (ed. Hemchand Gossai; London: T&T Clark, 2019), 106–21 (115–17).

7. For an example of the first position, see Mary Ann Beavis, 'A Daughter in Israel: Celebrating Bat Jephthah (Judg. 11:39d-40),' *Feminist Theology* 13 (2004): 11–25; for an example of the second, see Rhiannon Graybill, 'No Child Left Behind: Reading Jephthah's Daughter with *The Babylon Complex*,' *The Bible and Critical Theory* 11/2 (2015): 36–50 (45–47).

come up with an ethical framework that explains her character and why she makes those decisions. The variety of such characterizations gives us some idea of the complexity of ethical reflection in which interpreters engage, and in the following sections of the essay I will provide two different portrayals of the daughter's character in order to give a sense of at least some of the different kinds of ethical questions that interpreters' characterizations of even a very minor figure in a biblical narrative can raise for readers.

Jephthah's Ethical/Unethical Daughter

Constructions of the daughter's ethical character are inevitably contextualized in relation to the vow her father makes in 11:30-31 as he goes out to battle against the Ammonites; there he asks God for victory, offering to provide through sacrifice 'the one who goes out (אשר יצא)[8] from the doors of my house to meet me (לקראתי)' should he return in triumph. And since it is his daughter who יצאת לקראתו 'was going out to meet him' as he arrives home (11:34), she is the obvious candidate for the sacrificial victim Jephthah had vowed to give to God. Jephthah's immediate reaction in 11:35 to her appearance is to say אהה בתי הכרע הכרעתני,[9] and since in the

---

8. There is a small textual critical issue at this point. The Lucianic manuscript group and the Old Latin generally best reflect the OG of Judges, and have been influenced less by the *kaige* translational tradition and the Hexapla than the text of Judges in other manuscript groups that derived from the OG; see, e.g., Walter Ray Bodine, *The Greek Text of Judges: Recensional Developments* (HSM 23: Chico, CA: Scholars Press, 1980), 134-36; Natalio Fernández Marcos, 'Kritai/Iudices/Judges,' in *Introduction to the Septuagint* (ed. Siegfried Kreuzer; tr. David A. Brenner and Peter Altmann; Waco, TX: Baylor University Press, 2019), 155-64 (157-58). Given the evidence of the Lucianic Recension and the Old Latin for 11:31, the OG had no translation for a word corresponding to היוצא in the MT. It seems likely that this participle was added to the Masoretic tradition after it diverged from that behind the OG, and from the Masoretic tradition it spread to other versions of the LXX through the Hexapla. By adding it to the MT, a copyist thus has Jephthah's vow correspond more precisely to the daughter's emergence from the house in 11:34, which uses a participle from יצא to describe the daughter's actions. The opening of 11:31 in the OG, which reflects Hebrew והיה אשר יצא מדלתי ביתי, more likely corresponds to an original version of the text than the MT does.

9. The various translations in the LXX traditions appear to reflect the Hebrew root עכר for the final two words in that phrase rather than the MT's כרע. The Greek texts are largely divided between ἐμπεποδοστάτηκάς μεand ταραχῇ ἐτάραξάς με. The former suggests the translation of the Hebrew עכרתני (see 1 Chron. 2:7, where the same Greek root is used to translate a participle from עכר), while the latter reflects the same Hebrew verb and seems like an attempt to have the Greek correspond more closely to the syntax of the MT's textual tradition, in which the infinitive is followed by a finite form of the same root. The OG's Hebrew text, however, was likely altered under the influence of the word עכרי, which appears a bit later in the verse.

only other places where the verb כרע is used in the *hiphil* in biblical Hebrew it refers to killing,[10] it seems best to understand him as saying, 'Ah, my daughter, you have surely killed me.' Given this context, the next part of his speech in the same verse can be read as alluding to his death as well; 'you have become my troubler (עכרי),' he continues, using another root that appears elsewhere to refer to life-or-death situations.[11] Jephthah's speech in 11:35 is often understood as blaming the daughter for his emotional pain that will result from her death,[12] but with his statement that she has killed him, we can understand him as expressing his resolution to die rather than carry out his vow, now that he is aware of whom he would have to sacrifice. Biblical texts make no clear comment as to what might happen should Israelites fail to fulfill vows they have made to God, but it is reasonable to believe that they feared such action would lead to severe divine retribution and even to death, given that this was the belief in neighboring cultures.[13] 'I opened my mouth[14] to Yhwh and I cannot take it back,' Jephthah concludes in 11:35, and that means, as far as he is concerned, that he must die in place of his daughter.

The daughter begins to reveal her ethical character as she responds to her father's speech. 'You opened your mouth to Yhwh,'[15] she begins in 11:36, parroting

---

10. In Ps. 17:13, the psalmist asks in reference to the enemy that God might הכריעהו, which, the second part of that verse goes on to say, will be accomplished with the use of 'your sword.' In Ps. 78:31, God הכריע 'the chosen ones of Israel,' an act a parallel line of the verse defines by saying 'he killed their strongest.' In Ps. 18:40 [Eng. 39 = 2 Sam. 22:40], the only other passage in the Bible in which כרע appears in the *hiphil*, the psalmist uses the verb to refer to what God did to the enemy, which parallels the assertion of the previous verse that 'I struck them, they were not able to rise; they fell under my feet.'

11. See, for example, its use in Gen. 34:30, where Jacob uses it in the context of his fear that the Canaanites will kill his entire household, and in Josh. 7:25, where Joshua uses it twice, once to refer to the death of Israelite soldiers and again in an allusion to the coming execution of Achan.

12. E.g., Phyllis Trible, *Texts of Terror: Literary-Feminist Readings of Biblical Narratives*, OBT (Philadelphia: Fortress Press, 1984), 102; J. Cheryl Exum, 'Murder They Wrote: Ideology and the Manipulation of Female Presence in the Biblical Narrative,' in *The Pleasure of Her Text: Feminist Readings of Biblical and Historical Texts* (ed. Alice Bach; Philadelphia: Trinity Press International, 1990), 45–67 (47).

13. See, e.g., the Ugaritic and Akkadian texts discussed in Tony W. Cartledge, *Vows in the Hebrew Bible and the Ancient Near East* (JSOTSup 147; Sheffield: Sheffield Academic Press, 1992), 87–90, 113–14.

14. In the LXX versions of this verse, Jephthah says that 'I opened my mouth about you to Yhwh,' but the Hebrew עליך that lies behind the κατὰ σοῦ/ περὶ σοῦ we see in the LXX is likely an addition to the original text, since it explicitly connects the daughter to the vow.

15. Some witnesses to the LXX here reflect the MT's text, but others have the daughter begin her speech with εἰ ἐν ἐμοὶ ἤνοιξας τὸ στόμα σου πρὸς κύριον 'if you have opened your mouth to the Lord about me,' or words to that effect. This follows a later alteration of the

Jephthah's final words, but then her speech begins to diverge from his because she insists that she, not he, must die: 'do to me as it went out from your mouth,' she says. Neither of them appears aware of Deut. 12:29-31, the law that prohibits child sacrifice, nor of the law of Lev. 27:1-8 that would allow Jephthah to substitute a payment of silver for his daughter's life,[16] although some scholars argue that the wartime context of Jephthah's vow makes the possibility of such substitution an impossibility.[17] But debates about the law take up no space in this dialogue; 11:35-36 focuses instead on the daughter's decision that she will not permit her father to sacrifice his life to divine wrath by not fulfilling his vow. She understands her ethical duty as a daughter as one in which she must die for her father, and it is her position that prevails, since Jephthah makes no attempt to dissuade her. We see her speech continue in 11:37, although since that verse opens with the words, 'and she said to her father,' it appears to constitute a separate speech; we could imagine that, between her words in 11:36 and 37, Jephthah explains to her precisely what his vow entailed, but in 11:37 the daughter maintains her position that she and not her father must die. She now asks that she might go and spend two months in the mountains with her female companions, ואבכה על בתולי 'that I might mourn my virginity'. Some have understood this reference to virginity as indicating a transitional phase in the lives of ancient Israelite females from girls to women of marriageable age,[18] but such discussions normally focus on the possible senses of the Hebrew word בתולה, while the daughter actually uses the rarer word בתולים, one that mainly appears in legal texts with reference to proofs of a female's virginity (e.g., Deut. 22:14-20). She has no need to mourn her own life, for she goes to her death courageously, and wishes only to mourn the fact that, although she is legally eligible to marry and have children since she possesses her בתולים, she will now

text, however, since this introduction to the speech allows readers to clearly see that the daughter has made a logical leap that explains how she has made sense of Jephthah's initial – and to her, one might imagine, rather puzzling – words.

16. See, e.g., Robert B. Chisholm, Jr., 'The Ethical Challenge of Jephthah's Fulfilled Vow,' *BibSac* 167 (2010): 404-22 (414-15); Tal Ilan, 'Gender Difference and the Rabbis: Bat Yiftah as Human Sacrifice,' in *Human Sacrifice in Jewish and Christian Tradition* (ed. Karen Finsterbusch, Armin Lange, and K. F. Diethard Römheld; SHR 112; Leiden: Brill, 2007), 175-89 (184-85).

17. E.g., Susan Niditch, *War in the Hebrew Bible: A Study in the Ethics of Violence* (Oxford: Oxford University Press, 1993), 33-34; Sebastian Grätz, 'Jiftach und seine Tochter,' in *Geschichte Israels und deuteronomistische Geschichtsdenken: Festschrift zum 70. Geburtstag von Winfried Thiel* (ed. Peter Mommer and Andreas Scherer; AOAT 380; Münster: Ugarit Verlag, 2010), 119-34 (121).

18. E.g., Peggy Day, 'From the Child is Born the Woman: The Story of Jephthah's Daughter,' in *Gender and Difference in Ancient Israel* (ed. Peggy Day; Minneapolis: Fortress Press, 1989), 58-74; Mieke Bal, *Death and Dissymmetry: The Politics of Coherence in the Book of Judges* (CSHJ; Chicago: The University of Chicago Press, 1988), 46-48.

never be able to attain those social goods that, as Phyllis Bird points out, ancient Israelite culture believed were the desired ends of female existence.[19]

My work of characterization of the daughter in this interpretation creates her as an ethical actor who makes choices and sacrifices herself for the life of another. She wholeheartedly embraces the ethical goods of her culture, and courageously chooses death so that her father might live, and she largely does so with tranquility. She is trustworthy, since the narrator tells us in 11:38-39 that, when her father releases her to go to the mountains, she does not use this absence of parental control as an opportunity to escape death, but that she mourned her בתולים for two months and then returned to him, her only apparent regret being that she cannot actualize her potential to become a wife and mother as her society would otherwise expect of her. This reading defines the daughter as socially responsible, something that extends to her agreement with the cultural expectation that women marry and give birth to legitimate children. Assumedly, then, the annual festival of Israelite women that gathers to recount (לתנות) her (11:40) celebrates her socially upright character and the deeds that result from it. It is telling, then, that the last time readers of Judges have come across the verb תנה was in 5:11, where Israel 'recounted (יתנו) the righteous acts of Yhwh,' for in this reading the annual celebration of the daughter emphasizes her righteous character, entirely in agreement with social and divine will.

The daughter of this interpretation makes choices, but whether these are actually good choices depends on the ethical framework from which one operates, and so our work of characterization will depend upon our ethical analysis. The daughter may choose her speech and action but does so only within the confines of a patriarchal culture, as Cheryl Exum puts it,[20] which is why we do not hear her interrogate her father about the vow, ask about the possibility of the substitution of silver for her life, or wonder why he accepts her acquiescence to the sacrifice so readily. When the daughter mimics her father's words about the irrevocability of his vow and does not use her journey to the mountains as a chance to escape death at his hands, she seems like a victim trapped by a patriarchal belief system that only allows her to speak against her own interests.[21] At the heart of this character, in short, is her ethical impulse to sacrifice herself for her social superior, even when it results in her own death[22] in which she is treated as an animal would be.[23]

---

19. Phyllis Bird, *Missing Persons and Mistaken Identities: Women and Gender in Ancient Israel* (OBT; Minneapolis: Fortress Press, 1997), 37.

20. Exum, 'Murder They Wrote,' 62-63.

21. So, e.g., Bal, *Death and Dissymmetry*, 49-50; Dolores G. Kamrada, 'The Sacrifice of Jephthah's Daughter and the Notion of Ḥērem (חרם) (A Problematic Narrative against its Biblical Background),' in *With Wisdom as a Robe: Qumran and Other Jewish Studies in Honour of Ida Fröhlich* (ed. Károly Dániel Dobos and Miklós Kőszeghy; HBM 21; Sheffield: Sheffield Phoenix Press, 2009), 57-85 (83).

22. So Esther Fuchs, 'Marginalization, Ambiguity, Silencing: The Story of Jephthah's Daughter,' *JFSR* 5 (1989): 35-45 (38).

23. Ken Stone, 'Animal Difference, Sexual Difference, and the Daughter of Jephthah,' *BibInt* 24 (2016): 1-16 (5-7).

In this interpretation, the annual festival observed by 'the daughters of Israel' to commemorate her celebrates her willing submission to patriarchal authority,[24] the fact that she has made the ethical choice to become a martyr for this social good.[25] Exum argues, in fact, that the author's failure to name the daughter emphasizes her submission to patriarchal authority, since in this sort of interpretation she needs to be identified no further than as the female offspring of an Israelite man, a girl or woman who is acting in the ethical manner in which Israelite culture would expect of such a person.[26]

This work to place characters' decisions within an ethical context that explains why they make particular decisions is one part of interpreters' work of characterization, but to do that means that one must reflect upon that larger system to which the character's ethical choices do or do not correspond. In the case of my interpretation of the daughter's story, the worldview her character takes for granted is one in which a more marginalized social figure should be willing to die on behalf of a more powerful and central one; Jephthah, of course, is not only her father but is also the head of Gilead and its army (11:4-11). Within this belief system, Jephthah is a sympathetic character, someone who is faithful to God and his vow, someone who rightly takes his daughter's advice to fulfill it.[27] From this perspective, we can characterize the daughter as ethical because her actions are shaped by a worldview that prioritizes male leadership and control and privileges male lives. In this worldview, it was ultimately wrong of Jephthah to believe, as his words of 11:35 imply, that he should not fulfill his vow and so save his daughter's life, since biblical texts consistently point to the necessity to complete vows made to God (Num. 30:3 [Eng. 2]; Deut. 23:22-24 [21-23]; Eccl. 5:5-7 [4-6]). By the standards of this belief system, the daughter's ethical choice is clear and had to result in her death if she wanted to act as a good person does; her actions are ethically laudable because she recognizes her father's life is of more value than her own. As Deborah Rooke points out, when we compare this story to that of Genesis 22, where God intervenes to save Isaac's life from the sacrificial knife, or to 1 Samuel 14, where Israel rescues Jonathan from dying as a result of a vow his father made, we simply get the sense

---

24. See, e.g., J. Cheryl Exum, 'Feminist Criticism: Whose Interests are being Served?,' in *Judges and Method: New Approaches in Biblical Studies* (2nd ed.; ed. Gale A. Yee; Minneapolis: Fortress Press, 2007), 65–89 (75–76). A similar way of understanding the annual memorialization is Tikva Frymer-Kensky's, which sees it as preparing young women of marriageable age to enter into marriages with men whom their fathers choose and so to become parts of a world dominated by men who might do to them what Jephthah did to his daughter; see her *Reading the Women of the Bible* (New York: Schocken Books, 2002), 113–15.

25. E.g., Beavis, 'A Daughter in Israel'; Monroe, 'Disembodied Women,' 51–52.

26. Exum, 'Murder They Wrote,' 58–59.

27. So, e.g., Johanna Stiebert, *Fathers and Daughters in the Hebrew Bible* (Oxford: Oxford University Press, 2013), 90–101; see also Esther Fuchs, *Feminist Theory and the Bible: Interrogating the Sources* (Feminist Studies and Sacred Texts Series; Lanham, MD: Lexington Books, 2016), 87–88.

that in the ancient Israelite ethical worldview unmarried daughters, unlike sons, are expendable.[28] In such a context it was right of the daughter to insist that she die in her father's place, even if that meant she could not be given to another man and bear children for him, although the fact that she was not married simplified her ethical decision, as there was no other male who could legitimately oppose her will to die under this set of circumstances if her father opted to accept that choice. In this interpretation, the daughter believes that without marriage to a man and motherhood her life would have no real significance, but that the immediate ethical duty to her father outweighed other social obligations.

The ethical system that steers the decisions made by the character of the daughter I have created in my interpretation is one that I find to be repugnant in important ways, and a moral disconnect like this one between the worldview that explains a character's actions and our own moral systems might move us to further ethical analysis and push us to revisit our readings. So, for example, unsatisfied with my characterization of a figure who acts ethically according to her beliefs but unethically according to my own, I can point out that it is notable that neither God nor the narrator passes any judgment on the decisions the daughter and Jephthah make. In this rather different interpretation, the text – or the text as I have newly interpreted it, at any rate – has posed an ethical question for readers: absent authoritative judgment on the daughter's actions, how should they evaluate her moral character, or the larger moral belief system on which the character bases her actions? As I revisit my interpretation in light of the ethical reflection I have had to do in order to create the character of the daughter for my interpretation, in short, I find that the narrative that results from my exegesis is itself one that poses a difficult question for readers and urges them to engage in ethical reflection.

Jephthah's Ethical Daughter

The ethical dilemmas with which our interpretations leave us might cause us to conduct even more thorough revisions of our interpretations than the one I have just offered. Any such ethically driven reinterpretations will have to conform to interpretive principles that we understand to be good, but there is no particular reason why we cannot include ethical analysis as one principle of interpretation we find to be helpful, so long as it can coexist with others that we use.[29] When we do not do this, as Esther Fuchs argues, and arrive at interpretations that privilege

---

28. Deborah W. Rooke, 'Sacrifice and Death, or, the Death of Sex: Three Versions of Jephthah's Daughter (Judges 11:29-40),' in *Biblical Traditions in Transmission: Essays in Honour of Michael A. Knibb* (ed. Charlotte Hempel and Judith M. Lieu; JSJSup 111; Leiden: Brill, 2006), 249–71 (255–57).

29. For some, the sort of approach to interpretation I am suggesting might seem to raise the danger of readers feeling as if they can make the text mean anything they would like it to mean. I am operating, as I mention in note 3 above, with the presupposition that textual meaning can

characters and worldviews we judge to be immoral, then our refusal to do any sort of work that emphasizes such shortcomings only makes us complicit in this ethical failure.[30] The case might be that one can arrive at only one interpretation of a text, and if it is one like the first I presented above, in which my characterization of the daughter has her adhere to moral principles that my worldview leads me to reject, then I can, through ethical reflection, make a negative judgment of those principles an explicit part of my interpretive analysis. But my moral proclivities can lead me to look for different interpretations as well, and in this section of the essay I offer a very different reading of the character of Jephthah's daughter, one in which she is aware of the ethical shortcomings of her father and other powerful social figures and dedicates her life to a protest of an unjust social system, and in which her work is carried on in the annual festival of resistance that commemorates her opposition to social forces willing to sacrifice the daughters of Israel to protect the powerful.

I begin this reading of the character of the daughter by noting that it seems that she was aware of her father's vow before she exited the house to meet him. As others have suggested, we can understand Jephthah's vow in 11:30-31 as made publicly, perhaps as a way to demonstrate his resolve to his troops as he leads them into battle against Ammon.[31] The specific wording of his vow, in which he states that he will sacrifice 'the one who goes out (יצא) of the doors of my house to meet me (לקראתי),' tells us he was envisioning a human sacrifice,[32] for biblical Hebrew uses this combination of verbs only when referring to humans or, in the only exception to this rule, to an animal that has been anthropomorphized.[33] With such

---

only be realized through interpretation. This does not mean, however, that a given interpreter could assent to the validity of an infinite number of meanings for a text, since interpreters are always limited by the hermeneutical beliefs and practices acceptable to the communities to which they belong. Since textual meaning is always created in interpretation, but interpretation is always limited by communal interpretive practices, interpreters are never in the position of being able to say that a text could mean absolutely anything. For a much longer discussion of this point, see Stanley Fish, *Is There a Text in This Class? The Authority of Interpretive Communities* (Cambridge, MA: Harvard University Press, 1980), 303–21, 338–55.

30. Esther Fuchs, *Sexual Politics in the Biblical Narrative: Reading the Hebrew Bible as a Woman* (JSOTSup 310; Sheffield: Sheffield Academic Press, 2000), 20–22.

31. E.g., Danna Nolan Fewell and David M. Gunn, *Gender, Power, and Promise: The Subject of the Bible's First Story* (Nashville: Abingdon Press, 1993), 127–28; Pamela Tamarkin Reis, 'Spoiled Child: A Fresh Look at Jephthah's Daughter,' *Proof* 17 (1997): 279–98 (283).

32. So also, e.g., Reis, 'Spoiled Child,' 281–82; Chisholm, 'The Ethical Challenge,' 405–6; Monroe, 'Disembodied Women,' 35–36.

33. The combination of יצא followed by קרא appears thirty-four times in the Hebrew Bible, and in all but one case the subject of the action is a human. The single exception to this occurs in Job 39:21, part of God's speech to Job, and here it is a horse that goes out to meet the weapons of battle. This exception really proves the rule, however, since in God's discussion of the horse in 39:19-25 the animal is anthropomorphized; it is also said to speak (39:25) and to laugh (39:22).

a vow, in short, he tells his troops that he is potentially willing to sacrifice even a family member for triumph in battle, demonstrating how important this military clash is and so how much his soldiers should be willing to sacrifice to achieve victory. If this vow is public knowledge, however, such knowledge would act as a disincentive for anyone from Jephthah's household to go out and meet him upon his return. Pamela Tamarkin Reis suggests that part of Jephthah's plan was his hope that his family would hear of the vow and remain inside, forcing a slave to exit upon his arrival.[34] The daughter's first words to her father in 11:36, in fact, tell us that she already knows about his vow, even though the only thing he has told her about it is that 'I opened my mouth to Yhwh.' She immediately says to him, 'You opened your mouth to Yhwh; do to me just as it went out from your mouth, after which Yhwh gave you vengeance over your enemies, the Ammonites' (11:36). She does not need to ask her father what he means when he tells her he has opened his mouth to God, and without any explanation from him she demonstrates her awareness that his speech involved her, and that the vow immediately preceded Jephthah's victory in battle. It is difficult to explain how she could know all of this when her father has related none of these details to her unless she had previously been informed of the vow and its context.

As in any case of interpretation involving a human character, the decision on the part of Jephthah's daughter to exit the house is not one I can explain without ethical analysis of her character (or at least without assuming an ethical framework to which her character adheres). Since she knew what she was doing when she went out to meet him (יצאת לקראתו), she saves the life of some other innocent person who would otherwise have been the human sacrifice. Yet the ethical worldview I see her character as embodying here goes beyond that moral act; the daughter throughout her very short story forces her father and the leadership of the social group of which she is a member to confront the moral choices they are making. To understand this, it is important to remember that the elders of Gilead had originally asked Jephthah to lead the fight against the Ammonites (11:4-6), but that he agreed to do so only after they capitulated to his demand that he be made the head of Gilead if he were to be victorious (11:7-11). As a result, his vow of 11:30-31 can be read as self-serving, something that he believes will function as a payment to God to win not only victory for Israel but also a place for himself as the leader of Gilead. When his daughter goes out to meet him she does not simply walk out of the house, but comes out dancing and playing the tambourine (11:34), just like the women of 1 Sam. 18:6 who greet Saul and David upon their triumphant return from battle. Knowing of the vow Jephthah has made, one that he believed was necessary to achieve what he wanted, her celebration of his victory directly confronts him with a choice between what he has prioritized and what constitutes ethical action. With his vow he makes it clear that victory and the social and political advancement which that entails for his own person matters more to him

---

34. Reis, 'Spoiled Child,' 281-82.

than an innocent life does, but is that vow and its accompanying desiderata truly reflective of his ethical character, or can the daughter shame him into realizing how unethically he has acted? She takes control of the vow, as Danna Fewell and David Gunn put it,[35] and uses it to serve her ethical agenda, forcing Jephthah to confront the fact that with the vow he has prioritized his own power and control above the value of an innocent human life, even the life of someone from his own household.

And the fact that the elders of Gilead are now Jephthah's followers means that their ethical failure is exposed by the daughter along with Jephthah's. In 1 Sam. 14:24-46, Israel intervenes to save Jonathan's life when it appears to be threatened by a vow his father had made, but Gilead declines to do this on behalf of Jephthah's daughter, even though her fate must have been widely known, since she gathers companions from among the people to mourn for two months. With his victory, Jephthah has just won the leadership of Gilead, and Gilead has just won its freedom from Ammon, and the daughter's actions force both parties to make a moral choice as to whether or not they will prioritize an innocent life. Jephthah and the elders, however, apparently conclude that, since it is possible to understand God as having chosen the daughter to emerge to meet her father, indicating her divine election as sacrificial victim, it would be unwise to court the inevitable disaster that would accompany an unfulfilled vow.

Jephthah's first words in 11:35 upon seeing his daughter can be taken, as I argued in the previous section of the essay, as a declaration that he cannot sacrifice her and that he waits instead for God to kill him for his failure to fulfil the vow. The daughter seems uninterested in her father's initial claim that he is willing to die in her place, however; even though that might seem to provide her with the victory she desired, which is to say a radically ethical and unselfish response from her father, she decides to test his resolve in this matter. She knows her father, after all, and assumedly what she knows of his ethical character is troubling. That, at least, is the impression with which readers of Judges 11 are left, since 11:3 tells us that he had earlier surrounded himself with אנשים ריקים, and people whom biblical passages describe as ריק 'empty' are defined by unscrupulousness or shamelessness (Judg. 9:4; 2 Sam. 6:20; 2 Chron. 13:7), being empty of the sort of shame and sense of decency that restrain the behavior of the ethical. She has every reason to be suspicious of Jephthah's statement that he is willing to die in her place, given that he has just vowed to kill an innocent person, and with her speech in 11:36 – 'do to me just as it went out from your mouth' – she probes this first burst of remorse by presenting her father with a victim who appears willing to die. Will he alter his initial resolve to act in an ethical manner and privilege the life of his daughter once he sees she will readily submit to sacrificial murder? If not, will the elders of Gilead, the other social leaders in this story, be willing to step forward and put a stop to this? In 11:36, the daughter does not only claim to be willing to die, but refers as well to what Jephthah understands as the result of the vow: 'Yhwh gave you

---

35. Fewell and Gunn, *Gender, Power, and Promise*, 127-28.

vengeance over your enemies.' There is apparently a pause between her words here and that of 11:37 – as I mention above, the opening of that verse introduces another speech – and we can picture her staring at her silent father in the gap between the two verses, waiting for him to acknowledge that his vow had been unethical and to privilege her life over his, despite the fact that his sacrificial victim will apparently offer him no resistance and allow him to achieve the social advancement he desires. After he says nothing, however, the daughter can see that her worst fears about his character have been confirmed, and so she asks in 11:37 for two months to mourn her בתולים, giving him a long time to reflect on the matter, while news of it spreads throughout Gilead as her friends are called to accompany her.

Jephthah, however, does not change his mind, nor does Gilead intervene to put a stop to this immoral act. His story begins in Judges 11 as he surrounds himself with criminals who are אנשים ריקים, unethical people, and the elders of Gilead, Jephthah's new followers, demonstrate that this description applies to them, as well. And by returning to be sacrificed, the daughter forces Jephthah to publicly acknowledge what kind of person he is, and shows the rest of Gilead's leadership to be as unethical as he. In doing so, she becomes a martyr, the founder of an annual ritual of Israelite women who protest and so resist a social structure that values them so little that they seem of no more worth than the animals they eat and sacrifice, as Juliana Claassens and others have argued.[36] In this characterization, then, the daughter operates out of a moral worldview vastly different than the one I described in my first interpretation, but much closer to my own. In this ethical analysis, she is a courageous and moral agent, someone willing to risk her own life to condemn a misogynist social system that benefits men who are greedy for power and does not sanction those too cowardly to oppose them. The women of Israel who take up her cause operate with the same ethical beliefs that the daughter does, and see the stand she takes as so important that they create a national protest movement around her resistance by commemorating her stance against misogyny every year.

One could ask why, if we are to accept this interpretation, the daughter does not more clearly articulate in her speech the protest she is raising against social injustice, but a reasonable answer to this question involves pointing out that the narrator and God are equally lacking in direct speech that passes judgment, for they do not directly evaluate the ethical decisions of Jephthah and Gilead either. Without this, readers are placed in the same ethical situation as Jephthah and the elders of Gilead, forced by the daughter's actions to ask if God would truly approve of a father who sacrifices his own child and of a broader culture of leadership that

---

36. See, e.g., L. Juliana M. Claassens, *Claiming Her Dignity: Female Resistance in the Old Testament* (Collegeville, MN: Liturgical Press, 2016), 75–80; Lucía Riba, 'Memoriales de Mujeres: La Sororidad como Experiencia de Empoderamiento para Resistir a la Violencia Patriarchal,' *Franciscum* 58/165 (2016): 225–62 (238–40); Kimberly D. Russaw, *Daughters in the Hebrew Bible* (Lanham, MD: Lexington Books, 2018), 155.

stands silently by as this happens. In this interpretation, in which the ethical system that guides the daughter's actions has much in common with my own, neither Jephthah nor readers should need any explicit statement in regard to his ethical failure, for they should be able to see that what he is doing is immoral. But the divine silence of my interpretation here also pushes us to ask if the story this reading has produced does not indict God's character along with those of Jephthah and the elders of Gilead, since we see no divine action to halt child sacrifice here as we do in the story of the near-sacrifice of Isaac in Genesis 22;[37] as Deborah Sawyer points out, God's non-response to the sacrifice of the daughter comes in the midst of a book where God is constantly responding to Israel's evil,[38] yet Jephthah's action and Gilead's inaction do not merit so much as a single word of divine response.

Conclusion

Barton's basic observation about the role of ethical reflection in our readings of character is right; to restate it slightly, in our work of characterization we will be faced with issues of ethical analysis as we attempt to make sense of the characters we produce in our interpretations. Building upon that point, I have shown here that sometimes these attempts to explain the speech and action of even very minor characters can lead to complex ethical reflection. Insofar as any choice of any person is an ethical decision, we will have to understand the worldviews, the broader systems of belief, of the characters we create in interpretation if we want to make sense of what they do, and this involves ethical analysis. Decisions made by a prominent character in a narrative will sometimes seem to us a simple matter to explain, while it might take much more ethical analysis to suitably make sense of what a minor character is doing.

Since ethical analysis is part of any characterization in which interpreters engage, then we should be aware that such reflection is an important part of good interpretation. Depending on the sort of interpretation one is creating, this may mean that one has been able to persuasively describe the moral worldview that explains how a particular character acts, or that a disconnect between one's own ethical beliefs and those involved in characterization leads one to offer a critique of the failures of the worldview that drives the action in the narrative under discussion, or that this disconnect leaves one so unsatisfied with the character one has created that one feels compelled to revisit the original interpretation. Other outcomes of ethical analysis are possible as well and, for example, one might decide that analysis of an ethical worldview that explains characters we have created in our interpretations can be used to critique aspects of one's own set of moral beliefs. No characterization, however, will ever occur in an ethical vacuum, for interpreters

---

37. So, e.g., Trible, *Texts of Terror*, 105–6.
38. Deborah F. Sawyer, *God, Gender and the Bible* (Biblical Limits; London: Routledge, 2002), 74.

will always work within some moral system and will make sense of the characters they create in their interpretations by contextualizing them within what they understand to be those figures' ethical worlds. This does not mean that every creation of character in interpretation will result in complex ethical analysis, but some will, even when the character in question appears quite marginal in the larger narrative.

Chapter 9

DOMESTICATING SAMSON

Robert S. Kawashima

Samson is an ambiguous and liminal character. As such, and in spite of the fact that he is counted as a judge, he is not so much a hero as an anti-hero. Which is to say that, unlike most of the other judges in the book of Judges, he is a 'hero' who achieves certain 'heroic' deeds by accident, or even in spite of himself. Consider his one attempt at marriage (more on which below): 'And Samson went down to Timnah and saw a woman in Timnah of the daughters of the Philistines. And he went up and told his father and his mother and said, "A woman I have seen in Timnah of the daughters of the Philistines, and now, take her for me as a wife." And his father and his mother said to him, "Is there no woman among your kinsmen's daughters or in all my people that you should go to take a wife from the uncircumcised Philistines?" And Samson said to his father, "Her take for me because she pleases me"' (Judg. 14:1-3).[1] His desire to marry the daughter of an uncircumcised Philistine displeases his parents – they being good 'Jews' – because it transgresses a particularly significant ethnic boundary marker. And yet, we are next told, Samson's poor choice of a wife ultimately fulfils YHWH's will. For God, in effect, uses Samson as a type of 'pretext' for dealing with the Philistines. God works, in other words, toward the furtherance of the divine plan in spite of this judge's poor life choices. Indeed, I would go so far as to assert that this 'pretext' should provide the epitaph for Samson's grave: 'But his father and his mother did not know that it was from the LORD, for He sought a pretext from the Philistines' (14:4).

Jephthah as Precursor

Jephthah is arguably an anti-hero as well, and as such he sheds light on the character of Samson. No coincidence, in my view, that their stories – Judges

---

1. In honour of my teacher's recently completed translation of the Hebrew Bible, all translations are taken from Robert Alter, *The Hebrew Bible: A Translation with Commentary* (New York: Norton, 2018); I italicize whatever slight modifications I make to his translation for the sake a particular point.

11:1-12:7 (Jephthah) and Judges 13-16 (Samson) – are more or less contiguous. For the narrative accounts of these two anti-heroes lead to that premonarchical period of moral chaos with which the book of Judges concludes, and which anticipates or foreshadows the establishment of the monarchy in 1 Samuel: 'In those days there was no king in Israel, every man did what was right in his eyes' (Judg. 17:6; 21:25).[2] Jephthah, as is well known, infamously slaughters his own daughter in an abominable sacrifice to God. The reason for this unfortunate turn of events seems to originate in his unseemly parentage: he is 'the son of a whore-woman' (11:1). Jephthah, like Samson, thus has a questionable relationship to 'proper' kinship structure, the former because of his mother, the latter because of his wife. Not unlike Samson, who fails to consummate his marriage – which will be misinterpreted as a divorce – Jephthah is eventually disowned or 'driven out' by his brothers: 'And Gilead's wife bore him sons, and the wife's sons grew up and they drove [*waygaršu*] Jephthah out and said to him, "You shall not inherit in our father's house, for you are the son of another woman"' (11:2). (Tellingly, this disownment recalls Sarah's decision to disown Hagar and her son, Ishmael: 'And she said to Abraham, "Drive out [*gareš*] this slavegirl and her son, for the slavegirl's son shall not inherit with my son, with Isaac"' [Gen. 21:10].[3]) No wonder, then, that when his kinsmen come back to him and ask him to lead them into battle, he acquiesces, but only for a price: 'And [the elders of Gilead] said to Jephthah, "Come, be our captain, that we may do battle with the Ammonites." And Jephthah said to the elders of Gilead, "Did you not hate [*śěne'tem*] me and drive me out [*wattěgaršuni*] from my father's house,[4] and why do you come to me now when you are in distress?" ... And Jephthah said to the elders of Gilead, "If you bring me back to do battle with the Ammonites and the LORD gives them to me, it is I who will be your chief"' (11:6-9). Jephthah, it would seem, has something to prove, has a 'chip on his shoulder'. And his price is not cheap: he would be their 'chief'.

This backstory helps us understand why Jephthah ends up making his fatally rash vow: 'And the spirit of the LORD was upon Jephthah ... And Jephthah made a vow to the LORD and said, "If You indeed give the Ammonites into my hand, it shall be that whatever comes out of the door of my house to meet me when I return safe and sound from the Ammonites shall be the LORD's, and I shall offer it up as a burnt offering"' (11:29-31). Note, first, how the 'spirit of the LORD' falls upon Jephthah, and only then does he make his rash and extravagant vow to God.

---

2. Not coincidentally, Samson's bride was *'right in [his] eyes'* (14:3, 7).

3. This vague narrative connection is perhaps strengthened by a second narrative connection between Abraham and Jephthah, namely, child sacrifice.

4. In this sense, disownment closely resembles divorce. Thus, Samson's incredulous father-in-law must explain to Samson, who abandoned his daughter on their wedding night, that he has remarried her to another: 'I surely thought that you altogether hated her [*śano' śěne'tah*], and I gave her to your companion' (15:2). In other words, he interpreted Samson's hatred and disappearance – the mirror image of 'sending' a wife away from the house of the man who came to 'hate' her [Deut. 24:1-4] – as a *de facto* divorce.

This 'spirit' represents that charisma or gift – more on which below – bestowed by the deity upon his chosen judge in order to authorize the latter's entry into battle (see also Judg. 3:10; 6:34; 1 Sam. 11:6).[5] In other words, Jephthah has already been granted by God the means to achieve victory in battle. And yet, he still finds it necessary to make his ill-conceived vow. Why? Because he is so desperate to succeed, to be deemed worthy by those who once rejected him. In order to impress his extended family, he will tragically end up sacrificing a member of his nuclear family.

The 'spirit' of the LORD will also visit Samson on four different occasions. In none of these cases will it be associated with a proper military action. As a lad, 'the spirit of the LORD began to drive him in the camp of Dan between Zorah and Eshtaol' (13:25; see also 16:31) – note the liminal location between Zorah and Eshtaol – but it leads to no heroic deed. It would seem to represent his unspent youthful vigor – vaguely reminiscent, perhaps, of Onan son of Judah (Gen. 38). As a young man, he comes upon a lion: 'And the spirit of the LORD seized him, and he ripped it apart as one would rip apart a kid, with nothing in his hand' (14:6). Reminiscent of Heracles, he kills this lion with his bare hands.[6] As a newlywed, 'the spirit of the LORD seized him, and he went down to Ashkelon and struck down from among them thirty men and took their armor, and he gave the changes of garment to the explainers of the riddle' (14:19). In this case, Samson kills actual Philistines, but only because of the petty vindictiveness he feels toward them after his bride has betrayed to them the secret of his riddle (14:15-18), not from any sense of duty he feels toward the weal of the tribes of Israel. Finally, in the wake of a second vindictive rampage against the Philistines following this aborted marriage (15:7-8), the men of Judah find it necessary to hand him over to the Philistines: 'And they said to him, "We have come down to bind you, to give you into the hand of the Philistines." ... And they bound him with two new ropes and brought him up from the rock ... And the spirit of the LORD seized him ... and his bonds fell apart from upon his hands. And he found the fresh jawbone of a donkey and reached out his hand and took it, and he struck down a thousand men with it' (15:12-15). This second conflict with the Philistines is, again, more personal than

---

5. In the related case of Saul, the fact that he receives the spirit of the LORD implies that he is a 'charismatic' figure (a judge) rather than a 'traditional' authority (a king), and thus not destined to establish a dynasty. (I will define charismatic and traditional authority below.) Thus, this spirit causes Saul to prophesy (1 Sam. 10:6, 10) – charismatic authority, again. And his first military action similarly involves the divine spirit in the manner of a judge: 'And the spirit of God seized Saul' (1 Sam. 11:6). The 'spirit of the LORD,' it is true, is also said to fall upon David, but this represents the transfer of kingly anointing 'from that day onward' from Saul, from whom the 'spirit of the LORD had turned away,' replaced, what is more, by an 'evil spirit from the LORD' (1 Sam. 16:13-14).

6. See, with further references, James L. Crenshaw, *Samson: A Secret Betrayed, a Vow Ignored* (Atlanta: John Knox Press, 1978), 17.

communal, being in retaliation for the murder of his would-be wife and father-in-law (15:6). Indeed, Samson, unlike Israel's other judges, never leads an army. He works by himself and for himself. The closest he comes to mustering an army is when he unleashes a skulk of foxes (15:4-5).

Both of these skirmishes with the Philistines, as we have seen, have to do with Samson's poorly chosen wife. Indeed, he has a clear predilection for Philistine women. Thus, he chooses his bride 'from the uncircumcised Philistines' (14:3); the 'whore-woman' he visits is a Gazite; and, of course, Delilah is presumably a Philistine as well, not only because of her predecessors, but because of how she is immediately enlisted by the 'Philistine overlords' to work against her lover: 'Entice [*patti*] him and see in what his great power lies and with what we can prevail against him and bind him to torture him' (16:5).[7] What is more, Samson's questionable taste in women is reflected in his biography more generally, insofar as his story consists of repeated border crossings into Philistine territory. As Steve Weitzman has aptly observed, the Samson story constitutes a type of 'border fiction', one that unfolds in the 'borderlands' between Israel and Philistia.[8] Furthermore, Samson is not only a liminal figure travelling between Israel and Philistia, he is also and more precisely a type of 'wildman', a liminal figure inhabiting the border between nature and culture, a human who is perhaps more at home in nature than in culture. Or, as David E. Bynum has aptly observed, he is a 'biblical φὴρ ὀρεσκῷος': 'Nestor in the first book of the Iliad seems to mean this same race of sub-human beings [Centaurs] when he speaks of φηροὶ ὀρεσκῷοι, "wild (ones) who reside/are situated in the mountains".'[9] Samson's uncultured tendencies are related to his taste in women. For even if the Philistines are, as Mobley observes, more urban and technologically advanced than Israel,[10] their males are also uncircumcised – which is to say that their bodies are in a state of nature, untouched by a blade, like Samson's head – hence the contempt his parents have for his uncivilized bride. It is Samson's status as 'wildman', I maintain, that provides the key to understanding his characterization and his story.

---

7. I must admit, however, that her race is not made explicit.

8. Weitzman, 'The Samson Story as Border Fiction,' *BibInt* 10 (2002): 158–74.

9. Bynum, 'Samson as a Biblical φὴρ ὀρεσκῷος,' in *Text and Tradition: The Hebrew Bible and Folklore* (ed. Susan Niditch; Atlanta: Scholars Press, 1990), 66. Gregory Mobley builds on the work of Bynum (and others) in *Samson and the Liminal Hero in the Ancient Near East* (New York: T&T Clark, 2006). See also Susan Niditch, 'Samson as Culture Hero, Trickster, and Bandit: The Empowerment of the Weak,' *CBQ* 52 (1990): 608–24; and Stephen M. Wilson, 'Samson the Man-Child: Failing to Come of Age in the Deuteronomistic History,' *JBL* 133 (2014): 43–60.

10. Mobley, 30.

Samson and Fire

Samson's very name is instructive: Hebrew *šimšon* would seem to be etymologically related to *šemeš* or sun,[11] thus linking him to fire.[12] Fire, an ambiguous substance: on the one hand, a wild or natural destructive force; on the other, a domesticated constructive force that makes culture possible – cooking food, smelting metals, etc.[13] In particular, fire is necessary for burning offerings up to God. Not coincidentally, the annunciation type-scene that announces Samson's birth involves a fiery offering: 'And Manoah took the kid and the grain offering and offered them up on a rock to the Lord ... And it happened when the flame went up from the altar to the heavens, that the Lord's messenger went up in the flame of the altar, with Manoah and his woman watching, and they fell on their faces to the ground' (13:19f). This is domesticated fire in the service of cult and culture: cooking meat, sacrificing to God.

Conversely and more often, Samson is associated with wild, destructive fire.[14] First, note how Samson has a 'hot' temper; he is prone to lose his temper. For as the biblical Hebrew idiom demonstrates, wrath is associated with heat: 'And [Samson's] wrath flared [*wayyiḥar*], and he went up to his father's house' (Judg. 14:19).[15] Thus, Samson's bride is threatened with a fiery death, should she refuse to reveal the secret of her groom's riddle: 'And it happened on the fourth day that they said to Samson's wife, "Entice [*patti*] your husband that he explain the riddle or we will burn you and your father's house in fire"' (14:15; cf. 16:5). When Samson soon thereafter discovers that his bride, whom he abandoned on his wedding night, has been wedded to another, he torments her Philistine compatriots with a fire spread by foxes: 'And Samson went and caught three hundred foxes and took torches and turned tail to tail and put one torch between each two tails. And he set fire to the torches and sent them into the Philistines' standing grain and set fire to the stacked grain and the standing grain and the vineyards and the olive trees' (15:4-5). As a result, the Philistines, fulfilling their prenuptial threat, burn both her and her

---

11. See Crenshaw's overview in *Samson*, 15–16. The use of the recondite word *ḥeres* for 'sun' in Judg. 14:18, which occurs three times in the Bible, might be seen as an attempt to downplay the connection between Samson and sun. For, as Yair Zakovitch and Avigdor Shinan suggest, this 'relationship ... reflects some sort of pagan, mythological belief' (*From Gods to God* [Lincoln: University of Nebraska Press, 2012], 192), namely, that Samson derives from some sort of sun god or hero.

12. See Robert Alter, 'Samson Without Folklore,' in *Text and Tradition*, 50–51.

13. See Mieke Bal's different analysis of the ambiguity of fire in *Death and Dissymmetry: The Politics of Coherence in the Book of Judges* (Chicago: University of Chicago Press, 1988), 96–99. Others have noticed the opposition of nature and culture; see Crenshaw, *Samson*, 17–18.

14. See Mobley's similar observations in *Samson*, 70–71.

15. This metaphorical connection between heat and anger has a basis in human physiology. Anger leads to heightened blood pressure, elevated temperature, and so forth.

father 'in fire': 'And the Philistines said, "Who did this?" And they said, "Samson, the son-in-law of the Timnite, for he took his wife and gave her to his companion." And the Philistines came up and burned her and her father in fire' (15:6). Samson predictably exacts his revenge: 'And he struck them a great blow, hip on thigh, and went down and stayed in the crevice of the rock of Eitam' (15:8). As we have already seen, the men of Judah next agree to bind Samson and hand him over to the Philistines, which of course fails to constrain him: 'and the ropes that were on his arms became like flax burning in fire, and his bonds fell apart from upon his hands' (15:12-14). Finally, when Delilah seeks to hand Samson over to the Philistines: 'And the ambush was laid in her chamber. And she said to him, "Philistines are upon you, Samson!" And he snapped the cords as the wick of tow snaps when it touches fire, and the secret of his power was not known' (16:9). From fire to fire to fire to fire, a nearly uninterrupted sequence of fiery death and destruction.

Samson the Nazirite

The opposition between nature and culture, not coincidentally, corresponds to Samson's status as a Nazirite. For the holiness of the Nazirite derives from the various prohibitions imposed upon him: 'And a messenger of the LORD appeared to the woman and said to her, "Look, pray, you are barren and have born no child. But you shall conceive and bear a son. And now, guard yourself, pray, and drink no wine or strong drink and eat no unclean thing. For you are about to conceive and bear a son, and no razor shall touch his head, for the lad shall be a Nazirite of God from the womb"' (13:3-5). The restrictions against the consumption of wine and the cutting of hair amount to an 'eschewal of culture', to borrow Mobley's felicitous locution.[16] The restriction against eating any 'unclean thing' amounts to a partial renunciation of nature, insofar as the distinction between clean and unclean can only be established through language, is thus wholly human. The Priestly requirements for the Nazirite vow concur:

> Man or woman, should anyone act exceptionally to make a Nazirite vow to keep himself apart for the LORD, from both wine and strong drink he shall keep himself apart, neither wine vinegar nor liquor vinegar shall he drink, no grape steepings shall he drink, and grapes, whether wet or dry, he shall not eat. All the days of his Nazritehood, of anything made from the grapevine, from seeds to skin, he shall not eat. All the days of his Nazirite vow no razor shall pass over his head, until the days come to term. That which he sets apart for the LORD shall be holy [*qadoš*], to grow loose the hair on his head. All the days of his setting apart for the LORD, he shall not come to a dead person. For his father and for his mother and for his brother and for his sister he shall not be defiled for them

---

16. Mobley, 24. For an overview of the Nazirite vow, see Tony W. Cartledge, *Vows in the Hebrew Bible and the Ancient Near East* (Sheffield: Sheffield Academic Press, 1992), 18–23.

when they die, for the crown of his God [*nezer 'elohayw*] is on his head. All the days of his Naziritehood, he is holy to the LORD. (Num. 6:2-8)

Wine, razors, funerals – all aspects of culture.[17] And it is precisely this renunciation of culture that confers holiness upon the Nazirite. What is interesting, then, is that the holiness of the priest is associated instead with culture: temple, altar, burnt offerings, priestly garb, etc. The Nazirite is thus a type of mirror image of the priest. Whereas the former wears the 'crown of his God' in the form of his unsullied head of hair, the latter wears 'the *crown* of his God's anointing oil [*nezer* ... *'elohayw*]' (Lev. 21:12) in the form of 'a *holy* crown [*nezer-haqqodeš*] of pure gold' (Exod. 39:30). For the Nazirite, this crown consists of a natural outgrowth, for the priest, of a cultural anointing or adornment.

In order to analyse the underlying structure of this vow, we must turn to Max Weber, in particular, to his distinction between traditional and charismatic authority. 'Authority will be called traditional', Weber explains, 'if legitimacy is claimed for it and believed in by virtue of the sanctity of age-old rules and powers. The masters are designated according to traditional rules and are obeyed because of their traditional status.'[18] Conversely, 'the term "charisma" will be applied to a certain quality of an individual personality by virtue of which he is considered extraordinary and treated as endowed with supernatural, superhuman, or at least specifically exceptional powers or qualities. These are such as are not accessible to the ordinary person, but are regarded as of divine origin or as exemplary.'[19]

In the Bible, the charismatic figure is most clearly represented by the prophet, whose divine calling represents that charisma or gift bestowed by God upon his chosen messenger. Consider the calling of Isaiah son of Amoz:

In the year of the death of King Uzziah, I saw the Master seated on a high and lofty throne, and the skirts of his robe filled the Temple ... And I said,

'Woe to me, for I am undone,
  for I am a man of impure lips,
    and in a people of impure lips do I dwell.
My eyes have seen the King LORD of Armies.'

---

17. Regarding funerals, it is worth recalling that Thucydides, in his *History of the Peloponnesian War*, characterized the breakdown of proper burial rites during the plague of Athens as a type of 'lawlessness [*anomias*]' (2.53.1) – namely, a type of return to the savagery of nature.

18. Max Weber, *Economy and Society: An Outline of Interpretive Sociology* (Berkeley: University of California Press, 1978), 1.226.

19. Weber, 241. Weber posits a third form of authority, 'legal authority', but this need not concern us here.

And one of the seraphim flew down to me, in his hand a glowing coal in tongs that he had taken from the altar. And he touched my mouth and said, 'Look, this has touched your lips, and your crime is gone, your offense shall be atoned.' And I heard the voice of the Master saying, 'Whom shall I send, and who will go for us? And I said, 'Here I am, send me.' (Isa 6:1-8)

Isaiah's calling is a private and perhaps even a mystical experience that bridges the gap between heaven and earth, between the deity (or an angel) and the prophet, without the mediation of human institutions. It authorizes the prophet to speak precisely against traditional authority. Whence Amos's famous rejection of the priestly cult: 'I hate, I spurn your festivals / and smell no fragrance in your convocations. / Should you offer up to Me burnt offerings / or grain offerings, I will not accept them; / nor will I look on the well-being sacrifice of your fatted calves. / . . . / But let justice well up like water and righteousness like a steady stream' (Amos 5:21-24). Charismatic authority is the natural-born enemy of traditional authority, and vice-versa.

Insofar as traditional authority, in contrast, rests on the 'sanctity of age-old rules and powers,' it does not originate in an individual's unmediated gifts or calling, but is inherited from an established institution, and is thus typically passed down by inheritance as well. In the Bible, the two clearest examples of traditional authority are the monarchy (the sons of David) and the priesthood (the sons of Aaron) – both of which, not coincidentally, are centred in Jerusalem. Let us consider the case of the priesthood. The rules of the Aaronid priesthood consist largely of cultic rituals aimed at maintaining the separation of the sacred and the profane. No surprise, then, that the 'anointing' and 'consecration' (Lev. 8:12) of 'Aaron and his sons' (8:2) must gradually unfold in the course of Leviticus 8–9. These sixty verses – as opposed to the eight verses describing Isaiah's calling – recount sacrifices, anointings with oil, donning of official priestly garb, and so forth. The point of origin of the Aaronid priesthood thus involves a certain paradox: Which came first, the chicken or the egg? In order for Aaron, the first priest, to be anointed and consecrated, certain priestly rituals and paraphernalia needed already to exist; and yet how could these exist in the absence of an anointed and consecrated priest? Enter Moses. Neither quite prophet nor priest – even though his representation draws on aspects of both – he functions as a type of cultic 'midwife', who makes possible the ritual birth of the priesthood.

In this light, the Priestly description of the Nazirite vow would seem to be an attempt on the part of traditional authority to contain and control the lifelong charismatic authority enjoyed by Nazirites such as Samson and (most likely) Samuel. Thus, according to Numbers 6, the man or woman who feels called to make a Nazirite vow is beckoned to approach a priest at the temple at both the beginning and ending of his or her vow, making the appropriate sacrifices and so forth. Presumably, then, this Priestly legislation reflects an historical reality in which Nazirites existed and were revered by the general populace as a rival to priestly authority. As Israel Knohl relatedly observes: 'we may have here a polemic against a view that would assign permanent sanctity to someone outside of Priestly

This sequence of events recalls the narrative sequence in which the Hebrew slaves escape from Egypt, thanks to the LORD's 'deliverance': 'And the LORD on that day delivered [*wayyoša'*] Israel from the hand of Egypt, and Israel saw Egypt dead on the shore of the sea' (Exod. 14:30). In the wake of this victory: 'And Miriam sang out to them: "Sing to the LORD for He has surged, O surged, / Horse and its rider He hurled into the sea!"... And they went three days in the wilderness and did not find water. And they came to Marah and could not drink water from Marah, for it was bitter. Therefore is its name called Marah. And the people murmured against Moses, saying, "What shall we drink?" And he cried out to the LORD, and the LORD showed him a tree, and he flung [*wayyašlek*] it into the water, and the water turned sweet' (15:21-25).²⁷ Note the striking parallels between Exodus and Judges. After a great deliverance of God's people, a couplet is sung to the LORD in thanksgiving. Then, the very people whom God saved are threatened by thirst, a lack of drinkable water. God thus miraculously provides them with water. And as a result, the locale at which said miracle takes place is named via a wordplay. What this allusion means is not so much that Samson constitutes a second Moses – far from it. It establishes, rather, a spatial parallel between that liminal territory which Samson occupies between Israel and Philistia and that liminal space (and time) lying between Egypt and Canaan.

Samson Domesticated

Insofar as women in antiquity were associated with domestic indoor culture – recall, e.g., how Jacob the cook is associated with his mother and his tent – as opposed to the wild, outdoor nature of men – recall, e.g., that Esau the hunter is associated with the field and his father (Gen. 25:27-34) – it seems no coincidence that it is precisely two women – bringers of culture, like their ancestor, Eve (Genesis 3)²⁸ – who manage, where men fail, to bend Samson to their will: viz., the woman from Timnah and Delilah, Philistines both. It is no doubt for this reason that Samson fails to consummate his marriage. Doing so would have domesticated him, trapped him with the proverbial 'ball and chain'. Not coincidentally, both of these women manage to extract a secret from him.

First, the woman from Timnah. During their wedding ceremony, Samson poses a 'riddle' to her Philistine compatriots: 'And Samson said to them, "Let me pose you a riddle. If you actually explain it to me during the seven days of the feast and find the solution, I shall give you thirty fine cloths and thirty changes of garment. And

---

27. One also recalls a slightly later episode at Massah/Meribah: 'And the people thirsted [*wayyiṣmaʾ*] for water there...And Moses called out to the LORD...And the LORD said to Moses, "... Look, I am about to stand before you there on the rock in Horeb, and you shall strike the rock, and water will come out from it and the people will drink"' (17:3-6).

28. See, with further references, Robert S. Kawashima, '*Homo Faber* in J's Primeval History,' in *ZAW* 116 (2004): 483–501.

circles'.²⁰ The priests thus apparently concluded that this charismatic holiness must be subordinated to and redefined by and in relation to traditional holiness. Hence the authority exerted by the priests over the Nazirites in Numbers 6, and the merely temporary nature of this vow. For it is surely no coincidence that Samson, who is the only biblical character to be explicitly designated a Nazirite, is a lifelong Nazirite. Samuel, too, is presumably, if not explicitly, a life-long Nazirite, insofar as his mother Hannah makes a 'vow' to the effect that she would 'give him to the LORD all the days of his life [and that] no razor shall touch his head' (1 Sam. 1:11), and declares to Eli the priest that 'Neither wine nor strong drink have I drunk, but I have poured out my heart to the LORD' (1:15).²¹ Now, charismatic authority, as we have seen, derives from a gift or charisma, from a sense of calling. In the cases of Samson and Samuel, however, they themselves do not choose, they are not personally called, to be Nazirites. Rather, they inherit their charismatic calling from their mothers, in the manner of traditional authority. What is more, whereas Hannah makes her vow voluntarily, Samson's mother does not. Rather, she is placed under a type of involuntary calling: 'And now, guard yourself, pray, and drink no wine or strong drink and eat no unclean thing. For you are about to conceive and bear a son, and no razor shall touch his head, for the lad shall be a Nazirite of God from the womb. And he shall begin to *deliver* [*lĕhošiaʿ*] Israel from the hand of the Philistines' (13:4-5). Thus, whereas Hannah might be said to bequeath to her unborn son a type of charismatic authority, insofar as she voluntarily made her vow, felt called to make her vow, Samson's mother bequeaths to her son a type of hybrid, traditional-charismatic authority, an authority that did not derive from a voluntarily made vow. Which is to say that if the Nazirite is already a type of liminal figure, Samson's very relationship to this liminal figure is liminal, in turn.

Samson's liminal status as a Nazirite wildman is reflected in his choice of weapons.²² Not unlike Heracles, he does not wield a blade – just as no razor should ever touch his body. First, he kills a lion with his bare hands, reminiscent of how Heracles slays the Nemean lion. He later eats honey out of its carcass, honey being a type of liminal food: it is natural or raw, and yet produced by bees, long domesticated by human beings, and thus semi-cooked.²³ Whence the phrase, 'a

---

20. Israel Knohl, *The Sanctuary of Silence: The Priestly Torah and the Holiness School* (Minneapolis: Fortress Press, 1995), 160n.145. For a summary of the differences between the depiction of Samson as a Nazirite and the stipulations specified in Numbers 6, see Othniel Margalith, 'Samson's Riddle and Samson's Magic Locks,' *VT* 36 (1986): 230–31.

21. There are text-critical reasons for thinking that Samuel, too, was explicitly designated a Nazirite in the original text. See P. Kyle McCarter, *1 Samuel* (Garden City, NY: Doubleday, 1980), 49–50, 53.

22. See Bynum, 'Samson Story,' 62.

23. See Niditch's parallel but different interpretation of honey in *Judges* (Louisville: Westminster John Knox Press, 2008), 155–56.

land flowing with milk and honey' – milk, too, being a natural substance produced by domesticated beasts, namely, cows and goats.[24] Next, he burns the Philistines' fields and orchards by tying foxes to torches (15:4), thus combining a natural weapon (foxes) with an ambiguous wild/domesticated substance (fire). Shortly thereafter 'he found the fresh [or moist] jawbone of a donkey [*leḥi ḥamor ṭeriyyah*] and reached out his hand and took it, and he struck down a thousand men with it' (15:15). Not only does he use natural weapons, weapons provided by nature – not unlike milk and honey – he uses a fresh or moist weapon, a jawbone, we are meant to imagine, that still has flesh and sinew hanging off of it, rather than a jawbone cured by the sun. He has not yet quite entered into the stone age – uncannily reminiscent of the opening scene of Stanley Kubrick's *2001: A Space Odyssey*, in which a tribe of newly cultured hominids suddenly realizes, thanks apparently to a revelation from an extra-terrestrial monolith, that they can use bones as weapons to vanquish their merely natural enemies.

Samson Unbound

The thematic distinction between fresh and cured continues in the various attempts to bind and overpower Samson. Thus, when the men of Judah find it necessary to deliver Samson to the Philistines, they bind him with 'two new ropes [*'abotim ḥadašim*]' (15:13). Delilah similarly seeks to deliver him thus bound to his enemies: 'And Delilah said to Samson, "Look, you have mocked me and spoken lies to me. Now, tell me, pray, with what could you be bound?" And he said to her, "If they make sure to bind me with new ropes [*'abotim ḥadašim*] with which no task has been done, I would be weakened and become like any man." And Delilah took new ropes [*'abotim ḥadašim*] and bound him with them, and she said to him, "Philistines are upon you, Samson!"' (16:10-12). New ropes are more moist and supple than used ropes, dried and brittle from use and age. The earlier incident of mockery that Delilah refers to brings into play the same thematic distinction: 'And Delilah said to Samson, "Tell me, pray, in what your great power lies, and with what could you be bound to be tortured?" And Samson said, "If they were to bind me with seven moist thongs that had not been dried out, I would be weakened and become like any man." And the Philistine overlords brought up to her seven moist thongs that had not been dried out, and she bound him with them' (16:6-8). Presumably, these 'moist [*laḥim*] thongs' or cords or bowstrings – no doubt made out of animal tissue – are metonymically related within the narrative to the 'fresh [or *moist*] jawbone [*leḥi*]' Samson used just previously. New versus used, fresh versus cured, moist versus dry – water versus fire, Samson's element. Samson is thus consistently associated with something like the opposition between nature and culture, or at least between a primitive and a derivative state.

The opposition between nature and culture is similarly represented by Samson's relationship to geographical space. Just as he likes to travel between Israelite civilization and Philistine barbarism – preferring to cohabit with women from the latter – so too will he traverse the border between culture (indoors) and nature (outdoors), apparently preferring to inhabit the latter.[25] Thus, after he slays a number of Philistines in retaliation for their burning his wife and father-in-law, he 'went down and stayed in the crevice of the rock of Eitam' (15:8). In fact, cultured spaces threaten to trap or bind him. Thus, when Samson decides to spend the night with the 'whore-woman' in Gaza, the Gazites attempt to trap him within the town's gate: 'And they lay in ambush for him all night long at the town gate, and they plotted together all night long, saying, "At morning's light, we shall kill him." And Samson lay till midnight, and he arose at midnight and seized the doors of the town's gate and the two doorposts and pulled them free with the bolt and put them on his shoulders and took them up to the top of the mountain that faces Hebron' (16:2-3). In thus ripping out the town's gate, Samson undermines, if not eradicates, the distinction between culture and nature. In the same way, his relationship with Delilah – she who will finally succeed in defeating him by domesticating him – unfolds indoors, within her home – more on which later.

Samson's ambiguous relationship to geographical space is reinforced by a subtle, but I think clear and distinct, allusion to Exodus.[26] Let us return to his first 'great victory' over the Philistines:

And he found the fresh jawbone of a donkey and reached out his hand and took it, and he struck down a thousand men with it. And Samson said:

'With a donkey's jawbone, mound upon mound,
With a donkey's jawbone, I struck down a thousand men.'

And it happened when he finished speaking, that he flung [*wayyašlek*] the jawbone from his hand, and he called that place Ramath Lehi. And he was very thirsty [*wayyiṣma'*], and he called out to the LORD: 'You Yourself gave a great victory [or *deliverance*] [*hattĕšu'ah*] in the hand of your servant, and now should I die from thirst and fall into the hand of the uncircumcised?' And God split open the hollow that was in Lehi, and water came out of it, and he drank and his spirit returned and he revived. Therefore has its name been called Ein Hakkore to this day. And he led Israel in the days of the Philistines twenty years. (Judg. 15:15-20)

---

24. Milk and honey, then, constitute something like the 'fruit' of animals, which as such can be consumed raw, like the fruit of trees, and unlike the flesh of animals.

25. See Bynum, 'Samson Story,' 60–61.

26. I do not claim that the author(s) of the Samson story had before him/them some parts of Exodus, but I would maintain that he at least had a knowledge of the narrative traditions underlying Exodus and its sources.

if you are not able to explain it to me, you shall give me thirty fine cloths and thirty changes of garment." And they said to him, "Pose your riddle, that we may hear it." And he said to them: "From the eater food came forth, / and from the strong sweet came forth." And they could not explain the riddle for three days' (14:12-14). But a genuine riddle is a cleverly constructed question that one might, with a bit of cleverness, figure out. As Margalith observes: 'It is part of the essence of a riddle that the hearers have the answer within their knowledge though they are not conscious of it.'[29] Samson's so-called riddle clumsily amounts to a secret that one must simply be let in on, instead – although he does manage to produce a rather clever couplet. And as we know, he did not even tell it to his parents (14:6). Samson's riddle resembles, in this respect, the faux riddle that Bilbo Baggins unintentionally poses to Gollum in *The Hobbit*: '"What have I got in my pocket?" he said aloud. He was talking to himself, but Gollum thought it was a riddle, and he was frightfully upset.'[30] The Philistines, like Gollum, are upset by Samson's unfair 'riddle,' and so they threaten her and her father with a fiery death. Quite understandably, she attempts to manipulate her husband: 'And Samson's wife wept before him and said, "You only hate me and don't love me. You posed a riddle to my countrymen, but to me you did not explain it." And he said to her, "Look, to my father and my mother I did not explain it, and shall I explain it to you?" And she wept before him the seven days that they had the feast, and it happened on the seventh day, that he explained it to her, for she had badgered him [*heṣiqathu*]. And she explained the riddle to her countrymen' (14:16-17). In other words, she 'nagged him to death,' as the saying goes. Whereas the Philistine men sought to bind him, to overpower him with brute force, she manages to wear him down with an insistent force instead, in the way that water slowly but surely wears down rock in the course of geological time – witness the Grand Canyon.

Second, Delilah. She will similarly wear Samson down. As we have already seen, he lies to her twice: first, 'seven moist thongs' (16:7); second, 'new ropes' (16:11). The third lie takes an interesting turn: 'If you weave my head's seven tresses together with the web and drive them with a peg into the wall, I would be weakened and become like any man' (16:13). This time, Samson finally approaches the truth: he speaks of his hair. What is more, he speaks of weaving – a quintessentially feminine domestic task.[31] Symbolically speaking, she is about to domesticate Samson by weaving his tresses with a web, that is, by tainting the natural source of his holiness with culture. Finally, on her fourth try, she manages to extract the truth from him: 'And it happened when she badgered him [*heṣiqah lo*] with her words day after day and beleaguered him, that he was vexed unto the death. And he told her all that was in his heart, and he said, "No razor has touched my head, for I have been a

---

29. Margalith, 'Samson's Riddle,' 226.
30. J.R.R. Tolkien, *The Hobbit* (rev. ed.; New York: Ballantine Books, 1982), 78-79.
31. Recall how Helen weaves indoors, while the Trojan war takes place outdoors (*Iliad* 3.121-28); recall how Penelope weaves indoors, while her husband Odysseus fights for his homecoming (*Odyssey* 19.138-55).

Nazirite of God from my mother's womb. Were I shaven, my power would turn away from me and I would be weakened and become like any man"' (16:16-17). She, like Samson's bride, 'badgered him'. In this case, however, Delilah will also bring about his downfall by actually taming him, where other women have failed. Not only does this haircut invalidate his Nazirite status, it also functions as a type of rite of initiation, insofar as a razor touches his previously unsullied head and thus effectively domesticates him. In other words, he is no longer wild and thus no longer holy and thus no longer strong.

Time marches on, however, so that his hair begins to grow back: 'And the hair of his head began to grow as soon as it was shaven' (16:22). And with this hair, we are meant to understand, he ceases to be fully domesticated and starts to become wild and thus holy and thus strong once again. Nevertheless, his second great victory is represented as a gift from God, rather than as a purely natural expression of his brute strength:

> And Samson said to the lad who was holding his hand, 'Let me rest and feel the pillars on which the temple stands, that I may lean on them.' And the temple was filled with men and women, and all the Philistine overlords were there, and on the roof about three thousand men and women watching as Samson played. And Samson called to the LORD and said 'My Master, LORD, recall me, pray, and strengthen me just this time, O God, that I may avenge myself in one act of vengeance from the Philistines for my two eyes.' And Samson grasped the two central pillars on which the temple stood and pushed against them, one with his right hand and one with his left hand. And Samson said, 'Let me die with the Philistines!,' and he pushed powerfully, and the temple fell on the overlords and on all the people who were in it. And the dead that he killed in his death were more than he had killed in his life. (16:26-30)

It is not enough that his hair grows back; he must also pray to God, who apparently answers him.[32] What is more, asking to be allowed to rest upon the pillars of the Philistine temple is arguably the single truly clever act that Samson ever made. As a result, he manages, with his dying breath, to topple over the pillars of the temple in which he is being displayed and cause it to come crashing down upon his tormentors – striking image of nature (the wildman) subverting culture. In so doing, he finally kills more Philistines in his death than he did in his life – anti-hero, as I have said. Indeed, I would go so far as to argue that his epitaph, mentioned at the beginning of this chapter, should contain a second half: 'And the dead that he killed in his death were more than he had killed in his life' (16:30).

---

32. We noted earlier how the connection between Samson and sun 'reflects some sort of pagan, mythological belief' (Zakovitch and Shinan, 192), which needed to be attenuated in the biblical text. Here, too, the rather pagan notion that Samson's hair is the source of his strength is ultimately obscured by his prayer to God.

Chapter 10

DELILAH'S MYSTERIOUS ROLE IN SAMSON'S DESTINY: THE DYNAMICS OF POWER, KNOWLEDGE AND MYSTERY

Athena E. Gorospe

Birth and death mark the span of a person's life, encompassing the sphere in which his or her destiny is projected and realized. Destiny is commonly understood as a particular path that a person is to take in order to fulfil a certain purpose, mission or vocation. This path can be determined by the circumstances of one's birth, family, culture, history and education, plus one's personality, gifts, experiences and the people one meets. While destiny is often seen as predetermined, there is room for agency, since choices are still made even within the limitations and possibilities of one's existence.

Samson's birth and death are marked by such destiny. His pattern of life and his mission have been predetermined even when he was still in his mother's womb. Nevertheless, as he continually makes choices and exercises agency, there is a possibility of him missing his calling and not fulfilling the promise of his birth.

Two mysterious personalities suddenly appear at the junctures of birth and death in Samson's life. The first is a mysterious divine visitor who appears to his mother to announce his birth; the second is Delilah, whose actions lead to Samson's imprisonment and eventual death. The first initiates Samson's Nazirite status; the other ends it. While the first has no name and remains anonymous all throughout the story, the other one is named even as she speaks and acts. Their enigmatic characters are highlighted by the lack of detailed description regarding their identity. In this essay, I propose that Delilah is the counterpart of the mysterious divine visitor at Samson's birth. While the divine visitor announces Samson's destiny through a word of promise, Delilah is the one instrumental in fulfilling it.

Power, Knowledge and Mystery

The Delilah-Samson narrative, according to Carol Smith, primarily deals with 'the dynamics of power relationships,' and how 'different *kinds* of power are wielded by different people'.[1] These dynamics, however, operate in the rest of the Samson narrative as well. The most explicit form of power is physical power, as seen in Samson's enormous physical strength. This power is not inherent in Samson, but comes through the action of the spirit of YHWH (14:6, 19; 15:14) and his separated status as a Nazirite to the Lord (16:17).

But physical strength is also manifested in Philistine military superiority' over the Israelites in weapons and organization. This superiority, in turn, enables Philistine dominance over Israel in the form of political and economic control (13:1; 14:4b). Material power is also demonstrated in the fetters by which the Judahites, Delilah and the Philistines seek to constrain or radically reduce Samson's strength, whether with ropes or metal shackles, so that he can be captured (15:13; 16:11, 21). Some of the cords which Delilah used to tie Samson might even be regarded as having magical properties, with the physical bonds undergirded by what is believed to be supernatural power.

But there are other forms of power, aside from physical strength or bonds. In wit and riddles, the power of language is utilized to assert dominance in a verbal joust.[2] In the Samson narrative, this is played out in the tit-for-tat exchanges between Samson and the Philistines in the riddle incident, and in the coquettish interchanges between Samson and Delilah. In these interchanges, knowledge is used as a way of gaining advantage over the other, while the lack of knowledge puts one party in a more feeble and less defensible position. Aside from knowledge, however, the power of emotional and erotic attachments are exploited in order to put the other in a vulnerable position. Lastly, there is the power of the deities – Yahweh and Dagon. If the people who worship a particular deity gains victory, then that deity is regarded as more powerful than the one whose worshippers lose in battle.

However, the theme of power is intertwined with the theme of knowledge., The theme of knowledge is developed through the *leitwort* of tell/not tell (הגיד/לא־הגיד)[3] and know/not know (ידע/לא ידע).[4] 'Through these recurrent theme words the text makes explicit that in this story one knows only if one is told. If one is not told, one

---

1. Carol Smith, 'Samson and Delilah: A Parable of Power?', *JSOT* 76 (1997): 50.

2. Mieke Bal, *Death & Dissymmetry: The Politics of Coherence in the Book of Judges* (Chicago: Chicago University Press, 1988), 135–42.

3. הגיד is used eleven times in the riddle incident and seven times in the Delilah episode, all of which are used in connection with Samson's secret. The other three occurrences are a prelude to the riddle episode. See J. Cheryl Exum, 'Literary Patterns in the Samson Saga: An Investigation of Rhetorical Style in Biblical Prose' (PhD diss., Columbia University, 1976), 61–62 and 'Aspects of Symmetry and Balance in the Samson Saga,' *JSOT* 19 (1981): 4–5.

4. The use of יָדַע in the Samson narrative is mostly in relation to what is concealed (Judg. 13:16, 21; 14:4; 16:9, 20), except in one instance (15:11).

does not know.'[5] Related to this is the secrecy motif, which runs like an underlying thread that ties the different episodes together.[6] The riddle incident (14:11-19) provides dramatic interest that highlights secret knowledge, as Samson and the Philistines battle it out in veiled language, so that the surface meaning of the riddle is either obscured or exposed.

The intertwining of the two themes is developed through the repeated attempts to gain the knowledge of Samson's riddle and strength because the one who can conceal or reveal these secrets can claim supremacy over the other. Hence, 'there is a power struggle between those who know and those who do not know.'[7] Cheryl Exum makes a trenchant observation that, in the narrative, 'knowledge is power, and *women* are the ones who succeed in obtaining forbidden information in the story.'[8] Ilkani Latu Fakasiieiki explores this idea further in the Samson-Delilah episode using categories from Michel Foucault.[9] While Foucault is potentially illuminating, I will not be using him as my conversation partner in my analysis of Delilah's characterization. However, I will give special attention to the themes of knowledge and power.

Nevertheless, even when secret knowledge is uncovered, some things remain in the realm of mystery.[10] While both secret knowledge and mystery deal with what is hidden or concealed, a secret is potentially discoverable, while a mystery is inexplicable and unfathomable. Some things in the Samson narrative, for example, like the identity of the divine visitor and the definitive meaning of the riddle (or whether there are three riddles) are not fully resolved.[11] Lastly, even the whole Samson narrative itself expresses the enigma of a riddle, with its multivalent meanings and lack of closure.[12]

---

5. Edward Greenstein, 'The Riddle of Samson,' *Prooftexts* 1 (1981): 246.

6. James A. Wharton, 'The Secret of Yahweh: Story and Affirmation in Judges 13–16,' *Int* 27 (1973): 55–58.

7. Jacobus Marais, *Representation in Old Testament Narrative Texts* (Leiden: Brill, 1998), 123.

8. J. Cheryl Exum, 'Samson's Women,' in *Fragmented Women: Feminist (Sub)versions of Biblical Narratives* (Sheffield: Sheffield Academic Press, 1993), 81.

9. Ilkani Latu Fakasiieiki, 'Delilah: A Post-colonial Discourse Reading of Judg 16:4–22,' (PhD diss., Graduate Theological Union, 2015), 101–18. The narrative analysis, however, is superficial due to a lack of close reading of the Hebrew text and interaction with important works on the Samson narrative.

10. As pointed out by Marais (*Representation*, 130) and Exum ('Samson's Women,' 80), knowledge is elusive in the Samson narrative.

11. For the various proposals, see Philip Nel, 'The Riddle of Samson (Judg 14,14.18),' *Bib* 66 (1985): 536–39; Azzan Yadin, 'Samson's ḤÎDÂ,' *VT* 52.3 (2002): 407–10.

12. Greenstein, 'The Riddle of Samson,' 247, thinks that the 'meaning of the Samson story' is to 'be unravelled like a riddle'. Cf. Claudia V. Camp, *Wise, Strange and Holy: The Strange Woman and the Making of the Bible* (Sheffield: Sheffield Academic Press, 2000), 96–98; Jeremy Schipper, 'Narrative Obscurity of Samson's חידה in Judges 14.14 and 18,' *JSOT* 27.3 (2003): 343–48.

In this essay, I start with the characterization of Delilah in the events leading to Samson's death and then look at its significance in light of the appearance of a divine messenger in the announcement of Samson's birth.

Samson Loves Delilah

The beginning of the Samson-Delilah episode already hints of a power dynamic underlying the relationship of the two protagonists of the story: 'Afterwards, he [Samson] loved a woman in the valley of Sorek, and her name was Delilah' (16:4). At the onset, Samson's physical strength and virility gives him greater power in the relationship. However, the phrase 'Samson loved' suggests another dynamic operating in the relationship.

This relationship is clearly different from the other women in Samson's life, the timeline of which is delineated by the phrase 'afterwards' (אחרי־כן).[13] It is also the first time that the narrative describes Samson as 'loving' a woman. While Samson describes his feelings for the Timnite as 'she is right in my eyes' (14:3; cf. 14:7),[14] and the Timnite interpreted Samson's attraction towards her as love (14:16), the narrative never describes Samson as loving anybody else except Delilah. The converse, 'Delilah loved Samson,' is not mentioned, which may imply a one-sided relationship that puts Samson in a more vulnerable position.[15]

Susan Ackerman, however, argues that, when the verb אהב (to love) is used in interpersonal relationships, the subject is hierarchically superior to the object of love,[16] hence, the man is often the subject and seldom the woman.[17] A man's love may also become abusive, as in Amnon with Tamar (2 Sam. 13:1-14).[18] Nonetheless, there are instances where a woman loves a man, but the woman is not superior to the man.[19] Moreover, אהב is also used for the love of someone with equal or lower

---

13. Tammi J. Schneider, *Judges* (BO; Collegeville, Minn.: Liturgical Press, 2000), 219.

14. The expression 'right in one's eyes' (1 Sam. 18:20, 26; 2 Sam. 17:4; 1 Kgs 9:12; Jer. 18:4) has the sense of being 'pleased with' or 'approving of' a person or situation. It is not used as a synonym for 'love'. Cf. the adj. form in Judg. 17:6; 21:25, where ישר takes on a moral sense.

15. J. Cheryl Exum, *Plotted, Shot, and Painted: Cultural Representations of Biblical Women* (Sheffield: Sheffield Academic Press, 1996), 181–82.

16. Susan Ackerman, 'The Personal is Political: Covenantal and Affectionate Love ('ĀHĒB, 'AHĂBÂ) in the Hebrew Bible,' *VT* 52 (2002): 447.

17. Gen. 24:67; 29:18, 30; 34:3; 1 Sam. 1:5; 2 Sam. 13:1; 1 Kgs 11:1-2 ; Hos. 3:1; Est. 2:17; 2 Chron. 11:21.

18. Cf. Shechem (Gen. 34:2-4), although he 'loved her' after sexually humiliating her.

19. Shulammite (Song 1:7; 3:1-4); the metaphor of Israel as an unfaithful wife longing for other lovers (Hos. 3:1). Ackerman, 'Personal is Political,' 452–53, thinks that Michal (1 Sam. 18: 20, 28), as the king's daughter, is socially superior to David, although it can be argued that her love makes her vulnerable to David's political positionings. See Ellen White, 'Michal the Misinterpreted,' *JSOT* 31.4 (2007): 452–53. Cf. Exum, *Fragmented Women*, 45.

social status than the one loved.[20] Thus, rather than considering who is more vulnerable than the other, it is best to look at the different form/s of power being wielded by each character. My reading is that 'love' in 16:4 is used in an ironic way, in which 'love' is used to gain advantage in a relationship in which lovers seek to retain/gain power over the other.

Delilah is Named, but Remains a Mystery

Unlike other women in his life, including Samson's mother, Delilah's name is given, which may signal that a change is about to take place.[21] While named, however, her ethnicity, her social status or sphere of work, her family connections[22] – whether she's the daughter or wife or mother of someone – is not mentioned. Where she lives is given, but whether she is a native inhabitant or a sojourner in Sorek is not made explicit. The valley is located in the boundary of the territories of Israel and Philistia, so it is not clear whether she is a Philistine, an Israelite, or from another ethnic group.[23]

The fact that she is not connected to any man, as the mother, daughter, wife, concubine or slave of someone, makes her independent of any man who can give her status, acceptance, and identify her as belonging or attached to someone.[24] This makes it difficult to determine her interests and for whose benefit her actions and decisions are oriented. Even Deborah, who has the status of a prophetess and a judge, and who leads Israel into the battle, is mentioned in connection with her

---

20. Exod. 21:5 (slave); 1 Sam. 18:16 (king's subjects), Lev. 19:18 (the neighbour), Deut. 6:5; 11:1; Judg. 5:31 (loving God).

21. Gregory Mobley, *The Empty Men: The Heroic Tradition of Ancient Israel* (ABRL; New York: Doubleday, 2005), 191, and Caroline Blyth, *Reimagining Delilah's Afterlives as Femme Fatale: The Lost Seduction* (London: T&T Clark, 2017), 53–57, explore several proposals on the meaning of Delilah's name, but the lack of definitive agreement makes analysis of the name unhelpful for characterization. See also Barry G. Webb, *The Book of Judges* (NICOT; Grand Rapids: Eerdmans, 2012), 398.

22. Most of the women in Judges, except for one, are described in relation to a man or to a place: Achsah (1:11-13); Jael (4:17); Jephthah's daughter (11:34-40); Micah's mother (17:2-4), the Levite's concubine (Judg. 19); the virgins of Jabesh-Gilead (21:12-14); the daughters of Shiloh (21:21-23). The only exception is the woman who kills Abimelech (9:50-54).

23. Carol Smith, 'Delilah: A Suitable Case for (Feminist) Treatment?' in *Judges: A Feminist Companion to the Bible Second Series* (ed. Athalya Brenner; Sheffield: Sheffield Academic Press, 1999), 94–95, points out the ambiguity in her characterization. Cf. Mark Lackowski, 'Victim, Victor, or Villain? The Unfinalizability of Delilah,' *J Bible Recept* 6.2 (2019): 207–8, 213–14, 217; Latu Fakasiieiki, 'Delilah: A Post-colonial Discourse,' 144.

24. Exum, *Plotted, Shot, and Painted*, 181; Lilian Klein, 'The Book of Judges: Paradigm and Deviation in Images of Women,' in *A Feminist Companion to Judges* (ed. Athalya Brenner; FCB 4; Sheffield: JSOT Press, 1993), 61–62.

husband (Judg. 4:4). In contrast, Delilah is not even once referred to as 'Samson's woman/wife' nor is Samson described as 'her man/husband'. She is simply Delilah. But far from identifying who she is, her being named without additional details merely adds to the mystery of her personality and motivations. Unattached women at that time seemed an oddity since women were supposed to belong to a household, where they lived under the authority of the male head, either their father, husband or brother, who is to be the guardian of their sexuality.[25] Yet her being unattached to any male figure or household, her freedom to enter a sexual relationship, and her ability to contract financial transactions on her own cast her as an anomalous and strange figure.[26]

Perhaps, this is the reason why Delilah has often been portrayed as a prostitute, because she is not under the guardianship of any man.[27] However, there is nothing in the text that identifies her as such. Even though a prostitute is a sexually available woman operating 'on the street', meaning outside a patriarchal household,[28] she gets paid in money or valuables for engaging in sexual activity. While Delilah agrees to receive money from the Philistines, it is not in exchange for sexual services, and there is no indication that she receives payment from Samson for sexual favours. The relationship with Samson is not a short-term casual affair, as can be seen in the many days that Delilah pressured him before revealing his secret (16:16). In Mesopotamian non-literary texts, there is a term which is usually translated 'prostitute',[29] but may actually refer more broadly to a single woman who is not part of a household and whose sexuality, therefore, is not regulated by a male figure.[30] While prostitutes are classed in this category, not all women in this group

---

25. David Carr, 'Gender and the Shaping of Desire in the Song of Songs and its Interpretation,' *JBL* 119.2 (2000): 237. Because of this sexual guardianship of the husband, adultery is legally defined as sexual intercourse with a married or engaged woman and does not cover a married man's sexual affairs with an unmarried woman. Nevertheless, a father expects to be compensated by the man who has sex with his unmarried virgin daughter. Martha T. Roth, 'Marriage, Divorce, and the Prostitute in Ancient Mesopotamia,' in *Prostitutes and Courtesans in the Ancient World* (eds. Christopher A. Faraone and Laura K. McClure; Madison, WI.: University of Wisconsin Press, 2006), 25–26.

26. Blyth, *Reimagining Delilah's Afterlives*, 66–67.

27. Exum, *Plotted, Shot, and Painted*, 189–99, traces the reception history of Delilah being cast as a prostitute, as she is depicted in paintings, musicals, and films. Blyth, *Reimagining Delilah's Afterlives*, 72–74, shows some of the reasons why she has been characterized this way.

28. Roth, 'Marriage, Divorce, and the Prostitute in Ancient Mesopotamia,' 24; Marten Stol, *Women in the Ancient Near East* (Boston/Berlin: De Gruyter, 2016), 399–401.

29. The Sumerian word is *kar.kid*, which combines 'harbour' and 'to work', while the Akkadian is *ḫarīmtu*, 'a woman who is separated'. Stol, *Women in the Ancient Near East*, 399.

30. J. Assante, 'The *kar.kid/harimtu*, Prostitute or Single Woman?: A Reconsideration of the Evidence', *UF* 30 (1998): 5–96. She argues that a patriarchal bias in translations and lexical lists has caused scholars to eclipse the existence of this group of single women, and

circles'.[20] The priests thus apparently concluded that this charismatic holiness must be subordinated to and redefined by and in relation to traditional holiness. Hence the authority exerted by the priests over the Nazirites in Numbers 6, and the merely temporary nature of this vow. For it is surely no coincidence that Samson, who is the only biblical character to be explicitly designated a Nazirite, is a lifelong Nazirite. Samuel, too, is presumably, if not explicitly, a life-long Nazirite, insofar as his mother Hannah makes a 'vow' to the effect that she would 'give him to the LORD all the days of his life [and that] no razor shall touch his head' (1 Sam. 1:11), and declares to Eli the priest that 'Neither wine nor strong drink have I drunk, but I have poured out my heart to the LORD' (1:15).[21] Now, charismatic authority, as we have seen, derives from a gift or charisma, from a sense of calling. In the cases of Samson and Samuel, however, they themselves do not choose, they are not personally called, to be Nazirites. Rather, they inherit their charismatic calling from their mothers, in the manner of traditional authority. What is more, whereas Hannah makes her vow voluntarily, Samson's mother does not. Rather, she is placed under a type of involuntary calling: 'And now, guard yourself, pray, and drink no wine or strong drink and eat no unclean thing. For you are about to conceive and bear a son, and no razor shall touch his head, for the lad shall be a Nazirite of God from the womb. And he shall begin to *deliver* [*lĕhošia'*] Israel from the hand of the Philistines' (13:4-5). Thus, whereas Hannah might be said to bequeath to her unborn son a type of charismatic authority, insofar as she voluntarily made her vow, felt called to make her vow, Samson's mother bequeaths to her son a type of hybrid, traditional-charismatic authority, an authority that did not derive from a voluntarily made vow. Which is to say that if the Nazirite is already a type of liminal figure, Samson's very relationship to this liminal figure is liminal, in turn.

Samson's liminal status as a Nazirite wildman is reflected in his choice of weapons.[22] Not unlike Heracles, he does not wield a blade – just as no razor should ever touch his body. First, he kills a lion with his bare hands, reminiscent of how Heracles slays the Nemean lion. He later eats honey out of its carcass, honey being a type of liminal food: it is natural or raw, and yet produced by bees, long domesticated by human beings, and thus semi-cooked.[23] Whence the phrase, 'a

---

20. Israel Knohl, *The Sanctuary of Silence: The Priestly Torah and the Holiness School* (Minneapolis: Fortress Press, 1995), 160n.145. For a summary of the differences between the depiction of Samson as a Nazirite and the stipulations specified in Numbers 6, see Othniel Margalith, 'Samson's Riddle and Samson's Magic Locks,' *VT* 36 (1986): 230–31.

21. There are text-critical reasons for thinking that Samuel, too, was explicitly designated a Nazirite in the original text. See P. Kyle McCarter, *1 Samuel* (Garden City, NY: Doubleday, 1980), 49–50, 53.

22. See Bynum, 'Samson Story,' 62.

23. See Niditch's parallel but different interpretation of honey in *Judges* (Louisville: Westminster John Knox Press, 2008), 155–56.

land flowing with milk and honey' – milk, too, being a natural substance produced by domesticated beasts, namely, cows and goats.²⁴ Next, he burns the Philistines' fields and orchards by tying foxes to torches (15:4), thus combining a natural weapon (foxes) with an ambiguous wild/domesticated substance (fire). Shortly thereafter 'he found the fresh [or *moist*] jawbone of a donkey [*leḥi ḥamor ṭeriyyah*] and reached out his hand and took it, and he struck down a thousand men with it' (15:15). Not only does he use natural weapons, weapons provided by nature – not unlike milk and honey – he uses a fresh or moist weapon, a jawbone, we are meant to imagine, that still has flesh and sinew hanging off of it, rather than a jawbone cured by the sun. He has not yet quite entered into the stone age – uncannily reminiscent of the opening scene of Stanley Kubrick's *2001: A Space Odyssey*, in which a tribe of newly cultured hominids suddenly realizes, thanks apparently to a revelation from an extra-terrestrial monolith, that they can use bones as weapons to vanquish their merely natural enemies.

Samson Unbound

The thematic distinction between fresh and cured continues in the various attempts to bind and overpower Samson. Thus, when the men of Judah find it necessary to deliver Samson to the Philistines, they bind him with 'two new ropes [*'abotim ḥadašim*]' (15:13). Delilah similarly seeks to deliver him thus bound to his enemies: 'And Delilah said to Samson, "Look, you have mocked me and spoken lies to me. Now, tell me, pray, with what could you be bound?" And he said to her, "If they make sure to bind me with new ropes [*'abotim ḥadašim*] with which no task has been done, I would be weakened and become like any man." And Delilah took new ropes [*'abotim ḥadašim*] and bound him with them, and she said to him, "Philistines are upon you, Samson!"' (16:10-12). New ropes are more moist and supple than used ropes, dried and brittle from use and age. The earlier incident of mockery that Delilah refers to brings into play the same thematic distinction: 'And Delilah said to Samson, "Tell me, pray, in what your great power lies, and with what could you be bound to be tortured?" And Samson said, "If they were to bind me with seven moist thongs that had not been dried out, I would be weakened and become like any man." And the Philistine overlords brought up to her seven moist thongs that had not been dried out, and she bound him with them' (16:6-8). Presumably, these 'moist [*laḥim*] thongs' or cords or bowstrings – no doubt made out of animal tissue – are metonymically related within the narrative to the 'fresh [or *moist*] jawbone [*leḥi*]' Samson used just previously. New versus used, fresh versus cured, moist versus dry – water versus fire, Samson's element. Samson is thus consistently associated with something like the opposition between nature and culture, or at least between a primitive and a derivative state.

---

24. Milk and honey, then, constitute something like the 'fruit' of animals, which as such can be consumed raw, like the fruit of trees, and unlike the flesh of animals.

The opposition between nature and culture is similarly represented by Samson's relationship to geographical space. Just as he likes to travel between Israelite civilization and Philistine barbarism – preferring to cohabit with women from the latter – so too will he traverse the border between culture (indoors) and nature (outdoors), apparently preferring to inhabit the latter.[25] Thus, after he slays a number of Philistines in retaliation for their burning his wife and father-in-law, he 'went down and stayed in the crevice of the rock of Eitam' (15:8). In fact, cultured spaces threaten to trap or bind him. Thus, when Samson decides to spend the night with the 'whore-woman' in Gaza, the Gazites attempt to trap him within the town's gate: 'And they lay in ambush for him all night long at the town gate, and they plotted together all night long, saying, "At morning's light, we shall kill him." And Samson lay till midnight, and he arose at midnight and seized the doors of the town's gate and the two doorposts and pulled them free with the bolt and put them on his shoulders and took them up to the top of the mountain that faces Hebron' (16:2-3). In thus ripping out the town's gate, Samson undermines, if not eradicates, the distinction between culture and nature. In the same way, his relationship with Delilah – she who will finally succeed in defeating him by domesticating him – unfolds indoors, within her home – more on which later.

Samson's ambiguous relationship to geographical space is reinforced by a subtle, but I think clear and distinct, allusion to Exodus.[26] Let us return to his first 'great victory' over the Philistines:

> And he found the fresh jawbone of a donkey and reached out his hand and took it, and he struck down a thousand men with it. And Samson said:
>
> 'With a donkey's jawbone, mound upon mound,
> With a donkey's jawbone, I struck down a thousand men.'
>
> And it happened when he finished speaking, that he flung [*wayyašlek*] the jawbone from his hand, and he called that place Ramath Lehi. And he was very thirsty [*wayyiṣmaʾ*], and he called out to the LORD: 'You Yourself gave a great victory [or *deliverance*] [*hattěšuʿah*] in the hand of your servant, and now should I die from thirst and fall into the hand of the uncircumcised?' And God split open the hollow that was in Lehi, and water came out of it, and he drank and his spirit returned and he revived. Therefore has its name been called Ein Hakkore to this day. And he led Israel in the days of the Philistines twenty years. (Judg. 15:15-20)

---

25. See Bynum, 'Samson Story,' 60–61.

26. I do not claim that the author(s) of the Samson story had before him/them some parts of Exodus, but I would maintain that he at least had a knowledge of the narrative traditions underlying Exodus and its sources.

This sequence of events recalls the narrative sequence in which the Hebrew slaves escape from Egypt, thanks to the LORD's 'deliverance': 'And the LORD on that day delivered [*wayyošaʿ*] Israel from the hand of Egypt, and Israel saw Egypt dead on the shore of the sea' (Exod. 14:30). In the wake of this victory: 'And Miriam sang out to them: "Sing to the LORD for He has surged, O surged, / Horse and its rider He hurled into the sea!"... And they went three days in the wilderness and did not find water. And they came to Marah and could not drink water from Marah, for it was bitter. Therefore is its name called Marah. And the people murmured against Moses, saying, "What shall we drink?" And he cried out to the LORD, and the LORD showed him a tree, and he flung [*wayyašlek*] it into the water, and the water turned sweet' (15:21-25).[27] Note the striking parallels between Exodus and Judges. After a great deliverance of God's people, a couplet is sung to the LORD in thanksgiving. Then, the very people whom God saved are threatened by thirst, a lack of drinkable water. God thus miraculously provides them with water. And as a result, the locale at which said miracle takes place is named via a wordplay. What this allusion means is not so much that Samson constitutes a second Moses – far from it. It establishes, rather, a spatial parallel between that liminal territory which Samson occupies between Israel and Philistia and that liminal space (and time) lying between Egypt and Canaan.

Samson Domesticated

Insofar as women in antiquity were associated with domestic indoor culture – recall, e.g., how Jacob the cook is associated with his mother and his tent – as opposed to the wild, outdoor nature of men – recall, e.g., that Esau the hunter is associated with the field and his father (Gen. 25:27-34) – it seems no coincidence that it is precisely two women – bringers of culture, like their ancestor, Eve (Genesis 3)[28] – who manage, where men fail, to bend Samson to their will: viz., the woman from Timnah and Delilah, Philistines both. It is no doubt for this reason that Samson fails to consummate his marriage. Doing so would have domesticated him, trapped him with the proverbial 'ball and chain'. Not coincidentally, both of these women manage to extract a secret from him.

First, the woman from Timnah. During their wedding ceremony, Samson poses a 'riddle' to her Philistine compatriots: 'And Samson said to them, "Let me pose you a riddle. If you actually explain it to me during the seven days of the feast and find the solution, I shall give you thirty fine cloths and thirty changes of garment. And

---

27. One also recalls a slightly later episode at Massah/Meribah: 'And the people thirsted [*wayyiṣmaʾ*] for water there ... And Moses called out to the LORD ... And the LORD said to Moses, "... Look, I am about to stand before you there on the rock in Horeb, and you shall strike the rock, and water will come out from it and the people will drink"' (17:3-6).

28. See, with further references, Robert S. Kawashima, '*Homo Faber* in J's Primeval History', in *ZAW* 116 (2004): 483–501.

engage in sex as a profession. Thus, there is the 'woman who stands outside the patriarchal milieu and goes her own way, alone and self-sufficient',[31] and since she does not belong to a patriarchal household, she cannot claim a patronymic.[32] This fits the description of Delilah.

Unlike other instances in which the woman is said to be loved by the man, there is no physical description of Delilah. She is not presented as a sex figure, but neither is she depicted as sexually innocent.[33] Moreover, even though Delilah is loved by Samson, the text does not say that Samson took Delilah as his wife or concubine, brought her to his father's house, or ever paid a dowry for her. There is no further statement of how this love impacts him emotionally or how it is demonstrated in actual concrete actions.[34] Samson's love for Delilah does not seem to provide her with long-term security, protection, status or dignity. It is possibly a contractual relationship, in which there are no commitments on both sides.

Delilah as Pawn in a Power Game

We are not told how the Philistines know Delilah, but they seem to have a fair knowledge of Samson's activities and of Delilah's situation as well. In Samson's fling with the Gaza prostitute, the Philistines quickly gains the information about his whereabouts, and are able to assemble quickly to capture him (16:1-2). This highlights that the Philistines already possess the knowledge of Samson's apparent weakness regarding women, but this is not enough for them to defeat him, since their attempt is foiled by Samson's extraordinary strength (16:3). Nevertheless, they can use this knowledge to discover how he can be weakened.

Using women for their own purposes is not new to the Philistines.[35] By threatening to shame and take the life of Samson's Timnite wife and her family, the Philistines succeed in working out the puzzles behind Samson's riddle. This leads

---

so everybody is lumped together under the category of 'prostitute'. Cf. Hennie J. Marsman, *Women in Ugarit and Israel: Their Social and Religious Position in the Context of the Ancient Near East* (Leiden: Brill, 2003), 416–19, who thinks that Assante's proposition may be true of earlier texts, but not later ones. See also Roth, 'Marriage, Divorce, and the Prostitute,' 25–27; 31–32.

31. Stol, *Women in the Ancient Near East*, 417.
32. Assante, 'The *kar.kid/harimtu*,' 12.
33. Rebekah, Rachel, Tamar, Esther are described as attractive and beautiful, and their virginity is emphasized (Gen. 24:16; 29:17; 2 Sam. 13:1-2, 18; Est. 2:17).
34. While love presupposes 'a concrete inner disposition', it 'includes a conscious act in behalf of the person who is loved'. G. Wallis, ' אהב *'āhabh*,' *TDOT* 1:105. Isaac (Gen. 24:67), Shechem (Gen. 34:3-24), Elkanah (1 Sam. 1:5, 8) and Rehoboam (2 Chron. 11:21-22) express love through actions.
35. Women in the narrative, according to Exum (*Fragmented Women*, 86), 'are the pawns of men'.

to a tit-for-tat which eventually escalates to violent confrontations with Samson and to Philistine losses in lives and property (14:15-19; 15:1-8; 14-17). Their unsuccessful attempts to capture Samson, including using his own fellow Israelites against him (15:9-13), lead them to conclude that they can only put him down if they know the secret of his strength. The opportunity finally presents itself in Samson's relationship with Delilah.

But how can they get Delilah to cooperate in their plan? Utilizing a different approach, they make no threats to shame or kill Delilah. After all, Delilah does not seem to have any family to protect and so death threats and social pressure may not be the best tactics to get her on their side. Instead, they clearly lay out what they want her to do: 'Entice him (פתי אותו) and see (ראי) wherein his great strength [lies]' (במה כחו גדול) and 'how we can overpower him' (16:5) (במה נוכל לו). There is more at stake now than during the incident with the Timnite (cf. 14:15), since Samson continues to wreak havoc on the Philistine military and economy (14:19; 15:4-5, 7-8, 14-15). Thus, the combined force of the Philistine rulers come together to induce an unknown woman of no status or consequence to do something which they are powerless to do themselves.

The verb פתה D has the basic meaning of 'to persuade or convince' through words,[36] but it takes on a particular import in different contexts. In many cases, it has the sense of deceptive or manipulative persuasion; hence, it is often translated 'entice' or 'deceive' in English versions.[37] In a sexual context, it can have the sense of 'seduce', but this is rarely used.[38] In wisdom literature, the noun form refers to a gullible person, a simpleton who is easily deceived.[39] This implies that the Philistines see Samson as not smart enough, even though they are daunted by his colossal physical prowess.

The Philistines are upfront with Delilah about their goal – 'so we may bind him in order to debase him' (ואסרנהו לענתו). They believe that Samson's strength is magical in nature; thus the way to put his physical power under their control is to discover the proper binding ritual. In Mesopotamian religions, forms of binding and tying knots are part of incantation rituals that seek to immobilize or weaken an opponent.[40] They want Delilah to discover the magic ritual that would reduce his strength to the range of a normal human being. By approaching Delilah, the Philistines show what they think of her – a capable woman who makes her own decisions and can get the job done, a no-nonsense person who cannot be duped,

---

36. *HALOT* 3:985; *TLOT* 2:1038.
37. Deut. 11:16; 2 Sam. 3:25; Ps. 78:36; Jer. 20:10; Prov. 1:10; 16:29; 24:28.
38. Exod. 22:15 D; Job 31:9 N.
39. פתי is used fourteen times in Proverbs to describe someone who is 'credulous and weak-willed, easily seduced ... but capable of improvement'. Trevor Donald, 'Semantic Field of "Folly" in Proverbs, Job, Psalms, and Ecclesiastes,' *VT* 13 (1963): 287.
40. Mircea Eliade, 'The "God Who Binds" and the Symbolism of Knots,' in *Images and Symbols: Studies in Religious Symbolism* (New York: Sheed and Ward, 1969), 92–124, with Semitic parallels in 108–110.

and who would be attracted by a straightforward business transaction. Yet, at the same time, they expect her to have no qualms in betraying and deceiving Samson and, perhaps, even to use sexual wiles, to get him to open up.

The Philistines' end goal in binding Samson is 'to debase him' (לְעַנֹּתוֹ). ענה connotes a downward movement,[41] with ענה D having the sense of 'to humble' or 'humiliate'.[42] When used in relation to slaves, aliens, or the more vulnerable, it can mean to mistreat or oppress;[43] otherwise, it has the more general sense of 'to afflict'.[44] In sexual situations, it is commonly understood to stand for rape.[45] Disputing that the word means 'rape', Ellen van del Wolde shows that ענה in sexual situations connotes social debasement, as the woman is brought down from her honorable social status and is disgraced by her sexual violation.[46]

The objective of the Philistines then is not to kill Samson, but rather to humiliate him. This is confirmed when the Philistines paraded and ridiculed the blind Samson as public amusement to the Philistine aristocracy (16:25, 27).[47] The previous Samson-Philistine encounters show that the two are locked in a power contest, in which one party tries to show itself superior over the other.[48] By binding, imprisoning and then humiliating Samson, the Philistines are able to flaunt in the face of Samson and the Israelites that they are the ones in control, and that their and their deity's power is greater (16:23-24). As for Delilah, she may not be fully aware of the depth of the rivalry between Samson and the Philistines, but she knows that the Philistines do not intend to kill Samson.

Aside from stating Delilah's task and their objective with clarity, the Philistines are also clear-cut about the incentive – eleven hundred from each of the Philistine

---

41. Ellen van Wolde, 'Does *Innâ* Denote Rape? A Semantic Analysis of a Controversial Word,' *VT* 52 (2002): 531.

42. Deut. 8:2, 16; Isa. 58:3; 1 Kgs 11:39.

43. Gen. 15:13; 16:6; Exod. 1:11, 12; Deut. 26:6; Isa. 60:14; Exod. 22:21, 22; Gen. 31:50; 2 Sam. 7:10.

44. Num. 24:24; Isa. 53:4; Isa. 64:11 (E 64:12); Lam. 3:33; Nah. 1:12; Zeph. 3:19, where in some cases the subject is God. The nature of affliction here, however, can be understood in the sense of being brought to a low point, whether physically, emotionally or socially.

45. Gen. 34:2; Deut. 22:24, 29; Judg. 19:24; 20:5; 2 Sam. 13:12, 14, 22, 32.

46. van Wolde, *Innâ*, 543–44.

47. שׂחק D (16:25, cf. v. 27 G), means to laugh, play, or joke, but it can also have the sense of 'to mock' or 'ridicule'. *HALOT* 3:1314. As Robert Alter says, 'it seems more important for the Philistines to have him bound in order to be their plaything than actually to destroy him,' in 'Samson Without Folklore,' in *Text and Tradition*, ed. Susan Niditch (Atlanta: Scholars, 1990), 53.

48. The Samson-Philistine encounters follow a pattern: 1) it begins with Samson in an advantageous position; (2) the Philistines try to bring him down through trickery; (3) the Philistines' strategy seems to succeed and so Samson seems defeated; (4) however, Samson escapes from their trap and turns the table against them. See Athena E. Gorospe and Charles Ringma, *Judges* (Asia Bible Commentary; Carlisle: Langham Global Library, 2016), 187–89.

rulers – a huge amount,[49] which is enough to make Delilah financially independent for most of her life. Different motives have been proposed for why Delilah agrees to take money in exchange for information regarding Samson.[50] The most prominent is that she is simply a gold digger or a mercenary.[51] However, there are more positive interpretations of her actions. Bal, who thinks she's a Philistine, considers her a patriot,[52] while some class her with Jael, who lures Sisera, to save her own people.[53] But since the text does not clearly identify her as a Philistine, these interpretations are inconclusive.

However, if indeed Delilah belongs to a group of single women who are not part of a patriarchal household and do not have consistent income that comes from the land's produce, and if the relationship with Samson is a contractual arrangement that cannot provide her lifelong security, then it is understandable why Delilah feels the need to accept the Philistine offer. Caught as a pawn in the power game between two parties who are intent on ruining each other,[54] she is forced to choose the side which can give her long-term security and enable her to retain financial independence.

Who Deceives Whom?

Delilah is often regarded as betraying and deceiving Samson; this is also clearly what the Philistines' expect of her. However, Delilah exercises her independence by choosing to be straightforward with Samson, as can be seen in her opening appeal, which almost repeats word-for-word what the Philistines asked her to do: הגידה־נא לי במה כחך גדול ובמה תאסר לענותך (16:6; cf. v.5). If she wanted to deceive Samson, she would have been more indirect and not divulge the plan in such an explicit way. In addition, Delilah does not conceal the Philistines' involvement, for each time she cries out after binding him, 'The Philistines are upon you, Samson!' (vv. 9, 12, 14).[55]

---

49. If, as Robert Boling, *Judges* (AB; New York: Doubleday, 1975), 249, thinks, the 'rulers' are those of the five great Philistine cities, then the total amount is 5,500 shekels. This is three times the value of the rings from the Midianite kings (Judg. 8:26) and 550 times the annual wage of the Levite hired by Micah (Judg. 17:10).

50. Blyth, *Reimagining Delilah's Afterlives*, 79–81.

51. Webb, *Book of Judges*, 400.

52. Mieke Bal, *Lethal Love: Feminist Literary Readings of Biblical Love Stories* (Bloomington: Indiana University Press, 1987), 51; cf. Klein, 'Paradigm and Deviation', 63; Smith, 'Delilah: A Suitable Case', 109.

53. Schneider, *Judges*, 223; Susan Niditch, *Judges: A Commentary* (OTL; Louisville, Ky.: Westminster John Knox, 2008), 169.

54. Exum, 'Samson's Women', 86.

55. Betsy Merideth, 'Desire and Danger: The Drama of Betrayal in Judges and Judith', in *Anti-Covenant: Counter Reading Women's Lives in the Hebrew Bible* (ed. Mieke Bal; Sheffield: The Almond Press, 1989), 70. Cf. Exum, 'Samson's Women', 83; Bal, *Lethal Love*, 52.

Correspondingly, Samson's responses seems to indicate that he knows what is going on. First, he uses the third person plural for the subject: אִם־יַאַסְרֻנִי ('if they bind me...'; vv. 7, 11), when men are hiding in a room (vv. 9, 12), but uses the 2nd feminine singular when only Delilah is present (v. 13). Second, Samson's answers has to do with some form of binding, answering directly Delilah's question of how he can be bound. Instead of using the verb עִנָּה, however, Samson follows each binding ritual with חָלִיתִי וְהָיִיתִי כְּאַחַד הָאָדָם (vv. 7, 11, 13, 17) 'I shall be weak and become like any other man,' which is not part of the Philistines' bidding nor Delilah's entreaty. Samson seems to know that the Philistines' goal through Delilah is to weaken him and neutralize his supernatural strength.

If Samson is indeed cognizant of the plot, then he is the one repeatedly deceiving Delilah, rather than the other way around.[56] But if Samson is aware of the conspiracy, why then does he not put a stop to it and expose what is going on? Alter thinks that it is Samson's love for a high-stakes game that causes him to flirt dangerously close to the fire.[57] By winning such a game, he is able to establish his superiority over all.[58] The parallels with the riddle episode[59] highlight Samson's love for gaming, and how piqued he is when he loses. Thus, as Meredith suggests, the story is 'as much about Samson's pride and pretensions to immortality as it is about Delilah's harm to him'.[60] Samson wants to prove to everyone, especially to his opponents and to his lady love, that he is invincible and more powerful than all of them.

Games of Power

While the verbal interchange between Delilah and Samson (16:6-16) operates on several levels, the desire to be the one in control by possessing knowledge undergirds them all.[61] The most basic is that it is simply a game in which one player tries to discover what the other knows. The game ends when the player succeeds in gaining knowledge, or gives up after a few attempts. Samson, as the player with the secret knowledge, is confident, playful and amused at Delilah's misdirected efforts

---

56. Merideth, 'Desire and Danger,' 70-73.
57. Alter, 'Samson Without Folklore,' 50.
58. The same impulse is found in Samson's propounding of the riddle, which has to do with Samson trying to establish his superiority over the Philistines. Carl McDaniel, 'Samson's Riddle,' *Didaskalia* 12.2 (2001): 51-52.
59. Exum, 'Aspects of Symmetry and Balance,' 3-29.
60. Meredith, 'Desire and Danger,' 72.
61. For a detailed discussion, see Gorospe and Ringma, *Judges*, 199–204; J. Cheryl Exum, 'Harvesting the Biblical Narrator's Scanty Plot of Ground: A Holistic Approach to Judges 16:4-22,' in *Tehillah Le-Moshe: Biblical and Judaic Studies in Honor of Moshe Greenberg* (eds. Mordechai Cogan, Barry L. Eichler, Jeffrey H. Tigay; Winona Lake, IN: Eisenbrauns, 1997), 39–46.

and frustration at her repeated failures. Delilah, as the player seeking knowledge, is focused and persistent, guilt-tripping Samson into full disclosure. While these tactics are harmless and even amusing in a simple game where the strategy of each party is obvious to all, it becomes more serious when the game involves two people who seek to control each other in the guise of love, with knowledge as the decisive factor as to who win in the end. At the outset, Samson has the upper hand; not only is he immensely strong, he also possesses knowledge that Delilah wants. Hence, his attitude towards her is indulgently supercilious, like humouring a child. Delilah, at the receiving end of his condescending attitude, and repeatedly rebuffed, nevertheless continues to risk being mocked for the sake of attaining her goal.

Delilah has been characterized as a seductress[62] – a femme fatale – but the narrative does not show her using sex to gain Samson's trust,[63] even though the story itself implies a sexual relationship.[64] Rather, she uses the power of words – not flattery or inducement, but reproach. Thus, she repeatedly chides Samson for not taking her seriously and deceiving her: התלת בי ותדבר אלי כזבים ('You have trifled with me, and told me lies'; vv. 10, 13), which are all true. When this does not work, she then points to the inconsistency between his avowed love and his lack of total transparency: איך תאמר אהבתיך ולבך אין אתי ('how can you say you love me, if your heart is not with me?'; v. 15).

Nevertheless, when Samson finally gives in, it is not because he wants to prove his love for her, or that he feels guilty for deceiving her repeatedly. Rather, he responds to Delilah in the same way he did to his Timnite wife. In regard to his wife, who wept for seven days instead of rejoicing at her wedding feast, Samson finally gave in and 'he told her' (ויגד־לה) because she kept on pressing (הציקתהו) him (14:17). As for Delilah, Samson finally succumbs because she kept on pressing (הציקה) day after day (16:16), so that 'he told her' (ויגד־לה; 16:17). While the Timnite uses the power of tears, Delilah uses the power of her words.

The many parallels between the two episodes[65] highlight a personality trait in Samson when faced with intense pressure. The word for 'press' is קוץ H, which has the sense of driving someone into a corner.[66] Other incidents show how Samson wants to break free from anything that could possibly impede his freedom, like bonds and being closed in (15:14; 16:1-3).[67] Still, he submits to being bound by Delilah because he thinks he can always escape: 'I will go out as at other times, and shake myself free' (16:20, NRSV); and indeed twice, he tears off his bonds easily (16:9, 12). Samson's confidence is such that on Delilah's third attempt, he comes very close to the truth by mentioning his hair (16:13).

---

62. Blythe, *Reimagining Delilah*, 62–66; Lackowski, 'Victim, Victor, or Villain', 200–2.
63. Exum, 'Samson's Women', 86.
64. Scott B. Noegel, 'Evil Looms: Delilah – Weaver of Wicked Wiles,' *CBQ* 79 (2017): 196–97.
65. Exum, 'Aspects of Symmetry and Balance', 3–10.
66. *HALOT* 3:1014.
67. Mobley, *Empty Men*, 189.

Nevertheless, to have the feeling of being pushed into a corner becomes unbearable when prolonged. Thus, 'his spirit became impatient to death' ותקצר נפשו למות (16:16).[68] However, the literal meaning of קצר נפש 'life is shortened' suggests another nuance, that of diminishment or weakening.[69] So even as Samson is becoming impatient at being pressed, he is also weakening and is 'rendered so powerless that . . . he finally does reveal the secret of his strength'.[70]

We do not know how Delilah realized (ראה) that Samson had told her 'all his heart' (16:18, NRSV). ראה 'to see' is another *leitwort* in the Samson narrative,[71] and it can refer both to physical visibility or inner perception/recognition. In any case, what Delilah 'saw' makes her so confident that she boldly calls the Philistines, who seem to have left after her repeated failure, to 'come up this time'. And the Philistine rulers, believing that her claim is real, come back with her reward money (16:18).

Once Delilah gains the sought-for knowledge, the power advantage shifts to her side. This is indicated in the text when, as soon as Samson falls asleep after his revelation, she begins to debase (ענה) him (16:19). We do not know what form of humiliation she inflicts, whether this is physical pain or restricted movements (v. 20 seems to imply that he is bound in some way), but Delilah takes the control in the relationship, so that there is a reversal of gender positions.[72]

With the mystery of Samson's strength being shattered, there is now a convergence of perspectives among Samson, Delilah, the Philistines, and the readers. In a scenario where everyone has equal knowledge, Samson no longer has an advantage; it is the physical power of the Philistines which now dominates.

Delilah and the Mysterious Messenger

As for Delilah, she is never heard of again after the Philistines seizes Samson and binds him (16:21). In this, she is similar to the mysterious visitor who announces Samson's birth, who disappears after delivering and confirming his message (13:20-21). The numinous quality of the visitor is indicated in that while he 'appeared' to the woman (v. 3, ראה N), his identity is not known to the human characters. Like Delilah, the visitor is named, but very little is known about him. While he is called מלאך־יהוה (messenger or emissary of YHWH) in the narrative (vv. 3, 13, 15, 16, 17, 20, 21), Manoah and his wife simply refer to him as 'a man', 'the

---

68. The verb קצר 'to be short' when paired with נפש means 'to be impatient.' *DCH* 7: 286. Cf. Num. 21:4; Judg. 10:16; Zech. 11:8; Mic. 2:7; Job 21:4.

69. Robert Haak, 'A Study and New Interpretation of *qsr nps*,' *JBL* 101.2 (1982): 161–67.

70. Haak, '*qsr nps*,' 166.

71. Mark Greene, 'Enigma Variations: Aspects of the Samson Story (Judges 13–16),' *Vox Evangelica* 21 (1991): 61.

72. Delilah takes on the masculine role, while Samson is 'feminized'. See Exum, *Fragmented Women*, 84; Amy Beth W. Jones, 'The Stranger Within: Narrative Space and Identity Construction in the Book of Judges' (PhD diss., Drew University, 2014), 108–12.

man of God', or 'the man' (vv. 6, 8, 10, 11), indicating that they see him as a human person, possibly a prophet.

However, Manoah's wife senses the visitor's otherworldly character, describing his appearance (מראה, root ראה) as like the angel of God and נורא מאד ('greatly arousing fear'), so that she restrains herself from further inquiring about his identity (v. 6). Manoah, on the other hand, directly asks his name (v. 17). The answer of the emissary to Manoah's question both reveals and conceals – his name is פלאי, a word that refers to knowledge that cannot be attained – so wonderful that it cannot be explained or comprehended.[73] His identity is further obscured by other names used to refer to him: מלאך האלהים 'angel of God' (v. 9), YHWH (v. 19), while Manoah's designation is 'God' (v. 22), and his wife uses YHWH (v. 23). Thus, like Delilah, the visitor remains an enigmatic character.

Both the emissary of YHWH and Delilah are inextricably linked to Samson's destiny. It is the emissary who announces the coming child's distinctive identity – 'the boy will be a Nazirite to God from the womb' – as well as his mission – 'he will begin to deliver Israel from the control of the Philistines' (13:5). As a mark of his consecration, the boy's lifestyle is to be distinct from the rest – no alcohol from conception and his hair unshaved (vv. 4-5; cf. 7, 14). However, the emissary makes no mention of Samson's strength or its connection with his uncut hair. Nevertheless, the annunciation scene, the child's special vocation, and his mission of deliverance mark Samson as a child of promise, on whom the future hopes of the nation lie.

In the ensuing incidents, as Samson blurs the boundary lines of his separated lifestyle, his Nazirite status is no longer mentioned, and Samson operates as if he has no knowledge of it. Even when Samson's strength is unleashed against the Philistines through the action of the spirit, no mention is made of his hair or Nazirite status. This information and its significance seem to be deliberately withheld until the pivotal climax when Samson divulges it to Delilah.

It is through Delilah's persistent efforts that the connection between Samson's strength and his consecrated lifestyle as a Nazirite is finally revealed. Samson discloses what he may have known all along but has not shared with anyone – that his extraordinary strength can be attributed to his distinct calling as a Nazirite to God from the womb, as symbolized by his uncut hair (16:17). Yet Samson's confidence and sense of entitlement is such that, even after he says 'if my head were shaved, my strength would leave me, and I would become weak and be like any other man' (16:17), he does not seem to fully believe this would happen. Rather, he is convinced that he could escape as at other times (16:20a). Either he believes that the strength is inherent in him, despite what he says about the source of his strength, or he has taken for granted YHWH's favour, so that he thinks that no matter what he does, including abandoning his consecrated lifestyle, YHWH would never leave him. Thus, even after his big revelation, and despite Delilah's repeated attempts to

---

73. Prov. 30:18; Job 9:10; 37:5; 37:14; Ps. 118:23; 139:14. The root is also used for a difficult situation in which it is virtually impossible to find a solution for (Gen. 18:14; Deut. 17:8; Jer. 32:17, 27). The adj. is attested only in the feminine (Ps. 139:6).

bind him, he goes to sleep without any worry, and wakes up, 'not knowing' (לֹא יָדַע) that a fundamental change has taken place and 'that the LORD had left him' (16:20b).

The Real Mystery and Power: Beyond Human Knowledge

It is only when Samson is blinded that he finally comes to some self-insight. Before, he has always prided himself in being superior in knowledge and physical power. Thus, while Delilah's actions lead to his imprisonment and humiliation, they also enable Samson to gain true knowledge about the real source of his strength. Through Delilah, Samson is humbled (cf. 16:19) and forced to face up to what he has previously taken for granted. In his last action, he prays to Yahweh, whom he now realizes is his true strength, for a final surge of power so that he can avenge himself on the Philistines (16:28).

Thus, Delilah is the instrument of God's discipline and correction to a servant who has missed his calling, so that he can fulfil his mission to 'begin to deliver Israel from the control of the Philistines' and live up to the promise of his birth. Exum points out that Judg. 14:4 is ambiguous enough to allow for the היא in כי מיהוה היא to be translated 'she was from YHWH' instead of 'it was from YHWH'.[74] While the immediate context refers to Samson's attraction to the Timnite, it can be applied to Delilah as well. This is shown in succeeding events as YHWH uses Samson's imprisonment and death to strike a crippling blow to the Philistines, so that Samson kills more in his death than when he was alive (16:30).

This points to a mystery beyond human knowledge and control.[75] All the characters in the narrative, including Delilah, have limited knowledge and power. Despite the fact that they gain the coveted knowledge and power, they remain in the dark about the mysterious operation of YHWH who is working out a divine purpose in the very person and passions of Samson,[76] including his encounters with women (14:4). Inasmuch as Samson represents Israel,[77] his story in the context of Judges shows how Israel has been chosen by YHWH to live a consecrated life, distinct from the surrounding nations, and has been endowed with strength to fulfil God's mission. However, the people have failed to live up this destiny, and 'have become like any other man' because they have taken for granted YHWH's calling and endowment. Thus, God brings 'Delilahs' as instruments of judgement, discipline and self-insight.

---

74. Exum, 'Literary Patterns,' 122.

75. According to Exum ('Literary Patterns,' 61), 'the motif of knowing and not knowing draws attention to the mysterious ways of Yhwh, who works for Israel's benefit through and even in spite of the human participants with their limited vision.' Cf. Schipper, 'Narrative Obscurity,' 344.

76. Wharton, 'Secret of Yahweh,' 58–59.

77. Greenstein, 'Riddle of Samson,' 247–55; Lilian Klein, *The Triumph of Irony in the Book of Judges* (Sheffield: Almond Press, 1989), 116–18. See also, Gregory Wong's chapter in the present volume.

Chapter 11

SAMSON AS EVERYMAN IN ISRAEL[1]

Gregory T. K. Wong

The Anomalous Samson Cycle

Of the narratives of the six major judges that make up the bulk of the material about Israel's deliverers in Judges, the Samson narrative shows some unusual departures from the literary-rhetorical schema that brings these narratives together into a series of cycles.[2] Granted, some of these departures can be explained by the fact that the series of cycles that chronicles the heroics of these judges is not static but is subjected to an overarching progressively deteriorating trend. Therefore, it goes to reason that the Samson narrative, standing at the end of the series, would be affected by certain breakdowns of the established cyclical structure.

For example, according to the narrative framework constructed to introduce the major judges, each time Israel faced oppression by a foreign enemy, they would cry out to YHWH (3:9, 15; 4:3; 6:6-7; 10:10).[3] But in the Samson narrative, this

---

1. I am aware of the problem of using a gendered term like 'everyman' to inclusively refer to all people. I do not wish to perpetuate inappropriate gendered stereotypes, but the term is retained for three reasons. First, it is an established literary term to describe a 'type' of character (probably going back to the anonymous medieval play, *Everyman*). Second, it probably does not reflect an overly inaccurate perspective of the biblical authors, who would probably primarily mean *every man* by the use of the term everyman. Third, I am not the first to use this term to describe the various judges (see e.g., Lillian R. Klein, *The Triumph of Irony in the Book of Judges* [JSOTSup 68: Sheffield: Almond Press, 1988], 21). Thus, though it is a problematic term in our contemporary context it is retained here for its usefulness for this specific purpose.

2. Judges does not distinguish between the so-called 'major' and 'minor' judges. The designation of Othniel, Ehud, Barak, Gideon, Jephthah and Samson as 'major' in this article is mainly to reflect that only the lengthier narratives about these six judges are supplied with framework material that structures them into a series of cycles.

3. Although in the programmatic introduction to the cycles in 2:11-19, there is no mention of Israel crying out (צעק/זעק) but only that the situation had become distressing/

crying out is conspicuously absent. In fact, as the narrative unfolds, the people of Judah who represent Israel in this cycle have apparently accepted their subjugation to the Philistines and seem content to live under that status quo (15:11).[4] There was thus no crying out because as the cycles progress, Israel no longer sought deliverance.

Another example concerns the incompleteness of deliverance. While the narratives of the major judges that precede Samson all conclude with decisive victories over Israel's oppressors, Samson did not enjoy the same degree of success. In his birth narrative, the child to be born is already prophesied to only '*begin* to deliver Israel from the hand of the Philistines' (13:5). Hence, in his final act of vengeance against the Philistines, even though Samson is said to have 'killed many more when he died than while he lived' (16:30), unlike the concluding summaries of the other major judges (3:10, 30; 4:23-24; 8:24; 11:33), there is no explicit statement about the oppressors being decisively subdued.[5] That in the continuing Deuteronomistic account of the nation's history, the Philistines continue to be a major source of oppression for Israel until they were decisively subdued by David (2 Sam. 8:1) only confirms Samson's incomplete victory.

But while at first glance, such departures can readily be accounted for by the progressively deteriorating paradigm that affects even the cyclical structure that organizes the narratives of the major judges, upon closer reflection, these departures may in effect have undermined some of the carefully constructed literary-rhetorical schema that prevails throughout the book, including the aforementioned progressively deteriorating paradigm.

---

oppressive (צרר) to them, in each cycle except for the Samson cycle, Israel crying out is a constant element within the narrative framework. In the Jephthah cycle, the distress/oppressiveness (צרר) faced by Israel and Israel's crying out (זעק) even seems to be explicitly linked in a cause–result relationship (10:9-10). See also Neh. 9:27-28 where a similar relationship between these two terms exists in a passage that may be alluding to the cycles in Judges.

4. Serge Frolov ('Fire, Smoke, and Judah in Judges: A Response to Gregory Wong,' *SJOT* 21 [2007]: 130–31) suggests that the Judahites who turned Samson over to the Philistines were simply 'Judahite rabble' or 'a Judahite mob' that do not represent the tribe, let alone the nation. But is it plausible that, with the Philistines having already set up camp and their troops already spreading out (15:9), the ones who came to negotiate and with whom the Philistines consented to make a deal would be an unruly mob rather than those who had the authority to officially represent their tribe or the nation? In addition, Frolov's speculation that the Judahites who eventually handed Samson over to the Philistines were simply trying to force Samson to fight the aggressors and do what he was supposed to all along is entirely devoid of support from the text.

5. In the Othniel narrative, Othniel overpowered (עזז) the king of Aram (3:10). In the Ehud, Barak, Gideon and Jephthah narratives, the oppressors were all subdued (כנע) (3:30; 4:23; 8:28; 11:33) to the point of being cut off (4:24) (כרת), never to raise their head again (8:28) (ולא יספו לשאת ראשם).

Thematic and Theological Departures: Subverting the Cyclical Paradigm

Regarding the progressively deteriorating paradigm, I have written elsewhere about how this paradigm manifests itself not only through the breakdown of the cyclical structure that organizes the narratives of the major judges, but also through the development of numerous key themes traceable through the accounts of these judges.[6] One such theme involves the growing reluctance of YHWH to deliver his repeatedly sinning people.

In the narratives of the first major judges, Othniel, Ehud and Barak, the report of the people crying out to YHWH (3:9a,15a; 4:3) is followed almost immediately by a report of YHWH raising up for them a deliverer (3:9b,15b; 4:6-7). In the Gideon cycle, however, the people's crying out (6:6) is immediately followed by a prophetic rebuke from YHWH regarding the people's apostasy (6:7-10). It is only after the rebuke that Gideon is introduced (6:11-16). This suggests that YHWH was no longer as eager to provide quick relief to his people on account of their repeated relapses into apostasy after their deliverance in preceding cycles.

This reluctance on the part of YHWH to deliver his people is further exacerbated in the Jephthah cycle, where the people's crying out (10:10) is met with YHWH's personal rebuke and an initial refusal to help, telling them instead to cry out to the gods they were worshipping (10:11-14). It is only on account of Israel's unrelenting plea that YHWH was finally worn out by their badgering and gave in to their request.[7]

Given this progressively deteriorating relationship between YHWH and his people, one would naturally expect to see in the Samson cycle even greater reluctance or a more determined refusal on the part of YHWH to deliver his repeatedly sinning people. But surprisingly, just when the people seemed to have given up crying out altogether and have instead embraced their subjugation (15:11), YHWH took the initiative to raise up for them a deliverer. In allowing for such a plot twist, the progressively deteriorating trend concerning the relationship between YHWH and his people has effectively been reversed, thus subverting a theme that has taken five cycles to set up.

Not only so, but in the process, the very logic that underlies the cycles seems also to have been undermined. For the cyclical structure that organizes the narratives of the major judges is generally understood as comprising five stages: 1) Israel's apostasy, 2) YHWH's disciplinary action through the raising up of

---

6. Gregory T. K. Wong, *Compositional Strategy of the Book of Judges* (Leiden: Brill, 2006), 156–85.

7. Although the meaning of ותקצר נפשו בעמל ישראל in 10:16 is not immediately clear, in all four instances within the Hebrew Bible where the subject of קצר is נפש, the verb seems to carry the nuance of being worn out or becoming weary (Num. 21:4; Judg. 10:16; 16:16; Zech. 11:8). This is especially clear in the only other occurrence of this verb in Judges in 16:16, where Samson's becoming weary to the point of death is presented as a direct consequence of Delilah pressing (צוק) and badgering (אלץ) him about the secret of his strength.

oppressors, 3) Israel groaning in distress and crying out to YHWH, 4) YHWH raising up a deliverer-judge to alleviate the people's distress, and 5) peace being restored as the oppressors are subdued. It appears that in each cycle, motion is set in place by the first stage: Israel's apostasy. The subsequent stages all seem to flow out of the immediately preceding stage as a direct consequence of that stage. Thus, the raising up of oppressors (stage 2) is a direct consequence of Israel's apostasy (stage 1), the people's crying out (stage 3) is a direct consequence of oppression (stage 2), the raising up of deliverer-judges (stage 4) is a direct consequence of the people's cries of distress (stage 3), and the restoration of peace (stage 5) is a direct consequence of the raising up of deliverer-judges (stage 4).

Notice that under this scheme, the raising up of deliverer-judges (stage 4) effectively represents a reversal of YHWH's prior action in raising up oppressors (stage 2). The key that explains this reversal seems to lie in stage 3, the people's groaning and crying out to YHWH in distress. But in the Samson cycle, Israel apparently no longer feels distressed, as evident in the absence of any crying out and in their submissive acceptance of Philistine rule. If so, then what accounts for YHWH's stage 4 deliverance that reverses his stage 2 disciplinary action? With stage 3 in the cause-and-effect chain having gone missing, YHWH's action in stage 4 of the Samson cycle becomes somewhat inexplicable, such that a perspective distinct from that of the preceding cycles may have been introduced. Thus, notwithstanding the fact that the omission of stage 3 in the Samson cycle may seem on the surface to conform to the deteriorating trend that affects even the cycles, its absence may in fact have subtly subverted the theology that underlies the other cycles.

Departures in Characterization: A Flat Protagonist

Not only do the above plot twists in Samson cycle turn out upon closer examination to have possibly subverted some important themes, structures, and even theology that underlie preceding cycles, the way Samson is characterized within his cycle is also distinct from the way most other major judges are characterized.

As literary critics point out, concerning characterization in narratives, distinction is often made between flat (one-dimensional) and round (full-fledged) characters. According to Bar-Efrat, a flat character is static and is usually associated with a single character trait, whereas a round character is complex, demonstrates multiple character traits, and is perceived as changing and growing as the narrative progresses.[8] Hence, Berlin describes round characters as appearing like 'real people'.[9]

---

8. Shimon Bar-Efrat, *Narrative Art in the Bible* (trans. Dorothea Shefer-Vanson and Shimon Bar-Efrat; Sheffield: Sheffield Academic, 1989), 90.

9. Adele Berlin, *Poetics and Interpretation of Biblical Narrative* (Winona Lake: Eisenbrauns, 1994), 23.

Typically, protagonists in a narrative or narrative cycle are round characters, while characters occupying supporting roles such as agents and other functionaries usually remain flat. A possible exception is when a narrative unit is short and confined, so that the development of complex character traits or the demonstration of change and growth for the protagonist is often limited by insufficient narrative space. In such instances, a protagonist can appear rather flat. But in lengthier narratives or narrative cycles, the protagonist is almost invariably round.

Looking at how the major judges are characterized in Judges, it seems that the majority of major judges conform to expectation in terms of character type. Granted, the first judges, Othniel, Ehud and Barak, do come across as relatively flat, but this is likely due to the brevity of the narratives about them, thus not leaving sufficient room for character development.[10] But as the narratives of the next three major judges increase in length, narrative space opens up to allow for greater character development. Indeed, Gideon's transformation from timid and fearful before the battle against the Midianites to ruthless and assertive after his victory, and Jephthah's agony and regret regarding the rash and manipulative vow he made to secure a favourable outcome in war both testify to the fact that, with the opening up of greater narrative space, the protagonists emerge as round characters as protagonists should. But Samson appears to be an exception.

Although in terms of narrative space, the Samson cycle is comparable to those of Gideon and Jephthah, yet this protagonist is surprisingly flat.[11] In fact, one can argue that through the multiple episodes that make up the Samson cycle, almost no character development is detectable in Samson's portrayal, so much so that in terms of desire, type of action taken, and motivation, Samson hardly changed from his first appearance to his last. This is most clearly seen in two areas: his enduring obsession with Philistine women, and personal vengeance as primary motivation for actions taken against the Philistines.

Enduring Obsession with Philistine Women In Samson's first appearance, the first thing he did was to ask his parents to get for him a Philistine woman he saw in Timnah to be his wife. That this woman remains nameless throughout but is only characterized as Philistine (14:1-2) suggests that it is her ethnic rather than personal identity that is of significance. And it is precisely on account of her

---

10. The Othniel narrative comprises eighty words in the Hebrew text, the Ehud narrative 294, and the Barak narrative 419 excluding Deborah's Song in Judges 5. Judges 5 is excluded primarily because it is a poetic recounting of essentially the same events narrated in Judges 4 and does not represent a continuation of the narrative in Judges 4. Furthermore, as I have argued elsewhere (Gregory T. K. Wong, 'Song of Deborah as Polemic,' *Bib* 88 [2007]: 1–22), the nature of the song is polemical and is perhaps best taken as a commentary on the events of Judges 4, with its focus on the participation/non-participation of the tribes rather than on the exploits of Israel's deliverer judge.

11. The Gideon cycle (6:1–8:35) comprises 1709 words in the Hebrew text; the Jephthah cycle (10:6–12:7) 1099 words, and the Samson cycle (13:1–16:31), 1602 words.

being Philistine that Samson's parents initially expressed reservations about a marriage alliance, suggesting instead that an Israelite woman would have been a better choice (14:3). But Samson insisted. As it turns out, at their wedding feast, under threat from her fellow countrymen who had no intention of losing a bet regarding a riddle Samson had set for them, the woman nagged Samson day after day until he finally divulged the riddle's answer to her. Consequently, Samson lost his bet. Although Samson initially went away in anger and apparently did not consummate the marriage, he later returned to seek the woman out, likely intending to pick things up from where he left them. Rebuffed by the would-be father-in-law, who explained that the woman had already been given to another in marriage, Samson sought revenge by burning up the Philistines' harvest. The series of events that ensued culminated in Samson being bound and handed over to the Philistines to be killed. It was only when the Spirit of YHWH came upon Samson at the critical moment that he was delivered as he struck down a thousand Philistines with a donkey's jawbone.

One would have thought the unfolding of this series of events should have shown Samson the dangers of being enamoured with foreign women who are not beyond betraying him. But he never learned. In each of the two remaining narratives in the cycle, Samson continued to get involved with Philistine women, and echoes of his previous misadventure continue to appear in both narratives, highlighting a pattern of behaviour that seems to remain unchanged over time.

In the brief episode in 16:1-3, Samson went to Gaza, and there he sought the services of a prostitute. Although the text never specifies the ethnicity of the prostitute, it is only natural to assume she was Philistine, as Gaza was one of five main Philistine cities. The episode is extremely brief and tersely worded, but one can still find similarities with the preceding narrative involving Samson's would-be wife.

First, the opening of both episodes is remarkably similar. The preceding narrative opens in 14:1 with 'Samson went down to Timnah and saw a woman in Timnah among the daughters of the Philistines (וירד שמשון תמנתה וירא אשה בתמנתה מבנות פלשתים).' Here, 'to see (ראה)' and related concepts seem significant, for not only did Samson mention again in 14:2 that he saw (ראיתי) the Philistine woman when he asked his parents to get her for him, in response to their reservations, he justified his request by claiming that she was right in his eyes (כי־היא ישרה בעיני) (14.3). In fact, the narrator draws attention to this again as he highlights in 14:7 that the woman was right in Samson's eyes (ותישר בעיני שמשון). What this suggests is that Samson was a man ruled by his eyes, such that what drove him was what looked attractive to him.

Interestingly, this perspective appears to be subtly reinforced in the episode involving the Gaza prostitute. The opening of this episode in 16:1, 'Samson went to Gaza and saw a woman there, a prostitute, and he went to her (וילך שמשון עזתה וירא־שם אשה זונה ויבא אליה)' closely parallels 14:1. Now had the author simply wanted to convey the fact that Samson visited a prostitute in Gaza, he could have simply said, 'Samson went to Gaza and went to a prostitute' without needing to mention that he saw her before going to her. One therefore suspects that this detail about Samson first seeing the prostitute before going to her represents an attempt to link this incident to the preceding one, showing again that Samson's actions were driven by what he saw.

But there is more. Just as the series of events related to Samson's marriage to the woman in Timnah ended up bringing him nothing but trouble, eventually even imperilling his life, Samson's dalliance with the Gaza prostitute also brought a similar danger. For the people of Gaza, having found out that Samson was in town but apparently not knowing which house he was in, surrounded the town that night and lay in wait for him, intending to kill him when he leaves at dawn. But Samson eluded their ambush by leaving in the night, taking with him the doors of the city gate, which he tore off as a show of strength. So, this represents the second time Samson imperilled his own life on account of what looked to him to be an attractive Philistine woman.

But this was not to be his last. While Samson was able to remain largely unharmed the first two times he got involved with Philistine women, the third time proves to be his downfall. The narrative about Samson and Delilah resurrects many of the same themes that appeared in the narrative involving Samson's would-be wife, so much so that the Samson-Delilah narrative is almost set up as version 2.0 of the earlier narrative.

Like the Gaza prostitute, that Delilah was Philistine is never explicitly stated in the text. But the Valley of Sorek where she lived was Philistine territory at the time.[12] In fact, at the southern slope of this valley was Timnah where Samson's would-be wife lived. That Delilah had a cosy relationship with the Philistine rulers and was willing to collude with them to trap Samson reveal where her allegiance lay, thus making it likely that she was Philistine.[13]

---

12. Although according to Josh. 19:40-48, the area around the Valley of Sorek was allotted to the tribe of Dan, Josh. 19:47 and Judg. 1:34; 18:1 clearly indicates that Dan was unable to take possession of their allotted territory. The area originally allotted to Dan was apparently occupied by the Philistines through the period of the judges.

13. While James L. Crenshaw (*Samson: A Secret Betrayed, a Vow Ignored* [Atlanta: John Knox, 1978], 92) and most others accept the assumption that Delilah was Philistine, J. Cheryl Exum (*Fragmented Women: Feminist (Sub)versions of Biblical Narratives* [JSOTSup 163; Sheffield: JSOT Press, 1993], 69) wonders why Delilah cannot be Israelite, given her Hebrew name and the fact that she lived on the boundary between Israelite and Philistine territory. But that Delilah's name sounds Hebrew does not mean she cannot be Philistine. For although the Philistines probably originated from central to eastern Mediterranean, as Brent David, Aren M. Maeir, and Louis A. Hitchcock ('Disentangling Entangled Objects: Iron Age Inscriptions from Philistia as a Reflection of Cultural Processes,' *IEJ* 65 [2015]: 140–66) conclude in their examination of Iron Age inscriptions from Philistine-occupied areas, Philistine culture was eclectic and the people were probably multilingual owing to prolonged contacts with different ethnic groups throughout their migration history. That may be why words and names found in these inscriptions have variously been identified as having Semitic, Aegean, and other Indo-European (Anatolian) origins. This means a Philistine woman having a Semitic name may not be an unusual phenomenon.

Further similarities can be found between Delilah and Samson's would-be wife. Although when introducing Delilah, concepts relating to 'seeing' are no longer present, the statement that Samson 'loved' Delilah (16:4) reminds one of Samson's would-be wife, as both women ended up using Samson's love as leverage against him (14:16; 16:15).

Notwithstanding Samson's love for them, both women betrayed him at the behest of others: his would-be wife because her life and those of her household were threatened, and Delilah because she stood to gain a lucrative sum should she cooperate with the Philistine rulers.[14] While the impetus for each woman's betrayal may be different, the nature and means of their betrayals are similar as each was told to coax (Piel of פתה) a secret out of Samson (14:15; 16:5). So, while Samson's would-be wife wept before him every day at their wedding feast and accused him of hating her and not loving her (14:16-17) (רק־שנאתני ולא אהבתני), Delilah also nagged Samson every day and questioned his proclamation of love (16:15-16) (איך תאמר אהבתיך). And their strategies apparently hit Samson at his weak spot. For when Samson's would-be wife kept pressing him (הציקתהו) daily (14:17), and Delilah did the same with her words (הציקה לו בדבריה) to the point of wearying him to death (16:16), Samson gave in both times and divulged the secret that put him at a disadvantage in one case and imperilled his life in the other. This strong parallel between the two incidents thus shows that Samson never learned from his past experience: in spite of having once suffered from giving in to the persistent nagging of a woman he loved, he repeated the same mistake again.

Therefore, to the extent that Samson's repeated and reckless involvement with one Philistine woman after another constitutes an obsession, one can say that that enduring obsession that started from his first appearance and continued until his tragic death shows that there was little change or growth in the way he is characterized. In this respect, Samson the protagonist is uncharacteristically flat.

Personal Vengeance as Primary Motivation for the Actions Samson Took against the Philistines Not only is this lack of change or growth in Samson's characterization clearly on display in relation to his enduring obsession with Philistine women, it is equally so in relation to personal vengeance as primary motivation for the actions he took against the Philistines.

Although in his birth narrative, it is revealed that Samson would begin to deliver Israel from the hands of the Philistines (13:5), Samson never took this calling to heart.[15] From the three successive narratives chronicling his involvement

---

14. Although the text never discloses any personal information about Delilah, the fact that she consented to maintaining a relationship (and most likely a physical one) with Samson for financial gain casts her in the role of a prostitute. This creates a tantalising link that may well connect her with the Gaza prostitute in the preceding episode.

15. Citing the lack of any mention of Samson's future military role when Samson's mother reported her experience to her husband and noting how the angel also did not disclose this information again when Manoah requested instructions, Robert B. Chisholm Jr ('Identity

with Philistine women, it is clear that instead of seeking opportunities to deliver his people from Philistine oppression, all Samson wanted was to form relationships with their women. In fact, after Samson's parents expressed reservations about his desire to marry a Philistine in 14:3, the narrator's comment that they did not know Samson's request was from YHWH is telling. Rather than condoning Samson's request, a likelier explanation for this comment is that realizing how, left on his own, Samson would not have taken any action against the Philistines, YHWH was allowing the proposed marriage to proceed in order to create an occasion where Samson would end up striking the Philistines.

In support of this explanation, one simply needs to note that even though Samson ended up acting against the Philistines or Philistine interest on six occasions, on each, the action he took was reactive, motivated by personal vengeance in response to what the Philistines did or intended to do to him rather than proactively seeking the deliverance of his people.

Of the six occasions, two were out of self-defence in response to Philistine attempts to kill him when he was bound and handed over to them for slaughtering many of them (15:8-15) and when the Philistines set up an ambush against him in Gaza (16:2-3). In the former, he ended up killing a thousand Philistines with a donkey's jawbone, and in the latter, he dismantled and took away the doors of the city gate, thus weakening the city's defences.

But on the four remaining occasions, Samson's actions against the Philistines were all motivated by personal vengeance. On the first occasion, prompted by the spirit of YHWH, Samson went to Ashkelon and struck down thirty Philistines and took their garments to pay off the bet he lost when betrayed by his would-be wife (14:19). Although here, the text never explicitly describes Samson's action as motivated by vengeance, there are hints that it was so. First, before Samson set out for Ashkelon, his remarks about the Philistines ploughing with his heifer shows that he was aware that his Philistine groomsmen had used his would-be wife to obtain the answer to his riddle. Second, even after striking down the thirty Philistines and using their garments to pay off his bet, Samson was still burning with anger (14:9), so much so that he went straight back to his father's house without consummating the marriage. This shows the extent of his fury at having

---

Crisis: Assessing Samson's Birth and Career,' *BibSac* 166 [2009]: 150–55) argues that Samson was never aware of his role as YHWH's chosen deliverer. But this is an argument from silence. Surely Samson's parents must have told their son about the circumstances surrounding his birth, for when Samson divulged the secret of his strength to Delilah, he seemed keenly aware that he was נזיר אלהים from birth (16:17). It is unlikely that growing up, Samson never asked about the meaning and significance of a status he safeguarded, or that his mother, herself a victim of Philistine oppression when the angel first appeared to her, would forget the all-important announcement that her son would be the one to begin delivering her people from their oppressors. Besides, in Samson's first prayer to YHWH, he identified himself as 'your servant' (עבדך) when speaking of the victory he just had against the Philistines (15:18), thus showing that he was likely aware of the substance of his calling.

been betrayed. His attack against the Philistines in Ashkelon can thus reasonably be viewed as an act of personal vengeance against the Philistines for having made a fool out of him, and at his wedding, no less.

Next, in 15:3-5, we see Samson burning the Philistines' entire season of harvest. What precipitated this attack was Samson's discovery that his would-be wife had already been given to another so that he could no longer consummate his marriage with her. Samson's destruction of Philistine harvest was therefore an act of vengeance against the Philistines, likely brought on by the belief that they have colluded to deprive him of what should have rightfully been his. This, in fact, is also how the Philistines saw the matter, as their explanation for Samson's action confirms (15:6). In addition, I have argued elsewhere that there may have been a textual error in the MT in 15:3, such that Samson's declaration before he sprang into action may in fact read, 'This time I will avenge myself (נקמתי) against the Philistines when I do them harm' instead of 'I will be absolved (נקיתי) before the Philistines . . .'.[16] If so, then it is beyond doubt that Samson's action on this occasion was also motivated by personal vengeance.

Shortly thereafter, Samson struck down many Philistines in response to what they did to his would-be wife and father-in-law (15:7). When the Philistines found out it was Samson who destroyed their season's harvest but were unable to find him, they took it out on his would-be wife and her father by burning them to death. His anger against his would-be wife and father-in-law notwithstanding, Samson apparently took this as a personal affront. His explicit statement in 15:7 that he would avenge himself (נקם) against them for what they did again makes it clear that Samson's slaughter of the Philistines on this occasion was also motivated by personal vengeance.

Samson's final attack against the Philistines was after he was captured and blinded and made sport of in the aftermath of the Delilah affair. As he was brought out at Dagon's Temple to entertain those present, Samson prayed for strength, and in a suicide mission, pushed down the supporting pillars of the temple, thus killing himself and thousands of Philistines present. Although the narrator made it a point to note that on this occasion, Samson killed many more Philistines through his death than while he lived, Samson's final prayer makes it clear that even in his last hurrah, he was acting only out of personal vengeance and not out of concern for the deliverance of his people. For his prayer was for strength so that he could 'avenge myself (נקם) against the Philistines for my two eyes with one act of vengeance' (16:28).

Thus, even in death, Samson's concern was still just for himself, to seek vengeance for perceived wrong of a personal nature. Thus, one can say that Samson was merely an accidental deliverer for Israel, because from beginning to end, he never had the deliverance of his people in mind and may not have acted against the Philistines at all had they not first wronged him. And to the extent that he was

---

16. Gregory T. K. Wong, 'Unearthing Text-Critical possibilities through Lexical-Syntactic Analysis: A Case Study from Judg 15:3,' *BZ* 65 (2021): 299–307.

consistently motivated only by personal vengeance, such that he had neither given much thought to his calling nor grown into it, with respect to his life's mission, Samson's character is again static, and therefore, very flat.

Making Sense of the Anomalies

The above observations seem to indicate that the Samson cycle is more than just a cycle like those of the other major judges. Indeed, the many anomalies cited suggests that behind the Samson cycle lies an agenda that subtly stands out from that which governs the overall series of cycles. So, why is such an anomalous cycle included in the book and even used as a conclusion to the series of cycles? To answer this question, perhaps one should begin with the unusual flatness of Samson's characterization.

As mentioned earlier, in narratives, where narrative space permits, major characters, especially protagonists, are usually crafted as round characters with emotions and struggles and dynamic character developments. But on occasion, one does find major characters that remain rather flat throughout a narrative. When that happens, these characters often function more as a type than a true protagonist.

Take Abigail, for example. Although Abigail occupies a crucial role in 1 Samuel 25 as the heroine who singlehandedly averted potential disasters for all, functionally, she seems merely to typify the kind of wise and discerning woman who would make an ideal wife. For her character seems to revolve around this single character trait with little further character development. Indeed, after that narrative concludes with David taking her as wife, Abigail largely disappears from view and all further mentions of her within the Hebrew Bible (1 Sam. 27:3; 30:5; 2 Sam. 2:2; 3:3; 1 Chron. 3:1) have to do with her status as one of David's wives.

Another example is Jezebel. Given her role of antagonist par excellence within the Ahab-Elijah narratives, she is portrayed as consistently wicked. Unlike Ahab, her partner-in-crime who at least humbled himself before YHWH when rebuked for his role in the Naboth incident (1 Kgs. 21:27-29), not once has Jezebel veered from her villainous role. So, while she is undoubtedly a major character within those narratives, the flatness of her characterization signals that functionally, she typifies the idolatrous foreign wife who manages to turn Israel and her kings from following YHWH.

In fact, in very brief narratives where there is insufficient narrative space for character development, even a flat protagonist can also function as a type. That is why Othniel, the judge who begins the series of cycles in Judges, is often spoken of as typifying the ideal deliverer-judge who sets the standard against which all other deliver-judges are measured.[17]

---

17. Thus, Robert G. Boling, *Judges: A New Translation with Introduction and Commentary* (AB 6A; New York: Doubleday, 1975), 82; Daniel I. Block, *Judges, Ruth* (NAC 6; Nashville: Broadman & Holman, 1999), 149–50; J. Clinton McCann, *Judges* (Louisville: John Knox, 2002), 43.

Therefore, does Samson flatness indicate that he is being set up as a type? If so, what or who does he typify? As it turns out, Samson may have been crafted to typify Israel.

That Samson is Israel can be seen in two ways: from plot parallels between Samson's life and Israel's history, and from Samson's engagement in the same kind of action as the rest of the nation that brought chaos to Israelite society in those days.

Plot Parallels between Samson's Life and Israel's History

Regarding plot parallels between Samson's life and Israel's history, it has been well-noted that in many respects, the way the Samson narrative unfolds parallels the way Israel's history unfolds, so much so that one can say that Samson is a microcosm for the nation.[18] This can be seen in the following ways.

To begin, both Israel and Samson were chosen and set apart by YHWH even before they came into being. Where Samson is concerned, when the divine messenger appeared to his mother and gave her instructions about the child to be born, he told her, 'You are barren and cannot bear a child, but you will conceive and bear a son' (13:3). This suggests that Samson was not yet conceived when the message was delivered.[19] And yet, he was already marked out as a נזיר אלהים (13:5).

Because of this designation, and because the related stipulations regarding how Samson was to be raised closely parallel stipulations in Num. 6:2-21 concerning Nazirites, scholars generally take Samson to be a Nazirite. But perhaps there is room for reconsideration.

---

18. See detailed discussions by Edward L. Greenstein ('The Riddle of Samson,' *Proof* 1 [81]: 247–55). Others who hold a similar view include Kenneth R. R. Gros Louis, 'The Book of Judges,' in *Literary Interpretations of Biblical Narratives* (eds. Kenneth R. R. Gros Louis, J. S. Ackerman, and T. S. Warsaw; Nashville: Abingdon, 1974), 161-62, Barry G. Webb, 'A Serious Reading of the Samson Story (Judges 13–16),' *RTR* 54 (1995): 116–17, Dennis T. Olson, 'The Book of Judges,' in *New Interpreter's Bible*, Vol. 2 (Nashville: Abingdon, 1998), 842–43; 860–61, and Stephen M. Wilson, 'Samson the Man-Child: Failing to Come of Age in the Deuteronomistic History,' *JBL* 133 (2014): 57–59.

19. Chisholm ('Identity Crisis,' 148-49) argues that והרית in 13:3 can be translated as 'you *are* pregnant' instead of 'you will conceive'. But the fact that both the narrator (13:2) and the divine messenger (13:3) refer specifically to the woman's barrenness seems to cast the narrative as an annunciation of miraculous birth type scene. If the woman was already pregnant when the divine messenger appeared to her, and if, as Chisholm suggests, her pregnancy may have resulted from her having relations with Manoah shortly before the divine messenger appeared, then technically, she was not barren, and the divine messenger did not appear to announce a miraculous birth but simply to disclose information about the child to be born. In that case, it would have been entirely unnecessary to even bring up, let alone highlight, the barrenness issue.

First, as many have pointed out, other than the issue about the hair, Samson's supposed Nazirite status does not seem to play any role within the narrative. Thus, some have wondered if the designation נזיר אלהים may in fact be a later interpolation or if the cycle was a product of separate stories artificially joined together without enough attention being paid to overall coherence.[20]

Second, notwithstanding the similarities between the divine messenger's instructions to Samson's mother and the Nazirite stipulations found in Numbers 6, a closer look reveals differences that are not insignificant. While the prohibition from consuming product from the vine seems to apply in both cases, the prohibition against the consumption of unclean food, however, is not part of the Nazirite stipulations. Instead, the Nazirite stipulation concerning prohibition from contact with corpses that features prominently in Num. 6:6-12 is not mentioned at all in the instructions to Samson's mother.[21]

Furthermore, while according to Numbers 6, the Nazirite status was essentially voluntary and temporary, Samson's 'Naziriteship' was imposed upon him and life-long. But how does a life-long 'Naziriteship' actually work? For according to Numbers 6, on account of the voluntary and temporary nature of Naziriteship, if someone who has taken the Nazirite vow violates a key stipulation such as having contact with a corpse, that person's Naziriteship is immediately terminated, such that he/she needs to be reconsecrated for that status to be reactivated (Num. 6:9-12). But was that also true for Samson? After he ate honey from the lion's corpse, thus violating the prohibition from eating unclean food, did that affect his supposed Nazirite status? Did he need to, or did he do anything to keep or reactivate that status? And between when Samson's hair was shaved and when it eventually grew back, was he still a Nazirite? Or was that status essentially unaffected by the violation of any stipulation that came with it since it was life-long? Given the above differences, one has to concede that even if Samson was a Nazirite, he was not a Nazirite in the same sense as those described in Numbers 6.

How then should one understand Samson's status as a נזיר אלהים? To answer this question, one should note that the main idea behind the root נזר has to do primarily with separating from or being set apart for someone or something.[22] Hence, the

---

20. See, among others, Crenshaw (*Samson*, 73–74) for the first view and Marc Z. Brettler (*The Book of Judges* [London: Routledge, 2002], 43–44, 59–60) for the second.

21. This may be because such a stipulation would be unobservable for Samson, whose calling to deliver his people would naturally necessitate some killing of the oppressors.

22. The idea of separation can be seen in Lev. 15:31, where the Israelites were commanded to keep away (נזר) from women with bodily discharges, and in Judg. 16:3, where the word is used of abstaining (נזר) from products of the vine. As for being set apart or dedicating oneself for someone or something, in Hos. 9:10, Israel was rebuked for dedicating themselves to shameful idols (נזר לבשת). While these two nuances seem to convey somewhat opposing concepts, they may in fact be two sides of the same coin, since setting someone or something apart for a specific purpose will inevitably mean separating that someone or something from other competing commitments.

root connotes 'to consecrate', and by extension, 'to be chosen/elected' if that consecration is ordained from an external source. The Nazirites are thus so called because they have set themselves apart or consecrated themselves to YHWH (Num. 6:2).

Notice that although six out of sixteen instances of נזיר in the Hebrew Bible are found in Numbers 6 and refer specifically to the Nazirites, the term is also used in other instances to refer to those set apart who were not Nazirites. In Jacob's blessing in Gen. 49:26 and Moses' blessing of the tribes in Deut. 33:16, Joseph is referred to in both cases as 'the one set apart among his brothers (נזיר אחיו)'.[23] In Lam. 4:7, the word also seems to be referring to the chosen elite who were set apart from common folks within Israelite society and not to the class of Nazirites.[24] This means it is entirely possible that when Samson was designated as נזיר אלהים (13:5, 7) and when he disclosed his status as such to Delilah (16:17), what was conveyed was simply that he was someone set apart by/for God rather than specifically that he was a Nazirite in the Numbers 6 sense of the term.[25]

In support of this interpretation, note that Num. 6:2 has already made it clear that taking the Nazirite vow is for the purpose of setting oneself apart specifically for YHWH (להזיר ליהוה), so that in the remaining discussion of Nazirite stipulations, anyone who undertakes this commitment is simply referred to as נזיר/הנזיר without further qualifiers. But in Judg. 13:5, 7; 16:17, Samson is consistently referred to as נזיר אלהים, the genitive qualifier 'to God' being somewhat superfluous if indeed, the class of Nazirites is in view. But if instances of נָזִיר within the Samson cycle simply refer to someone who is chosen or set apart, then the genitive qualifier would not be redundant as it serves to clarify who set him apart ('by God') or the purpose for which he was set apart ('for God').

As for the similarities between the instructions associated with Samson and the Nazirite stipulations as outlined in Numbers 6, it may simply represent an attempt to present Samson as someone set apart by/for God much like the Nazirite were without necessarily equating the two, the differences between the two sets of rules serving to distinguish them from each other. This emphasis on Samson being

---

23. Although in these two verses, נזיר is often given the nuance 'prince' in lexicons and is so translated in the NIV and NRSV, support for such a translation is lacking both from usage and from cognate languages.

24. The editors of BHS have proposed reading נזיריה (her chosen ones) in 4:7 as נעריה (her young men). But this proposed emendation is highly conjectural as it has no manuscript support.

25. Incidentally, LXX[B] (Codex Vaticanus) renders נזיר אלהים in Judg. 13:7 and 16:17 as ἅγιον/ἅγιος θεοῦ ('a holy one of God'). Although various explanations have been offered for this variant, it is possible that an ancient reviser of the Greek translation understood the Hebrew term as merely referring to Samson's status as someone consecrated by/for God rather than in the technical sense as a Nazirite. Among contemporary English translations, NET also consistently renders נזיר אלהים in Judges as 'dedicated to God' without using the term 'Nazirite'.

someone set apart by/for God much as the Nazirites were may in fact be for the purpose of presenting him as a type of Israel.[26]

For just as Samson was set apart by/for God even before his conception, Israel too was set apart as YHWH's chosen people even before they became a nation. In Deut. 7:6, Israel is said to be a people holy to YHWH as they were chosen out of all the peoples on earth to be YHWH's treasured possession. Deut. 10:15 further explains that Israel's election was due to the fact that YHWH has set his affection on their forefathers and loved them, so that Israel as their descendants was chosen above the nations. That YHWH promised to make Abraham's descendants into a great nation and to establish a covenant with them to be their God even before Abraham had a son (Gen. 12:2; 17:7) means that before Israel came into being, it was already set apart by/for YHWH.

Unfortunately, neither Samson nor Israel took their calling and election to heart. In fact, certain episodes within the Samson cycle mirror some of the history of Israel's failures as a nation.

For example, after Samson had just experienced a great deliverance when the spirit of YHWH enabled him to kill a thousand Philistine with a donkey's jawbone, he complained to YHWH about his thirst. Playing on the word 'hand' (יד), he reminded YHWH that even though YHWH had just worked a great deliverance by his hand (ביד־עבדך), should he die of thirst, he would then fall back into the hand of the uncircumcised (ביד הערלים) from whom he was just delivered (15:18). In other words, what Samson was asserting is that should YHWH fail to relieve his thirst, then the great deliverance he had just accomplished would effectively be nullified and rendered pointless. No wonder Exum characterizes Samson's prayer as an attempt to 'bait the deity'.[27]

This echoes a similar series of events in Israel's history that also involves a pressing need for water to drink. In Exod. 15:22–17:7, three incidents are recorded that concern the provision of food and water soon after Israel crossed the Red Sea and was free of their Egyptian pursuers. That the three incidents are intended to be taken together as a series can be seen in that not only are they united by the same subject matter distinct from those of the immediately surrounding narratives, they are also introduced similarly, each with a brief progress report indicating the starting point of that stage of Israel's journey to the place where the incident occurred. Moreover, the three incidents also seem to be structured chiastically, with the central and most detailed incident involving the provision of quail and

---

26. In his discussion, Greenstein ('The Riddle,' 247, 249) sees Samson's Naziriteship as representative of Israel's covenant with YHWH. But perhaps a better parallel would be to focus on both being set apart by/for YHWH. After all, a covenant is generally entered upon by both parties, whereas in Samson's case, he did not have a choice in terms of his status. Besides, as discussed above, there are still too many questions regarding whether or not Samson was in fact a Nazirite.

27. J. Cheryl Exum, 'Aspects of Symmetry and Balance in the Samson Saga,' *JSOT* 19 (1981): 23.

manna (Exod. 16:1-36) bracketed by two shorter accounts of provisions of water to drink (Exod. 15:22-27; 17:1-7). A closer look reveals several similarities between this series of events and Samson's prayer for water.

First, both Israel's and Samson's complaints about their respective physical needs came not long after YHWH had accomplished a significant deliverance for each. Yet their complaints so soon after experiencing deliverances betray a lack of faith in their deliverer.

Second, both complaints mentioned the prospect of imminently death by thirst, these being the only time in each book 'to die' מות and 'thirst' צמא are used together, with the latter functioning as the cause of death through the ב preposition. But not only is the phrasing similar, the role 'dying by thirst' plays within each narrative is also similar. While Samson was trying to force YHWH's hand by reminding him that the deliverance he had just accomplished would be rendered pointless if he allows Samson to die of thirst, in Israel's case, their grumbling that Moses had brought them out of Egypt to have them die of thirst (Exod. 17:3) also implies the rendering of the deliverance YHWH had just accomplished pointless because they would die anyway. Thus, in both cases, 'dying of thirst' represents the prospect of the nullification of recent deliverances.

Third, despite this lack of faith in YHWH on the part of Samson and Israel, YHWH still responded to their complaints by providing water for each to drink, and both times from rocky formations.[28] In fact, in both narratives, the report that 'water will come out/came out from it (ויצאו ממנו מים)' (Exod. 17:6; Judg. 15:19) represents the only two times this combination of words appears in the Hebrew Bible. And both narratives also end with an etiological note about the place being named to reflect what had taken place (Exod. 17:7; Judg. 15:19).

From the above, it seems clear that in the praying-for-water episode, Samson was intentionally cast in the mould of Israel, such that the whole incident is evocative of Israel's lack of faith soon after they experienced a great deliverance out of Egypt.

But lacking in faith was apparently not Israel's only problem, nor was it Samson's. Although Israel was set apart for YHWH to be a people exclusive to himself, Israel seems to have an obsession for things foreign, especially foreign gods.

In the programmatic introduction to the cycles (2:7) as well as in the framework material for every major judge (3:7, 12; 4:1; 6:1, 10:6; 13:1), it is mentioned that Israel 'did evil in the eyes of YHWH'. That this evil refers primarily to idolatry can be seen in that in the majority of occurrences of this description in the Hebrew Bible, context clearly identifies the evil as idolatry.[29] Within Judges, the evil is likewise specified in 2:11, 3:7, 10:6 as worshipping the Baals and the Asherahs.

---

28. In Samson's case, YHWH provided water by splitting open the מכתש, a rare noun that only occurs elsewhere in the Hebrew Bible in Prov. 27:22, where it refers to a basin-like mortar for grinding grain. Thus, in Judg. 15:19, it most likely refers to a basin-like rocky structure.

29. See, for example, Deut. 4:25; 9:16-18; 17:2-3; 1 Kgs. 11:6-7; 14:22-23; 16:25-26, 30-31; 21:25-26; 22:51-53 (Eng); 2 Kgs. 17:17; 21:2-3, 6, 20-21; 2 Chron. 33:2-3, 6, 22.

But not only did Israel have a penchant for serving foreign gods, this tendency may even have reached obsessive proportions. After all, even though Israel's pursuit of foreign gods never brought them anything but grief as their waywardness kept provoking YHWH to anger so that he kept giving them over to their oppressors, still Israel never stopped running after these gods. Surely, such reckless pursuit of something to the point of ignoring all resulting harm is a clear sign of obsession.

But if Israel was suffering from a bad case of obsession, so was Samson. As has already been pointed out, despite the fact that every involvement Samson had with Philistine women either imperilled his life or brought him trouble, he seemed unable to resist being drawn to them. Considering how in the Hebrew Bible, involvement with idols is often spoken of in the language of having illicit relationships with undesirable women, Samson's obsessive pursuit of Philistine (hence, foreign and undesirable) women may indeed be symbolic of Israel's obsessive pursuit of foreign gods.[30]

There is one final possible plot parallel between Samson and Israel, and it concerns the manner of Samson's downfall. In the Delilah incident, after Samson revealed the secret of his strength, Delilah had his hair shaved while he was sleeping. In what may be the sorriest statement of the whole narrative, when Samson awoke to Delilah's call that the Philistines were upon him, he thought he could simply go out against them as before, entirely unaware that YHWH had left him. The pathos of that statement reminds one of Israel's downfall when the nation fell to the invading Babylonians. For far too long, Israel had taken for granted the protection YHWH afforded them, so that they firmly believed that as long as YHWH resides in his temple in Jerusalem, they would be protected from attacks of invaders. Not only was this thinking reflected in some of the Songs of Zion (e.g. Pss. 46; 47), it was also evident through the dismissal of prophetic warnings by those who resorted to the mantra, 'This is the Temple of YHWH, the Temple of YHWH, the Temple of YHWH' (Jer. 7:2-11). It was only belatedly revealed after the nation had gone into exile that unbeknown to them, the glory of YHWH had already departed from his Temple and the city on account of their sin shortly before the arrival of the invaders (Ezek. 10–11).

To be sure, whether Samson's oblivion of YHWH's departure that precipitated his downfall was crafted to typify Israel's similar oblivion of YHWH's departure that precipitated hers depends to large extent on when the Samson narrative was composed/redacted. If, as many scholars believe, Judges, and by extension the Samson cycle, was composed/redacted in the exilic period, and if its author/redactor was well aware of prophetic traditions associated with Jeremiah and Ezekiel, then it is indeed possible that the account of Samson's

---

30. For the use of זנה 'to engage in illicit relationships/harlotry' to describe involvement with foreign gods, see Exod. 34:15-16; Lev. 17:7; 20:5-6; Deut. 31:16; Judg. 2:17; 8:27, 33; 1 Chron. 5:25; 2 Chron. 21:11; Jer. 3:6, 8; Ezek. 6:9; 20:30; 23:30; Hos. 4:12.

downfall was crafted to symbolize the fall of Jerusalem and Judah under similar circumstances.[31]

But even if this last parallel is tentative, the other parallels cited above between Samson's life and Israel's history should suffice to show that the unusually flat characterization of Samson may indeed be to portray Samson as a type of Israel, a nation who spurned their status as a people set apart for YHWH and whose obsession with things foreign, especially foreign gods, imperilled themselves and ultimately brought about their downfall.

Samson's Engagement in the Same Kind of Action as the Rest of the Nation that Brought Chaos to Israelite Society

But not only is the role of Samson as Israel discernible through the many plot parallels between Samson's life and Israel's history, that Samson is Israel can also be seen in the way Samson engaged in the same kind of action as the rest of the nation that brought chaos to Israelite society in those days. In establishing this connection between Samson and the rest of the nation, the author/final redactor of Judges has effectively used the Samson cycle as a bridge to connect the two main parts of the book into a unified whole.

This connection between Samson and the rest of the nation in the era of the judges is established primarily through a rhetorical link between the Samson cycle and the refrain in the last five chapters of Judges. The link itself is relatively straightforward and will be presented momentarily. But to fully grasp the significance of this link and the crucial role it plays in uniting the book into a unified whole, one must first understand the challenge that exists regarding whether the judges cycles and the last five chapters of the book should be read together as constituent parts of the same book.

Critical scholars often speak of Judges as consisting of three independently composed parts that were artificially joined together into its current final form.[32] That the cycles that make up the bulk of the book and the final chapters that contain the bulk of the remaining narrative material are often thought to have no direct relationship with each other is not hard to understand. After all, in four main areas, the two parts of the book seem to show some significant disconnections.

---

31. Dennis T. Olson ('The Book of Judges,' in *The New Interpreter's Bible: Old Testament Survey* [eds. Walter Brueggemann; Nashville: Abingdon, 2006], 110), for example, thinks Judges was redacted for those who had experienced the Babylonian exile. Critical scholars who see Judges as a part of Deuteronomistic History are generally also of the opinion that DH or portions of DH were initially redacted or later revised in the exilic period.

32. Noth (*Deuteronomistic History*, 23–24, 77), for example, sees both Judg. 1:1–2:5 and 17:1–25:25 as later additions to the Deuteronomistic core of the book. Likewise, A. D. H. Mayes (*Judges* [Old Testament Guides; Sheffield: JSOT Press, 1985; repr., 1989], 13–16) sees the prologue and epilogue of the book as deriving from a hand different from that responsible for the judges cycles.

First, in a book titled Judges, the judges featured in the cycles have altogether disappeared in the final chapters. Instead, two Levites whose tribe has not been mentioned in the cycles have now occupied prominent roles in the two extended narratives that make up these chapters. Second, the five-stage cyclical framework of apostasy, foreign oppression, crying out for deliverance, raising up of a deliverer, and restoration of peace around which the cycles are organized also disappears in the final chapters, replaced instead by a refrain that punctuates the two extended narratives that make up these chapters. Third, while the cycles primarily concern deliverances from the nation's foreign oppressors, in the final chapters the foreign oppressors too disappear. The focus instead falls on the moral, social, religious, political and military chaos that were generated entirely from within. And finally, while the cycles feature judges most of whom are named and supplied with family lineages, the final chapters feature a slew of nameless characters, only two of whom are named.[33] Because taken together, these disconnections involve significant departures in subject matter, focus, narrative structure and style, they seem to suggest that the two parts of the book indeed came from different hands.

But as substantial as these differences seem to be, the two parts are nonetheless not without points of connection. First, although in the final chapters, the cycles, the foreign oppressors, and the judges have all disappeared from view, yet oppression has not ceased but continues to pervade these chapters as Israel is shown stealing, robbing, raping, fighting and slaughtering each other. If the lives of Israelites were miserable under foreign oppression, what these final chapters show is that even without the foreign oppressors, their lives fared no better because they were also oppressing each other.

But more importantly, the second point of connection is that, surprisingly, the root cause behind both forms of oppression turns out to be the same.

Consider the cycles. As has already been pointed out, each cycle is set in motion by the first stage of the cycle: Israel's apostasy. Each successive stage that follows basically flows out of the immediately preceding stage as a consequence of that stage, until the final stage is reached and peace is restored. Notice that unlike the stages within each cycle where a directs cause–effect relationship exists that governs the progression of the stages, no such relationship exists between the final stage of one cycle and the first stage of the next, so that the end of one cycle does not necessitate the beginning of another. If only Israel could stay away from idols once peace is restored, the recurrence of cycles can conceivably come to an end. What this means is that the key that repeatedly sets one cycle in motion after another is none other than Israel's repeated return to their idols. Thus, the

---

33. Othniel (3:9), Ehud (3:15), Shamgar (3:31) (though there is doubt as to whether Anath is indeed the name of Shamgar's father), Barak (4:6), Gideon (6:11), Tola (10:1), Jephthat (11:1), Abdon (12:13) and Samson (13:2) are all introduced with the names of their fathers. In contrast, the anonymity in the final chapters seems to suggest that the events narrated, while involving specific individuals, are not unique to those individuals, but can potentially occur anywhere and to anyone in Israel in those days.

statement, 'The sons of Israel did what is evil in the eyes of YHWH (ויעשׂו בני־ישׂראל הרע בעיני יהוה)' effectively communicates the root cause behind the constant recurrences of cycles and the miseries each cycle brings.

Although, unlike the cycles, there is no direct explanation for the chaos and oppression narrated in the last five chapters, through a refrain that punctures these narratives, a root cause is nonetheless strongly hinted at.

The refrain that punctuates the final chapters takes two forms. A full refrain that occurs towards the beginning (17:6) and at the very end (21:25) of these chapters brackets a shorter version that twice occurs (18:1; 19:1) at major transitions. The short version only includes the first part of the full refrain: 'In those days, Israel had no king.' However, the repetition of the full refrain towards the beginning and at the end of these chapters that functions almost as bookends, and the close proximity between the occurrences of the first long and short refrains encourage the supply in the short refrain of what is missing from the long. In fact, because the short refrain on its own does not seem to provide any direct logical connection with what immediate precedes and follows in either of its two occurrences, whereas the part omitted from the long refrain, namely, 'Everyone did what was right in his own eyes,' seems to provide a more reasonable transition by serving as a commentary that sums up what precedes and previews what follows, a case can be made that the omission actually represents a deliberate attempt to draw attention to what is missing by having the audience go back to find and supply the missing part in order to make better sense of the transition. If so, then what is omitted in the short refrain may in fact hold the key to understanding the chaos and oppression recounted in these final chapters.

While the respective keys to understanding the cycles and the final chapters are admittedly not identical, there is a sense in which conceptually, doing what is evil in the eyes of YHWH and doing what is right in one's own eyes actually communicate the same thing. After all, one of the most prominent pairs of oppositions in the Hebrew Bible is between doing what is right and doing what is evil in the eyes of YHWH. In fact, the almost formulaic pair, 'He did what is right in the eyes of YHWH (ויעשׂ הישׁר בעיני יהוה)' and 'He did what is evil in the eyes of YHWH (ויעשׂ הרע בעיני יהוה),' used repeatedly in Kings and Chronicles to describe good and bad kings, involves identical constructions in Hebrew but for the interchange between ישׁר ('right') and רע ('evil').[34] Thus, doing what is evil in the eyes of YHWH is the equivalence of not doing what is right in his eyes.[35]

---

34. Compare, for example, the positive statement in 2 Kgs. 14:3; 15:3, 34; 18:3; 22:2; 2 Chron. 25:2; 26:4; 27:2; 29:2; 34:2 and the negative in 1 Kgs. 15:26, 34; 22:53; 2 Kgs. 3:2; 8:18, 27; 13:2, 13; 14:24; 15:9, 18, 24, 28; 17:2; 21:2, 20, 32, 37; 24:9, 19; 2 Chron. 21:6; 22:4; 33:2, 22; 36:5, 9, 12.

35. In fact, in 2 Kgs. 16:2 and 2 Chron. 28:1, where one would expect the statement about Ahaz to be 'He did what was evil in the eyes of YHWH,' what one finds instead is 'He did not do what was right in the eyes of YHWH.' Hence, 'doing what is evil' in the eyes of YHWH is the same as 'not doing what is right' in his eyes.

But doing what is right in one's own eyes also appears to stand in opposition to doing what is right in the eyes of YHWH. This can be seen in Deuteronomy 12, where the focus is on worshipping and offering sacrifices to YHWH at the right place and in the right way. In Deut. 12:2-14, Moses cautioned Israel against following the practices of the nations by worshipping at locations of their choice. Instead, once they have taken possession of the land, they must conduct their cultic activities only at the place YHWH would choose as a dwelling for his name. Part of this caution is expressed in Deut. 12:8 by prohibiting Israel from continuing their current practices, where each person did what was right in his own eyes (לא תעשון ... איש כל־הישר בעיניו). This formulation is substantially similar to the second half of the full refrain in Judg. 17:6; 21:25, which has איש הישר בעיניו יעשה. After further instructions concerning the eating of meat, the section in Deuteronomy 12 closes in with a reiteration of the instructions already given, urging obedience in 12:28 because that would be doing what is good and right in the eyes of YHWH their God (תעשה הטוב והישר בעיני יהוה אלהיך). From this, one can see that there is a sense in which doing what is right in one's own eyes stands in contrast to doing what is right in the eyes of YHWH. If so, that means both the oppression Israel suffered from their foreign enemies as seen in the cycles and those they suffered from their own people as recounted in the final chapters of the book are in fact rooted in the same thing: a failure to do what is right in the eyes of YHWH.

However, notwithstanding the shared theme of oppression and a common root cause behind the oppressions recounted in both parts of the book, given the many disconnections cited earlier between the two parts, there still needs to be some form of direct rhetorical link between them before a credible case can be made to justify reading both parts of the book together as a unified whole. As it turns out, the key lies within the Samson cycle.

As one of the recurring cycles, the Samson narratives clearly belong to the cyclical part of the book. But within this cycle also lies a subtle connection with the final chapters. When Samson first requested that his parents get the Philistine woman from Timnah for him as wife, he told his parents, 'She is right in my eyes (היא ישרה בעיני)' (14:3). Then in reporting that Samson went down to Timnah to talk with the same woman, the narrator also comments that 'she was right in the eyes of Samson (ותישר בעיני שמשון)' (14.7).

Now as Greenstein points out, the use of the root ישר to describe a woman's physical attractiveness is unusual. Elsewhere within the Hebrew Bible, a woman's beauty is most frequently described using some form of טובה or יפה.[36] In fact, Judg. 14:3, 7 are the only two times within the Hebrew Bible that ישר is used to describe a woman's physical attractiveness. This suggests a deliberate attempt to create a rhetorical link with the refrain in the final chapters of the book. But what is the point of this link?

---

36. Greenstein, 'Riddle,' 249–50.

As already mentioned, in the cycles, the root cause behind the foreign oppression of Israel is idolatry as the nation did what is evil in the eyes of YHWH. Because the judges were raised by YHWH to deliver the nation from this oppression, and because each cycle seems to begin anew only after the passing of a judge (2:19), the impression conveyed is that the judges stood apart from and above the rest of the sinning nation. But while the judges' non-involvement in idolatry is implicitly understood and explicitly shown in the case of Gideon, who demolished the altar of Baal and the Asherah pole beside it (6:25-28), that Samson, the final judge in the series, is nonetheless presented as going after what was right in his own eyes as the rest of the nation means that Samson, at least, is not above the nation but very much a part of it. Thus, while Samson may not have done what is evil in the eyes of YHWH by participating in idolatry like the rest of the nation, he still failed to do what is right in the eyes of YHWH by going after what was right in his own eyes like the rest of the nation. And to the extent that doing what is right in one's own eyes is presented as the root cause behind the chaos and oppression the people of Israel suffered from what they were doing to themselves, Samson thus became just as much a part of the problem as anyone else as the nation was engulfed in moral, social, religious, political, and military chaos. In other words, Samson is Israel not only in that his life represents a microcosm of the history of his nation, but also in that he acted exactly as the nation did in that specific slice of time when he lived.

In fact, a case can be made that in the end, Samson became more than just a type of Israel. As the final judge in the series of cycles, Samson may also have come to represent the judges that preceded him. For as it turns out, Samson going after what was right in his eyes may have become a pointer that invites further exploration into how and what other actions he took that constitute doing what was right in his own eyes. And as I have written about elsewhere, such an exploration eventually leads to the discovery that for each bizarre episode in the final chapters that confounds the mind and that constitutes an example of people doing what was right in their own eyes, one can find shadows of one of the judges – not just Samson, but also Ehud, Gideon and Jephthah.[37] Thus, it seems that the two judges with flat characterizations who bookend the cycles each typifies those who held the same office. While Othniel, the first judge, whose brief and formulaic introduction may be designed to typify the ideal deliverer-judge, Samson, the concluding judge with his extended narratives, seems to sum up and typify the reality about what Israel's judges turned out to be, and they were anything but ideal. And the fact that Samson typifies both Israel and the judges at the same time poses no problem. For in the end, Samson, and by extension, Israel's judges, except perhaps for Othniel, all turned out to be not above those they delivered but very much a part of them. In fact, one can no longer be certain whether the people did what was right in their own eyes because their judges did, or whether the judges

---

37. As this insight requires extensive explanation that falls outside the scope of this article, for details, see Wong, *Compositional Strategy*, 79–141.

did what was right in their eyes because that was how everyone in society acted. But perhaps that is ultimately not important. For while it is specifically through Samson that one comes to understand more clearly the problem of Israel, there is a sense in which Samson, and by extension, the judges for whom he serves as representative, were Israel too.

Tying up Loose Ends

At the beginning of this article in the discussion of the anomalies of the Samson cycle, two issues having to do with possible subversions of the cyclical paradigm were raised. These will be addressed briefly as follows.

One of the issues concerns whether the omission of stage three of the cycle, the crying out of the people, would result in a theology that differs from, and hence, subverts that which is conveyed through the cyclical framework. The answer to that actually depends to a large extent on how one takes the missing stage three: whether the crying out represents repentance on the part of Israel, or whether it is just a cry for help out of distress. Those who see a strong Deuteronomistic influence behind the editing of the cycles tend to see the crying out as an implicit sign of repentance, as it is generally recognized that a significant tenet of Deuteronomistic theology is the principle that apostasy leads to punishment by oppression while repentance is rewarded with deliverance.[38] But this view has also been challenged by some who see the crying out simply as a cry for help out of distress that does not necessarily imply an accompanying repentance.[39]

As the detailed arguments of these two positions fall outside the scope of this article, I will simply state my preference for the non-repentance view as it seems to be more in line with the evident presented in Judges. After all, in Judg. 10:10-16, YHWH's initial refusal to deliver came *after* Israel cried out to him, and it was only after YHWH's initial refusal that Israel got rid of their foreign gods. This shows that Israel's cry in 10:10 cannot be one of true repentance, nor was it seen as such by YHWH. Besides, that YHWH told Israel to go and instead cry out (זעק) to the gods they have chosen (10:14), using the same word that describes their action towards him, makes it quite clear that YHWH took Israel's cry only as a cry for help and not of repentance. Otherwise, why would YHWH tell Israel to go and repent before their foreign gods? Finally, in 2:18 in the programmatic introduction to the cycles, it is already clearly stated that YHWH's decision to send judges to

---

38. Thus, Serge Frolov and Mikhail Stetckevich ('Repentance in Judges: Assessing the Reassessment,' *HS* 60 [2019]: 130. Frolov and Stetckevich also provide in the accompanying footnote a list of scholars who hold such a view.

39. For a recent proponent of such a view, see JoAnna Hoyt, 'Reassessing Repentance in Judges,' *BibSac* 169 (2012): 143–58. For other who hold a similar view, see Frolov and Stetckevich, 'Repentance,' 131, n.4.

deliver his people was a result of the people's groaning (נאקתם) before their oppressors. That all three other occurrences of 'groaning (נאקה)' within the Hebrew Bible (Exod. 2:24; 6:5; Ezek. 30:24) refer only to the kind of moaning that comes from oppression but that does not require repentance indicates that the deliverance YHWH sent in response to the people's crying out in Judges is to be construed primarily as an act of compassion on the part of YHWH, unrelated to whether or not repentance was present.

Of course, if one holds to the repentance view of the crying out, then in the Samson cycle, YHWH's decision to raise up Samson to begin delivering his people despite the absence of Israel's repentance can indeed be construed as introducing a different theology from that which, up to that point, underlies the rest of the cyclical framework. But if the crying out never involves any repentance, then the absence of any crying out in the Samson cycle is not in discord with the overall theology of the cyclical framework. For if YHWH's saving acts were from the beginning based not on what Israel did but solely on his compassion towards them, then while it is true that in the cyclical framework, YHWH's deliverance is a result of the people crying out, that crying out is, however, not a necessary condition for deliverance. In fact, if anything, YHWH's decision to provide deliverance for Israel in the Samson cycle despite the absence of any crying out only serves to highlight and reinforce the compassion of YHWH that from the beginning underlies the theology of the cyclical framework. If so, then the Samson cycle turns out not to be as subversive as initially thought, and certainly not anomalous with respect to the theology that underlies the cycles after all.

Besides, if Samson is indeed a type of Israel, then YHWH's compassion rather than Israel's repentance as a basis for deliverance can also be seen through Samson. For as has already been pointed out, Samson's request for strength in his final prayer to YHWH was still motivated primarily by personal vengeance and not out of a desire to fulfil his calling to deliver the people. If this signals a lack of change and growth that contributes to the flatness of Samson's characterization, it is at the same time also an indication of Samson's failure to turn from self-interest to an interest in the divine agenda, and hence, represents a lack of repentance. Yet, YHWH still consented to answer Samson's prayer and allowed his death to begin accomplishing Israel's deliverance as he killed many more Philistines when he died than when he lived. In so doing, YHWH has thus shown through Samson his willingness to respond graciously and compassionately to his people's cry for help even when that cry does not proceed from repentance.

The second issue raised earlier is somewhat related to the first, and concerns the problem posed by the apparent reversal of the progressively deteriorating relationship between YHWH and Israel within the cycles. If the deteriorating relationship between YHWH and his people primarily aims at showing YHWH's dissatisfaction with a people who repeatedly refused to respond to his deliverances with true and lasting repentance, then through the progression from immediate deliverances (3:9, 15; 4:3-7) to a deliverance preceded by a rebuke through an intermediary (6:7-10) to YHWH's personal rebuke and initial refusal to deliver

(10:10-14), this theme may have reached its end.[40] For the next logical step in this progression would be for YHWH to resolutely refuse to deliver. But if that were to happen, then it would have subverted the key theme developed through the cycles of YHWH's compassion towards his people as the basis for his repeated deliverances.[41] Therefore, rather than seeing the initiative YHWH took in the Samson cycle to deliver his people despite the absence of crying out as a reversal of the progressively deteriorating relationship between YHWH and his people, it is perhaps preferable to see this as an attempt to return to the theme of YHWH's compassion by showing that despite his frustration at his people's lack of repentance, in the end, it was his compassion that triumphed over his wrath, such that he would provide deliverance even when deliverance was undeserved and not sought. In other words, what initially appears to be a reversal or subversion of a progressively developed sub-theme turns out to be a reinforcement of a larger overarching key theme of the book.

Conclusion

In this article, I have explored features of the Samson narrative that set it apart from accounts of the other major judges within the cyclical framework of the book. I have focused for the most part on the unusually flat characterization of Samson and have shown how this flatness may represent a conscious attempt to cast our protagonist in the role of a type. While many have already noted how parallels between events in Samson's life and events in the history of the nation point strongly to the fact that Samson typifies Israel, that, however, is not the only way in which Samson is representative of the nation. Through a rhetorical link that shows Samson going for what was right in his owns eyes just as the nameless individuals that represent Israelite society at large in the final chapters of the book were also doing, not only has the author/final redactor of Judges managed to bring two seemingly unrelated parts of the book together, he has also shown in the process that Samson indeed represents the nation because he was also acting in the very same way the nation was in that slice of time when they both lived. And if one follows the hint this provides and explores further how Samson and the Israelites in his days were acting similarly in going after what was right in their own eyes,

---

40. Notice that while YHWH's decision to save was rooted in his compassion and not the people's repentance, that does not mean, however, that YHWH no longer requires repentance on the part of his people. It seems that repentance is always expected as a proper response to grace even if not as a condition for receiving grace, so that a lack of true repentance *after* being shown compassion is reason enough to justify wrath and further discipline.

41. Note that even though in the Jephthah cycle, YHWH initially refused to deliver his people, yet the fact that he eventually did still testifies to his compassion, even if that compassion was severely tried and the eventual deliverance was only reluctantly given.

one may be surprised to discover that almost every bizarre act that reflects the people doing what was right in their own eyes in the final chapters is subtly linked to acts of a similar nature associated with one of the major judges recounted in the cycles. Hence, in Samson, one sees not only the path Israel has trodden in their historical development, but also how Israel was acting in that particular slice of time in history, and not just in terms of how common folks in Israelite society were acting, but also how Israel's leaders were acting – doing what was right in their own eyes. And in this respect, one can truly say that Samson was everyman in Israel.

Chapter 12

MOTHER'S LITTLE HELPER: MICAH AND HIS BIG IDEA

Robin Baker[1]

Introduction: You Do Not Need To Be Gruesome To Be Gross

By the time readers of Judges have absorbed the tales of Gideon, Abimelech, Jephthah and Samson to reach chapter 17, their sense of searing discomfort is dulled by the enormity of gore, lust and horror they have traversed. Episode upon episode of violent betrayal, fratricide, brutality, blood-pollution and the rank obtuseness of the Israelites' understanding of the covenant relationship with their ancestral god take their toll. The unremitting corrosion of the covenantal ideal brings in train a dilution of moral outrage in the reader as much as in the people the work describes. It takes the gang-rape, murder and dismemberment of the Levite's concubine in its final section, events so obscene that its sin-brutalized characters exclaim, 'Nothing like this has taken place or been seen since the day the sons of Israel came up from the land of Egypt until now!' (Judg. 19:30), to reignite emotions of shock and disgust in the reader. Thus, in the grim landscape of human corruption and devastation that unfolds in stages from chapter 6, it is reasonable to evaluate the account of Micah and the Levite for hire, the drifter-cum-grifter Jonathan, as offering not much more than a tale 'filled with irony, humor, and ambiguity that ridicule[s] [Israel's cultic] decline'.[2]

That the Micah section is primarily a satire on idolatry is a conclusion many scholars have reached. Although the two chapters end with the slaughter of a community that seems prelapsarian in its innocence and contain a study of the casual but systematically recounted violation of the principal precepts of

---

1. I am grateful to the book's editors and to Caroline Smith for insightful comments on earlier drafts of this essay.

2. Gale A. Yee, 'Ideological Criticism: Judges 17–21 and the Dismembered Body', in *Judges and Method: New Approaches in Biblical Studies* (2nd edn; Minneapolis MN: Fortress, 2007), 138–60 (149).

God,³ the chapters represent for these commentators a relatively light-hearted interlude in the dark narrative sweep of Judges.⁴ Others take a different view. For them the chapters offer historiography that charts cultic developments in Israel.⁵ Half a century ago, Arthur Cundall cautioned against this interpretation, observing that Judges is concerned to cast Jonathan and the Danites unsympathetically.⁶ If the pericope is historiography, its intent is polemical. Exegetes such as C. F. Burney, who read the piece as a neutral rendering of an episode in Israel's early history, misunderstood the ideology of the section.⁷

That said, these competing claims are each valid up to a point. Humour and irony are never far from the surface in Judges. Equally, Micah's story, which boasts the only datable reference in the book – the Assyrian exile of Israel – comes as close to explicit historical record as Judges offers.⁸ Appraising Judges 17–18 as a single stratum of narrative-meaning driven by a single rhetorical purpose, however, underestimates its literary and theological sophistication. It is a composition of layered complexity.⁹

---

3. J. Clinton McCann, *Judges* (Interpretation; Louisville KY: Westminster John Knox Press, 2003), 120.

4. David Marcus, 'In Defence of Micah: He Was Not a Thief,' *Shofar* 6 (1988): 72–80 (72); Trent C. Butler, *Judges* (WBC 8; Nashville TN: Nelson, 2008), 381; Barry G. Webb, *The Book of Judges* (NICOT; Grand Rapids MI: Eerdmans, 2012), 424; K. Lawson Younger, Jr., *Judges and Ruth* (NIVAC; Grand Rapids MI: Zondervan, 2002), 344.

5. Frank Moore Cross, *Canaanite Myth and Hebrew Epic: Essays in the History of the Religion of Israel* (Cambridge MA and London: Harvard University Press, 1997), 197–99; H. H. Rowley, *Worship in Ancient Israel: Its Forms and Meaning* (London: SPCK, 1967), 78; H. W. Hertzberg, *Die Bücher Josua, Richter, Ruth* (4th edn; ATD 9; Göttingen: Vandenhoeck & Ruprecht, 1969), 238; J. Alberto Soggin, *Judges: A Commentary* (2nd edn; trans. John Bowden; OTL; London: SCM Press, 1987), 267; Yairah Amit, 'Hidden Polemic in the Conquest of Dan: Judges XVII-XVIII,' *VT* 40 (1990): 4–20 (7, 15); Susan Niditch, *Judges: A Commentary* (Louisville KY: Westminster John Knox Press, 2008), 185; Jason S. Bray, *Sacred Dan: Religious Tradition and Cultic Practice in Judges 17–18* (LHBOTS 449; New York: T&T Clark, 2006), 5.

6. Arthur E. Cundall and Leon Morris, *Judges, Ruth* (London: Tyndale Press, 1968), 192.

7. C.F. Burney, *The Book of Judges with Introduction and Notes* (2nd edn; London: Rivingtons, 1920), 416; cf. E. Aydeet Mueller, *The Micah Story: A Morality Tale in the Book of Judges* (SBL 34; New York: Lang, 2001), 29; Avraham Biran, 'Tel Dan: Biblical Texts and Archaeological Data,' in *Scripture and Other Artifacts: Essays in Honor of Philip J. King* (ed. Michael D. Coogan et al.; Louisville KY: Westminster John Knox, 1994), 1–17 (5).

8. Amihai Mazar, *Archaeology of the Land of the Bible 10,000–586 B.C.E.* (Cambridge: Lutterworth, 1993), 495; Yifat Thareani, 'Revenge of the Conquered: Paths of Resistance in the Assyrian City of Dan,' *Semitica* 60 (2018): 473–92; Webb, *Book of Judges*, 450; Bray, *Sacred Dan*, 22.

9. J. Cheryl Exum, 'The Centre Cannot Hold: Thematic and Textual Instabilities in Judges,' *CBQ* 52 (1990): 410–31 (410); Yairah Amit, *The Book of Judges: The Art of Editing*

What is unarguable is that, due in part to its comparatively muted tone, the pericope has attracted less commentary than other major stories in Judges.[10] For Jason Bray, it 'feels like a text left behind.'[11] This essay addresses that neglect from a particular angle. It analyses what the text reveals of Micah's character and considers the way it goes about characterization. In the process the essay exposes some of the pericope's layers of meaning as well as several of the characteristic literary devices the book employs. Ultimately, we discover that, in the mind of the Judges writer, Micah and his circle do not merit their relative obscurity. What they do deserve just as much as other unsavory characters he parades before us is infamy.

Where Is Wilderness, Where Is God?

By the standards of Judges, the Micah segment is an exercise in understatement. This applies as much to the characterization as to its scene-setting with each typically reinforcing the other. The opening scene is a study in domestic banality, a descriptor that one can rarely apply to this book. 'A man Micaiah' (17:1) is at home with his mother where they are having a quiet if intense conversation. The house, we learn, is located in a peaceful, supportive and anonymous neighbourhood in Israel's geographic heart, the hill country of Ephraim. Here the writer departs from his custom of careful topographical specification. H. W. Hertzberg notes the 'general placing' of the scene.[12] In the context of Judges, what is remarkable about Micah is that he is actually unremarkable. The story of Micah is the story of Everyman, a conclusion that is reinforced by the recapitulation of 'a man Micaiah' in 17:1 in the programmatic 'a [that is, 'every'] man did what was right in his own eyes' in 17:6. The writer marks him out from his two swashbuckling predecessors chiefly by his ordinariness.

Jephthah and Samson operated violently in the marches of Israelite territory and/ or beyond them and, like all major male characters in Judges including our Levite Jonathan, undertook journeys.[13] By contrast, although the narrative shows him to

(trans. Jonathan Chipman; BIS 38; Leiden: Brill, 1999), 12–13; Robin Baker, *Hollow Men, Strange Women: Riddles, Codes and Otherness in the Book of Judges* (BIS 143; Leiden, Boston: Brill, 2016), xi, 12 n. 60, 30, 38–39, 294.

10. David M. Gunn, *Judges* (Malden MA and Oxford: Blackwell, 2005), 232; Bray, *Sacred Dan*, 4.
11. Ibid., 15.
12. Hertzberg, *Bücher*, 239; see also Amit, 'Hidden Polemic,' 12.
13. Shmuel Vargon, 'Saul's Pursuit of David in the Land of Judah and the Geographical Background,' in *Marbeh Ḥokmah: Studies in the Bible and the Ancient Near East in Loving Memory of Victor Avigdor Hurowitz* (2 vols; ed. S. Yona et al.; Winona Lake IN: Eisenbrauns, 2015), 1:559–85 (563–64).

live near, or perhaps on, a main thoroughfare, Micah is not tempted to see the world. The furthest he travels is to a spot 'some distance from Micah's house' (18:22), and he goes that far only because he was provoked into a frenzied dash to reclaim his stolen items. The last we see of Micah is his returning dejected to the house where his story began (18:26). Otherwise, when he appears at all, he is either in or close to his dwelling. In this story, though, immobility does not denote inactivity.

The subtext is plain: if the sinful and destructive deeds Micah commits are perpetrated by an Israelite undistinguished except for a fine Yahwistic name and a rich mother, at home in an anonymous community in the middle of the Promised Land, nowhere/no one is immune.[14] His story tells the reader that the typological wilderness of 'the peoples round about,' the forbidding space that constantly threatened Israel's stability and integrity (Judg. 2:12-14), has permeated the heart of their geography and citizenry. This is not all: the center is now the margin.[15] Thanks to Micah, the center becomes a producer and exporter of iniquity in the form of his cultic innovations to the original periphery.[16] They reach the territory of the peoples round about, in this case Laish,[17] marking the ultimate cultic inversion and scandal (cf. Deut. 6:14; 13:7-8 [Eng. 6-7]).

These remarks begin to point up the paradox of Micah's character. He holds no formal leadership position, he lacks military prowess in a militaristic society, any influence he possesses is limited to his local community, and in a patriarchy he has no father and does not seem to understand fatherhood. The narrative ascribes no particular skill to him, and certainly no virtue. He is the antithesis of the charismatic leadership type that commentaries associate with Judges. Yet the book implies in 18:30-31 that Micah's impact on his people's future was, in the long run, more profound than that of all the foreign armies and Israelite leaders whom it describes, combined.

The Judges writer has been experimenting incrementally with the figure of the Israelite anti-hero since chapter 4, beginning with his portrait of Israel-aligned Jael. It is the unfolding plot of Judges that motivates these experiments since, with the progressive loosening of Israel's adhesion to YHWH and its concomitant of their enveloping sinfulness, each episode calls for an apposite anti-hero to limn the national decline. In the figure of Abimelech, the author gives us the book's seemingly most conventional anti-hero type.[18] While some similarity exists

---

14. Daniel I. Block, *Judges, Ruth* (NAC 6; Nashville TN: B&H, 1999), 474.

15. Cf. Mary Douglas, *Purity and Danger* (Harmondsworth: Penguin, 1966), 137–38, 145.

16. Lillian R. Klein, *The Triumph of Irony in the Book of Judges* (JSOTSup 68; Sheffield: Almond Press, 1988), 143–44.

17. Mazar, *Archaeology*, 492; Avraham Biran, 'The High Places of Biblical Dan,' in *Studies in the Archaeology of the Iron Age in Israel and Jordan* (ed. Amihai Mazar; JSOTSup 331; Sheffield: Sheffield Academic Press, 2001), 148–55.

18. The reality is not so clear-cut; see Robin Baker, *Mesopotamian Civilization and the Origins of the New Testament* (Cambridge and New York: Cambridge University Press, 2022), chapter 5.

between his characterization and Micah's, as an approach to characterization the treatment of the latter is unique and uniquely bold. Yet it is consistent with the rhetorical strategy the writer employs in the pericope. Just as physical space has been turned inside out in this tale to present the center as periphery and the periphery as center so characterization has been turned inside out to reveal the most consequential leading figure in Judges to be someone who possesses no quality of or claim to leadership.

To achieve this, the writer makes Micah the focus of the story while portraying him as not especially dynamic. His technique is to have Micah participate in only a third of the pericope's forty-four verses and yet have his name run through the entire account. The initial verse (17:1) provides its first mention and the final verse (18:31), the last. In all, 'Micah'/'Micaiah' occurs eleven times (10+1) and the phrase 'house of Micah'/'Micaiah' figures a further ten times (9+1). In this way, even when he is absent from the action, he evidently remains the plot's catalyst. Although he departed defeated and distraught from the drama in 18:26, the chain of events his and his mother's acts set in motion eventually engulfs the entire nation of Israel.[19] The reverberations of his deeds only cease with the death of the nation and the loss of its ancestral lands.

A comparison of the pattern of mentions of Micah/Micaiah with the treatment of the person and name of YHWH in the story elucidates this point. Judges 17–18 is the only substantial section of the composition in which YHWH is not explicitly engaged.[20] Notwithstanding, he is mentioned, and names with the theophoric element *yah*/*yahu* are more in evidence here than in any other segment, with its main characters, Micaiah 'Who is like YHWH?' and Jonathan 'YHWH has given,' bearing such a name.[21] By the way it treats the divine name, the narrative signals that, as the story develops, what relevance YHWH had for its actors and those they represent diminishes. The first indication of this is the change in the principal character's name from Mîkāyəhû with its full Yahwistic theophoric element to the hypocoristic Mîkâ. The change happens immediately after the production of the two silver images in 17:4. To underline that the truncation of the divine name is no scribal shorthand, an analogous expression of the development occurs. Less than halfway through the pericope, the free-standing Tetragrammaton ceases to appear. It is gradually replaced or, perhaps more accurately, swallowed up by the generic *ĕlōhîm* 'god/s,' as Table 12.1 demonstrates.

Another device the writer uses to insinuate Micah as consequential for the narrative and Israel's later history is the predicates that are attached to him. The deployment of the verb *'āśâ* 'to do, make' is exemplary.[22] Again, the contrast with

---

19. Block, *Judges*, 477.

20. P. Deryn Guest, 'Judges,' *Eerdmans Commentary on the Bible* (ed. James D. G. Dunn and John W. Rogerson; Grand Rapids MI and Cambridge: Eerdmans, 2003), 190–207 (203).

21. Baker, *Hollow Men*, 61–63.

22. This verb is pregnant for the book's coda sections because the locution 'every man *did* what was right in his own eyes' (17:6; 21:25) introduces and concludes them.

Table 12.1 Occurrences of the nouns 'YHWH' and 'ĕlōhîm' in Judges 17–18

YHWH	'ĕlōhîm
17:2	17:5
17:3	18:5
17:13	18:10
18:6	18:24 'my gods'
	18:31

YHWH is enlightening. The great divine creator ostensibly makes nothing and does nothing. Micah's 'making,' on the other hand, is the inclusio framing the report of cultic deviance that Micah and his mother initiated and that drives the story (17:3; 18:31). The narrative deploys 'āśâ twelve times. In five of these, Micah is instrumental in making something, matching the number of times 'ĕlōhîm is mentioned. And what this very ordinary creator makes is 'ĕlōhîm (18:24).[23] Here we confront possibly the most audacious inversion in Judges: Everyman makes gods in place of the God who made every human being. The section's final verses highlight the opposition: 'Jonathan ben-Gershom ben-Moses and his sons were priests to the Danite tribe until the day of the exile of the land. They erected for themselves Micah's *pesel* 'graven image' that he had made ('āśâ) all the time the house of the god (hā'ĕlōhîm) was in Shiloh' (18:30b-31).[24]

Three other predicates that denote actions performed by Micah – šûb 'to return, turn back,' rā'â 'to see,' and yāda' 'to know' – also serve as heuristics. Each assists in his characterization and illuminates aspects of the wider drama. The exchange between Micah and his mother contains a flurry of three (Hiphîl) šûb forms in two verses (17:3-4) with mother and son each returning the tainted silver to the other in a confusing jumble. The other time √šûb is found with Micah is when he 'returns' to his house, his final reported act (18:26). A 3+1 pattern of this kind in Judges frequently signifies that the word and/or event is negatively ominous.[25] √šûb occurs in two pivotal verses in Judges, 2:19 and 8:33, where it functions to record the Israelites' descent into apostasy.[26] By means of this intra-textual referencing to

---

23. Block, *Judges*, 480.

24. J. Alberto Soggin (*Judges*, 264) remarks, '*pesel* stands for the idolatrous image *par excellence* mentioned in the Decalogue, Ex. 20.4-5//Deut. 5.8-10, and Deutero-Isaiah, cf. Isa. 40.18-20; 44.14-20.'

25. On the generally fateful nature of the 3+1 figure in Judges, see Baker, *Hollow Men*, 38, 60, 86–93 passim; idem, '"A Dream Carries Much Implication": The Midianite's Dream (Judges VII), Its Role and Meanings,' *VT* 68 (2018): 349–77 (353–77).

26. BDB, 997. Cf. the deverbal substantive *məšûbâ*, Biblical Hebrew's regular term for 'apostasy' (ibid., 1000).

preceding material, a common device in the book,[27] the writer provides an additional layer of commentary on the significance of the exchange between Micah and his mother and its portentous nature. Micah may return to his house, now devoid of idols and the accoutrements of his home-made cultus, but he is never absolved from Israel's decay and destruction any more than Israel ever escapes the consequences of Everyman's apostasy.

The first rendition of the refrain 'a man did what was right in his own eyes' planted in the opening verses of the Micah account points to the risks inherent in seeing in Settlement-era Israel. Micah saw the silver and stole it; he later saw its potential for manufacturing idols; he saw the itinerant Levite and saw his potential to be his priest. But in none of these cases is the predicate 'see' (*rā'â*) used. The sole occasion when Micah 'sees' is when he 'saw' that he was no match against the Danites (18:26). It is at this moment that his eyes were finally opened and he appeared as nakedly helpless as the primordial couple in their sin. All that he had prized to give him security, prosperity and status had vanished. His idols and his priest had not helped him and would not help him, and YHWH had not done him good in reward for his cultic observances (17:13). His entire enterprise had carried his mother's curse after all. Micah's seeing as he exits the stage was as tragic for his life as Samson's blinding was for his.[28]

'Seeing' and 'knowing' both recall the first apostasy against the Creator that was triggered by the incentive, "Your eyes will be opened and you will be as god/s knowing (√*yāda'*) good and bad." The account continues, 'And the woman saw (√*rā'â*) that the tree was good for food and was pleasing to the eyes' (Gen. 3:5-6).[29] Micah's one instance of 'knowing,' which is conveyed in the section's single soliloquy, was equally wrong-headed and likewise ended badly: 'Now I know that Yahweh will do good to me because I have a Levite as a priest' (17:13). Judges serves subtle notice of this bad outcome by the predicate *yāda'* evincing a 3+1 configuration. In 17:13 it applies to Micah; the other citations refer to the Danites. So concerned is the writer to stress the idea of knowing that he produces a linguistic mini-*tour de force* on the verb root. On each occasion the root appears, it models a

---

27. David M. Gunn, 'Joshua and Judges,' in *The Literary Guide to the Bible* (ed. Robert Alter and Frank Kermode; London: Fontana, 1987), 102–21 (105–7); Baker, *Hollow Men*, 81, 114.

28. The text invites us to make the connection. For both characters, realization of their true spiritual condition comes when they are finally confronted by their weakness (16:20-21; 18:26).

29. Judges abounds in intertextual references to episodes in Genesis (Moshe Garsiel, 'Homiletic Name-Derivations as a Literary Device in the Gideon Narrative: Judges VI–VIII,' *VT* 43 [1993]: 302–17 [314–16]; Martin Buber, *Kingship of God* [3rd edn; trans. Richard Scheimann; New Jersey, London: Allen & Unwin, 1967], 71–72; A. Graeme Auld, 'Gideon: Hacking at the Heart of the Old Testament,' *VT* 39 [1989]: 257–67 [257–58]; Robin Baker, 'Double Trouble: Counting the Cost of Jephthah,' *JBL* 137 [2018]: 29–50 [46–48]).

different finite form. These alternate between indicatives and modals: 'I know' (perfect indicative); 'we may know' (cohortative) (18:5); 'do you know?' (perfect interrogative) (18:14); 'Know!' (imperative) (18:14).

This peculiar datum raises the question why the writer seems so concerned to emphasize the importance of 'knowing' for the pericope, given that its principal character is said to 'know' only once. Together with many scholars, I understand the ephod and teraphim which Micah commissioned to have a divinatory function.[30] In other words, their role was knowledge production. The pattern of occurrences of *yāda'* in Chapter 18 corroborates this conclusion. Whenever the Danites speak of 'knowing' it is in the context, indeed the proximity, of the ephod and teraphim. Jonathan's initial contribution to their mission was an oracular utterance. Admittedly, it was, like its speaker, vacuous,[31] but whereas Micah's knowledge quickly proved false, the knowledge the Danites accepted from Jonathan, so far as they were concerned, was authentic. Their folly took longer to be revealed but when it was exposed, the consequences were cataclysmic. The 3+1 configuration buttresses what the text implies: the knowledge was profane and proved lethal first to the Laishites and then to Israel. Sacred knowledge, the knowledge of YHWH, had been abandoned or abused by the generation of Israelites to which Jonathan and Micah belonged: 'And all that generation was gathered to their fathers, and another generation sprang up that knew neither Yahweh nor [a literal translation] the made-things he made for Israel. And the sons of Israel made evil in Yahweh's sight' (2:10-11).

Fatherless Patriarchy

The key role that the second chapter of Judges evidently fulfils for interpreting the work thus compares the Israelites of Micah and Jonathan's generation unfavorably with their fathers.[32] Joshua was buried in the territory where Micah's story begins (2:8-9). Micah is so alien to the standard of Joshua bin-Nun and the fathers, however, that not only has he not learnt from them, he appears utterly cut off from them. To underscore the point, he lacks a father and even a patronymic. From the first chapter of Judges the father-figure features strongly (with Achsah and Othniel) in various permutations, as one would expect in a patriarchal society. All the main

---

30. Julius Bewer, 'The Composition of Judges, Chaps. 17, 18,' *AJSLL* 29 (1913): 261–83 (264); T. J. Lewis, 'Teraphim,' *DDD*, 844–50 (846-50); Niditch, *Judges*, 181, 183; Block, *Judges*, 481–82; Younger, *Judges*, 338; John Gray, *The New Century Bible Commentary: Joshua, Judges, Ruth* (Grand Rapids MI: Eerdmans, 1986), 340; Mueller, *Micah Story*, 60.

31. Robert Polzin, *Moses and the Deuteronomist: A Literary Study of the Deuteronomic History*, Part One (New York: Seabury, 1980), 198; Yee, 'Ideological Criticism,' 150.

32. David M. Gunn and Danna Nolan Fewell, *Narrative in the Hebrew Bible* (The Oxford Bible Series; Oxford: Oxford University Press, 1993), 120.

male characters are referenced against their fathers, some extensively like Gideon, Abimelech and Samson, and some simply by means of a patronymic, for instance, Ehud, Baraq. This comes to a sudden halt in Micah. So removed is Micah from his paternal line, we do not know his clan affiliation or even his tribal membership.

A variation on the theme of uncertain tribal affiliation cleaves to Jonathan, whose tribal membership is a perennial *crux* for exegetes.[33] Only the Danites, a concubine tribe that in Judges epitomizes Israel's dereliction of the Yahwistic ideal, are presented as clear about, and proud of, their paternal line, naming the town Laish ('Lion'; cf. Deut. 33:22) after 'Dan their father who was born to Israel' (18:29).[34]

The other conspicuous Judges character who lacks a father but whose mother is prominent is Israel's feared enemy Sisera. His story casts light on Micah. It ends with the son failing to rob Israelites of goods he planned to give to his mother (5:27-31). In an intra-textual chiasm, Micah's story begins with Micah robbing his Israelite mother to give to himself. This act elicits the third explicit curse in Judges. The first occurs in the battle against Sisera when Deborah and Baraq curse Meroz (5:23). The second, Jotham's, is levelled at a son who dishonored his father (9:20, 56-57). Micah's mother's curse threatens a son who dishonored his mother. All of them are engendered by a breakdown in Israel's social mores. The first two are aimed at egregious outliers. The third takes place at the society's core.

It is not that Micah is oblivious of his need for a father, any more than he is unaware of his need for YHWH's blessing in his life. He perceives the Levite 'lad' (*na'ar*) Jonathan as a creative solution to both. He can be Micah's 'father' and his 'priest' and – an unexpected bonus – he becomes 'like one of [Micah's] sons' (17:10-11). This bewildering set of status/identity switches reinforces the message of the story's first few verses in which Micah dishonors his mother by purloining her silver. The fifth commandment, 'Honour your father and your mother, so that your days may be long in the land that the LORD your God is giving you' (Exod. 20:12), is no longer observed or understood. Deviance and delinquency are normalized. Essential familial relations – maternal, paternal, and filial – are hopelessly disfigured.[35] It is terror at the curse, not contrition at breaking the commandment or rejecting basic morality, that prompts the mother-robbing Micah to acknowledge his crime and return the silver (17:2-3).[36] And the writer traces this violation of the fifth commandment to its logical end, namely, the reduction of days 'in the land,' in the pericope's denouement (18:30-31). It is at the tale's climax, too, that he at last introduces patronymics, with the startling disclosure that the Levite lad's name is

---

33. David Z. Moster, 'The Levite of Judges 17–18,' *JBL* 133 (2014): 729–37 (731–33).
34. Burney, *Judges*, 427; *HALAT* 2:503; BDB, 539.
35. Block, *Judges*, 488.
36. Ibid., 479; C. A. Faraone, B. Garnand and C. López-Ruiz, 'Micah's Mother (Judg. 17:1-4) and a Curse from Carthage (*KAI* 89): Canaanite Precedents for Greek and Latin Curses against Thieves?,' *JNES* 64 (2005): 161–86 (176).

Jonathan ben-Gershom ben-Moses.[37] Whatever YHWH has given and whatever Moses produced have been corrupted to the point that it is impossible to discern the nature of the giver or the benefit in the gift. In a final twist, it is this father-son whose sons maintain the forbidden cultus of Dan until Israel, 'to whom their father Dan was born,' is swept away (18:29-30).

Using symbolic numbers to shed light on characters and plot is a favored literary device in Judges. Five is an especially loaded number in this story and its pervasive presence is surely deliberate. There are five Danite spies, five times Micah's god-production activity is cited, and the related substantive *ĕlōhîm* also occurs five times. References to the ephod and teraphim are pentadic. Micah is five times termed 'man', and Jonathan five times 'lad'. We would underestimate the writer's ingenuity, though, to assume that the abundance of pentads serves solely to point up the significance of the fifth commandment for the story. His delight in polyvalent associations validates looking for additional analogues.

Biblical Israel's enemy is sometimes pentepartite: five kings of Midian (Num. 31:8); five kings of the Amorites who hid in the cave and were hung on the trees (Josh. 10); and in Judges itself 'the five lords of the Philistines' (3:3), the book's only mention of 'five' outside chapters 17–18. The composite image comprising five elements that Nebuchadnezzar espied in his dream (Dan. 2:31-36) may indicate that the symbolic connotation of five as Israel's enemy entered Judaic scribal consciousness. In this case, the monstrous pentad was destroyed by the indivisible Yahwistic stone-cum-mountain, recalling the Shema, 'YHWH your god is one YHWH'.[38] All the pentads I have listed for the Micah section may plausibly be considered enemies of YHWH. Cumulatively they posed a greater threat to the integrity of his people than the last external enemy discussed in Judges (14–16), the Philistine pentapolis.

In the number symbolism of Judges, seven is pregnant. Typically, it symbolizes the divine or that which is perceived as divine.[39] It is telling, then, that the noun *kesep* 'silver, shekel, money' forms a heptad in our story (17:2 twice, 3 twice, 4 twice, 10). Cash may not be king in pre-monarchic Israel, but for Micah silver is literally god. While the icing on his religious cake was boasting a Levite as priest, in Micah's estimation of value, and sacrality, Jonathan ranks below the various costly images that Micah fashioned. His initial exchange with the Levite, in which he immediately embarks on a commercial negotiation, together with his larceny expose the centrality of material wealth in his worldview. Indeed, his sin with the idols springs from the desire to materialize the immaterial.

---

37. Robert H. O'Connell, *The Rhetoric of the Book of Judges* (VTSup 63; Leiden: Brill, 1995), 6-7; cf. Meir Sternberg, *The Poetics of Biblical Narrative: Ideological Literature and the Drama of Reading* (Bloomington: Indiana University Press, 1985), 259; Irving Finkel, *The Ark before Noah: Decoding the Story of the Flood* (London: Hodder & Stoughton, 2014), 182.

38. Cf. Michael Fishbane, *Biblical Myth and Rabbinic Mythmaking* (Oxford, New York: Oxford University Press, 2003), 167.

39. Baker, 'A Dream Carries,' 365-67, 377.

The monetary incentive he offers Jonathan, which the latter perceives as 'hire' and is pleased to accept, is ten silvers a year, as against two hundred silvers expended on the graven and molten images, not to mention the 1100 that Micah stole from his mother. It is conceivable that Jonathan does not carry off the molten image (*massēkâ*) when he snatches the other items from Micah's house (18:20; cf. v. 18) simply because its silver content rendered it too heavy for him to carry. Two hundred shekels would keep Jonathan for twenty years, the temporal phrase that concludes the Samson section and that supplies the bridge to the Micah narrative.[40] When the Danites rob Micah, it is the loss of the silver articles that he most laments, not the human capital.[41] The narrative leaves the reader in no doubt as to Micah's value hierarchy, which the number symbolism reinforces.

Daniel Block proposes that Micah's mother operates as a foil in his characterization.[42] In my view, she stands closer than that to the subject. Micah's morality and her own are indistinguishable, he is 'mother's little helper'. After her questionable blessing of her son (17:2), the two characters seem to morph before our eyes into one thieving, idol-producing conglomerate. Hence we have the scrambled giving back and forth of the silver between them and the ambiguity surrounding the identity of the commissioner of the *pesel* and *massēkâ* that complicates the storyline. The mother appears to have been the prime mover and yet the narrator attributes the creation of the *pesel* (and implicitly the *massēkâ*) to Micah (18:31). One might even question whether the son is Micaiah and the morphed son-mother amalgam becomes 'the man Micah' since this name first appears immediately following the mother's receding from the narrative having gifted 'the house of gods' (17:4-5). Thanks to its –*â* ending, outwardly the appellation Micah is grammatically feminine. We have already noted the significance of names in this pericope, a significance intimated by the fact that, save for a fleeting mention of Phinehas in 20:28, Micah and Jonathan are the last named individuals in Judges. Leaving 'Micah' aside, onomastic –*â* is evinced in Judges only with Achsah, Deborah and Delilah, three of the four named female characters in the book. The fourth – Jael – has a rhetorically loaded masculine name. The Judges writer delights in manipulating gender and subverting gender stereotypes.[43] He feminizes patently masculine characters such as Samson and Abimelech and masculinizes female ones, not least by plays on names (Samson, Lappidoth, as well as Jael). Appraised thus, a bi-gendered 'man Micah' would be an audacious variation on the gender distortion encountered elsewhere in the work.

---

40. Cf. S. R. Driver, *A Treatise on the Use of the Tenses in Hebrew and Some Other Syntactical Questions* (3rd edn; Oxford: Clarendon, 1892), §76. The 1100 shekels also link the Micah and the Samson sections (Baker, *Hollow Men*, 81).

41. Webb, *Book of Judges*, 445.

42. Block, *Judges*, 482.

43. Ken Stone, 'Gender Criticism: The Unmanning of Abimelech,' in Yee, *Judges and Method*, 183-201; Klein, *Triumph of Irony*, 42; Susan Niditch, 'Samson as Culture Hero, Trickster, and Bandit,' *CBQ* 54 (1990): 608-24 (617); Baker, *Hollow Men*, 50-55, 236-37.

Be this as it may, it is Jonathan who is Micah's foil. The features that distinguish them and those they share help to define Micah's character. Both individuals fit the description *'ănāšîm rêqîm* 'hollow/empty men' (cf. Judg. 9:4; 11:3), although the writer does not expressly apply it to them. Against formidable competition, for instance the minor judge Elon,[44] they may indeed be the quintessential examples of the type. Like Abimelech and Samson, they are empty of understanding, morality and scruple. Unlike them, however, they are also empty of courage and skill. Both are avaricious.[45] They do whatever strikes them as personally expedient,[46] and possess no loyalty. Just as Micah 'took' his mother's silver, so Jonathan 'took' the items fashioned from that silver, which belonged to his father/son Micah (17:2; 18:20). On the other hand, Micah displays greater initiative, not least in initiating conversations,[47] and, ironically, he is a little more sensible of the spiritual dimension than the Levite Jonathan, as his soliloquy reveals.

Trial by Interrogative: A Biblical Who's Who

One of the Micah section's most striking traits is the prominence it affords to existential questions, specifically, 'who?' and 'what?' Micaiah bears a name that poses the question 'Who is like YHWH?' In ancient Israelite culture, the notion *nomen est omen* had currency.[48] Accordingly, Micaiah's mother's naming him was a performative act and she and he appear to believe that his destiny is to image YHWH. Moreover, Micah not only imagines that he comprehends who YHWH is,[49] he also 'knows' what will induce his blessing. The interrogative pronouns 'who' and 'what' (*mî* and *mâ*) punctuate the pericope. The Danite spies' first utterance is one 'who?'-question followed by two 'what?'-questions. The rarity of this configuration highlights its importance to the narrative (cf. 1 Sam. 20:1).[50] So does the fact that the answer to their initial question is 'Micah.' In Micah's final recorded

---

44. Baker, *Hollow Men*, 151, 154–55.

45. Moster, 'The Levite,' 735.

46. Marc Zvi Brettler, 'The Book of Judges: Literature as Politics,' *JBL* 108 (1983): 395–418 (409).

47. Moster, 'The Levite,' 733–34.

48. Bill T. Arnold, 'Word Play and Characterization in Daniel 1,' in *Puns and Pundits: Word Play in the Hebrew Bible and Ancient Near Eastern Literature* (ed. Scott B. Noegel; Bethesda MD: CDL, 2000), 231–48 (243–45); Roland de Vaux, *Ancient Israel: Its Life and Institutions* (trans. John McHugh; London: Darton, Longman & Todd, 1961), 43; Peter W. Coxon, 'Shadrach, Meshach, Abednego,' *ABD* 6:1150; William Johnstone, *1 and 2 Chronicles. Volume 2. 2 Chronicles 10-36: Guilt and Atonement* (JSOTSup 254; Sheffield: Sheffield Academic Press, 1997), 269; Otto Kaiser, *Isaiah 1-12: A Commentary* (trans. R.A. Wilson; OTL; London: SCM Press, 1972), 90–91.

49. Guest, 'Judges,' 203.

50. Moster, 'The Levite,' 734.

utterance he despairs, 'What remains to me?' (18:24).[51] These interrogative statements stand as sharp reminders that axiomatic questions that were supposed to have been resolved during the forty years in the wilderness – who is YHWH and what is the appropriate response to living in covenant with him? – and that may well have been grasped by the fathers' generation, have again become abstruse. The writer guides his readers to realize that Micah, for all his efforts and confidence in his destiny, creates a hubristic fantasy that will contribute to the destruction of the tribes of the Northern Kingdom.

The prophet Micah the Morashtite had perceived this destruction and its causes. He frames his oracle announcing Israel's destruction with the interrogative pronoun *mî*: 'What [who] is Jacob's transgression? Is it not Samaria? ... Therefore I will make Samaria a heap of rubble ... All her idols [*pesel*s] will be broken to pieces; all her temple gifts will be burned with fire; I will destroy all her images' (Mic. 1:5-7 NIV). Given the Judges author's proclivity for intertextual allusion, it seems probable that as he composed the story of an individual named Micah the words of his older near-contemporary, Micah's namesake, informed his thoughts.[52] The Morashtite's oracles went on to answer the 'what' question and in doing so, at least in part, exposited the 'who' question signalled in his own name: 'He has announced to you, people, what is good and what YHWH seeks from you; namely, to do justice, to love loving-kindness and to walk humbly with your God' (Mic. 6:8). None of the human dramatis personae of Judges 17–18 adheres to the tenets of this prescription. Actually, they do not display the vaguest appreciation of them. The Micah tale offers a lesson in the validity of Graeme Auld's maxim that it is 'good to probe what is involved in men's claims of faithfulness to their god'.[53]

The pericope's 'who?'/'what?' open questions also function to reveal the personalities of the main characters. We may infer that Jonathan's reply to the Danites' 'what are you doing in this place?' was so vapid that the narrator makes do with the summary 'this and that' (18:3-4). The Danites' uncouthness and their ruthless focus on securing land are encapsulated in their terse question to the returning spies, 'What you?' (*mâ 'attem*) (18:8).[54] A 'what'-interrogative triggers Micah's barely coherent outburst against the Danites in which he recasts the Danites' 'what's with you?' into three articulations of 'what' in rapid succession

---

51. Block, *Judges*, 445.

52. 'The Micah collection' was remembered in Jerusalem a century later (Jer. 26:17-19) (Karel van der Toorn, *Scribal Culture and the Making of the Hebrew Bible* [Cambridge, MA: Harvard University Press, 2007], 174; Delbert R. Hillers, 'Micah, Book of,' *ABD* 4:807–10 [808]).

53. A. Graeme Auld, *Joshua Retold: Synoptic Perspectives* (Edinburgh: T&T Clark, 1998), 122.

54. Cf. Burney, *Judges*, 428; Soggin, *Judges*, 273.

55. Baker, 'Double Trouble,' 40.

(thus creating a 3+1 figure) (18:23-24). This constitutes the only occasion that Micah exhibits deep emotion.

Of Ponds and Pebbles: The Kinetic Aspect of Retribution in Judges 17–18

A central irony of Judges is that non-standard figures, the Kenizzites/Edomites Othniel and Achsah, the southpaw Ehud and the woman-leader Deborah are presented as models of virtue, whereas the archetypal son of Israel, Micah, the bearer of a splendid Yahwistic name who hails from the heart of the Promised Land, epitomizes vice.

This tale's scope is, however, much bigger than Micah, Jonathan, the Danites and even the idols with their pretension to divinity and marvelous knowledge. Ultimately, it backlights the wholly silent and apparently absent YHWH, thereby helping the reader to comprehend the answer to the question posed in the segment's first verse, *mîkāyəhû*, who is YHWH/what is he like?

Micah believed that by producing his cultic innovations he was resolving the meaning of this name and revealing the nature of God. This proved to be a grotesque misapprehension with catastrophic results. The account shows how an ordinary individual who is ignorantly and stubbornly wedded to an evil conception contains the seeds of epic destruction in him/herself. Micah's sin was a pebble lobbed into the immense lake of the Northern Kingdom's history. The ripples it created ultimately contributed to its cataclysmic demise.

In Judges 9, the fratricide and the dishonoring of the father determine the fate of all those implicated in the crime, a fate that an execration defines. In that tale, too, YHWH is remote from the action. He is not absent, however. An evil spirit is his agent in realizing the curse upon Abimelech and his accomplices (9:23). The narrative is explicit: God made it happen (9:56-57). In that tale, though, the sin was eliminated by the blood of its perpetrators.[55] The transgressions of Micah and his associates contravene nearly all the Decalogue's precepts.[56] They worship images, manufacture idols, dishonor parents, covet, steal, murder and take YHWH's name in vain.[57] To the charge-sheet, one can add vow-breaking. Seen in this light, they exceed the iniquity of Abimelech and his erstwhile supporters in scope. Judges 17–18 does not disclose what became of Micah. We might infer that he returned to banal existence in Ephraim's hill country. In his story, no transgressor death is recorded, only the flow of generations. But then suddenly the nation itself dies violently as the ultimate purgation.[58]

The Micah section takes the idea of the remoteness of the rejected and offended deity further than any other part of Judges does. YHWH's determination of the sin

---

56. McCann, *Judges*, 120.

57. Marc Z. Brettler, 'Micah,' *ABD* 4:806–7; Younger, *Judges*, 344.

58. Mieke Bal, *Death and Dissymmetry: The Politics of Coherence in the Book of Judges* (Chicago: Chicago University Press, 1988), 1.

59. Soggin, *Judges*, 277.

and execution of its consequences are eerily static, and removed, to the extent that condign retribution for grievous trespass against the commandments assumes an automatic quality. From this perspective, divine punishment possesses a kinetic energy that continues until the sin and the sinners are obliterated. This feature of catastrophic inevitability is in fact encoded in the pathology of Micah's characterization since it too contains a 3+1 pattern. There are four characters with whom he is significantly involved and who, in different ways, lay bare his character. With three of them he is in dialogue: his mother, Jonathan, and the Danites, who speak as one to non-Danites. The fourth is YHWH, whom Micah speaks of but never speaks to, and never hears from. While the three variously amplify Micah's deviance, the Judges reader's accumulated knowledge of the fourth exposes the deviance for what it is and supplies the theological framework to interpret its consequences.

On one level, Judges 17–18 is an exploration of the morbidity of idolatry and covenant-breaking. It describes a chain of causality that has as its touchstone the Decalogue and as its endpoint the Assyrian destruction of tribal Israel. It portrays a theodicy that seemingly takes on an existence of its own.[59] To this is added a complementary hermeneutical layer in the form of Micah's characterization. The plot intimates that we are no different from him: ordinary persons whose impact will be determined by the choices we make and by the standards to which we adhere. This is not all. The Micah story serves notice that the consequences of our choices do not necessarily end with us. They may reverberate down the generations.

Chapter 13

A MOTHER, A SON, A LEVITE AND A TRIBE
(JUDG. 17–18)

Susanne Gillmayr-Bucher

Three interlinked stories tell about the efforts of Micah, a Levite and the tribe of Dan to consolidate their existence in the land. Micah tries to establish a house for himself, the Levite is looking for a place to stay and the Danites are searching for land to settle. Links between these narratives arise due to random encounters opening new possibilities for the narrated characters. The randomness of the sequence of events contributes significantly to the construction of the world of this text. It emphasizes the initial aimlessness of the depicted actions as well as the self-centredness of the narrated characters. This creates the impression of a time in which guidelines, laws, or common goals are lacking. Compared to the previous stories in the book of Judges, the textual world of Judg. 17–18 is clearly different. The schematic framework that shapes the narratives in Judg. 3–16 disappears, there is no hero who rescues the people from enemies, and the idea of a tribal solidarity seems not to exist. Instead of the charismatic figures who take responsibility for the people, Micah is presented as an individual figure caring for his own house and family. And instead of a coalition of several tribes, a single tribe focuses on its own problems. Furthermore, Judg. 17 also omits the common evaluation of the circumstances at the beginning of the stories. Only after the first sequence of events, the narrative voice adds an assessment of the narrated world emphasizing the self-centeredness of all people (v. 6).

This sudden change in the world of the text in the book of Judges makes it difficult to assess the figures, as familiar patterns are not available at first. Top-down processes, in which readers subsume the information given on a figure in the text under a given category, are not easily available. They rather need to accumulate textual information 'until it can be connected with prior knowledge or turned into a category or schema itself'.[1] In order to gather this information, it is necessary to

---

1. Jens Eder, Fotis Jannidis and Ralf Schneider, 'Characters in Fictional Worlds: An Introduction,' in *Characters in Fictional Worlds. Understanding Imaginary Beings in Literature, Film, and Other Media* (ed. Jens Eder, Fotis Jannidis and Ralf Schneider; Berlin, New York: De Gruyter, 2010), 3–64, 35.

pay close attention to the way the figures are presented by the narrative voice or by other figures and also to the various constellations in which they appear. Characters usually do not tend to appear on their own in narratives but are part of constellations which shape their portrayal and offer the readers the possibility to perceive them in different roles.[2] Furthermore, it is worthwhile to ask for the worldview of the individual figures. Although they all share the world created in the text, each of them has his or her own (relative) world. They differ from each other by what they know, wish for or plan to do, they have different obligations or moral standards. Thus, the challenging conflicts of a story can originate from a conflict within a figure (if e.g. a wish and a moral obligation are mutually exclusive), or from conflicting interests of two or more figures.[3] The readers can also recognize conflicts between the worldview(s) of a figure and the values and standards of the world of the text and add it to the characterization of a figure. 'Characterisation (in the wide sense) can then be defined as the process of connecting information with a figure in a text so as to provide a character in the fictional world with a certain property, or properties, concerning body, mind, behaviour, or relations to the (social) environment.'[4]

In order to assess the behaviour of the characters, readers need information about the world of the text. This is normally provided in the text to the extent that the characters and their actions are comprehensible to the readers. However, single biblical stories are embedded in the larger textual world of a biblical book, which can also offer important information for the characterization. Furthermore, cross-book comparisons can prove helpful: what seems to be 'normal' behaviour in one text, can be explicitly rejected or even be prohibited in other books.[5] If the readers

---

2. Cf. Eder, Jannidis, Schneider, 'Characters in Fictional Worlds,' 26; see also Benjamin J. M. Johnson, 'Character as interpretive Crux in the Book of Samuel,' in *Characters and Characterization in the Book of Samuel* (ed. Keith Bodner and Benjamin J. M. Johnson) London: T&T Clark, 2020), 1–13, 5.

3. See Andrea Gutenberg, *Mögliche Welten. Plot und Sinnstiftung im englischen Frauenroman* (Heidelberg: Universitätsverlag C. Winter, 2000); Ansgar Nünning and Vera Nünning, 'Multiperspektivität aus narratologischer Sicht. Erzähltheoretische Grundlagen und Kategorien zur Analyse der Perspektivenstruktur narrativer Texte,' in *Multiperspektivisches Erzählen. Zur Theorie und Geschichte der Perspektivenstruktur im englischen Roman des 18. bis 20. Jahrhunderts* (ed. Ansgar Nünning and Vera Nünning; Trier: Wissenschaftlicher Verlag Trier, 2000), 39–77; Susanne Gillmayr-Bucher, *Erzählte Welten im Richterbuch. Narratologische Aspekte eines polyfonen Diskurses* (BIS 116; Leiden: Brill, 2013), 10–16.

4. Eder, Jannidis, Schneider, 'Characters in Fictional Worlds,' 32.

5. In the canonical order, the book of Judges is placed in a larger context ranging from the narratives of the Exodus from Egypt and the conquest of the land to the beginnings of the monarchy, and thus shares in the text world of these books. Regardless of possibly underlying ancient narrative traditions and their originally independent text worlds, readers also perceive the narratives of the Book of Judges as part of this larger text world.

come across (serious) differences, the perspective on characters or a whole narrative may change as readers must decide whether the texts present different sets of obligations, or, whether readers are asked to critically consider the textual world at hand by the standards of another.

The constellation of figures in Judg. 17–18

The stories in Judg. 17–18 mention eight figures or groups of figures, who appear in different roles and with different frequency. The only figure given a name is Micah, the others are identified either by their relation to Micah (his mother, his sons), or by their tribal affiliation (Levite,[6] Danites), the town they live in (inhabitants of Laish), their trade (refiner = gold/silversmith) or their temporary task (scouts). This already emphasizes that Micah is given a special role in these stories. He, his house and his sanctuary are shown as an intersection and a transit point where others linger, meet, depart, but which they also exploit. Nevertheless, the stories do not only focus on Micah, they rather present different scenes in which different constellations of figures are prominent.

- The first scene (17:1-6) provides a short glimpse into Micah's family: Micah, his mother and his sons, who are mentioned, but not developed as characters, and it also mentions a silversmith.
- This nuclear family is extended by the arrival of a Levite, whom Micah engages as a priest (vv. 7-13).
- Chapter 18 then introduces the tribe of Dan looking for a place to settle. Thus, five men from the tribe are sent out as scouts to explore a new settlement area. When they set out on their mission, they pass Micah's house. However, Micah is not involved in this encounter, instead the Levite meets the scouts (vv. 3-6). After a short stay, the scouts move on until they come to the town of Laish and recognize it as an ideal settlement area (v. 7). They persuade their tribe to set out and to conquer Laish (vv. 8-12).
- On their way there, they come to Micah's house again (vv. 14-17). They first meet the Levite (vv. 18-20), but now as Micah enters the scene, he meets the Danites, as they are about carry away his cult objects from the sanctuary (vv. 22-26). Furthermore, the Levite joins the Danites and leaves Micah.
- The story continues with a summary of the tribe of Dan's successful conquest of Laish (vv. 27-31). In the end, Micah's accomplishments serve the Danites, and the stability he had desired for his home and his family, likewise passes to the Danites.

---

6. Judg. 18:30, a later addition identifies the unnamed Levite from Bethlehem with Jonathan, a grandson of Moses. Implicit in this attribution is a criticism, since it would mean that the second generation after Moses had already turned to this pernicious cult of images. See Walter Groß, *Richter* (Herders Theologischer Kommentar Altes Testament; Freiburg i. Br.: Herder, 2009), 793.

Micah, his Mother and his Sons (Judg. 17:1-6)

Judges 17 explicitly starts a new story introducing a man from the hill country of Ephraim, named Micah.[7] However, instead of providing some more information on the village, Micah's family or tribal affiliation,[8] the next verse brings the reader into the middle of a dialogue between Micah and his mother as they discuss 1,100 pieces of silver. Micah is returning this considerable amount of silver to his mother, but why he possesses the money to which his mother is entitled and why he is returning it is not explained. The origin of the money and its further whereabouts remain unclear and cast doubt on the integrity of the characters. Such a considerable amount of money raises the suspicion that it could be a reward for an act of treason or an assault, hush money or a bribe.[9] But not only does Micah's mother seem dubious, Micah's honesty could also be in doubt, as it is not explained how Micah came into possession of the money.[10] Micah declares that the silver, which has been taken for his mother,[11] and which she has protected with an oath, is now with him.[12] He further explains that he took it. This statement can be understood either as an admission of guilt that it was he who took the silver, or as an explanation of why the silver is now with him, i.e., that he took the silver from the one who stole it from his mother. Regardless of how one understands this statement, the

---

7. Only in v. 1 the longer form of the name מיכיהו ('who is like YHWH') is used; all further references use the shorter form מיכה.

8. Such information is usually given, cf. Judg. 13:2; 19:16; 1 Sam. 1:1; 9:1. In the book of Judges, Micah is the only main character whose father is not named. See Mercedes García Bachmann, *Judges* (Wisdom Commentary 7; Collegeville: Liturgical Press, 2018), 198.

9. The first allusion points to the lords of the Philistines, each of them offering Delilah 1,100 pieces of silver for finding out the origin of Samson's strength (Judg. 16:5). In Gen 20:16, Abimelech gives Abraham 1,000 pieces of silver as a covering for the eyes of all those who are with Sarah and for vindication. In 2 Sam. 18:12, 1,000 pieces of silver would not be enough to commit murder; 2 Kgs 15:19, king Menahem tries to bribe Pul, king of Assur with 1,000 pieces of silver.

10. Many exegetes suspect that Micah stole the money from his mother. See e.g. Renate Jost, 'Der Fluch der Mutter. Feministisch-sozialgeschichtliche Überlegungen zu Ri 17,1–6,' in Renate Jost, *Feministische Bibelauslegungen. Grundlagen – Forschungsgeschichtliches – Geschlechterstudien* (Internationale Forschungen in Feministischer Theologie und Religion. Befreiende Perspektiven 1) Berlin: LIT Verlag, 2014), 123–129, 124–125; Jason Bray, *Sacred Dan. Religious Tradition and Cultic Practice in Judges 17–18*, (LHBOTS 449; London, New York: T&T Clark, 2006), 32; Trent Butler, *Judges* WBC 8; Nashville: Thomas Nelson, 2009), 377–78; García Bachmann, *Judges* (Wisdom Commentary 7; Collegeville: Liturgical Press, 2018), 199.

11. The phrase לקח־לך 'been taken for you,' which only occurs here, is not the same as לקח מן 'take away from.'

12. Cf. Ina Willi-Plein, *Opfer und Kult im alttestamentlichen Israel* (Stuttgarter Bibelstudien 153; Stuttgart: Katholisches Bibelwerk, 1993), 9–11.

circumstances of how the silver disappeared and was recovered remain obscure. Nonetheless, the mother's reaction to this announcement is favourable. The formulation ברוך ... ליהוה expresses gratitude for solidarity shown (cf. Ruth 2:20; 3:10; 1 Sam. 23:21; 2 Sam. 2:5). So it seems that the mother approves Micah's action.[13] The next verse briefly mentions that Micah hands over the money to his mother as announced. Thereupon, the mother takes the initiative and determines the destination of the money, consecrating it to YHWH and specifying that a cult image and cast image (פסל ומסכה) should be made. She also includes her son as a beneficiary of her actions and wants him to manage the money. When he refuses, she does not hesitate, but takes 200 pieces of silver and commissions a silversmith.[14] Once the פסל ומסכה have been made, Micah's mother and the rest of the money disappear from the narrative.

Nevertheless, her character deserves attention; her decisions not only set the following events in motion, but her attitude and world view also establish a basic attitude for the narrative.[15] Micah's mother is presented as a self-confident, pragmatic woman who knows what to do. She does not hesitate to evaluate a situation or to make a decision. The mother's words also allow a glimpse into her religious beliefs. Twice she mentions YHWH – blessing her son and dedicating the money – thus establishing a relationship that marks her as a worshipper of YHWH. In her imagination, the production of cult images also seems to be compatible with the cult of YHWH, and neither the narrative voice nor any other character criticizes this understanding. Nonetheless, what seems to be justified from the perspective of Micah's mother raises doubts among the readers: her unexplained wealth and her commissioning of cult images does not meet the expectations of other biblical texts.[16] Thus, at this point of the story, the readers have two sets of information: According to the text, Micah's mother appears as a

---

13. Jost interprets this short dialogue even further and means that the mother takes back the oath and thus shows mercy to her son. Jost, 'Der Fluch,' 125. See also Barry Webb, *The Book of Judges* (NICOT; Grand Rapids: Eerdmans, 2012), 424.

14. These objects probably represented YHWH in an anthropomorphic or theriomorphic shape. Walter Groß, 'Michas überfüllte Hauskapelle. Bemerkungen zu Ri 17+18,' in *Studien zum Richterbuch und seinen Völkernamen* (ed. Walter Groß and Erasmus Gaß; Stuttgarter biblische Aufsatzbände Altes Testament 54; Stuttgart: Katholisches Bibelwerk, 2012), 72–88, 83.

15. Cf. Gillmayr-Bucher, *Erzählte Welten*, 198.

16. See the explicit rejection in Deut. 27:15; Nah. 1:14; Isa. 42:17; Hab. 2:18. To make a מסכה, a term often used for images of other deities, is also prohibited in Exod. 34:17; Lev. 19:4; as a negative example it is used in 1 Kgs 14:9 and 2 Kgs 17:16. A פסל is also rejected in Exod. 20:4; Deut. 4:16.23.25; 5:8; Lev. 26:1; cf. also Isa. 44:9.10.15.17; for a negative example of erecting a פסל see 2 Kgs 21:7; 2 Chron. 33:7. Nonetheless, in Judg. 17 the פסל ומסכה probably are cultic representations of YHWH, but not a clear sign of idolatry (see Groß, *Richter*, 759). The מסכה par excellence is the golden calf (Exod 32), which is often remembered as a negative example (cf. Deut. 9:16; 2 Kgs 17:16; Neh. 9:18). Cf. Bray, *Sacred Dan*, 64–66.

capable woman with clear – and at first sight – honorable plans. However, if the readers include information from other biblical texts, her attitude and her actions appear questionable.

The role of Micah serves to give his mother room for maneuver, as he knows about the whereabouts of the silver. Although the story does not explain in any detail how Micah is connected to the money, he seems to be interested only in returning it to his mother, but not in taking it for himself.

Before the narration continues, a summary is added pointing out the effect of the previous events for Micah: 'and the man Micah, for him (was) a house of God(s) (בית אלהים)' (v. 5).[17] This commentary interprets the result of the mother's actions as the establishment of a sanctuary for Micah[18] and thus attributes great importance to these events. Again, seen in the context of the instructions for the installation of a sanctuary formulated in the book of Deuteronomy, Micah's sanctuary does not meet the expectations. The prohibition of idols but also the instruction that God has to choose the place is violated.[19] Like the judges in the chapters before, the figures in this text seem to be in the dark on how to understand YHWH.[20]

After that, Micah becomes active and has more cult objects made, an אפד and תרפים.[21] In this way, Micah continues his mother's initiative, and he further enhances the sanctuary.[22] In the light of other biblical texts, the cultic installations are ambivalent at best. While the ephod is usually mentioned as a legitimate cult object, the teraphim are viewed more critically.[23] Although Micah does not make any plans of his own, he proves to be very adept at assessing the possibilities of a situation and taking advantage of them. And after Micah has assembled the cult

---

17. Only v. 5 mentions the 'house of God(s)' (בית אלהים), otherwise the idols are placed in the house of Micah or the house of the Levite.

18. Cf. also Judg. 18:31, where the only other 'house of God(s)' (בית אלהים) in this story is located in Shiloh.

19. Cf. Deut. 12:5.11.14.18.21.26; 14:24.25; 15:20; 16:2.6.7.11.15.16; 17:8; 18:6; 26:2; 31:11; see also Neh. 1:9; 2 Chron. 7:12.

20. Cf. Robert Polzin, *Moses and the Deuteronomist. A literary study of the Deuteronomic History* (New York: Seabury, 1980), 173.

21. The ephod and the teraphim can be used for divination, cf. 1 Sam. 23:9-12; 30:7-8; Ezek. 21:26; Zech. 10:2.

22. The spatial relation between and Micah's house and the 'house of God(s)' is not elaborated. These could be different buildings; however, Micah's 'house of God' could have also been a "cult corner" or 'cult niche', a 'part of a room or courtyard' within a house that was designated for religious purposes and that thus contained a constellation of religious objects and furnishings.' Benjamin Cox and Susan Ackerman, 'Micah's Teraphim,' *JHS* 12, Art. 11 (2012): 1–37, 19.

23. Hos 3:4 is the only other text mentioning ephod and teraphim as legitimate cult objects. Cf. Groß, 'Michas überfüllte Hauskapelle,' 83; Cox and Ackerman, 'Micah's Teraphim,' 15.

objects, he goes one step further and appoints one of his sons as a priest for the sanctuary (v. 5).[24] In this way, he establishes a family tradition, in which the initiative of Micah's mother is continued by Micah and his son.

Micah's role as a son and father in these verses emphasizes that he is building his own house, he is restructuring his family around the sanctuary. He is trying to establish a center. Setting this first scene in a larger context, critical aspects become obvious. Micah's efforts allude to other stories dealing with the construction of a sanctuary, e.g. 1 Kings 12:28-29, the implementation of Jeroboam's sanctuaries in Dan and Beth El,[25] albeit on an individual level. Like Jeroboam, Micah establishes a sanctuary with his own idols, which provide representations of YHWH,[26] and he also appoints any priest at hand (cf. 1 Kgs 12:31; 13:33; 2 Chron. 13:9). Micah's sanctuary is neither carefully planned nor approved by YHWH, it rather just happens to come into existence, and Micah interprets the successful completion as a sign that God will prosper him (v. 13).

A general comment on the era concludes the first scene in this story and further enhances the critical questions and doubts the readers might have: 'In those days there was no king in Israel. Everyone did what was right in his own eyes' (v. 6).[27] While the story mostly presents the perspective of the narrated characters, this commentary shifts the perception of the readers and encourages them to apply well known schemas from other biblical stories to their evaluation of the figures of the text. In this way it becomes obvious that self-determined actions are not usually seen in a positive light, and the decision on what is right or wrong is not considered to be an individual choice,[28] so that this attitude is not consistent with the ideals found in other biblical books.

Micah Meets a Levite (vv. 7-13)

The second scene starts like the first with the introduction of a new character: a young man (נער), a Levite, from Bethlehem in Judah enters the scene. The information provided on this man's origins describes him as a landless and thus

---

24. The expression 'to fill the hand of someone' is a technical term for ordaining a person to serve as a priest (e.g. Exod. 28:41; 29:9.29; Lev. 8:33; 21:10; Num. 3:3). See Butler, *Judges*, 382.

25. Cf. Nadav Naaman, 'The Danite campaign northward (Judges XVII–XVIII) and the migration of the Phocaeans Massalia (Strabo VI 1,4),' *VT* 55 (2005): 47–60, 51.

26. Cf. Susan Niditch, *Judges: A Commentary* (OTL; Louisville: Westminster John Knox, 2008), 181; see also Butler, *Judges*, 382.

27. Amit points out that the critique of this statements is twofold: 'On the one hand, it constitutes a critical summary of what was related earlier . . . on the other hand, it constitutes an opening, throwing negative light on what will appear further on.' Yairah Amit, *Hidden Polemics in Biblical Narrative* (BIS 25; Leiden: Brill, 2000), 101.

28. Cf. Prov. 12:15; 21:2; for a cultic context see e.g. Deut. 12:8.

socially dependent person: He is from a family (מִשְׁפָּחָה) of Judah, but he also is a Levite and he is living in Bethlehem as a sojourner (גֵּר).[29] This description already hints that the young man does not have strong roots in Judah, and v. 8 shows him on the way, looking for a new place to stay as a גֵּר. He sets out without a clear destination, and so he comes to the hill country of Ephraim.[30] Although the Levite plays an important role in the following events, he remains without a name.[31]

When he passes Micah's house, Micah involves him in a conversation. The Levite answers his questions, emphasizing his search for a place to stay. Micah invites the Levite to stay with him as a priest (vv. 9-10), offering him a salary, garments and livelihood.

So Micah seizes the chance meeting as an opportunity to further improve his sanctuary. Micah's invitation offers an interesting insight into his hopes: he offers the Levite not only the role of priest but also of a father.[32] This shows that Micah is looking for guidance.[33] But his expectation that the Levite might provide orientation is not fulfilled. Rather, the still inexperienced Levite becomes like one of his sons (v. 11). This commentary indicates a discrepancy between Micah's desires and the resources available to him; Micah, according to the narrative voice,

---

29. Groß points out that מִשְׁפָּחָה can not only denote a family or a tribe, but also a larger group of people (Groß, *Richter*, 775–76); or מִשְׁפָּחָה may even refer to the territory of a family (Herrmann Niemann, *Die Daniten. Studien zur Geschichte eines altisraelitischen Stammes* [Forschungen zur Religion und Literatur des Alten und Neuen Testaments 135; Göttingen: Vandenhoeck & Ruprecht, 1985], 65). The verb גּוּר is attributed to an Israelite who does not reside his native place (cf. Markus Zehnder, *Umgang mit dem Fremden in Israel und Assyrien. Ein Beitrag zur Anthropologie des Fremden im Licht antiker Quellen*, BWANT 168 (Stuttgart: Kohlhammer, 2005), 285). Furthermore, a גֵּר can also denote an economic dependence (cf. Christoph Bultmann, *Der Fremde im antiken Juda. Eine Untersuchung zum sozialen Typenbegriff 'ger' und seinem Bedeutungswandel in der alttestamentlichen Gesetzgebung* [Forschung zur Religion und Literatur des Alten und Neuen Testaments 153; Göttingen: Vandenhoeck & Ruprecht, 1992, 134]).

30. In Judg. 19, another Levite makes a similar journey; he is living in the hill country of Ephraim and travels to Bethlehem.

31. He is called a young man (17:7.11.12; 18:3.15), a Levite (17:7.9.10.11.12.13; 18:3.15) and a priest (17:10.12.13; 18:4.6.19.17.18.20.24.27).

32. אָב can be used as an honorific form of address, emphasizing respect and referring to a special relationship (cf. 1 Sam. 24:12; 2 Kgs 2:12; 2 Kgs 6:21; Gen. 45:8). See Butler, *Judges*, 388.

33. Micah's expectation of the Levite is reminiscent of Deut. 33:8-11, where the proclamation of the Torah, and thus instruction for a successful life, is presented as one of the main functions of the Levites. However, the combination of priest and father is uncommon. Usually, a father, a priest and a Levite have different roles (e.g. in Ezra 1:5; 3:12; 8:29; Neh. 8:13; 2 Chron. 19:8 the heads of the fathers, the priests and Levites, are listed as responsible for the people). Micah summarizes all these expectations in the hope he holds for the young man.

does not assess things correctly. After this comment, the story allows another glimpse into Micah's perspective, and reveals that he still considers the presence of a Levite as a guarantee for YHWH's lasting attention and support (v. 13).[34] Furthermore, in this statement Micah mentions YHWH for the first time, thus indicating that he, like his mother, sees himself as a worshipper of YHWH.

In view of the quite unusual appointment of the Levite as a priest, this estimation of the situation again raises doubts about Micah and his worship. The phrase 'to become a priest for someone' (היה ל לכהן) is used throughout this narrative,[35] by which the priesthood of the Levite is not stated in general terms but is explicitly connected with Micah and later the tribe of Dan.[36] This special relation between Micah and his priest is unusual and reinforces the readers' doubts about the cult Micah installs. The allusions to other occurrences of this phrase in 2 Kgs 17:32, 2 Chron. 13:9 provides a critical perspective, reminding the readers that appointing priests for oneself like the peoples of the lands is not a desirable practice.

Micah, however, seems to be unaware of such critical thoughts. Following in the footsteps of his mother, he aims to consolidate his sanctuary and he knows how to take advantage of opportunities. He is living in his small world, which consists of his sanctuary, house and family. Nonetheless, he is not isolating himself, but willing to include new persons if they fit into his concept. In contrast, the Levite is portrayed as a figure still on its way, literally and figuratively. He does not pursue a goal but leaves it to chance where he will end up, readily following the suggestions of others. The Levite seems to lack any ambitions and even his decision to accept Micah's offer (v. 11) is only summarized by the narrative voice.

The Danite Scouts Find the Levite (Judg. 18:1-21)

After Micah's confident summary of his situation, a new story starts in Judges 18. It begins with a general statement about the narrated time, and in this time a new protagonist, the tribe of Dan, is introduced in search of an inheritance (v. 1). As in Judges 1, when the tribes were looking for land to settle, the Danites set out again to conquer their territory.[37] This plan is justified by the explanation that no inheritance (נחלה) had fallen to Dan, a statement which contradicts Josh 19:40-

---

34. Niditch points out that a Levite is considered to be a mediator between God and humans, and to have divinatory abilities. From this perspective, it is great luck for Micah to find a Levite. See Niditch, *Judges*, 182.

35. The phrase is found in the appointment of the son as priest 17:5; in Micah's speech ('for me,' vv. 10, 13), the summary of the narrative voice ('for him,' v. 12), in the Levite's answer to the Danites (18:4), likewise in the Danites' speech (18:19) and in the summary at the end of the narrative (18:30).

36. Cf. Groß, *Richter*, 778.

37. Compared to the beginning of the book of Judges, it is noteworthy that their war campaign is not legitimized by YHWH but their own idea. Cf. García Bachmann, *Judges*, 204.

48.[38] Judges 1 also assumes that a land was granted to the Danites, but vv. 34-35 report that the Amorites prevented the Danites from advancing into their lot; the Danites thus appear weak and unsuccessful. Comparing these texts it is obvious that the unflattering portray of Dan in Judg. 1 gives way to a more favorable image of Dan in Judg. 18. In this story the Danites are no longer incapable of securing their land but they prove to be strong and assertive. Before the tribe sets out, they appoint five men and commission them to scout out a new settlement area (vv. 1-2). On their way they come to Micah's house and in this way the two stories are linked together. Within the story of Micah, the appearance of the Danites and their plan opens a new arc of suspense.

The five scouts are particularly capable men (אנשים בני־חיל) acting proactively and with great competence. On their way they pay close attention to every detail. This first becomes evident when they pay attention to the voice of the Levite. The scouts are able to recognize that he does not belong to this place, which attracts their interest, so they turn to the house of Micah and ask the Levite for the reason of his presence. What first appears as a random element soon turns out to be a valuable information. Once their interest is aroused, they get to the bottom of things asking the Levite interrogation-like questions (v. 3). In addition, they also use the newly acquired information immediately in their favour, using the cultic competence of the Levite to make sure of the success of their mission.

This encounter also adds further information on the characterization of the Levite. It is only in this situation, when the five Danites ask him to consult God (v. 5), that he is shown to act as a priest in Micah's sanctuary.[39] The Danites, who at first still recognized the Levite as a young, dependent man (נער), ask him for an oracle only after they have learned of his installation as priest. Now they take him seriously in his new role. When the narrative voice introduces his oracle in v. 6, it also calls him a priest. Thus, the Levite develops from a נער, a socially dependent person,[40] to a priest (כהן).

Instead of giving a clear answer to the scouts' question whether their journey will succeed, the Levite's information remains ambivalent. The first statement is an assurance to 'go in peace' (לכו לשלום) referring both to the further journey of the scouts and to their relationship with the Levite; and the following words describe the way of the men as one that is before God (נכח יהוה). This spatial metaphor points to God's special attention, which can be read in terms of both supportive

---

38. The book of Judges does not present a list of the land allotted to the tribes but presupposes the information in the book of Joshua. According to Josh. 19:40-48, the tribe of Dan received a share of the land, but later lost it. They then moved north and captured the city of Leshem, which they renamed Dan.

39. Cf. Gillmayr-Bucher, *Erzählte Welten*, 199.

40. Stähli understands the designation נער not only as a 'young man' but as an occupational designation, as a kind of 'sacerdotal servant'. Hans-Peter Stähli, *Knabe – Jüngling –Knecht. Untersuchungen zum Begriff נער im Alten Testament* (Beiträge zur biblischen Exegese und Theologie 7; Frankfurt a. M.: Peter Lang, 1978), 208–11.

and critical attention.⁴¹ The further course of the narrative confirms a positive reading, the way of the scouts will be successful. Thus, the Levite proves to be a capable priest who can deliver an oracle.

In this scene, the presence of the Levite links the narrative of Micah to the narrative of the tribe of Dan, for it is through him that the scouts become aware of Micah's sanctuary, and it is to him and the sanctuary he administers that the scouts return with the warriors from their tribe. And only then it becomes obvious that the scouts did not only discover Micah's sanctuary, but they were also able to estimate its value and its vulnerability. Although the Levite does not seem to actively pursue any goals of his own, he has a central position in the narrative, which is due to the appreciation of his role by other characters. To Micah and the Danite scouts alike, the Levite seems to be of interest only insofar as his presence completes a sanctuary and offers the possibility to communicate with God. So, as a Levite this man is in high demand and others make use of him for their own plans; his character, however, is hardly developed.

After their encounter with the Levite, the scouts continue their journey until they come to Laish. They quickly recognize that this city would be an ideal settlement area for the Danites.⁴² The narrator's assessment of the area is presented from the scouts' perspective only (v. 7). Their perception is entirely shaped by their mission, focusing on the readiness of the inhabitants to defend the city and possible support from nearby people. What they see is a peaceful and defenceless population which seems to be easy prey. Once they return, they encourage their people to take advantage of their discoveries (v. 9). Before they even tell what they have seen (v. 10), they are already urging departure. In their detailed report, they emphasize the fertility of the land and the weakness of its inhabitants, but they also assure the people of God's support and emphasize that the deity has given the land into their hands. Thus they are offering a theological interpretation of their trip as well.⁴³ Nonetheless, their certainty of success is only their subjective interpretation, for there is no explicit indication that God has given this land to the Danites.

The portrait of the Danite scouts clearly refers to the men sent out by Moses in Num. 13, who provide a negative foil in relation to which the five Danites can be viewed. Compared to the scouts in Num. 13, it is noticeable that the observations of the Danites are told in reverse order. While the scouts in Num. 13 first pay attention to the fertility of the land (Num. 13:23) and only in their report address the military strength of the inhabitants (Num. 13:28-29), it is exactly the opposite

---

41. A similar formulation is found only in Prov. 5:21 'For before the eyes of YHWH (are) the ways of a man' (נכח עיני יהוה), here with a critical function.

42. The portrait of the Danite scouts clearly is constructed in contrast to the scouts in Num. 13. These five Danites are presented as exemplary scouts.

43. The phrase נתן ביד is frequently used in the book of Judges. If God has already given somebody into the hands of Israel, this phrase firmly encourages the audience to assess a given situation as advantageous.

in Judg. 18. The Danite scouts are at first mainly interested in the military defence situation (v. 7), and only later report about the attractiveness of the land as a whole (v. 10). As in Num. 13, the decision whether the people will dare to conquer depends on the report of the scouts. Unlike Num. 13, the Danite scouts present the situation quite optimistically: the land is conquerable, and the resident population is not prepared for a fight. In this respect, the five men prove to be not only good scouts but also ideal supporters of the tribe's desire for a new settlement area.

After their successful report, the scouts assume the task leading the tribe's warriors towards Laish (v. 11). Although Micah's house is not the destination of the Danites, they pass it on their way. But it is only when they have arrived there that the scouts point out the existence of the sanctuary together with its cult objects to the others. This second visit shows that the scouts also consistently apply the knowledge they gained during their exploration for the benefit of their tribe.[44] First they address their companions with a rhetorical question: 'Do you know that in these houses there are ephod and teraphim?' (v. 14), which emphasizes their exclusive knowledge. The scouts share their knowledge, but in contrast to the clear request in v. 9, they now leave it to the others to use this knowledge accordingly. What they want to achieve remains ambivalent. In the light of their previous visit, it could be an invitation to ask for an oracle. However, the rhetorical question can also be an indirect invitation to take possession of these objects – and this happens in the further course of the story.

The focus of this scene is yet another dialogue with the Levite (vv. 18-19), in which the scout's plans become obvious. When the Levite tries to prevent the Danites from taking away the cult objects, they rebuff his resistance by curtly commanding him to be silent (v. 19), but they also add the offer to join them and become a father and priest for the Danites. Thus they make the same offer as Micah (17:10). Although they do not offer him a salary, their rhetorical questions aim at comparing the current situation and the offer made by the Danites. Explicitly pointing out the larger sphere of influence, they ask the Levite to see the advantages for himself. They succeed and overcome his resistance. The narrative voice even goes one step further by providing an insight into the Levite's emotional reaction (v. 20), which shows that he gladly agrees to the new opportunity: 'And the heart of the priest became glad' (וייטב לב הכהן).[45] Immediately afterwards, it is reported that the Levite takes the cult objects and joins the Danites. Webb points out that 'both acts have symbolic significance. By taking these tokens of priestly office from the five men, he effectively accepts reconsecration at their hands, and by moving into

---

44. Cf. Gillmayr-Bucher, *Erzählte Welten*, 203.

45. The phrase: 'to make the heart glad' is mostly used in contexts that mention a glad heart in combination with good food and drink (e.g. Judg. 19:6, 9.22; Ruth 3:7; 1 Kgs 21:7; also Eccl. 11:9); it describes a state of freedom from worries and an emotional affirmation of the situation. This phrase also connects Judg. 18 with the next chapter, were another nameless Levite frequently makes his heart glad or is invited to do so.

the midst of the migrating Danites he symbolically cuts himself off from Micah and accepts them as his new constituency.'[46]

Once the takeover of the cult objects and the Levite is secured, the scouts disappear from the story; they have fulfilled their function.

Micah Confronts the Danites (18:22-27)

It is only after the Danites have left Micah's property together with the Levite and the objects from Micah's sanctuary that Micah comes into view (v. 22). The alarm is raised, and men are summoned to take up the chase together with Micah. They catch up with the Danites and get their attention, but they are unable to recover the stolen items. A short dialogue with the Danites shows that they argue from a position of strength and do not accept other arguments.[47] When Micah charges them with theft and describes the situation from his perspective, they reject him brusquely.[48] Micah's claim to the preservation of one's possessions and the right of the strongest, as enforced by the Danites, collide.[49] The threat of the Danites (v. 25) leaves no doubt that they will use their superior strength. For the sake of emphasis, they even refer to themselves as 'men of bitter disposition' (אנשים מרי נפש);[50] they see themselves as fierce men who will stop at nothing. In view of this threatening situation, Micah takes no further risk and turns back without having achieved anything. In contrast to the people of Dan, Micah is not described as brave, nor is he transformed into a hero (like Gideon, Judg. 6).

Once the Danites took away the gods Micah had made and the Levite (18:24), there is nothing left for Micah. While at the beginning, the cult images and the priest were a part of Micah's house, they are increasingly taking center stage as Micah's rhetorical question 'and what (remains) for me? ' points out (v. 24). 'His gods'[51] and the Levite have become the center of his world. Although Micah's worship is directed towards YHWH, the cult, nevertheless, is shown as self-made and lacks divine approval. It is noteworthy, however, that Micah is not punished by God, he is not given into the hands of strangers, rather, another tribe of the

---

46. Webb, *Judges*, 442.

47. Cf. Gillmayr-Bucher, *Erzählte Welten*, 201.

48. Bray points out that the series of short phrases in Micah's answer (v. 24) imitates his breathlessness. Bray, *Sacred Dan*, 39.

49. Cf. Webb, *Judges*, 444-45.

50. See David's men (1 Sam. 22:2) or Hushai's description of David's heroes (2 Sam. 17:8).

51. The phrase Micah uses in his claim: 'My gods that I have made for myself,' is turned into an accusation in Jer. 2:28: 'Where are your gods that you have made for yourself?'; see also Amos 5:26.

Israelites desires his achievement and deprives him of the symbols of his confidence and faith.[52]

In the estimation of the Danites, Micah's sanctuary appears to be something they consider desirable.[53] However, they do not mimic the idea of building a sanctuary but take the relevant cult objects and cult personnel to install in their shrine. For the readers, however, it is obvious that this is a questionable attitude at best. It not only contradicts the commandment of the Decalogue 'you shall not covet' and 'you shall not steal'. Furthermore, the concept of a sanctuary built not only with randomly available objects and people, but even with stolen property, is an obvious contrast to the dignity of a sanctuary. The portrait of the Levite further complements this upside-down image of a sanctuary and completes this idea of a twisted world. He is unable to provide the necessary guidance in the name of YHWH. The later ideal image of the Levite protecting the tradition of the Torah and encouraging the observance of its obligations is lacking.[54]

The Inhabitants of Laish and the Danites

The portrayal of the Danites and the inhabitants of Laish could not be more different. The Danites are not settled but on the move, searching for a place to live. They are determined and they have 600 well-equipped warriors (vv. 11, 16, 17), demonstrating their strength and superiority. The inhabitants of Laish are the exact opposite: they live peacefully and safely in their city and land; they are quiet and guileless, without conflicts but also without protection (v. 7).[55] The description of these people is first given form the scouts' point of view (v. 7) and it is then repeated by the narrative voice (v. 27), emphasizing that the people of Laish and their land really emanate well-being and wealth. In the perspective of the narrative voice, the description of this people and their way of life resembles the life in the land promised to Israel (cf. Lev. 25:18-19; 26:5; Deut. 12:19).[56] This description of the inhabitants of the city of Laish deviates significantly from the usual description

---

52. Cox and Ackerman point out that especially the teraphim could not be replaced easily. These figurines represent the deceased ancestors who 'participate in the safeguarding of the familial patrimony through their presence in their descendants' homes or extended household compounds.' They thus have a special role in the well-being of a family. Cox and Ackerman, 'Micah's Teraphim,' 27.

53. Susanne Gillmayr-Bucher, 'Images of Tranquility in the Book of Judges,' in *History, Memory, Hebrew Scriptures. A Festschrift for Ehud Ben Zvi* (ed. Ian Wilson and Diana Edelman; Winona Lake: Eisenbrauns, 2015), 35–47, 41.

54. Cf. Reinhard Achenbach, 'Levitische Priester und Leviten im Deuteronomium,' *Zeitschrift für Altorientalische und biblische Rechtsgeschichte* 5 (1999): 285–309, 285.

55. The phrase מציל ואין (v. 28) usually refers to the situation of someone whose last and only stronghold is YHWH. Cf. Gillmayr-Bucher, *Erzählte Welten*, 204–205.

56. Gillmayr-Bucher, *Images of tranquility*, 43–44.

of foreign peoples in the book of Judges. This city and its inhabitants are not presented as a menace to Israel; on the contrary, their peaceful and reserved way of life poses no threat to anyone. When the narrative voice thus describes the inhabitants of Laish with sympathy and admiration, this portrayal influences the portrait of the Danites. Their attack does not show them as brave warriors or even heroes, but rather as ruthless conquerors, overrunning defenceless people. The allusion to Deut. 20:10 and the requirement to offer peace before fighting a city further emphasizes this critical view. But despite all discrepancies, the Danites successfully conquer a place for themselves, they give the town a new name, Dan, and they also establish a sanctuary.

Summary

The world and the characters presented in the stories of Judg. 17–18 unfold without providing a secure point of view for the readers. The combination of different aspects – the sanctuary of Micah in the mountains of Ephraim, the unconventional foundation of the sanctuary in Dan, the lack of leadership and the self-centredness the people – is used to portray a twisted world. Traditional points of view are turned upside down: 'Micah, who practices hospitality and provides lodging to the five able men from Dan, is punished; the Levite, who drives a hard bargain and abandons values of loyalty and gratitude, ends up benefiting; while the Danites, who plunder others, end up victorious and achieving their goal.'[57] Nevertheless, the way the figures are portrayed is not totally negative; evoking sympathy for the twisted world belongs to the persuasive strategy of the narration. In this way, the characters are more understandable, and thus they do not only reaffirm the readers in their superior position but also challenge the readers' own attitudes.

Throughout the narrative, each of the figures follows its own plans, but no one is portrayed as a driving force behind all the events. Micah is shown as a man who reacts to various events but rarely takes the initiative.[58] He blends into his mother's plans, develops them, and creates his own world out of them. However, despite his hopes, his house does not become a stronghold but a waypoint where others are passing through. The Levite travels aimlessly and inadvertently acts as a catalyst, connecting people and triggering events. Like the Levite, the Danites are looking for a place to live wherever they might find it; and similar to Micah, they take advantage of the circumstances they encounter.[59] But they aggressively enforce their interests and ruthlessly exploit every weakness in their favour. In addition, it is striking that YHWH appears only in the words of the figures: Micah (17:13), his mother (17:2.3) and the Levite (18:6), but God's perspective is not mentioned by

---

57. Yairah Amit, *The Book of Judges: The Art of Editing* (BIS 38; Leiden: Brill, 1999), 333; see also Polzin, *Moses*, 198.
58. Gillmayr-Bucher, *Images of Tranquility*, 38.
59. Cf. Amit, *The Book of Judges*, 332.

the narrative voice, nor are his words quoted. Thus, the images of YHWH in this story only mirror the figures' thoughts and their subjective idea of God and worship, but YHWH does not appear as an authority which guarantees order or orientation.[60]

The characterization of the figures gains its dynamics from the relationships between the figures. In the course of the story, the various constellations of figures show the characters in different contexts and social roles. It is primarily in the interaction between them that the problematic nature of their attitudes and actions becomes clear; even seemingly justified actions can then appear problematic. The presentation of these figures leaves the readers somewhat perplexed. However, the story only works if it is told for readers who are familiar with religious and social principles that enable them to review this story critically.[61] The story itself does not build up such principles, as the narrative voice mostly withholds explicit evaluations,[62] it rather assumes that the audience already shares them and in this way encourages them to critically reflect their own attitude.

---

60. Cf. Gillmayr-Bucher, *Erzählte Welten*, 204.
61. Cf. Gillmayr-Bucher, *Erzählte Welten*, 208.
62. Cf. Matthias Ederer, "Ein jeder tat das in seinen Augen Gerade' (Ri 17,6). Das Israel der Richterzeit in der Perspektive von Ri 17–21. Das Richterbuch (Teil 4)," *Bibel und Liturgie* 88.4 (2015): 313–19, 314–15.

Chapter 14

'OF ALL THE CHARACTERS IN SCRIPTURE, SHE IS THE LEAST': THE LEVITE'S CONCUBINE AND THE DISCOURSE OF SILENCE

Francis Landy

'Of all the characters in scripture, she is the least.' So Phyllis Trible writes of the Levite's concubine in her by now canonical feminist reading from 1984.[1] She does not speak; only three actions are attributed to her, of which only one is undisputed. She is pure victim, 'alone in a world of men'. Trible adds that, unlike Jephthah's daughter, 'she has no friends to aid her in life or mourn her in death'.[2] Yet, for someone who is so entirely eclipsed by the narrative, she has generated an enormous amount of commentary, and, I might say, retrospective mourning. Cheryl Exum memorably argues that recounting the story reproduces the rape; the narrator's condemnation facilitates a pornographic gaze, 'without guilt'.[3] Adele Reinhartz, in her fine study of anonymity in biblical narrative, comments that her 'anonymity symbolizes (the) denial of her identity and personhood' but at the same time – as with the other anonymous characters in the story – it 'lends her a legendary paradigmatic quality'.[4] Along the same lines, Alice Keefe thinks that her fragmented body symbolizes that of Israel in the book of Judges. Both of these play a part in my interpretation.[5]

1. Phyllis Trible, *Texts of Terror: Literary-Feminist Readings of Biblical Narratives* (Philadelphia, Fortress, 1984), 80.
2. *Texts of Terror*, 81.
3. J. Cheryl Exum, *Fragmented Women: Feminist (Sub)versions of Biblical Narrative* (London: Bloomsbury, 2nd ed. 2016), 158. See also *Plotted, Shot, and Painted: Cultural Representations of Biblical Women* (Sheffield: Sheffield Academic Press, 1996), 19–53 esp.28.
4. Adele Reinhartz, *'Why Ask My Name?' Anonymity and Identity in Biblical Narrative* (Oxford: Oxford University Press, 1998), 126. For the complexity of anonymity in our story, see also Don M. Hudson, 'Living in a Land of Epithets: Anonymity in Judges 19–21', *JSOT* 62 (1994), 49–66. Katherine Southwood, *Marriage by Capture in the Book of Judges* (Cambridge: Cambridge University Press, 2007), 14, comments that 'she could be *any* woman of such a status'.
5. Alice A. Keefe, 'Rapes of Women/Wars of Men' *Semeia* 61 (1993): 79–97. See also Susan Niditch, 'The 'Sodomite' Theme in Judges 19–21: Family, Community, and Social

I have two interests in this essay. The first is to trace how at every point the narrator focuses our attention on the woman's subjectivity, but only indirectly. In other words, silence speaks. The second is to follow Rhiannon Graybill's plea for an 'unhappy' reading of the story. An 'unhappy' reading is one that responds to the unhappiness of the text, that notes how it affects us, emotionally and sensually; it does not seek to tell the story, so as to leave it behind; it is not a monument. It sticks with the details of the story however horrible, so as *not* to leave it behind. But it is also 'unhappy' in that it is unhappy with itself; it resists the temptation to make a good story. To quote Graybill: '*Speaking as or not speaking on behalf of can be acts of violence. And we should not demand that the Levite's concubine speak.*'[6]

I have two problems with this. One is the sheer brilliance of the narrator. The story is beautifully crafted; I cannot but admire the subtlety of the telling even as I don't want the story to be told. The second is that there is something in the story that resists analysis, namely the woman's silence. How does one interpret a figure who is so thoroughly occluded by the text? One has to acknowledge the mystery, the unfathomability, of the self. As Graybill suggests, giving her a voice risks betrayal. Yet the narrator insistently directs our attention to her presence, while systematically avoiding it.

I assume that the character of the *pilegesh* is complex and multi-levelled, like every character, even if it is almost entirely concealed from us.[7] At the deepest level, she is defined by a sense of self, an intimate and ineffable psychic reality, which accompanies her throughout her life. One can imagine her being born, growing up, there in Bethlehem, and having all the affective experiences that constitute us as persons, and then that life, that reality – which Lacan memorably

---

Disintegration' *CBQ* 44 (1982): 365–78, who comments, citing Mary Douglas, that 'In the OT, inappropriate or forced alliances always lead to larger social disintegration' (368), and Susan Niditch, *Judges: A Commentary* (OTL; London and Louisville: Westminster/John Knox, 2008), 190, that 'the family is a symbol for the family of Israel.' For Pamela Tamarkin Reis, 'The Levite's Concubine: New Light on a Dark Story' *SJOT* 20 (2006): 146, the anonymity of the characters illustrates 'the disintegration and dehumanization of society.'

6. Rhiannon Graybill, *Texts after Terror: Rape, Sexual Violence, & the Hebrew Bible* (Oxford: Oxford University Press, 2021), 167. Italics original.

7. Benjamin J. M. Johnson, 'Character as Interpretive Crux in the Book of Samuel' in *Character and Characterization in the Book of Samuel* (ed. Keith Bodner and Benjamin J. M. Johnson; London: Bloomsbury, 2020), 1–13 (5). Similarly, Helen Paynter, *Telling Terror in Judges 19* (London and New York: Routledge, 2020), 37, says that the concubine, whom she calls Beli-Fachad, 'is not a one-dimensional literary device, but a complex, ambiguous individual'. In contrast, Cynthia Edenburg, *Dismembering the Whole: Composition and Purpose in Judges 19–21* (Atlanta: SBL, 2016), 16, thinks that she is presented 'in uncritical fashion'. Much depends on how one interprets ותזנה in v. 2.

calls 'the mystery of the unconscious'[8] – being utterly erased. On another level, she is constituted by her relationships, or lack thereof. Finally, there is the symbolic level, resulting from her status, as *pilegesh,* as woman, as daughter, and as a Bethlehemite, and from her intertextual relationships with other figures in Judges and beyond, especially female ones. She thus becomes a figure for the personality of Judges, its sexual and tribal politics.

'And it was in those days, when there was no king in Israel, that there was a man of Levi, sojourning in the far reaches of Mt. Ephraim, and he took for himself a woman, a concubine,[9] from Bethlehem of Judah' (Judg. 19:1).

Like every marriage in Judges, this has theological and political implications. It promises the union of the two major tribes, Ephraim and Judah, representing north and south, and thus a pan-Israelite identity. The notation, 'when there was no king in Israel,' not only sets the narrative in the anarchic past, from the point of view of the reader, but it also inserts the monarchy proleptically into the text. This transaction is a sign of the future. Its significance is underlined by her provenance from Bethlehem, the birthplace of David. However, its promise is subverted. She is a *pilegesh*, a secondary wife. In the absence of a first wife, we do not know exactly what this means, but at any rate she is something less than a full wife, the union is not quite complete. Using Graybill's vocabulary, it is 'icky' if not 'sticky'.[10] Perhaps the Levite wants her for sexual gratification, but is unwilling to pay a full bride price. She is uneasily between roles, her indeterminate status reinforced by the apparent lack of children. As Isabelle Hamley argues, *pilagshim* in the HB are characterized by vulnerability, sexual transgression and liminality.[11] The only other *pilegesh* in Judges is the mother of the fratricide Abimelech, and thus associated with the first abortive attempt at a kingdom. Like Jephthah's prostitute mother, she is a strange woman,

---

8. Jacques Lacan, *Encore: The Seminar of Jacques Lacan Book XX. On Feminine Sexuality, the Limits of Love and Knowledge*, 1972–1973 (ed. Jacques-Alain Miller; tr. Bruce Fink; New York and London: W. W. Norton, 1999), 131.

9. The meaning of *pilegesh* is much discussed, particularly since Mieke Bal's thesis that it refers to patrilocal as opposed to virilocal marriage (Mieke Bal, *Death and Dissymmetry: The Politics of Coherence in the Book of Judges* [Chicago: Chicago University Press, 1988], 84–86). In my view, the conventional translation, 'concubine', is adequate, since in classical times at least it referred to a legal arrangement. In this essay, I use *concubine* and *pilegesh* interchangeably.

10. 'Icky' is, I think, quite clear. 'Sticky' refers to the aptitude of affects to stick to objects, as well as the uncomfortable feeling that we experience when something is sticky. The rhyme is important.

11. Isabelle M. Hamley, 'Dis(re)membered and Unaccounted For: *Pilegesh* in the Hebrew Bble' *JSOT* 41 (2018): 415-34 (415). See also Hamley *Unspeakable Things Unspoken: An Irigirayan Reading of Otherness and Victimization in Judges 19-21* (Eugene, OR: Wipf & Stock, 2019), 137: 'There are no good stories of פלגש: they are all dark tales.'

living outside the comfortable patriarchal home among Gideon's many wives (8:30-31), in the half-indigenous enclave of Shechem. That the woman in our text is a *pilegesh* is already a sign that ours will not be a happy story.

The Levite, too, is fraught with significance.[12] He belongs to a tribe that has no territory, that is sacred but marginal. He is a stranger in Ephraim, who comes from its 'far reaches' (ירכתי), from the back of beyond.[13] That he is a stranger makes the union of Judah and Ephraim still more problematic. The Levite, as the divine representative, might evoke the ideal unity of Israel and its Yhwhistic affiliation.[14] But the image of Levites in Judges has already been tarnished by the previous story in chapters 17–18, in which a meretricious Levite from Bethlehem of Judah goes to Mt Ephraim and is stolen by migrating Danites to serve as priest in their sacrilegious shrine in Dan.[15] The two stories are mirror images of each other. Levites travel in opposite directions between Judah and Ephraim, and are involved in sordid stories of apostasy and rape.

The woman is traded, an object of exchange between father and Levite, a transaction in which she apparently has no say. As a *pilegesh*, moreover, she is of less value, presumably, than a regular wife. We do not know why, or what she makes of her status. Does she feel depreciated? Her father might wish to discard her, at any price, with whatever effect on her morale; the Levite might look down on her. She is doubly a stranger, both in being translocated, and by appertaining to a man who is himself a stranger. She is in-betwixt-and-between, neither a full wife nor a

---

12. A number of scholars think that the identification of the man as a Levite is not integral to the story and was added as a redactional bridge to chs 17–18. See, for example, Yairah Amit *The Book of Judges: The Art of Editing* (tr. Jonathan Chipman; Leiden: Brill, 1999), 353, and 'Editorial Considerations Regarding Ending' in *In Praise of Editing in the Hebrew Bible: Collected Essays in Retrospect* (Sheffield: Sheffield Phoenix Press, 2012), 157. Sara J. Milstein, *Tracking the Master Scribe: Revision through Introduction in Biblical and Mesopotamian Literature* (Oxford: Oxford University Press, 2016),193–94 thinks that the Levite is a stand-in for Saul, in a polemical recasting of an 'original Saul complex.' Edenburg, *Dismembering the Whole*, 20, comments on the irony in the presentation of the Levite.

13. David Moster, 'The Levite of Judges 19–21' *JBL* 134 (2015), 721–30 (724) notes that he is the only character in the HB to be described as coming from ירכה, the 'edge' of a place, and that it already establishes his marginality.

14. See my essay 'Between Centre and Periphery: Space and Gender in the Book of Judges in the Early Second Temple Period' in *Centres and Peripheries in the Early Second Temple Period* (ed. Ehud Ben Zvi and Christoph Levin; Tübingen: Mohr Siebeck, 2016), 133–62 (142). Mark Leuchter, *The Levites and the Boundaries of Israelite Identity* (Oxford: Oxford University Press, 2017) argues that the Levites, as a priestly caste, were among the principal agents in the emergence of Israelite identity in the late premonarchic period (see especially pp. 81–92).

15. Hamley, *Unspeakable Things Unspoken*,132; Landy, 'Between Centre and Periphery,' 148–50.

prostitute, or even a maidservant (אמה), and consequently suspect.[16] Ickiness, to cite Graybill again, sticks to her. She is lower class, whatever that entails.

Suspicions are borne out by the following words:

ותזנה עליו פילגשו ותלך מאתו
'And his concubine fornicated against him, and went from him.' (19.2a)

Whatever this means, and great are the confabulations, she seizes the initiative; the centre of attention shifts from him to her. Clearly, the couple are estranged; if she is promiscuous, it is more, so the preposition 'against' suggests, a sign of alienation from him rather than intimacy with anyone else. That she leaves and goes back home does not portend any lasting attachment.

A long commentarial tradition, novelistically summarized in Margaret Atwood's *The Testaments*,[17] has seen in the story a lesson for wayward women. According to this reading, the concubine suffers ghastly poetic justice for her unfaithfulness.[18] Cheryl Exum, for instance, writes that 'the message that the story of Bath-sheber (*her name for the Levite's concubine*) gives to women is that the consequences of sexual autonomy ... are terrible or deadly'.[19] Others sanitize the text, through adopting one or other of the Septuagint readings,[20] or proposing alternative meanings for זנה,[21] or even suggesting that the Levite pimps her.[22] These create a black-and-white morality tale, in which the concubine is the only innocent character. As Helen Paynter says, this assumes that 'a "real" victim must be "guiltless".'[23] That she may be sexually active makes her character more interesting, more ambiguous, perhaps more desperate. We glimpse her as a morally responsible subject, whose eclipse is consequently the more poignant.

זנה is a key metaphor in Judges, and the Deuteronomistic History generally, for Israel's betrayal of YHWH. Thus the concubine is both a representative, a symbol,

---

16. Hamley, *Unspeakable Things Unspoken*, 137.

17. Peter J. Sabo and Rhiannon Graybill, 'Arcane Energy: An Afterword on the Bible and *The Testaments*' in Rhiannon Graybill and Peter J. Sabo, *"Who Knows What We'd Make of It, If We Ever Got Our Hands on it?" Margaret Atwood and the Bible* (Tübingen: Mohr Siebeck, 2020), 409–21 (413–14). See also Brandon M. Hurlbert, 'Cut & Splice: Reading Judges 19 Cinematically' *BibInt* (advanced articles), 1–25 (1–2).

18. Hamley, 'What's Wrong with Playing the Harlot?', 55–56.

19. Exum, *Fragmented Women*, 146.

20. LXX[A] has 'she became angry'; LXX[B] 'she left him.' This is adopted by Edenburg, *Dismembering the Whole*, 16, NSRV and others.

21. Thus it is frequently emended to זנח, 'scorned', or alternative meanings are proposed, such as 'leave'. For details, see Hamley, 'What's Wrong with Playing the Harlot?', 47–52. Bal, *Death and Dissymmetry*, 88, thinks it refers to the tension between patrilocal and virilocal marriage, to both of which the woman is unfaithful.

22. Reis, 'The Levite's Concubine,' 128–31.

23. Paynter, *Telling Terror*, 36.

for perfidious Israel, and marginalized, as woman, as *pilegesh*, as a stranger married to a stranger. That she takes charge, in Hamley's Irigarayan reading, effects a Copernican revolution.[24] Man is no longer the centre of the universe. One can imagine the cost to the Levite's masculinity, in one way or another. Not only might he be cuckolded, but his aspiration for establishing a house in Israel is thwarted.

However, the motif is entirely undeveloped. She goes home, exchanging one patriarchal domain for another: 'to her father's house, to Bethlehem of Judah'. This is perhaps a safe place, somewhere she can resume her old life. The amplification, 'to Bethlehem of Judah', suggests that it is more than her father's house to which she returns, it is to a landscape, a dialect, a society, and to a symbolic site, whose meaning is yet to unfold, but which is surely implicit, at least in the mind of the reader. But home might also be uncanny, in the Freudian sense, as a place which is both intimately familiar and strange.[25] One cannot go back without the knowledge of everything that has happened in between. There is much speculation about how her father welcomes her, why he does not enforce the Deuteronomic law against adulterers.[26] Is a *pilegesh* subject to the same restrictions as a full wife? What do her friends think? In any case, she comes back under a cloud, and perhaps with a reputation (though who knows what her life was like before her departure, and what were sexual mores in ancient Israel, at least on the evidence of the Song of Songs). Was it only men who 'did what was right in their own eyes'?

There is no mother in view; she may have died, or simply be effaced by the narrator, for whom a house is the patriarchal institution *par excellence*. The absence of the mother, at least textually, renders the domestic space unsafe, a void where maternal nurture once was. Mieke Bal asks 'Where is Clytemnestra?'[27] The empty house is haunted, either by the dead mother or her textual absence. What memories are there, for father and daughter? Bal's answer is that the figure of Clytemnestra is displaced onto the various murderous women of Judges: Jael, the woman with the millstone, Delilah. The displacement is a sign of repression. Hamley comments, 'There is no mother to provide a female genealogy. She is cut off and rootless.'[28]

---

24. *Unspeakable Things Unspoken*, 138. Hamley's first chapter is an exemplary introduction to Irigiray's work, and her second discusses and evaluates her influence on biblical studies (*Unspeakable Things Unspoken*, 1–62).

25. Sigmund Freud, 'The Uncanny' in *The Penguin Freud Library. Vol. 14: Art and Literature* (trans. James Strachey; London: Penguin, 1990), 335–76.

26. See for example, Edenburg, *Dismembering the Whole*, 244–45, who, despite her adoption of an alternative meaning for זנה, thinks that the choice of the homonym creates an intertextual echo; Karla G. Bohmbach, 'Conventions/Contraventions: The Meaning of Public and Private for the Judges 19 Concubine' *JSOT* 23 (1999): 83–98 (90); Paynter, *Telling Terror*, 33, who notes the contrast. In my view, it illustrates the disconnect between the legal codes and actual practice.

27. *Death and Dissymmetry*, 197. In Aeschylus' tragedy *Agamemnon*, Clytemnestra murders her husband, Agamemnon, to avenge his sacrifice of their daughter, Iphigenia.

28. *Unspeakable Things Unspoken*, 139.

Four months pass, in which nothing happens. Periods of time are pregnant; we do not know what she thinks and feels. Day follows day; the addition of ימים, 'days', to ארבעה חדשים, 'four months', gives one a sense of repetition, normality, perhaps even tedium. It could drag on forever; if so, there would have been no story. If only the Levite had not come to fetch her. It is the first of the counter-factuals, ways not taken, that render the story pathetic. Perhaps distance makes the heart grow fonder, perhaps the domestic space becomes more uncomfortable, especially if, as Mieke Bal suggests, it unconsciously signifies the mother's womb.[29] Relationships between fathers and daughters throughout the book of Judges are fraught and perilous. Two daughters are immolated in their father's houses; other daughters are raped; the apparently perfect daughter, Achsah, obtains something associated with fertility from her father and gives it to her husband, who, as her uncle, himself embodies the possibility of incest. Ideally, daughters are 'sent out' from the paternal home and other daughters brought in, as in the case of the so-called minor judge, Ibzan (12:8-9). A daughter who stays home, or worse, returns home, threatens the system of exchange through which Israelite identity is constructed. Not a word passes between father and daughter in our text, but who knows what possibilities remain unspoken?

After four months the Levite comes, 'to speak to her heart'. Whatever the alienation between them, he tries to cross it. Speaking to the heart suggests tenderness, affection, the choosing of words which will appeal to her and re-establish intimacy. It is sweet-talk. We might expect to hear what he says, and, even more important, her reaction. Will she take him back, if one reads according to the Ketiv? Will he bring her back, if one follows the Qere?[30] The effort involved is indicated by the succession of verbs, formulaic as they are: 'And her husband rose up, and went after her.' It is quite an expedition, accompanied as he is by a servant and two donkeys. Why it takes him so long, we do not know, nor is it our business, in an essay concerned with her character, except insofar as we see it through her eyes. The very possessive, אישה, 'her husband,' as Helen Paynter says,[31] uniquely makes her the focus of the relationship, and implies reciprocity. She may be surprised to see him, she may wonder at his dilatoriness, she may be pleased or anxious. Her heart may be all a-flutter. As with every instance of reconciliation after a breach, it is against a background of tension, of unresolved conflict. For the moment, the text uses its rhetorical resources to give him the benefit of the doubt, perhaps in her eyes also.

---

29. *Death and Dissymmetry*, 196.

30. The Ketiv, or written Masoretic text, reads להשיבו, 'to bring him back'. The Qere, or text as traditionally read, goes להשיבה, 'to bring her back'. For the different readings, ignored in most commentaries, see Paynter, *Telling Terror*, 37.

31. *Telling Terror*, 34. Paynter notes that in every other case where the construction is used, it is a sign of strong female agency.

At any rate, there seems to be no question. She comes out to meet him, and brings him into her father's house.³² This is her last action before the denouement; thereafter the text constantly refers to her, so as to keep her before our eyes, for example by calling her father 'the father of the girl', but without allowing her any subjectivity. We watch her disappearing into the background. The detail, 'she brought him into her father's house', captures this moment of fade-out. Presumably she greets him in some way, and he answers her back; they must look at each other. She brings him across the threshold, into the intimate space of the house, which, as we know, has become strange and uncanny. It is no longer a refuge. However, he seems to leave her outside. She watches her father rejoice to see him; perhaps the father smiles, and the two men engage in a drinking bout that lasts for five days. Brandon Hurlbert comments that hers is a 'felt absence'.³³ What happens between father, daughter and Levite we do not know. The 'threshold', as Jennifer Matheny writes, is a key term in our text, anticipating the threshold at the climax.³⁴ The threshold symbolically marks the difference between the public and the private, and the turning point. She quotes Bakhtin saying that, metaphorically, the threshold 'is connected with the breaking point of life, the moment of crisis, the decision that changes a life'.³⁵ Once he crosses the threshold, the Levite cannot go back. In her dramatic representation of 'Beth the movie',³⁶ Mieke Bal describes how 'the long scene will slowly move into uncanniness'.³⁷ The uncanniness is caused by 'a split between what the actors do and what they feel'. Meanwhile, Beth is 'sitting, waiting, anxious'.

She has a hermetic function. She introduces the Levite into the house, which is representative, a microcosm of Bethlehem, 'the house of bread', and thus of the future destiny of Israel. There he will have nourishment. But she also introduces us, as well as the characters in the story, to an alternative story, insofar as she is representative of Israel. The inner space, the matrix, is also a sexual space, into which the man intrudes. The 'house of bread', then, is associated with fertility and blessing, notably, of course, in the accompanying story of Ruth. Life, with all its promises, turns into death.

---

32. Bal, *Death and Dissymmetry*, 91, thinks that she does not come out of the house, but that is surely wrong. Some translations, e.g. NRSV, follow the Septuagint in seeing the Levite as the subject.

33. Hurlbert, 'Cut & Splice,' 11–12. Hurlbert, like Bal, imagines how the scene might be filmed, with the camera constantly switching between the different faces.

34. Jennifer M. Matheny, 'Mute and Mutilated: Understanding Judges 19–21 as a משל of Dialogue' *BibInt* 25 (2017): 625–46 (38).

35. Matheny, 'Mute and Mutilated,' 638, citing, Mikhael M. Bakhtin, *The Dialogic Imagination: Four Essays* (tr. Caryl Emerson and Michael Holquist; Austin: Texas University Press, 1981), 248.

36. Feminist critics delight in inventing names for the woman. Bal calls her 'Beth', Exum 'Bath-sheber', Paynter 'Beli-Fahad'.

37. *Death and Dissymmetry*, 189.

But that is to run ahead of ourselves.

The men eat, drink, sleep. Whatever they talk about, the bonhomie is strained, as the repeated injunctions by the host that the Levite should 'feast his heart' and that his heart should be 'good' suggest. The father urges the guest to stay, to enjoy his hospitality; the son-in-law resists, but complies, until it is too late. There is of course an irony, that father's solicitude for the Levite's heart contrasts with the Levite's failure to talk to the woman's heart. Apparently, male bonding, the camaraderie of father-in-law and son-in-law, takes precedence over any affection for the wife and daughter. That is indeed the patriarchal construction of marriage, as an exchange between men, in which women are purely instrumental.[38]

The father's motives are much discussed.[39] The Levite may be an asset, as in the previous story of Micah (Judg. 17–18); the father may be suspicious after the previous estrangement; he may want to hang on to the daughter. He may want to restore the family's good name, and erase the past. Who knows? But the daughter is trapped. If home is unsafe, and the Levite is unsafe, she has nowhere to go.[40] The men compete for her, and exclude her.

Retardation induces an affect of slow motion. Everything happens in an alcoholic haze, as the father plies more and more drinks. The Levite may also feel trapped. 'One imagines (the Levite) thinking, "If I don't leave now, I never will".'[41] For the *pilegesh*, it may be boring, as well as suspenseful. In Graybill's terms, it is 'icky' as well as 'sticky'. Affects stick to each moment of the sequence, as one dwells on the incidents, the passing words and thoughts. This is especially so in moments of anticipation and surprise. For example in v. 5, they 'get up early in the morning' (וישכימו בבוקר) and one can contemplate the excitement of departure, the early morning freshness, a strange clarity despite the previous day's inebriation, only for inertia to settle in once again.

The Levite and the concubine may have sex, since they pass the night. If so, it will consummate the reconciliation, but at an indeterminate emotional cost. For

---

38. For the Irigarayan Marxist-oriented view of the role of women in patriarchal economy, see Hamley, *Unspeakable Things Unspoken*, 18-19: 'women become both goods and objects of exchange between men' (19). See also *Unspeakable Things Unspoken*, 118-21.

39. See, for instance, Danna Nolan Fewell and David M. Gunn, *Gender, Power & Promise: The Subject of the Bible's First Story* (Nashville: Abingdon, 1993), 133, who think that the father may being showing solicitude for his daughter, and on the contrary, Reis, 'The Levite's Concubine', 131-34, who considers him to be indifferent to her fate. Bal, *Death and Dissymmetry*, 90-91, sees the issue as being patrilochy. I discuss the different possibilities in 'Between Centre and Periphery', 147. See also Edenburg, *Dismembering the Whole*, 19.

40. For the reversal of public and private in the narrative, see Bohmbach, 'Conventions/ Contraventions': 'Just as the woman is not safe in public, neither is her private positioning any guarantee of safety' (97). But see Hamley, *Unspeakable Things Unspoken*, 123, who questions whether the public/private distinction might not be anachronistic.

41. 'Between Centre and Periphery', 147.

her, it might be a surrender of whatever drove her away in the first place. The father may feel ambivalent about having another man sleeping with his daughter in his own house, especially if he harbours incestuous desires. Or, on the contrary, they may not have sex, in which case one wonders what has actually happened. If there is no wooing, no seduction, no intercourse, there is perhaps no relationship. She may feel jealous, frustrated, or relieved. If they do not have sex, it suggests that the problems between them have not been resolved. Or perhaps the Levite merely feels inhibited in the presence of the father. His adoption into the familial nest turns him into a quasi-brother, a surrogate son, and hence evokes the spectre of incest, at one remove.

Off they go, late in the day, on the fateful journey home. Again, she has no say, even though she may think, like her father, that it is stupid. She is part of his entourage, like the servant and the donkeys. As they come to the vicinity of Jerusalem, she is mentioned parenthetically, in tandem with the beasts, in a neat chiastic parallelism: ועמו צמד חמורים חבושים ופלגשו עמו, 'and with him the pair of laden donkeys, and his concubine with him' (v. 10). Hamley suggests that she is 'a mere afterthought', following the donkeys,[42] but the point is that both are encompassed by him, just as the singular verbs – 'and he rose, and he went, and he came' – governs all of them, so that he is the sole actor. More important, the passing reference, for the last time until v. 19, draws attention to the role of the servant in vv.11-13. The servant's common sense not only exposes the Levite's lack of it,[43] but may make us wonder what the woman thinks, or not. She is entirely eclipsed by the narrative, silent and invisible.[44] It gets darker and darker; they find themselves in the square of a strange city, houseless and unwelcome; no one asks her opinion or seems to notice her. Night is associated with terrors, 'the fear of the night' (Song 3:8; Ps. 91:5). Nocturnal dread lacks an object; throughout the text the oncoming night is regarded with foreboding, the danger of which is unspecified, and has something primeval about it. One can imagine, from the woman's point of view, there in the shadows, that familiar shapes become unfamiliar, uncanny. Night is

---

42. *Unspeakable Things Unspoken*, 139. See also Bohmbach, 'Conventions/Contraventions,' 87. However, the relationship between the A and B clauses in a parallelism is less definitive. The B clause may indicate that they are of equal status, or it may be climactic.

43. The Levite is an ironic 'exemplar of misplaced piety' cf. Landy, 'Between Centre and Periphery,' 153. Jan P. Fokkelman, 'Structural Remarks on Judges 9 and 19' in *Sha'arei Talmon: Studies in the Bible, Qumran, and the Ancient Near East Presented to Shemaryahu Talmon* (ed. Michael Fishbane and Emanuel Tov; Winona Lake: Eisenbrauns, 1992), 33–45, comments that the refusal to spend the night in Jerusalem is the turning point that reveals that all values are reversed, that, for example, the servant is right, contrary to convention (44–45).

44. Lilian R. Klein, *The Triumph of Irony in the Book of Judges* (JSOTS 68; Sheffield: Sheffield Academic Press, 1988), 164.

the realm of the unconscious, of ghosts and demons.[45] To be unsheltered at night, especially in a public place, surrounded by eyes that refuse the demand for recognition, by closed doors, evokes a lack of the primal human need for containment, for community.[46] But there is no indication as yet that the woman fears risk to herself. Such things are not done in Israel.

And then salvation comes, an old Ephraimite, like the Levite a stranger, but settled enough to have a field and a house. The concubine surfaces momentarily as the Ephraimite's 'handmaid' (אמה), an expression into which I read no more than common politeness, since the Levite includes himself among the Ephraimite's servants.[47] Equally politely, he claims he will be of no trouble and expense, since he has fodder for the animals and bread and wine for the humans. Everything seems quite normal; the Levite provides the concubine with the basics. Whatever the dynamics between the Ephraimite and the Levite, she may be reassured of her sustenance. The Levite puts on a good show. Of course, the echo of Gen.19:1-3 may alert the suspicious reader; Cynthia Edenburg, in particular, notes the contrasts.[48] But the concubine may have no such anxieties.

So they enter the house, wash their feet, eat and drink, and they 'make their heart merry'. We have no reason to think that the concubine does not share in the general well- being.[49] All's well that ends well. Washing the feet associates our text with the hospitality type-scene, particularly Gen. 18:3; 19:2 and 24.32;[50] it marks the transition from the outside to the inside, it is the first act of a good host. Metonymically, as well as sensually, it signifies the end of the journey, the weariness, grime, and sweat of the road. One can feel the water against the skin, especially in an era when water was precious, and the sense of relief. It is a sociable experience, shared by all the participants; one can imagine, for instance, that she has good

---

45. There are any number of spooky nocturnal tales in the Hebrew Bible, for example Jacob's struggle with the angel in Gen. 32:23-33 and Moses' encounter with Yhwh in Exod. 4:24-26. The only equivalent I can think of in Judges is Gideon's victory over the Midianites in 7:9-23, though that, of course, is entirely positive from the narrator's point of view. Alice Bach, 'Rereading The Body Politic: Women and Violence in Judges 21,' *BibInt* 6 (1998): 1–27 (6) comments that night is not always sinister in the Hebrew Bible, citing Gen. 32:23-31, the visions of Zechariah, and the Witch of Endor! I venture to disagree.

46. According to the psychoanalyst Wilfred Bion, the sense of being contained is essential to infantile development. For a useful introduction to Bion's work, see Joan and Neville Symington *The Clinical Thinking of Wilfred Bion* (London: Routledge, 1996). For the concepts of container and contained, see especially pp.50–58.

47. Hamley, *Unspeakable Things Unspoken*, 139–40, thinks that an אמה is less than an עבד, but I do not see the evidence for this. Lapsley, *Whispering the Word*, 44, comments that usually in the HB אמה is a self-designation. The Levite's appropriation of the term exceeds his prerogative.

48. *Dismembering the Whole,* 175–76.

49. Some, however, do harbour doubts, for instance, Lapsley, *Whispering the Word,* 45.

50. For the hospitality type-scene, see Edenburg, *Dismembering the Whole,* 15, esp. n.22.

feelings for her companions. Of course, as Sara Ahmed says, happiness is precarious;[51] any anxiety might be relieved by alcohol. Happiness sticks to things; it pervades the room. The alienation suggested by the Levite's failure to speak to the pilegesh's heart, and the father's repeated appeals that he gladden and feast his heart, seems to be resolved. The heart (לבם) is a collective entity, a conviviality in the literal sense.

It does not last long. There is a hammering at the door. The sons of Belial make their scandalous request.[52] The scandal is intensified by the Levite's status as a member of the sacred tribe, whose inheritance is YHWH, and thus dishonours the deity. This is clear from the parallel with the Sodom story, in which the guests are divine emissaries. As Bal says, the house becomes a prison.[53] In demanding to open the door, they want to break open the prison; they have become a lynch mob. The concubine hears the threat to her husband, and may react in different ways, with astonishment, panic, or even worry for him; the consternation is contagious. Teresa Brennan writes, 'Is there anyone who has not, at least once, walked into a room and felt the atmosphere?'[54] There is a sea-change in mood, as if a gusty wind blows through the door. But for the moment at least there is no direct danger; she can try to make herself inconspicuous. The old man goes to the door; perhaps he will save the situation.

The host makes his equally surprising offer. It is a long speech, and she has time to absorb its implications. Again it is not our business here to discuss the Ephraimite's motives, his construction of his duty, whether he exceeds his authority; only how she might understand it. She is at his disposal, with no capacity to object. As the Ephraimite expatiates on their fate, 'and rape them and do to them what is good in your eyes', we can imagine the two women listening, assuming that the walls are not too thick. Each word is experienced viscerally, as something that might happen, if he gets his way, with all the accompanying outrage. The *pilegesh* is de trop; the real import of the Ephraimite's words is that he is prepared to sacrifice that which is most valuable to him, his family's principal asset, for the sake of his guest.[55] That, of course, is what Lot offers. The *pilegesh* is expendable, worthless, an extra little treat. That is what her life has come to. She may expect the Levite to

---

51. Sara Ahmed, "Happy Objects' in *The Affect Theory Reader* (ed. Melissa Gregg et al. Cambridge: Cambridge University Press, 2010), 29–51 (33).

52. James Harding, 'Homophobia and Masculine Domination in Judges 19–21' *BCT* 6 (2018): 41–73 (54), wonders whether ידע might actually be ambiguous here, and that the Gibeahites might simply wish to get to know the Levite. This seems scarcely plausible to me, especially in view of what follows.

53. *Death and Dissymmetry*, 183.

54. Teresa Brennan, *Transmission of Affect* (Ithaca: Cornell University Press, 2004), 1.

55. Milstein, *Tracking the Master Scribe*, 176, thinks that the virgin daughter is 'a blind motif', since she does not appear again, and only introduced to make the connection with Gen. 19. I think that the opposite is the case: the daughter is the real point of the Ephraimite's offer.

protect her, but he does not. The crowd refuses the proffered gift: 'the men did not want to listen to him' (v. 25). Rejection compounds abjection; she is worthless and not worth having. That could be a relief. But that is not what transpires.

As Hamley says, the Levite throws her 'to the wolves'.[56] It says, ויחזק האיש בפילגשו ויצא, אליהם החוץ, 'and the man took hold of his concubine and brought her out to them outside'. ויחזק can mean 'force'; it is not a single act of ejection; one can imagine him dragging her outside. That requires determination, as well as suggesting her resistance.[57] It would take some seconds, or maybe more, to push her out, in which time her eyes would be opened to the true character, and indeed masculinity, of her man (איש) and the value of their relationship. His is the first violation.

And what follows:

וידעו אותה ויתעללו בה כל הלילה עד הבקר
'And they knew her, and worked their will on her, all night till morning.'

Here we reach the limit of our unhappy reading. The euphemism for sex, ידע, 'know', designates an act of un-knowing, non-recognition. If 'knowing' connotes intimacy, this is as impersonal as possible. She is raped as a substitute for the Levite, but also as a defiled and subjugated body. Rhiannon Graybill writes of the temptation to make of this a 'sad story', even the worst of stories, and, especially among feminist critics, to give the woman a voice, for example through her speaking body.[58] But she is voiceless. Helen Paynter says that it is possible that 'she *cannot* speak; her experience has rendered her incapable of speech'.[59] She quotes Elaine Scarry that 'physical pain does not simply resist language but actively destroys it' and causes 'a reversion to the sounds and cries a human being makes before language is learned'.[60] All we can do, Graybill says, is to 'stay with the story

---

56. *Unspeakable Things* Unspoken, 134. Graybill, *Texts After Terror*, 160, thinks it is ambiguous whether the Ephraimite or the Levite throws her out. Moster, 'The Levite', 728, argues that the subject is most likely the Ephraimite, and in general tries to exculpate the Levite. However, Hamley adduces many reasons why it has to be the Levite, of which the syntactical one is the most important.

57. L. Juliana M. Claassens, *Claiming Her Dignity: Female Resistance in the Old Testament* (Collegeville: Liturgical Press, 2016) understandably does not mention our text. As Paynter says (*Telling Terror*, 30), 'few of these acts of resistance can be said to apply to (the concubine)'. However, perhaps here we do have a trace of resistance.

58. *Texts After Terror*, 157.

59. *Telling Terror*, 48. Italics original.

60. The quotation is from Elaine Scarry, *The Body in Pain* (Oxford: Oxford University Press, 1985), 324.

and its difficulties',[61] without foreclosing it, without attempting to speak on behalf of the woman, to give her a voice.[62]

Yet, as she also says, I cannot resist 'the pull of its sadness'. I have been writing and avoiding writing this section. Paynter writes, helpfully, of Judith Butler's 'notion of grievability'.[63] One can grieve for the *pilegesh* without finding words for one's grief. Paynter thinks that the pain is 'in the mind of the narrator, who has given her an obituary'.[64] In this it is typical of the book of Judges, which is a book of grief.[65]

James Harding argues that the story exemplifies masculine domination.[66] The woman is raped so as to assert the Gibeahites' power over the Levite as well as the woman's body. Reducing it to an object symbolically displays their phallic supremacy, both over women and over enemies.[67] Juliana Claassens writes movingly how rape 'destroys the innermost core of the human being'[68] and that this is the source of the perpetrator's pleasure. 'The new world of the perpetrator is built on the ruins of the victim's world … Through the rape the perpetrator becomes invincible and removed from any earthly law; he becomes a law unto himself.'[69]

The story exemplifies the interfusion of sex and violence endemic in human culture as well as in the book of Judges, a metaphorical equivalence as terrifying as that of knowing and unknowing. It is not plausible that the men of Gibeah are not sexually excited: how else would they get an erection? Or that the sexual excitement is distinguishable from that of violence. The sadistic fantasy plays out endlessly, at least all night, on the woman's body, and thereafter in the their imagination, perhaps beyond the grave. And that fantasy means evoking the woman's subjectivity, so as to destroy it again and again. The more she cries, the more she resists, the greater the pleasure.

Where do we see this in the text? After 'they knew her' the text continues ויתעללו בה כל הלילה עד הבקר, 'and worked their will on her, all night until morning'. The root עלל refers to deeds, generally bad, often cruel. They don't just rape her, but they perpetrate all sorts of acts on her; not once, but the entire night. The Hitpael ויתעללו, in particular, is associated with waywardness and torture (e.g. Num. 22:29; 1 Sam. 31:6); they use her body as a sex toy, in a ghastly parody of foreplay, thus

---

61. *Texts After Terror*, 157.
62. *Texts After Terror*, 165–66.
63. *Telling Terror*, 51. The full discussion is on 51–52.
64. *Telling Terror* 52.
65. I agree here with Deryn Guest's recent psychoanalytic reading, *YHWH and the God of Israel: an Object-Relations Analysis* (Cambridge: Cambridge University Press, 2018), though I disagree fundamentally with her interpretation of that grief.
66. Harding, 'Homophobia and Masculine Domination'.
67. Bach, 'Rereading The Body Politic', 1.
68. *Claiming Her Dignity*, 41
69. Claassens is quoting Louise du Toit, but does not give a reference.

demonstrating, as with any torturer, absolute power over the female body. They do it to elicit a response (whimpers, cries, screams), investing themselves in the body of the other as the site of pain and pleasure. And it goes on all night, boring, interminable.

And we, what do we feel? If we adopt her subject position? Perhaps two things:

1. Dissociation. This isn't really happening to me. I am somewhere else, in a land without pain or fear.
2. Consciousness. I am who I am, despite all that they do to me.[70] They cannot really touch me.

Perhaps there is just pain, horror, disintegration. Anyway, at dawn, like the night demons they are, they let her go, and she crawls back to the threshold. It is here that we reach the end of our journey, since I cannot bear to carry on. Mieke Bal, in her cinematic reading, brilliantly describes what it looks like from below.[71] She looks up at the man as he comes out, nonchalantly or not, in the morning, and says, 'Get up, let's go.' Her hands are the focus of attention, as if imploring or trying to reach that threshold of safety, and as witness to her incapacity. We do not know if she is alive or dead. She does not answer, ואין ענה. She may see the man, now called 'her lord,' stepping out into the new day. Bal imagines his legs over her. But it is all 'dreamlike',[72] a world on a journey she can never again enter. She sees the life that she had, the entire misadventure, slipping away. I imagine her opening her eyes, wondering, hovering between life and death, too weak to care.

He hoists her on the donkey, they go home, he cuts her up into twelve pieces. We do not know if she is alive, dead, unconscious. Perhaps she dies on the way. I don't want to go there.[73]

What do we make of all this in terms of character and characterization? Obviously, there is rather little to work with. She is not a character with a fully developed trajectory, like Saul, David, or Samson. Robert Alter typically,

---

70. I do not have any references for these speculations, but I am thinking of the wonderful description of gang rape in Bernardine Evaristo's novel, *Girl, Woman, Other*.

71. *Death and Dissymmetry*, 195-96. See also Hurlbert ('Cut & Splice,' 15-16), who thinks it is focalized entirely through the eyes of the Levite. Hurlbert seems unaware of Bal.

72. *Death and Dissymmetry*, 195.

73. There is no indication in the text that she is alive and conscious. Graybill, *Texts after Terror*, 159-61, insists that rape is not murder. 'People survive rapes, even gang rapes' (161). But some people do not. Paynter movingly compares our text to the story of Jyoti, the young woman who died of her rape in India in 2012 (*Telling Terror*, 59-60). Of course, we may react affectively to the Levite's dissection of the *pilegesh*. Meir Sternberg, *The Poetics of Biblical Narrative* (Bloomington: Indiana University Press, 1985), 239, thinks that the ambiguity serves to implicate both the Gibeahites and the Levite in the death, in a characteristically masculinist reading. But from the woman's point of view, the story is mercifully over.

magnificently, comments on the 'art of reticence' in biblical characterization; and that 'though biblical narrative is often silent where later modes of fiction choose to be loquacious, it is *selectively* silent' (my italics).[74] I am always astonished at the Hebrew Bible's capacity to bring a character alive with a few words, and to give (almost) everyone their due, even those it portrays as fools or enemies.[75] It is an extraordinarily generous text. What I have tried to do is to show how the narrator invests in the character of the concubine, through all the odd details – why is she a *pilegesh*? What is the meaning of זנה? Why does she bring him in? – so as the more radically to occlude her. Secondly, I suggest that she remains the focus of attention throughout the story, as we wonder why she is not consulted about a lodging place, how she reacts to the Ephraimite's outrageous offer, and so on; the servant is there precisely to make us aware of her exclusion from the dialogue. Thirdly, I argue that she is interesting because she is morally ambiguous. She is not a pure innocent victim. As Helen Paynter says, the assumption is that a 'real' victim must be guiltless. Her action, whatever it is, asserts her independence, her alienation from the situation in which she finds herself, and briefly turns the patriarchy on its head. It may be, as Cheryl Exum argues, that the Gibeahites exact patriarchy's revenge.[76] But we know what the narrator thinks of them, since he calls them בני בליעל, 'scoundrels', not to speak of the unspeakable Levite!

Her promiscuity, if such it is, renders her typical of the world of Judges. It is a morally compromised world, in which people make their way as best they can. That she is human, with a past, suggests that she is not unsullied by life, social conditions, fate, and nonetheless worthy of compassion. She is like the rest of us.

Her character is constituted by her life experiences and her relationships. What is important is her isolation, from her father, her lover, even the servant, the absence of a mother, of female friends. But, like the rest of us, she was also a dreamer. She had her imaginary world, which connected her social, conscious self to the unconscious processes of thinking and feeling, which constituted her subjectivity,[77] and to the fantasy life of ancient Israel. We have no access to that world; she left no poems or diaries; but we have an ethical responsibility to acknowledge it, and its erasure.

And finally, there is the symbolic dimension. She is in touch with the deepest forces of life and death. Alice Keefe writes of the female body as the 'site of the

---

74. Robert Alter, *The Art of Biblical Narrative* (New York: Basic Books, 1981). 'Characterization and the Art of Reticence' is his chapter 6 (pp. 114–130). The second quotation is from p. 115.

75. Examples are when Nabal says 'Who is David? Who is the son of Jesse … ?' (1 Sam. 25:10) and one sees matters from the perspective of a well-established landowner; or when Jezebel dies with dignity.

76. *Fragmented Women*, 151–52.

77. For the creative function of dreaming, I am indebted to Thomas H. Ogden, *Reclaiming Unlived Life: Experiences in Psychoanalysis* (London: Taylor and Francis, 2016), 30–35.

power of life, and the Israelite community as that in which life is sustained and encompassed'.[78] What is violated is 'the sacrality of the female body as the source and matrix of ... life'. The woman is connected intertextually to all the other women, daughters and mothers, of Israel, especially, but not only, the victims. Structurally, she corresponds to Jephthah's daughter in Judges 11.[79] There is a further correlation: with Rachel, the arch-mother of the Benjaminites, who died giving birth to them.[80] Rachel is a houseless ghost throughout the Hebrew Bible. I have noted Bal's suggestion that the absent mother haunts the text. The absent mother is recollected in the childless daughter, in the children she will never have. As the text goes on, the void gets bigger and bigger, sucking in the bodies of ever more raped and traumatized women and murdered men, women and children. The vagina as the source of life becomes the hollow which destroys Israel. This is a terrible fantasy, and we have to evoke the narrator imagining it, inhabiting the body of the woman as one of his personae, writing and protesting. But this leads us elsewhere. For she connects YHWH and the land. She is a displacement of the Levite, as the object of the Gibeahites' desire, and thus of YHWH, but she also represents the land, and hence the trauma of conquest. She enacts the tension between endogamy, going back to the father with its incestuous implications, and exogamy, denoted by the verb זנה. As Matheny writes, the future is 'founded on rape and dismemberment'.[81] In my view, this is the essential problem of the book of Judges, the reason why it tells the same story again and again. Israel has to occupy the land, wiping out its inhabitants, but at the same time, it has to marry into the land, to make it truly its own. This is an impossible predicament, whose implications are worked out in the disastrous final chapters.

78. 'Rapes of Women/Wars of Men,' 89.
79. Fokkelman, 'Structural Remarks on Judges 9 and 19.'
80. Landy, 'Between Centre and Periphery,' 158, 160.
81. Matheny, 'Mute and Mutilated,' 627.

Chapter 15

SIX CHARACTERS IN SEARCH OF A DEITY: TALKING ABOUT GOD IN THE BOOK OF JUDGES[1]

Keith Bodner

Readers familiar with the Genesis account will recall a vivid scene where the younger Jacob impersonates his older fraternal twin Esau. Although his father is nearly blind, Isaac's sense of smell remains intact, and thus Jacob wears his older brother's clothes and presumably modulates his voice as he seeks to secure the blessing of primogeniture from his aged father. When Isaac inquires as how he hunted game and prepared a meal so quickly, Jacob does not flinch: 'Indeed, YHWH your God caused an encounter before me!' (cf. NRSV, 'Because the LORD your God granted me success' Gen. 27:20). Commentators have long paused over this response, as it seems to be a disingenuous use of the divine name that furthers the deception and serves to secure the paternal blessing for Jacob instead of Esau. This is far from the only example of deploying a divine name in direct speech in Genesis, and one might compare a later instance in another deceptive circumstance. When the brothers of Joseph are invited to dine at the prime minister's residence in Egypt they are wracked with fear and guilt, appealing plaintively to the chief steward ('the one over the house') as they declare their innocence in regard to the silver that was returned in their baggage. In response, the steward reassures them: 'Shalom to you, don't be afraid, your God and the God of your father has given you treasure in your bags. Your silver has come to me' (Gen. 43:23). Without poring over the details, one might note that the steward's use of the divine name when speaking to the nervous brothers has a different purpose from when Jacob deployed the divine name(s) when hoodwinking his father. How characters *talk about God*, in other words, has implications for interpreting the narrative and provides a measure of insight into the rhetoric of characterization that is at work in the story.

---

1. The idea for this chapter, including the title that plays on Luigi Pirandello's experimental drama *Six Characters in Search of an Author* (the inaugural performance of which was infamously marked by a brawl and shouts of 'madhouse'), was prompted by conversations and correspondence with Cheryl Exum.

This short essay explores the way that characters talk about God in the book of Judges, paying attention to the content of various speeches and the purposes that such discourse might serve. There is no shortage of interesting options, but this study is limited to six examples from various sectors of Judges. At one level we will be evaluating how talking about God is used as a technique of characterization and how it facilitates comparisons between the various figures in the story. At another level, it is worth analysing how such God-talk contributes to the larger thematic contours of the narrative. For instance, interpreters have often discussed the book's framework that outlines a relentless cycle of apostasy: the Israelites are guilty of violating the covenant, then are oppressed by an adversary, but cry out for deliverance and enjoy a measure of relief by the hand of a judge, yet soon slide back into the same pattern of misery. More recent scholarship is drawing attention to some enhanced complexities in the book as a whole, and Ken Stone provides a starting point:

> While this theological framework is important for understanding the book of Judges, the stories inserted into the framework often reveal a more complicated world. Here we find individuals whose actions cannot always be characterized neatly as righteous or wicked, moments at which God's actions or intentions are either unclear or troubling, ambiguous or fluid boundaries between 'Israelite' and 'non-Israelite', conflicts among the Israelite tribes themselves, and unexpected developments that are often related to matters of gender. If one reads the individual tales of the judges while asking how clearly those stories illustrate the theological framework, one discovers much variation. Thus the theological significance of Judges cannot be derived only from the orthodox interpretive framework. Rather, the complicated structure of Judges encourages readers to acknowledge, and to grapple with the theological implications of, the tension that usually exists in religious traditions between stable orthodox frameworks and the heterogeneous realities of the lives of the people of God.[2]

While this essay is just a preliminary undertaking, it could be that direct speech from various characters that include some mention of the divine could provide a sliver of insight into the kinds of 'heterogeneous' dimensions that readers can find in Judges. Analysing *how* various figures use divine name(s) unveils a measure of perceived experiences and projection, and, as an element of characterization, merits some brief attention in a volume such as this. If characters can represent their own entanglements and complexities – not mere ciphers for a putative author's viewpoint but perhaps endowed with degrees of independence – then their words can be filtered accordingly.[3] Theorists seem increasingly comfortable

---

2. Ken Stone, 'Judges,' 87–96 in *Theological Bible Commentary*) (ed. Gail R. O'Day and David L. Petersen; Louisville: Westminster John Knox Press, 2009), 87.

3. For a helpful caution on the motives of the prophet Samuel in 1 Sam. 12, see Deryn Guest, *YHWH and Israel in the Book of Judges: An Object-Relations Analysis* (Cambridge: Cambridge University Press, 2019), 91.

with such distinctions, and in this essay I am content to proceed along such lines of inquiry.[4]

A King

Some enigmatic kings can be found in the pages of the Primary History in the Hebrew Bible. Melchizedek's encounter with Abram immediately springs to mind, as does Og of Bashan and his sizeable sleeping apparatus (in Deut. 3:11 his bed is thirteen and a half feet long and six feet wide by the standard measure).[5] To this list one might add Adoni-bezek from Judges 1, who is afforded the first words of an individuated character in the book. After the tribe of Judah launch a strike against Bezek, the leader Adoni-bezek – whose name might be a title meaning 'lord of Bezek' – flees the scene but is duly apprehended. The mutilation of this ruler is a grim introduction to a persistent pattern in Judges, as body parts pile up over the course of a long narrative where Israelite society seems to be gradually dismembered.[6] In the immediate context, Adoni-bezek's disfigurement leads to what sounds like a kind of royal soliloquy:

> Adoni-bezek fled, but they chased after him: they seized him, and sliced off his thumbs and big toes. Adoni-bezek said, 'Seventy kings – with their thumbs and big toes sliced off – were scavenging under my table! Just as I have done, so God has repaid me.' They brought him to Jerusalem, and he died there. (Jdg. 1:6-7)

It is not immediately clear who Adoni-bezek is addressing in these tantalizing words that preface the final journey to his death in Jerusalem. Presumably he is speaking to his captors, and as he has nothing to gain, it sounds as though he has a prophetic accent. The retrospective survey of his career has a startling denouement: he receives a penalty for his own acts of violence. His claim to have subdued seventy kings is certainly grand – much like the dimensions of Og's bed – and Adoni-bezek paints an incredible tableau of scavenging dogs with a mere handful

---

4. Cf. John Frow, 'Character,' in *The Cambridge Companion to Narrative Theory*, ed. Matthew Garrett (Cambridge: Cambridge University Press, 2018), 109: 'The work done by fictional character is a function of its ability to engage us affectively – to do emotional as well as representational work. Its figural pattern asks us to respond with curiosity about a destiny: What happens next; what will the fate of this character be? Because its work is that of enticing the reader's interest, it is 'as much a reconstruction by the reader as it is a textual construct" (citing Philippe Hamon, 'Pour un statut sémiologique du personnage,' in Roland Barthes, Wolfgang Kayser, Wayne Booth and Philippe Hamon, *Poétique du récit* [Paris: Seuil, 1977], 119).

5. On the latter, see Maria Lindquist, 'King Og's Iron Bed,' *CBQ* 73 (2011): 477–92.

6. Note Karolien Vermeulen, 'Hands, Heads, and Feet: Body Parts as Poetic Device in Judges 4–5,' *JBL* 136 (2017): 801–19.

of words.[7] Most intriguing is his declaration of divine retribution: we can probably assume that he is referring to the God of Israel, and if so, then his 'central theme is that power comes and goes, for the mighty fall. He who inflicts punishment may, with God's will, become the afflicted.'[8] Susan Niditch makes the compelling observation that this chastened king now experiences the treatment he once administers to his enemies: 'Now facing the same fate, he identifies with them. The rhythmic proverb, "As I did, so God has repaid me," is less an expression of Israelite or Judahite triumphalism than a warning, colored with pathos, about the vagaries of power.'[9]

Furthermore, Adoni-bezek's words take on a different hue later on, after reading the whole story until the end of 2 Kings 25. Scholars have pointed out an intriguing comparison with Jehoiachin, the last surviving king of Judah who is at the table of a foreign king having been exiled. Gunn and Fewell suggest that Adoni-bezek's episode can be 'recognized as a parable of Israel's relationship with YHWH,' and should the Israelites break the covenant, they can expect certain consequences.[10] The reversal of fortune makes a larger thematic point in light of the narrative beyond the book of Judges: 'In the parable Adoni-Bezek is Israel. The Canaanite is an Israelite. Not such a strange thought, from Jehoiachin's point of view since, in the event, YHWH had the Assyrians and Babylonians do to the Israelites – dispossess them – just what the Israelites in this part of the story are enjoined to do to the Canaanites.'[11] Considering the possibility of these parabolic contours, the words of this forlorn king carry a more ominous tone, as he (thumblessly) points to himself as a cautionary tale for the entire nation of Israel.

A Prophet

If Adoni-bezek's caveat about divine retribution carries a prophetic edge, then the words of Deborah – unique among the judges, as she actually is pictured in a judicial role at the outset – enhance the prophetic quotient in the narrative. The familiar pattern of apostasy recurs in Judges 4, and on this occasion the oppression takes the form of King Jabin's nine hundred chariots of iron. Deborah's description is elaborate, designating her as a prophet holding court under the 'Palm Tree of

---

7. For the significance of *seventy*, see Francis Landy, 'Judges 1: The City of Writing, the Sacred, and the Fragmentation of the Body,' 37–50 in *Voyages in Uncharted Waters: Essays On the Theory and Practice of Biblical Interpretation in Honour of David Jobling* (ed. Wesley J. Bergen and Armin Siedlecki; HBM 13; Sheffield, Sheffield Phoenix Press, 2006), 46.

8. Susan Niditch, *Judges: A Commentary* (OTL; Louisville: Westminster John Knox, 2008), 39.

9. Niditch, *Judges*, 40.

10. David M. Gunn and Danna Nolan Fewell, *Narrative in the Hebrew Bible* (Oxford: Oxford University Press, 1993), 162.

11. Gunn and Fewell, *Narrative in the Hebrew Bible*, 163.

Deborah' in the hill country of Ephraim. Her first words are a call to Barak of Naphtali, who previously has not been introduced in the narrative: 'Has not the LORD God of Israel commanded you? Go! Draw out to Mount Tabor, and take with you ten thousand men from the descendants of Naphtali and Zebulun. I will draw out Sisera, captain of Jabin's armed forces and his chariots and his multitude to you, to the Kishon Valley, and I will give him into your hand' (4:6-7).

Much has been made of Barak's hesitation in response to Deborah's imperatives, with some interpreters arguing that Barak exercises wise caution by insisting on prophetic accompaniment into battle, while others are more scathing with accusations of cowardice. Of more interest here is Deborah's confident articulations of strategy and outcome, and her use of the divine name is conveyed in the form of a question (although the Hebrew construction is rendered as an imperative by the NRSV). She does not seem to have been expecting Barak's demurral, and hence her subsequent modification that the climactic 'honour' will not be conferred to him. Bruce Herzberg has compiled a list of parallels between Deborah and Moses throughout Judges 4–5, noting: 'The story of Deborah has much in common with the story of the Israelites crossing the Reed Sea in Exodus 14–15. In both stories, the Israelites defeat a better-armed force equipped with chariots, in both the Israelites are led by a prophet, and both are followed by a victory song.'[12] Whether or not one goes as far as Herzberg – who suggests that Deborah is characterized as an 'avatar' of Moses himself – her words certainly have a Moses-like quality, certainly elevating her status in the narrative.[13]

A Hacker

Deborah poses a (rhetorical) question that prompts the reader to believe that God had already granted success in the upcoming battle. Our next example has similar kind of question, but a decidedly more ambivalent construal. The name 'Gideon' is derived from the verbal root *to hack*, a memory of the injunction to *hack down* idolatrous installations upon taking possession of the land (e.g. Deut. 7:5).[14] In light of the later revelation that Gideon's own father has a Baal altar (6:25), the name carries a certain irony.[15] The first use of the divine name from Gideon occurs

---

12. Bruce Herzberg, 'Deborah and Moses,' *JSOT* 38.1 (2013): 15–33 (16). For the idea of Deborah as 'counterpart to Jacob,' see Rannfrid Irene Thelle, 'Matrices of motherhood in Judges 5,' *JSOT* 43 (2019): 436–52 (442–43).

13. Other Exodus parallels and the 'Divine Warrior' motif are listed in Richard D. Nelson, *Judges: A Critical and Rhetorical Commentary* (London: Bloomsbury T&T Clark, 2017), 84.

14. A. Graeme Auld, 'Gideon: Hacking at the Heart of the Old Testament,' *VT* 39 (1989): 257–67.

15. Considering the recent work of Diane M. Sharon, 'The Gideon Cycle and the Deuteronomist's Critique of Hereditary Monarchy: An Intertextual Perspective,' in *Ve-'Ed Ya'aleh (Gen 2:6): Essays in Biblical and Ancient Near Eastern Studies Presented to Edward L.*

in a dialogue earlier in chapter 6, as he is threshing wheat on a winepress in order to conceal it from the Midianite oppressors. In response to the greeting ('The LORD is with you, you mighty warrior!') from the angelic messenger who does not disclose his identity, Gideon's questions have a rather different tone than Deborah: 'Excuse me, my lord? Sure, the LORD is with us! So why has all *this* found us? Where are all his wonderful deeds that our ancestors have recounted to us, saying, "Didn't the LORD bring us up from Egypt?" But now, the LORD has left us, and given us into the grip of Midian!' (6:13). Just a couple of chapters earlier the iron chariots of Sisera dominated the landscape, and yet Deborah speaks of divine rescue. Here in chapter 6 Gideon's sarcastic frustration emits a sense of defeat and despair. In his recital there is an absence of miraculous acts, and divine abandonment tips the blame for the present crisis toward God with scant acknowledgement of any culpability on Israel's part.

Is Gideon's response a singular opinion in Judges 6, or to what degree are his sentiments representative of the larger community? A second example of Gideon's 'God-talk' might therefore be helpful, taking place at end of his career in Judges 8 (after the bulldozing of his father's Baal installation, fleece test, and defeat of the same Midianites with the trumpets and torches). A darker side of Gideon is increasingly apparent in his pursuit of the royal Midianite fugitives Zebah and Zalmunna, and the brutal treatment of his previously critical compatriots.[16] Most telling is his response to the offer of dynastic leadership: 'Then the Israelites said to Gideon, "Rule over us – you, your son, and your son's son – for you have saved us from the hand of Midian!" Gideon said to them, "I will not rule over you, and my sons will not rule over you – the LORD will rule over you"' (8:22-23). On the surface such a refusal sounds impressive, but given that Gideon then straightaway asks for donation of gold that he makes into an ephod (that he places in his hometown of Ophrah, where it becomes a snare for both the nation and his own house), a shadow is cast over his *character zone*.[17] Combined with the disclosure of Gideon's many wives and a concubine, this questionable manufacturing of an ephod is similar to the criticism of Solomon, as Moshe Garsiel has pointed out.[18] Solomon likewise has

Greenstein, Volume 1 (edited by Peter Machinist, Robert A. Harris, Joshua A. Berman, Nili Samet and Noga Ayali-Darshan; Atlanta: SBL Press, 2021), 595–609, it raises the interesting question about whether the hereditary issue in the Gideon stories is foregrounded quite early in the narrative.

16. L. Juliana M. Claassens, 'The Character of God in Judges 6–8: The Gideon Narrative as Theological and Moral Resource,' *HBT* 23 (2001): 51–71 (64) remarks that Gideon treats 'the rest of the characters as objects to be used and mistreated as he desires'.

17. For proposals on the ephod, see Trent C. Butler, *Judges* (WBC 8; Grand Rapids: Zondervan, 2009), 315; Niditch, *Judges*, 105.

18. Moshe Garsiel, 'Homiletic Name-Derivations as a Literary Device in the Gideon Narrative: Judges vi-vii,' *VT* 43 (1993): 302–17 (306–7).

an orthodox façade that hides a syncretistic industry. Consequently, Gideon's use of the divine name must be considered dubious in Jdg. 8:23, and perhaps there is a degree of similarity to Jeremiah's complaint about the citizens of Jerusalem: 'you are near to their lips but far from their kidneys' (Jer. 12:2).

A Negotiator

After the sordid reign and incendiary demise of Gideon's son Abimelech, the rise of Jephthah is framed by a neighbouring adversary and a looming crisis: 'Judges 10:6-18 forms the backdrop of the story, and portrays the Ammonite threat as affecting not only Gilead but also the tribes of Judah, Benjamin, and Ephraim.'[19] At the end of Judges 10 the local Israelite commanders recognize their problem, and seek a military solution that revolves around a new leader: 'Who is the man that will begin to fight against the Ammonites? Let him be head over all the residents of Gilead!' Their declaration sets the stage for the introduction of Jephthah, who is the outcast son of a prostitute, but has undeniable combat credentials and a reckless gang that has gathered around him. Nonetheless, the elders of Gilead sound hesitant to commit their future into Jephthah's hands, and he engages in a protracted negotiation to secure the promise of being 'head' over Gilead after securing victory against the Ammonites. This lengthy negotiation in turn anticipates one of the longest exchanges in the book of Judges when Jephthah later sends a messenger to the Ammonite king in 11:12-28. Prior to any battle, Jephthah is presented in the narrative as the consummate talker, an element worth noting because his name means something like *he who opens wide (his mouth)*.[20]

In several places during the negotiation and afterwards, God-talk is used by Jephthah and the elders of Gilead, although the degree of sincerity for both sides might be open for debate. The example of interest here is Jephthah's response in 11:9, and consider the NRSV rendering: 'If you bring me home again to fight with the Ammonites, and the LORD gives them over to me, I will be your head.' Alternatively, Jephthah's response can be translated as a question ('If you are bringing me back to fight against the Ammonites and the LORD gives them before me, will I *really* be your head?'), but either way the issue of insecurity is foregrounded. Jephthah's lack of trust in the leadership of Gilead is understandable in the light of his past treatment (vv. 2-3, '"You won't have an inheritance in our father's house, for you are the son of another woman!" Then Jephthah fled from the presence of his brothers, and lived in the land of Tob'). Despite the offer of headship

---

19. J. Cheryl Exum, *Tragedy and Biblical Narrative: Arrows of the Almighty* (Cambridge: Cambridge University Press, 1992), 46.

20. Elie Assis, *Self-Interest or Communal Interest: An Ideology of Leadership in the Gideon, Abimelech and Jephthah Narratives (Judg 6–12)* (VTSup 106; Leiden: Brill, 2005), 216. For some trends in Jephthah research of late, see Kelly J. Murphy, 'Judges in Recent Research,' *CBR* 15 (2017): 179–213 (187–89).

over Gilead in v. 8, Jephthah's response in v. 9 – whether translated as a question or an emphatic affirmation – seems to be a request for an oath. Jack Sasson helpfully summarizes the matter:

> Many commentators are puzzled by Jephthah's statement. The elders have just offered him the post unconditionally. He needed only to go back with them to battle Ammon, and he is their chief. So why does he complicate matters by making his accession conditional? Does it foreshadow his lack of self-confidence, which will soon make him utter a famous vow? (11:30-31)[21]

The importance of *language* in the Jephthah narrative is certainly underscored in this initial exchange with the elders of Gilead. In their final response it can be observed that the elders seal the deal with an oath in v. 10 ('The LORD will be the one who hears between us, if we do not do just as you have said.') and this oath is ill-advised for at least two reasons.[22] First, it is a prologue to Jephthah's own oath later in the chapter that will consume his own daughter: Abimelech earlier slaughtered his own brothers, and now Jephthah's language destroy his own child. Second, Jephthah's 'headship' results in later bloodshed at the fords of Jordan, with the kind of excess that resembles both Gideon and Abimelech.[23] Glancing back at our previous discussion, Gideon earlier uses the divine name in a duplicitous manner, and a similar tactic can be noticed in Jephthah as well. Similar uses, with obvious political expedience, will be apparent in other leadership debates such as 2 Sam. 5:1-3 when the northern tribes meet with David and Hebron and offer him the kingship only *after* losing a nasty civil war. Matters of God-talk in Judges, therefore, carry interpretive implications for other sectors of the Hebrew Bible.

A Mother

The first instalment of the Micah narrative takes place in the hill country of Ephraim in Judges 17. Rather cryptically, Micah's story begins with a confession to his mother: 'The eleven hundred silver pieces that were taken from you, about which you uttered a curse in my hearing – behold the silver is with me. *I* took it.'

---

21. Jack M. Sasson, *Judges 1–12: A New Translation with Introduction and Commentary* (AB; New Haven, Yale University Press, 2014), 423.

22. Robert H. O'Connell, *The Rhetoric of the Book of Judges* (VTSup 63; Leiden: Brill, 1996), 180.

23. See Robin Baker, 'Double Trouble: Counting the Cost of Jephthah,' *JBL* 137 (2018): 29–50. Other remarks on the reception history of this section can be found in David M. Gunn, *Judges* (Blackwell Bible Commentaries. Oxford: Blackwell, 2005), 133–69; N. Scott Amos, "Do to Me According to What Has Gone Out of Your Mouth': A Reformation Debate on the Tragedy of Jephthah and his Daughter,' *Reformation & Renaissance Review* 21 (2019): 3–26.

No background data is provided for the theft, but coincidentally, the same number occurs in the Delilah transaction in the previous chapter (the amount offered by each of the Philistine rulers in 16:5). Rather than identifying Delilah as the (otherwise unnamed) mother of Micah, the mention of *eleven hundred* continues the theme of betrayal in this present narrative context. A longer form of Micah's name (*Micahyehu*, 'who is like YHWH?') is used early in the story, but gradually disappears after the idolatrous dialogue between him and his mother. The example of God-talk of interest here is from Micah's mother, in one of her sentences after Micah gives back her stolen silver in 17:3-5. After her initial elation ('May my son be blessed by the LORD!') with her son's actions, she continues:

> His mother said, 'I solemnly devote the silver to the LORD from my hand to my son, in order to make an idol and a molten image. So now, I am returning it to you!' He returned the silver to his mother, and she took 200 silver pieces and gave them to the refiner. He made it into an idol and a molten image, and they were in Micah's house. As for the man Micah, he had a house of God. He made an ephod and teraphim. He filled the hand of one of his sons, and he was a priest for him.

Commentators often underscore that the mother's response reveals a syncretism at work, as she blesses her son using Israel's covenantal name for God, but then dedicates the returned silver for illicit cultic objects: 'This strange conjunction of devotion to Yahweh and idolatry, and disconnection between word and act, gives the episode a satirical quality which, as we are about to see, turns out to be characteristic of the whole narrative.'[24] In terms of the wider Judges story, the presence of vows and curses are reminiscent of Jephthah's oath and Jotham's fable. More specifically in chapter 17, the mother's response helps explain where the silver came from in the first place: Micah has a shrine, and evidently it is lucrative affair as other Israelites were willing to part with their own silver for whatever benefits were derived. Perhaps Micah returns the silver out of fear of the curse his mother utters, and maybe she too is motivated by the same fear in her words of blessing and subsequent dedication of the silver: 'Motherly love and happiness about having the silver back, or compassion upon hearing Micah's confession of guilt may play a role, but the primary motive for the blessing seems to be fear. That is why, after the blessing, the mother takes further precautions to ensure Micayhu's safety. She dedicates the silver to YHWH, and she specifies that it be used for a

---

24. Barry G. Webb, *The Book of Judges* (NICOT; Eerdmans: Grand Rapids, 2012), 424. Cf. J. Cheryl Exum, 'Judges,' in *Harper's Bible Commentary* (ed. James L. Mays; San Francisco: Harper & Row, 1988), 259: 'Molten images are forbidden in Exod. 20:4-6; Deut. 5:8-10; Exod. 34:17; and Deut. 27:15; and warnings about the dangers of syncretism appear in Judg. 2:1-5; 6:7-10; and 10:10-15.'

sculptured and a molten image.'[25] To what extent the syncretistic God-talk of Micah's mother mirrors the surrounding Israelite society could be the subject of another study, but traces of her words have been seen previously in the narrative. Indeed, the notice of an ephod in Micah's well-equipped shrine has echoes of Gideon's actions of crafting an ephod with a deleterious outcome: 'and all Israel prostituted themselves to it there, and it became a snare to Gideon and to his family' (Judg. 8:27 NRSV). Micah is excited when he secures a Levite for his house ('Now I know that the LORD will be good to me, because the Levite has become a priest for me', 17:13), but such excitement is short-lived as the Levite later becomes complicit in another theft. After stealing his mother's silver, Micah's silver images are stolen in turn by a gang of marauding Danites, despite the ample language of 'blessing' from both Micah and his unnamed mother.

A Tribe

During a time when 'there was no king in Israel', a group of roving Danites are introduced in Judges 18.[26] In the previous chapter the young Levite was on the move seeking a preferable living arrangement, and in chapter 18 the tribe of Dan is likewise in search of a better opportunity. To that end, the group of spies are dispatched, and alight upon Micah's house. The Danites recognize the Levite, but whether it is because of a distinct accent or because their paths have crossed previously is not clarified in the narrative. They make an inquiry through the Levite, although the response ('Go in *shalom*! The journey that you are going on is before YHWH') could be interpreted by the reader as deeply ambivalent in the circumstances. The Danite spies do not raise any questions the oracle, but instead venture to Laish. After scoping out this isolated and secure city, they return and report to their fellow Danites. The God-talk in their speech is of interest here, as the spies produce their own kind of oracle, overflowing with a divine assurance of success and sounding like Joshua as they describe the land and the opportunity at hand:

> Arise, and let us go up against them! For we have seen the land, and behold, it is very good. But you are unresponsive! Do not be sluggish to go, to enter in and possess the land: when you enter, you will come to a secure people, and the land is wide on both hands, because God has given it in your hand – a place where there is no lack of anything that is in the land! (18:9-10)

25. E. Aydeet Mueller, *The Micah Story: A Morality Tale in the Book of Judges* (New York: Peter Lang, 2001), 58.

26. Gregory T. K. Wong, 'Judges,' in *The Baker Illustrated Bible Commentary* (ed. Gary M. Burge and Andrew E. Hill; Grand Rapids: Baker, 2012), 236: 'The inability of the Danites to take possession of their allotted land has already been disclosed in Joshua 19:47 and Judges 1:34. What the tribe has done to compensate for that inability is now described in detail in 18:1b–31.'

This comparatively long utterance from the spies has the intended effect of rousing other Danites, who, armed and dangerous, set out for Laish. While on the journey, the spies speak up again upon reaching the region of Micah's house, adumbrating the cultic contents of shine and indirectly proposing a quick detour. Enticing the Levite with a better offer, the Danites loot the place, and Micah's fruitless chase after the armed bandits ultimately reveals the emptiness of the religious platitudes voiced by his mother and himself. They earlier sounded confident in their affirmations of divine blessings, but the vacant shrine is a testimony to their ineffective syncretism. A kind of *measure for measure* retribution unfolds in the storyline: the stolen silver is dedicated for crafting idolatrous accoutrements, only to be stolen in turn by the gang of Danites (with the hired Levite as an accomplice, no less).[27] Lest one thinks that the Danites get away with stolen shrine, the account ends with a notice of their own measure for measure experience: the Danites invade the homes of Micah and Laish, but in the end they are themselves invaded on the day of exile (18:30), and once more the silver is stolen and the cultic items are consigned to exilic oblivion. Their confident words ('God has given it in your hand') eventually prove to be just as misguided as those of Micah and his mother, and a complete antithesis to Deborah back in chapter 4. Assuming that the 'captivity of the land' in 18:30 is a reference to the Assyrian invasion of 2 Kings 17, the words of the Danites sound quite different when the end of the narrative is considered. Perhaps the lament of Adoni-Bezek comes to mind ('Just as I have done, so God has repaid me'). Of course, the story is not quite that heavy-handed, but it is difficult for the reader to quickly dismiss that implication.

Conclusion

Of necessity this essay is just a short study in how characters talk about God or use the divine name in direct speech in several sectors of the book of Judges. Numerous other examples could have been chosen, ranging from Ehud's *secret* (3:19-20) or the angel's curse of Meroz (5:23), or the apparent lack of any obvious divine references in Jotham's fable (9:8-15), and so on. But by way of conclusion, I might suggest that this topic can further developed in at least two ways.

First, 'God-talk' is a technique of characterization that merits attention, and could be fruitfully explored in longer works of analysis. Along with attention to individual characterization and distinctive speech accents, comparisons among the various figures within Judges can be undertaken. A few preliminary comments have been made above, but there is ample scope for more rigorous discussion. Furthermore, one might also compare God-talk in Judges with other portions of the Deuteronomistic History, from Rahab's declaration about the assurance of the conquest (Josh. 2:9-13) all the way to the bombast of Sennacherib's field commander

---

27. For a list of parallels between Micah in chapter 17 and the Danites in chapter 18, see Yairah Amit, *The Book of Judges: The Art of Editing* (BIS 38; Leiden: Brill, 1999), 334–35.

outside the wall of Jerusalem as he exhales about the inevitability of the city's destruction in 2 Kings 18. When assessing the direct speech of a character, utterances that involve uses of the divine name can provide a host of insights into the various figures who appear across a much larger narrative canvas.

Second, more research could be devoted to the question of whether or not God-talk operates at thematic level of the larger narrative of Judges. It is well-documented, to cite one example, that the image of Achsah on her donkey is a case in point.[28] In Judg. 1:13-14 Achsah rides her donkey to make a request for better land from Caleb her father. Such positive images are abominably inverted in 19:25-28 when the nameless woman is cast upon a donkey by the Levite after a night of horrific abuse. This horrible inversion indicates the corruption and social disintegration of the covenant community over the course of the narrative. It is possible that God-talk might also be used as an index of gradual degeneration in the community. Although only a short sample has been canvassed in this essay, one wonders if the systemic social and spiritual deterioration in Judges can be further traced through how characters talk about God in increasingly self-serving ways.

---

28. E.g., Danna Nolan Fewell, 'Deconstructive Criticism: Achsah and the (E)razed City of Writing,' in *Judges and Method: New Approaches in Biblical Studies* (2nd ed. edited by Gale A. Yee; Minneapolis: Fortress, 2007), 130.

AFTERWORD

J. Cheryl Exum

I have accepted the difficult remit of writing a *brief* Afterword to this volume. Since this afterword is intended to be a supplement to the volume rather than a formal response, I shall not be engaging with the individual contributions but rather limiting my comments to the volume as a whole.

What strikes me immediately about this collection is how appreciative the contributors are about the portrayals of the characters they discuss (apart from Abimelech and those who appear in the more disagreeable stories of Judges 17–19). The stories of the judges abound with humorously entertaining anecdotes that, among other purposes, allow readers to see the strengths and foibles of each of the characters, whereas Judges 17–21 favours satire and irony (Kaminsky). Ehud is a hero who deceives and defeats his stronger opponent, and readers who question his actions and the morality of the story in terms of their own ethical standards would do better to approach the story on its own terms as an expression of the ancient writer's worldview (Andersson). Deborah is a prophet, a judge, a gifted and charismatic leader, a wise woman, and a 'mother in Israel'[1] – a commanding figure although she is not described as a warrior and must share the limelight with two other human heroes, Jael and Barak (Amit). Jael is a resourceful and courageous figure who functions as a warrior in command, overturns expectations, and – though some ambiguity remains regarding her motive for killing Sisera – serves as an instrument of God (Backfish).

Gideon represents the traditional type of hero found in epic tales from various cultures. He is a guerrilla warrior, the leader of a resistance movement – a complex character who matures from an insecure, divinely inspired young man into a capable, self-assured national leader who does not seek advancement for himself or his family (Niditch). His son Abimelech is a complex character. Neither judge nor deliverer of Israel, he first becomes king over Shechem and later appears as ruling over Israel. He has no allegiances, is ill-suited to rule and predisposed to violence (Johnson). Samson is a liminal character, a Nazirite wild man inhabiting

---

1. Amit sees a 'mother in Israel' as 'one who brings liberation from oppression, provides protection, and ensures the well-being and security of her people,' citing an article I wrote in 1985. Since then I have changed my view (see below).

the border between nature and culture. Domesticated when his hair is cut, he becomes wild, and thus strong again, as a result of his prayer to God in which he asks for strength. More anti-hero than hero, his crowning act is to kill more Philistines in his death than he killed in his life (Kawashima). Samson's flat characterization and the parallels between events in his life and in the history of Israel indicate that Samson is a type: he represents Israel as well as the Israelites of the time, who were doing what was right in their own eyes and failing to do what was right in the eyes of God (Wong). Two enigmatic characters in the Samson story, the divine messenger who announces Samson's birth to his parents and Delilah, are both linked to Samson's destiny, with Delilah serving as an instrument of divine judgement who enables Samson to understand the meaning of his calling (Gorospe).

Jephthah does not appear in such a positive light. Rather than taking charge, Jephthah responds to the actions of others; he seeks to avoid conflict by means of negotiation, and he habitually presents himself as the innocent party. He becomes a problematic character when he makes the vow that seals his daughter's fate (Schneider). If Jephthah's words in 11:35 mean that he would rather die himself than carry out his vow,[2] his daughter's decision to be sacrificed can be seen as either ethical (she sacrifices her life in order to protest an unjust social system that prioritizes power and status over the value of innocent human life) or unethical (she sees it as her duty to die in her father's place since his life is more important than hers) (Janzen).

The ways various characters – Adonibezek, Deborah, Gideon, Jephthah, Micah's mother, the Danites – speak about the deity point to the complexity of his characterization. Deborah's use of the divine name in 4:6-7, for example, expresses her confidence that God will give Israel victory, whereas Gideon expresses doubt (6:13), and the way characters (beginning with Gideon) speak about God in increasingly self-serving ways contributes to the picture of gradual social and spiritual deterioration in Judges (Bodner).

The range of approaches taken to the book of Judges in this volume open up challenging areas for further exploration; in particular I would like to see more instances of resistant readings – readings that take issue with the ideology of the book of Judges. According to this ideology, Israel has been given the land of Canaan by their god and thus has the right to possess it and to take it forcibly from others who are also living there. As Jephthah puts it, 'Will you not possess what Chemosh your god gives you to possess? All that Yahweh our god has dispossessed before us, we will possess' (11:24). By and large, the contributors read the stories of the judges according to the ideology of the biblical narrator. They are 'resistance stories' in which the Israelite underdogs get the better of their militarily superior oppressors and the biblical text shows a hearty approval of it all. No doubt this

---

2. This interpretation of 11:35 seems unlikely to me. I would translate: 'Ah, my daughter, you have brought me very low and have become the source of my trouble. I have opened my mouth to Yahweh and I cannot take it back.'

interpretation is true to the spirit of these stories. But what about the other side of the story?

We are dealing in these narratives with an ideology of 'us' versus 'them', those on the 'right' side, the Israelites and their god, and those on the 'wrong' side, the other peoples, the oppressors, the enemy and their gods. In a biblical book that advocates fighting to possess contested territory, should we not be raising questions about the problem of 'othering' and maligning the 'other' (including ethnic humor at their expense)? I am not arguing that we should not appreciate, even enjoy, these stories in terms of their epic and folkloric qualities, qualities well described by Niditch. I am saying that we need to acknowledge the problem of othering those who do not belong to 'us' and the question of what this says about us.

The situation is different in Judges 17–19, chapters whose relationship to Judges 1–16 has long been debated. Here we no longer find the ideology of 'us' versus 'them'. Israel is now divided against itself, and a pro-monarchal ideology casts its shadow over the stories (though the issue of pro- and anti-monarchal ideology in Judges is, as Johnson's discussion of Abimelech shows, a complex issue). Not surprisingly, the characters in chs 17–18 have little to commend them. Micah is undistinguished apart from his Yahwistic name; he is not a warrior, holds no leadership position, has no particular skill and no virtue, yet his actions are consequential. He and those associated with him are disreputable, immoral, and unscrupulous characters, whose various undertakings set in motion events that lead to Israel's demise (Baker). The problematic nature of the attitudes and actions of Micah and the other figures in chs 17–18 is revealed in the interaction among them. They are not portrayed as totally negative but rather as reflections of the twisted world in which they live. They are self-centred individuals who, in the absence of rules and common goals, exploit whatever opportunities arise (Gillmayr-Bucher).

Unlike the other characters represented in this volume, the Levite's wife of Judges 19 is a victim. She is not an enemy of Israel, but she is an 'other' a voiceless dispensable unnamed female victim whose point of view – unlike that of Jephthah's daughter, whatever we think of it – is withheld by the narrator. Landy's reading of ch 19 is a notable example of resistant reading in this volume, resistant because Landy is not content with the story as told by the narrator.[3] He sets himself the difficult task of writing about the Levite's wife and the way the story affects us without foreclosing interpretive possibilities or co-opting the woman's voice. His comments about the painful experience of writing the essay well describe the experience of reading it: 'I don't want the story to be told,' 'I cannot bear to carry on.'

Landy's essay exemplifies the kind of approach I am advocating here: an approach that recognizes the point of view of the 'other' in our interpretations of biblical texts – points of view that are typically suppressed in the interest of the biblical writer's ideology. They are not necessarily successfully suppressed, and I

---

3. Cf. Gillmayr-Bucher's observation that, in the light of the description of the inhabitants of Laish as peaceful and posing no threat to anyone, the Danites who destroy their city come across as 'ruthless conquerors overrunning defenceless people'.

offer here two examples of places in the book of Judges where the text itself provides the reader the opportunity to consider the events from the perspective of the 'other.' Judges 5:28-30 presents a poignant vignette of a mother's experience of waiting for her son to return safe from battle. The mother is Sisera's, and we observe her through the window out of which she peers, watching for him and troubled by his delay. The text vividly captures her anxiety – 'Why is his chariot so long in coming? Why so tardy the clatter of his chariots?' – as, assured by her attendants, she desperately attempts to convince herself of his heroic return: 'Her wisest companions answer, indeed, she answers herself, "Are they not finding and dividing the spoil?"' We lose sympathy with the Canaanite women, however, when they callously imagine the plunder of their enemy and the rape of innocent women.[4]

Gabriel Josipovici observes that this is the only time in the book of Judges when one character displays an awareness of what it feels like to be another; the singer of Judges 5, he notes, 'has given us a sense of the silent victims as well as of the exultant victors'.[5] Sisera's mother is given greater interiority than any other character in the story, and the finely crafted portrait of her is both moving and chilling.[6] Readers are likely both to sympathize with her anxiety and to be appalled by the vision of rape and pillage that she relies on to allay her fears.[7]

Sisera's mother serves as the mouthpiece for the male ideology of war in which pillage and rape go together. To the victor belong the spoils.[8] By placing these words in the mouth of Sisera's mother, the 'singer' of Judges 5 not only presents women approving of war for profit but also has a mother endorse the rampant rape of other women and their daughters ('a womb or two for every hero'). In addition, he puts Sisera's mother and her attendants in the position of approving their own imminent rape.[9] In the male ideology of war, rape is a weapon of terror

---

4. Danna Nolan Fewell and David M. Gunn, 'Controlling Perspectives: Women, Men, and the Authority of Violence in Judges 4 & 5,' *JAAR* 58 (1990): 389–411 [406–409].

5. Gabriel Josipovici, *The Book of God: A Response to the Bible* (New Haven, CT: Yale University Press, 1988), 130.

6. Witness the sympathy, albeit qualified, for Sisera and his mother in the commentaries.

7. Fewell and Gunn, 'Controlling Perspectives,' 406–409; J. Cheryl Exum, 'Feminist Criticism: Whose Interests Are Being Served?,' in *Judges and Method: New Approaches in Biblical Studies* (2nd edn, ed. Gale A. Yee; Minneapolis, MN: Fortress Press, 65–89 [72–74]; Exum, 'Shared Glory: Salomon de Bray's *Jael, Deborah and Barak*,' in *Between the Text and the Canvas: The Bible and Art in Dialogue* (ed. J. Cheryl Exum and Ela Nutu; Sheffield: Sheffield Phoenix Press, 2007), 11–37 [32–35]; Exum, *Art as Biblical Commentary: Visual Commentary from Hagar the Wife of Abraham to Mary the Mother of Jesus* (London: T&T Clark, 2019), 168–196 [194–96].

8. Whether the embroidered garments are Sisera's or his warriors' or his mother's is not clear; see Jack M. Sasson, *Judges 1–12: A New Translation with Introduction and Commentary* (New Haven, CT: Yale University Prerss, 2014), 310.

9. Fewell and Gunn, 'Controlling Perspectives,' 408.

and revenge.[10] Is there any reason to expect that Israelite victors ('us') would treat the defeated men's women any better than their Canaanite counterparts (the 'other') are pictured as doing?[11]

The attention given to Sisera's mother invites comparison with the other mother in the story, Deborah, the 'mother in Israel'. Deborah is portrayed as a mother who gives life to Israel, as Amit observes, but she also sends her 'sons' off to war, where many of them will die. It is not difficult to imagine other mothers in Israel experiencing the anxiety and loss of Sisera's mother. In the portrayal of Sisera's mother peering through the window, hoping against hope that she will soon spy her son returning triumphantly, the text opens a window for its readers to look through the other's eyes, and to catch a glimpse of the inescapable horrors of war.

My other example, Judg. 16:23-24, presents the Philistine view of Samson: 'Our god has given our enemy into our hand, the ravager of our country, who has killed many of us' (v. 24). Keeping in mind that one group's freedom fighter is another group's terrorist, what, we might ask, has Samson done to the Philistines compared to what they have done to him?[12] It is Samson who initiates a chain of reprisals and counter-reprisals by posing a riddle that his wedding guests cannot answer without cheating. Whether the riddle contest is harmless entertainment or a matter of honour and shame, in order to discover the answer, the guests resort to threatening Samson's wife, whom they hold partly accountable: 'Have you invited us here to impoverish us?' (14:15). Samson's response to losing his wager is out of proportion to his guests' chicanery. He kills thirty men in Ashkelon, who have done nothing to him, so that he can use their garments to pay off his debt.

Another terrorist act on Samson's part is his burning of the Philistines' grain fields and olive orchards. What provokes this deed? Samson's father-in-law, who not unreasonably believed that Samson had effectively divorced his daughter, gave her to another man. Here, too, innocent people, in this case children as well as men and women, are victims of substantial, unjustifiable devastation with serious long-term effects. The Philistines respond by punishing not Samson but rather their own people, the ones they hold responsible for inciting Samson to destroy their

---

10. If one wished to argue that the narrator is using Sisera's mother's speech to condemn rape, one would have to say he is also condemning plunder, and thus condemning war. Israel's mission, however, is to dispossess and despoil the Canaanites, and this is what the Song of Deborah and the book of Judges is about.

11. Israelite men took women prisoners for their sexual use, as we know from the law in Deut. 21:10-14. This law attempts to place restrictions on male behavior toward female captives, but does not deal with women who were raped on the spot and abandoned or killed.

12. On Samson as a terrorist, see J. Cheryl Exum, 'The Many Faces of Samson,' in *Samson: Hero or Fool?* (ed. Erik Eynikel and Tobias Nicklas; Leiden: Brill, 2014), 13–31 [17–20]; reprinted in Exum, *Samson and Delilah: Selected Essays* (Sheffield: Sheffield Phoenix Press, 2020), 283–301 [287–90]; Joseph R. Jeter, Jr, *Preaching Judges* (St Louis, MO: Chalice Press, 2003), 116.

crops. Samson takes the Philistines' retaliation against his wife and her father personally and, in revenge, slaughters many Philistines (15:8). His tactics place his own people in danger, as the actions of terrorists often do. When the Philistines attack the people of Judah, it is only to coerce them to hand Samson over to them. They abandon the raid when the men of Judah comply rather than suffer for Samson's self-appointed acts of revenge. Although it appears that Samson is finally in their power, Samson turns the tables on them and kills a thousand Philistines with the jawbone of a donkey (15:15).

The Philistines' rather feeble attempts to rid their country of a fierce destroyer pale in comparison to Samson's vendettas against them. Not without cause do the Philistines see Samson as the ravager of their country and an adversary responsible for the deaths of many of their people. Their eventual capture of Samson, with the help of Delilah, leads to Samson's ultimate terrorist act: pulling down the temple of Dagon and killing himself along with 'all the people who were in it' (16:30). Destruction on such a huge scale would have included many innocent people, men and women who had never had any dealings with Samson directly (children are not mentioned apart from the young boy who leads him, 16:26). Since Samson is an instrument in the plan of a god who is 'seeking a pretext to act against the Philistines' (14:4), and since it is this god who enables Samson to pull down the temple by granting him strength, Samson can be seen as the ancient equivalent of a suicide-bomber, an assassin sent by his god on a mission to destroy as many Philistines as possible.[13]

The elephant in the room is the god-character. Admittedly the lack of attention to the characterization of the deity in this volume is understandable: the contributors focus on specific individual characters of their choice. But because God plays such an important role throughout the book of Judges (except ch. 19), consideration of his characterization has a good deal to contribute to our understanding of Judges as a whole (and, especially, in my opinion, from the point of view of a resistant reader). As the character with whom most of the other characters interact directly or indirectly, he is ultimately responsible – either through his actions or his failure to act – for the series of events that begins with Israel's successes and failures in battles against various enemies and culminates in internecine war and the near extinction of an Israelite tribe. In his innovative essay, Bodner examines the deity as seen by other characters in Judges, with what they say about him serving as an indirect form of interaction. The result is fascinating, but a character as complex as Israel's god (as he is constructed by the biblical narrator) will always merit further scrutiny, and so I offer a few observations here.

---

13. Kaminsky notes that some modern readers might draw a parallel between Samson and a 'contemporary suicide bomber/terrorist' but he does not consider this option. Readers might be interested in the controversial 2009 production of Saint-Saëns's *Samson et Dalila* by the Flanders Opera Company. Israeli Omri Nitzan and Palestinian Amir Nizar Zuabi, the stage directors, portray Samson as a suicide bomber who dons a belt of dynamite sticks to enact the final destruction, at which point the curtain falls (available on DVD, Antwerp, 2011).

The biblical narrator expects the reader to read with the ideology of the text and to view God, however mysterious, as beyond reproach and Israel alone as responsible for its suffering. When God comes to Israel's rescue it is not because Israel has deserved it but because God is compassionate. This ideology is the basis of the framework (apostasy > punishment > cry for help > deliverance) and appears throughout the book of Judges. What is needed in a study of the characterization of God is the kind of critical approach one brings to the study of other literary characters.

In an article published some years ago, I argued that the god-character is as much to blame as Israel for the chaos and dissolution progressively depicted in Judges and with which the book ends.[14] More recently, Deryn Guest uses object relations theory to explore the deity's dysfunctional relationship with Israel. God is portrayed as the dominant parent who punishes because he loves, and Israel as the wayward child whose anxiety and anger at 'the unfulfillable demands this larger-than-life divine parent imposes' is suppressed by the biblical scribe in order to create an ideal child who is loyal, obedient, and submissive. The scribe 'encourag[es] his readers to engage with his identity formation project and willingly sacrifice autonomy and authority in order to retain a continued and effective relationship with YHWH'.[15] Guest identifies six salient character traits of this god: earth's landlord, supreme military strategist and commander, grand manipulator of circumstances, fertility fixer, the dominant male to whom human males must submit, and jealous deity.[16]

How does the biblical narrator construct God? Because Judges is about war – Israel's battles to take possession of the promised land – it is not surprising that the most prominent role this god holds is that of the supreme leader of the Israelite troops, sometimes entering the fray, at other times controlling events from the sidelines. In Judges 4–5 he appears in his role of divine warrior, the 'Most High Male',[17] who, as Amit and Backfish observe, is the real hero of the tale.[18] How does the biblical narrator have God present himself? He reduces the number of Gideon's

---

14. J. Cheryl Exum, 'The Centre Cannot Hold: Thematic and Textual Instabilities in Judges,' *CBQ* 52 (1990): 410-31.

15. Deryn Guest, *YHWH and Israel in the Book of Judges: An Object–Relations Analysis* (Cambridge: Cambridge University Press, 2019), citations from pp. 145 and 156. It is impossible to do justice here to this pioneering study and its challenge to traditional interpretations of Judges.

16. Deryn Guest, 'Judging Yhwh,' in *The Oxford Handbook of Biblical Narrative* (ed. Danna Nolan Fewell; New York: Oxford University Press, 2016), 180-91.

17. I refer to the god-character as 'he' because he is male-identified. As David Clines points out, he is the supreme masculine character of the Bible, the 'Most High Male', a character who in one figure incorporates the masculinity of Hebrew culture; David J. A. Clines, 'The Most High Male: Divine Masculinity in the Bible,' in *Hebrew Masculinities Anew* (ed. Ovidiu Creangă; Sheffield: Sheffield Phoenix Press, 2019), 61-82.

18. In Backfish's view, Jael as an instrument of Yahweh 'enables women to identify with the divine Warrior metaphor so commonly employed in the Hebrew Bible.' I wonder, Do women want to identify with the divine warrior? Do men?

troops because 'The troops with you are too many for me to give the Midianites into their hand. Israel would only take the credit away from me, saying, "My own hand has delivered me"' (7:2). What does this tell us about his ego? What do we learn about this god from his controlling, though behind-the-scene, role in the life of Samson, who is repeatedly animated by this god's spirit? And how might we interpret his remarkable aloofness in chapters 17–19, followed by his pronounced involvement in the internecine war in chapters 20–21?

The deity's role is particularly perplexing in the two most scandalous stories in Judges, those of Jephthah's human sacrifice and the rape, abuse, and dismemberment of the Levite's wife, both of which have parallels elsewhere in the Bible. There are a number of distressing aspects of God's dealings with the judge Jephthah. For one thing, Jephthah's vow is made under ambiguous circumstances. The spirit of God comes upon him shortly before he makes the vow, thus raising the question whether or not he utters the vow under its influence (11:29-31). According to Judg. 11:32, 'Jephthah crossed over to the Ammonites to fight against them; and God gave them into his hand' (see also 12:3). If not a tacit acceptance of the terms of Jephthah's vow, this statement at least implicates the deity. There is otherwise no divine action in the story and, disturbingly, no divine judgement regarding human sacrifice. The imposition of the vow between the coming of the spirit of God upon Jephthah and the victory renders it impossible to determine whether victory comes as the result of the spirit, or the vow, or both.[19] Inexplicably Jephthah does not try to find an alternative means of honoring his vow.[20] Most disturbing is the fact that God does not intervene at the crucial moment to prevent the sacrifice, as he did when Abraham prepared to sacrifice his son Isaac (Gen. 22).[21]

Whereas in Genesis 19 God intervenes to save Lot's guests from an unruly mob, in the gruesome counterpart in Judges 19 the deity is conspicuous by his absence. The outrage at Gibeah of Benjamin – or, more precisely, the Levite's account of what happened there, which differs from the narrator's version – leads to internecine war in which God plays a crucial and perplexing role. Why, for example, does he promise victory but send the Israelites to defeat by the Benjaminites

---

19. J. Cheryl Exum, 'Jephthah: The Absence of God,' Chapter 3 in *Tragedy in Biblical Narrative: Arrows of the Almighty* (Cambridge: Cambridge University Press), pp. 45-69. See also Exum, *Fragmented Women: Feminist (Sub)versions of Biblical Narratives* (2d edn; Bloomsbury T&T Clark, 2016), 1-23.

20. Jephthah is not an unsympathetic character. As his response to the one who greets him indicates, he did not expect it to be his daughter (see above n. 2).

21. Janzen raises the possibility that the divine silence could be an indictment of God along with Jephthah. He also raises the possibility of resistant reading when he speaks of a potential conflict between the moral worldview one finds in a story and one's own ethical beliefs.

(vv. 23-25)? The hostilities result in the near extinction of an Israelite tribe and rape and murder on a grand scale.[22]

As is noted in the introduction to this volume, there are rich insights to be gained by a focus on characterization in Judges. The topic is virtually inexhaustible. As such, a volume like this one can only ever be an entry point not an end point and this volume will no doubt stimulate further investigations of Judges' motley cast of characters. I would like to see future studies take the kinds of analyses offered here and move beyond to question the ideologies of the narrative and to resist some of its perspectives along the critical lines that I have indicated in my brief comments above.

22. As a feminist, I have made it a policy throughout my career to draw attention to language I would like to see avoided, in particular the use of 'man' as though it were generic, but also the unnecessary feminine ending --ess (e.g. seamstress, stewardess, manageress etc.). Thus I mention here my problem (about which the editors are aware) with the use in this volume of 'man' for humanity, 'prophetess/es' (does anyone not know that the prophet Deborah is a woman?).

BIBLIOGRAPHY

Achenbach, Reinhard. 'Levitische Priester und Leviten im Deuteronomium.' *Zeitschrift für Altorientalische und biblische Rechtsgeschichte* 5 (1999): 285–309.
Ackerman, James S. 'Prophecy and Warfare in Early Israel: A Study of the Deborah-Barak Story.' *BASOR* 220 (1975): 5–13.
Ackerman, Susan. *Warrior, Dancer, Seductress, Queen: Woman in Judges and Biblical Israel.* New York: Doubleday, 1998.
Ackerman, Susan. 'The Personal is Political: Covenantal and Affectionate Love (ʾĀHĒB, ʾAHĂBÂ) in the Hebrew Bible.' *VT* 52.4 (2002): 437–58.
Ahmed, Sara. 'Happy Objects.' Pages 29–51 in *The Affect Theory Reader*. Edited by Melissa Gregg et al. Cambridge: Cambridge University Press, 2010.
Aitken, James K. 'Fat Eglon.' Pages 141–53 in *Studies on the Text and Versions of the Hebrew Bible in Honour of Robert Gordon*. Edited by Geoffrey Khan and Diana Lipton. Leiden: Brill, 2012.
Alonso-Schökel, Luis. 'Erzählkunst im Buche der Richter.' *Biblica* 42 (1961): 143–72.
Alter, Robert. 'Samson Without Folklore.' Pages 47–56 in *Text and Tradition*. Edited by Susan Niditch. Atlanta: Scholars, 1990.
Alter, Robert. *The David Story: A Translation with Commentary of 1 and 2 Samuel*. New York: W.W. Norton & Co., 1999.
Alter, Robert. *The Art of Biblical Narrative*. New York: Basic Books, 1981; rev. ed. 2011.
Alter, Robert. *The Hebrew Bible: A Translation with Commentary*. New York: Norton, 2018.
Amit, Yairah. 'Hidden Polemic in the Conquest of Dan: Judges XVII-XVIII.' *VT* 40 (1990): 4–20.
Amit, Yairah. *The Book of Judges: The Art of Editing*. BIS 38. Leiden: Brill, 1999.
Amit, Yairah. *Judges: Introduction and Commentary*. Mikra Leyisraʾel. Tel Aviv: Am Oved, Jerusalem: The Magnes Press, The Hebrew University, 1999 (Hebrew).
Amit, Yairah. *Reading Biblical Narratives*. Minneapolis: Fortress, 2001.
Amit, Yairah. 'Judges.' Pages 355–91 in *The New Oxford Annotated Bible*. New Revised Standard Version With The Apocrypha. New York: Oxford University Press, 2010.
Amit, Yairah. *In Praise of Editing in the Hebrew Bible: Collected Essays in Retrospect*. Sheffield: Sheffield Phoenix Press, 2012.
Amos, N. Scott. '"Do to Me According to What Has Gone Out of Your Mouth": A Reformation Debate on the Tragedy of Jephthah and his Daughter.' *Reformation & Renaissance Review* 21 (2019): 3–26.
Andersson, Greger. *The Book and Its Narratives: A Critical Examination of Some Synchronic Studies of the Book of Judges*. Örebro Studies in Literary History and Criticism 1. Örebro: Universitetsbiblioteket, 2001.
Andersson, Greger. 'A Narratologist's Critical Reflections on Synchronic Studies of the Bible: A Response to Gregory T. K. Wong.' *SJOT* 21.2 (2007): 261–74.
Andersson, Greger. *Untamable Texts: Literary Studies and Narrative Theory in the Books of Samuel*. London: T&T Clark, 2009.

Andersson, Greger. 'The Problem of Narratives in the Bible: Moral Issues and Suggested Reading Strategies.' Pages 59–72 in *Narrative Ethics*. Edited by Jakob Lothe, Jeremy Hawthorn. Amsterdam: Rodopi, 2013.

Andersson, Greger. 'Stories about Humans in a Complicated World: The Narratives of the Hebrew Bible.' Pages 51–71 in *God and Humans in the Hebrew Bible and Beyond: A Festschrift for Lennart Boström on his 67th Birthday*. Edited by David Willgren. Sheffield: Sheffield Phoenix Press, 2019.

Arnold, Bill T. 'Word Play and Characterization in Daniel 1.' Pages 231–48 in *Puns and Pundits: Word Play in the Hebrew Bible and Ancient Near Eastern Literature*. Edited by Scott B. Noegel. Bethesda MD: CDL, 2000.

Assante, Julia. 'The *kar.kid/harimtu*, Prostitute or Single Woman?: A Reconsideration of the Evidence.' *UF* 30 (1998): 5–96.

Assis, Elie. 'The Hand of a Woman: Deborah and Yael (Judges 4).' *JHS* 5, Article 19 (2005): 1–14.

Assis, Elie. *Self-Interest or Communal Interest: An Ideology of Leadership in the Gideon, Abimelech and Jephthah Narratives (Judg 6–12)*. VTSup 106; Leiden: Brill, 2005.

Assis, Elie. 'Man, Woman and God in Judges 4.' *JSOT* 20 (2006): 110–24.

Auld, A. Graeme. 'Gideon: Hacking at the Heart of the Old Testament.' *VT* 39 (1989): 257–67.

Auld, A. Graeme. *Joshua Retold: Synoptic Perspectives*. Edinburgh: T&T Clark, 1998.

Bach, Alice. 'Rereading The Body Politic: Women and Violence in Judges 21.' *BibInt* 6 (1998): 1–27.

Backfish, Elizabeth H. P. 'Nameless in the Nevi'im: Intertextuality between Female Characters in the Book of Judges.' Pages 71–88 in *Reading Gender in Judges: An Intertextual Approach*. Edited by Paul Kim, Shelley Birdsong and Cornelis de Vos. Atlanta, GA: SBL Press, 2023.

Baker, Robin. *Hollow Men, Strange Women: Riddles, Codes and Otherness in the Book of Judges*. BIS 143. Leiden, Boston: Brill, 2016.

Baker, Robin. 'Double Trouble: Counting the Cost of Jephthah.' *JBL* 137 (2018): 29–50.

Baker, Robin. '"A Dream Carries Much Implication": The Midianite's Dream (Judges VII), Its Role and Meanings.' *VT* 68 (2018): 349–77.

Baker, Robin. *Mesopotamian Civilization and the Origins of the New Testament*. Cambridge and New York: Cambridge University Press, 2022.

Bakhtin, Mikhael M. *The Dialogic Imagination: Four Essays*. Translated by Caryl Emerson and Michael Holquist. Austin: Texas University Press, 1981.

Bal, Mieke. *Lethal Love: Feminist Literary Readings of Biblical Love Stories*. Bloomington: Indiana University Press, 1987.

Bal, Mieke. *Death and Dissymmetry: The Politics of Coherence in the Book of Judges*. CSHJ. Chicago: The University of Chicago Press, 1988.

Bal, Mieke. *Murder and Difference – Gender, Genre, and Scholarship on Sisera's Death*. Bloomington & Indianapolis: Indiana University Press, 1988.

Bal, Mieke. *Narratology: Introduction to the Theory of Narrative*. 3rd ed. Toronto: University of Toronto Press, 2009.

Bar-Efrat, Shimon. *Narrative Art in the Bible*. Sheffield: Almond, 1989. Republished: London: T&T Clark, 2004.

Barton, John. 'Characterization and Ethics.' Pages 1–16 in *Characters and Characterization in Kings*. Edited by Keith Bodner and Benjamin J. M. Johnson. LHBOTS 670. London: T&T Clark, 2020.

Beavis, Mary Ann. 'A Daughter in Israel: Celebrating *Bat Jephthah* (Judg. 11:39d-40).' *Feminist Theology* 13 (2004): 11–25.

Beldman, David J. H. *The Completion of Judges: Strategies of Ending in Judges 17–21.* Siphrut; 21. Winona Lake, IN: Eisenbrauns, 2017.
Berger, Peter. 'Christian Faith and the Social Comedy.' Pages 123–33 in *Holy Laughter: Essays on Religion in the Comic Perspective.* Edited by M. Conrad Hyers. New York: Seabury, 1969.
Berger, Peter. *A Rumor of Angels.* Expanded Edition. New York: Doubleday, 1990.
Berlin, Adele. *Poetics and Interpretation of Biblical Narrative.* Winona Lake, IN: Eisenbrauns, 1994.
Bewer, Julius. 'The Composition of Judges, Chaps. 17, 18.' *AJSLL* 29 (1913): 261–83.
Biddle, Mark E. *A Time to Laugh: Humor in the Bible.* Macon, GA: Smyth & Helwys, 2013.
Biran, Avraham. 'Tel Dan: Biblical Texts and Archaeological Data.' Pages 1–17 in *Scripture and Other Artifacts: Essays in Honor of Philip J. King.* Edited by Michael D. Coogan et al. Louisville KY: Westminster John Knox, 1994.
Biran, Avraham. 'The High Places of Biblical Dan.' Pages 148–55 in *Studies in the Archaeology of the Iron Age in Israel and Jordan.* Edited by Amihai Mazar. JSOTSup 331. Sheffield: Sheffield Academic Press, 2001.
Bird, Phyllis. *Missing Persons and Mistaken Identities: Women and Gender in Ancient Israel.* OBT. Minneapolis: Fortress Press, 1997.
Bledstein, Adrian. 'Is Judges a Woman's Satire of Men who Play God.' Pages 34–54 in *A Feminist Companion to Judges.* Edited by Athalya Brenner. Sheffield: JSOT Press, 1993.
Block, Daniel I. 'The Period of the Judges: Religious Disintegration under Tribal Rule.' Pages 39–58 in *Israel's Apostasy and Restoration: Essays in Honor of R.K. Harrison.* Edited by A. Gileadi. Grand Rapids, MI: Baker, 1988.
Block, Daniel I. 'Deborah among the Judges: The Perspective of the Hebrew Historian.' Pages 229–53 in *Faith, Tradition, and History: Old Testament Historiography in Its Near Eastern Context.* Winona Lake, IN: Eisenbrauns, 1994.
Block, Daniel I. *Judges, Ruth.* NAC 6. Nashville, TN: B&H, 1999.
Bluedorn, Wolfgang. *Yahweh Versus Baalism: A Theological Reading of the Gideon-Abimelech Narrative.* JSOTSup 329. Sheffield: Sheffield Academic Press, 2001.
Blyth, Caroline. *Reimagining Delilah's Afterlives as Femme Fatale: The Lost Seduction.* London: T & T Clark, 2017.
Boda, M. J. 'Recycling Heaven's Words: Receiving and Retrieving Divine Revelation in the Historiography of Judges.' Pages 43–68 in *Prophets, Prophecy, and Ancient Israelite Historiography.* Winona Lake, IN: Eisenbrauns, 2013.
Bodine, Walter Ray. *The Greek Text of Judges: Recensional Developments.* HSM 23. Chico, CA: Scholars Press, 1980.
Bohmbach, Karla G. 'Conventions/Contraventions: The Meaning of Public and Private for the Judges 19 Concubine.' *JSOT* 23 (1999): 83–98.
Boling, Robert G. 'Jephthah.' *ABD* 3: 680–82.
Boling, Robert G. *Judges: A New Translation with Introduction and Commentary.* Garden City: Doubleday, 1975.
Boling, Robert G. *Joshua: A New Translation with Introduction and Commentary.* AB 6. Garden City, NY: Doubleday, 1982.
Boogaart, T.A. 'Stone for Stone: Retribution in the Story of Abimelech and Shechem.' *JSOT* 32 (1985): 45–56.
Bray, Jason S. *Sacred Dan: Religious Tradition and Cultic Practice in Judges 17–18.* LHBOTS 449. New York: T&T Clark, 2006.
Brennan, Teresa. *Transmission of Affect.* Ithaca: Cornell University Press, 2004.

Brenner, Athalya. *The Israelite Woman: Social Role and Literary Type in Biblical Narrative.* Sheffield: JSOT Press, 1985.

Brenner, Athalya. 'A Triangle and A Rhombus in Narrative Structure: A Proposed Integrative Reading of Judges 4 and 5.' Pages 139–59 in *A Feminist Companion to Judges* 4. Sheffield: Sheffield Academic Press, 1993.

Brettler, Marc Tzvi. 'The Book of Judges: Literature as Politics.' *JBL* 108 (1989): 395–418.

Brettler, Marc Tzvi. *The Book of Judges.* Old Testament Readings. London: Routledge, 2002.

Brettler, Marc Tzvi. 'Micah.' *ABD* 4: 806–7.

Brison, Ora. 'Jael, 'eshet heber the Kenite: A Diviner?' Pages 139–60 in *Joshua and Judges.* Texts@Contexts. Minneapolis: Fortress Press, 2013.

Brison, Ora. 'Between Biblical Heroines and the Divine Sphere: Female Heroics as Intermediaries between the Human and the Divine.' PhD Diss., Tel Aviv University, 2015.

Brown, Michael L. 'ברך.' Pages 757–67 in *NIDOTTE.* Vol. 1. Edited by Willem A. VanGemeren. Grand Rapids, MI: Zondervan. 1997.

Brueggemann, Walter. *Theology of the Old Testament: Testimony, Dispute, Advocacy.* Minneapolis, MN: Fortress Press, 1997.

Buber, Martin. *Kingship of God.* 3rd ed. Translated by Richard Scheiman. New York: Harper & Row, 1967.

Bultmann, Christoph. *Der Fremde im antiken Juda. Eine Untersuchung zum sozialen Typenbegriff 'ger' und seinem Bedeutungswandel in der alttestamentlichen Gesetzgebung.* Forschung zur Religion und Literatur des Alten und Neuen Testaments 153. Göttingen: Vandenhoeck & Ruprecht, 1992.

Burney, Charles F. *The Book of Judges.* New York: Ktav Publishing House, 1970.

Butler, Trent. *Judges.* WBC 8. Nashville: Thomas Nelson Publishers, 2009.

Bynum, David E. 'Samson as a Biblical φὴρ ὀρεσκῷος.' Pages 57–73 in *Text and Tradition: The Hebrew Bible and Folklore.* Edited by Susan Niditch. Atlanta: Scholars Press, 1990.

Camp, Claudia V. *Wise, Strange and Holy: The Strange Woman and the Making of the Bible.* Sheffield: Sheffield Academic Press, 2000.

Carman, Jon-Michael. 'Abimelech the Manly Man? Judges 9.1-57 and the Performance of Hegemonic Masculinity.' *JSOT* 43.3 (2019): 301–16.

Carr, David. 'Gender and the Shaping of Desire in the Song of Songs and its Interpretation.' *JBL* 119.2 (2000): 233–48.

Carroll, Noël. *Beyond Aesthetics. Philosophical Essays.* Cambridge: Cambridge University Press, 2001.

Cartledge, Tony W. *Vows in the Hebrew Bible and the Ancient Near East.* JSOTSup 147. Sheffield: Sheffield Academic Press, 1992.

Chalcraft, David J. 'Deviance and Legitimate Action in the Book of Judges.' Pages 177–201 in *The Bible in Three Dimensions.* Edited by David J. A. Clines, Stephen E. Fowl and Stanley E. Porter. Sheffield: JSOT Press, 1990.

Chisholm, Robert B., Jr. 'Identity Crisis: Assessing Samson's Birth and Career.' *BibSac* 166 (2009): 147–62.

Chisholm, Robert B., Jr. 'The Ethical Challenge of Jephthah's Fulfilled Vow.' *BibSac* 167 (2010): 404–22.

Chisholm, Robert B., Jr. *A Commentary on Judges and Ruth.* KEL. Grand Rapids, MI: Kregel, 2013.

Chun, S. Min. 'To Reform or Not to Reform: Characterization and Ethical Reading of Josiah in Kings.' Pages 250–68 in *Characters and Characterization in the Book of Kings.*

LHBOTS 670. Edited by Keith Bodner and Benjamin J.M. Johnson; London: Bloomsbury T&T Clark, 2020.

Claassens, L. Juliana M. 'The Character of God in Judges 6-8: The Gideon Narrative as Theological and Moral Resource.' *HBT* 23 (2001), 51-71.

Claassens, L. Juliana M. *Claiming Her Dignity: Female Resistance in the Old Testament*. Collegeville, MN: Liturgical Press, 2016.

Claassens, L. Juliana, and Sharp, Carolyn J. 'Introduction: Celebrating Intersectionality, Interrogating Power, and Embracing Ambiguity as Feminist Critical Practices.' Pages 11-38 in *Feminist Frameworks and The Bible: Power, Ambiguity, and Intersectionality*. Edited by L. Juliana Claassens and Carolyn J. Sharp. LHBOTS 630. London: Bloomsbury, 2017.

Conway, Mary L., *Judging the Judges: A Narrative Appraisal Analysis*. Pennsylvania: Eisenbrauns, 2020.

Coogan, Michael D., ed. *The New Oxford Annotated Bible*. Oxford: Oxford University Press, 2018.

Cox, Benjamin and Susan Ackerman, 'Micah's Teraphim.' *JHS* 12, Art. 11 (2012): 1-37.

Coxon, Peter W. 'Shadrach, Meshach, Abednego.' *ABD* 6:1150.

Craig, Kenneth M., Jr., 'Judges in Recent Research.' *CBR* 1.2 (2003): 159-85.

Crenshaw, James L. *Samson: A Secret Betrayed, a Vow Ignored*. Atlanta: John Knox Press, 1978.

Crenshaw, James L. 'Wisdom.' Pages 225-64 in *Old Testament Form Criticism*. Edited by John Hayes. San Antonio: Trinity University Press, 1974.

Cross, Frank Moore. *Canaanite Myth and Hebrew Epic. Essays in the History of the Religion of Israel*. Cambridge, MA: Harvard University Press, 1973.

Cundall, Arthur E. and Leon Morris. *Judges, Ruth*. London: Tyndale Press, 1968.

David, Brent, Aren M. Maeir, and Louis A. Hitchcock. 'Disentangling Entangled Objects: Iron Age Inscriptions from Philistia as a Reflection of Cultural Processes.' *IEJ* 65 (2015): 140-66.

Davidson, E. T. A. *Intricacy, Design and Cunning in the Book of Judges*. Philadelphia: Xlibris, 2008.

Davies, G. Henton. 'Judges VIII 22-23.' *VT* 13.2 (1963): 151-57.

Day, Peggy. 'From the Child is Born the Woman: The Story of Jephthah's Daughter.' Pages 58-74 in *Gender and Difference in Ancient Israel*. Edited by Peggy Day. Minneapolis: Fortress Press, 1989.

Day, Peggy, ed. *Gender and Difference in Ancient Israel*. Minneapolis, MN: Fortress, 2006.

Derrida, Jacques. 'Structure, Sign and Play in the Discourse of the Human Sciences.' Pages 351-70 in *Writing and Difference*. Translated by Alan Bass. London: Routledge, 2001.

De Temmerman, Koen. *Crafting Characters: Heroes and Heroines in the Ancient Greek Novel*. Oxford: Oxford University Press, 2014.

De Vaux, Roland. *Ancient Israel: Its Life and Institutions*. Translated by John McHugh. London: Darton, Longman & Todd, 1961.

Dolansky, S., S. Shectman, S. Ackerman, A. L. Joseph, M. Leuchter & M. Warner. 'Gendered Historiography: Theoretical Considerations and Case Studies.' Edited by Shawna Dolansky and Sarah Shectman. *JHS* 19 (4) (2019).

Donald, Trevor. 'Semantic Field of "Folly" in Proverbs, Job, Psalms, and Ecclesiastes.' *VT* 13.3 (1963): 285-92.

Dorson, Richard M. 'Introduction.' Pages 1-6 in *Heroic Saga and Epic: An Introduction to the World's Great Folk Epics*. Edited by Felix J. Oinas. Bloomington, IN: Indiana University Press, 1978.

Douglas, Mary. *Purity and Danger*. Harmondsworth: Penguin, 1966.
Driver, S. R. *A Treatise on the Use of the Tenses in Hebrew and Some Other Syntactical Questions*. 3rd Edition. Oxford: Clarendon, 1892.
Dundes, Alan. *Interpreting Folklore*. Bloomington: Indiana University Press, 1980.
Edenburg, Cynthia. *Dismembering the Whole: Composition and Purpose in Judges 19–21*. Atlanta: SBL, 2016.
Eder, Jens, Fotis Jannidis and Ralf Schneider. 'Characters in Fictional Worlds: An Introduction.' Pages 3–64 in *Characters in Fictional Worlds. Understanding Imaginary Beings in Literature, Film, and Other Media*. Edited by Jens Eder, Fotis Jannidis and Ralf Schneider. Berlin, New York: De Gruyter, 2010.
Ederer, Matthias. '"Ein jeder tat das in seinen Augen Gerade" (Ri 17,6). Das Israel der Richterzeit in der Perspektive von Ri 17–21. Das Richterbuch (Teil 4).' *Bibel und Liturgie* 88.4 (2015): 313–19.
Eliade, Mircea. 'The "God Who Binds" and the Symbolism of Knots.' Pages 92–124 in *Images and Symbols: Studies in Religious Symbolism*. New York: Sheed and Ward, 1969.
Exum, J. Cheryl. 'Literary Patterns in the Samson Saga: An Investigation of Rhetorical Style in Biblical Prose.' PhD. Dissertation Columbia University, 1976.
Exum, J. Cheryl. 'Aspects of Symmetry and Balance in the Samson Saga.' *JSOT* 19 (1981): 3–29.
Exum, J. Cheryl. '"Mother in Israel": A Familiar Figure Reconsidered.' Pages 73–85 in *Feminist Interpretation of the Bible*. Oxford: Basil Blackwell, 1985.
Exum, J. Cheryl. 'The Centre Cannot Hold: Thematic and Textual Instabilities in Judges.' *CBQ* 52.3 (1990): 410–31.
Exum, J. Cheryl. 'Murder They Wrote: Ideology and the Manipulation of Female Presence in the Biblical Narrative.' Pages 45–67 in *The Pleasure of Her Text: Feminist Readings of Biblical and Historical Texts*. Edited by Alice Bach. Philadelphia: Trinity Press International, 1990.
Exum, J. Cheryl. 'Jephthah: The Absence of God.' Pages 45–69 in *Tragedy in Biblical Narrative: Arrows of the Almighty*. Cambridge: Cambridge University Press, 1992.
Exum, J. Cheryl. *Fragmented Women: Feminist (Sub)versions of Biblical Narratives*. Sheffield: Sheffield Academic Press, 1993.
Exum, J. Cheryl. 'Samson's Women.' Pages 61–93 in *Fragmented Women: Feminist (Sub)versions of Biblical Narratives*. Sheffield: Sheffield Academic Press, 1993.
Exum, J. Cheryl. *Plotted, Shot, and Painted: Cultural Representations of Biblical Women*. Sheffield: Sheffield Academic Press, 1996.
Exum, J. Cheryl. 'Harvesting the Biblical Narrator's Scanty Plot of Ground: A Holistic Approach to Judges 16:4–22.' Pages 39–46 in *Tehillah Le-Moshe: Biblical and Judaic Studies in Honor of Moshe Greenberg*. Edited by Mordechai Cogan, Barry L. Eichler, Jeffrey H. Tigay. Winona Lake, Ind.: Eisenbrauns, 1997.
Exum, J. Cheryl. 'Shared Glory: Salomon de Bray's Jael, Deborah and Barak.' Pages 11–37 in *Between the Text and the Canvas: The Bible and Art in Dialogue*. Edited by J. Cheryl Exum and Ela Nutu. Sheffield: Sheffield Phoenix Press, 2007.
Exum, J. Cheryl. 'Feminist Criticism: Whose Interests Are Being Served?' Pages 65–89 in *Judges and Method: New Approaches in Biblical Studies*. Edited by Gale A. Yee, 2nd ed. Minneapolis: Fortress, 2007.
Exum, J. Cheryl. 'Deborah.' Pages 189–90 in *The HarperCollins Bible Dictionary*. 3rd edition. New York: HarperCollins Publishers, 2011.
Exum, J. Cheryl. 'Judges: Encoded Messages to Women.' Pages 112–27 in *Feminist Biblical Interpretation: A Compendium of Critical Commentary on the Books of the Bible and*

Related Literature. Edited by Louise Schottroff and Marie-Theres Wacker. Grand Rapids, MI: William B. Eerdmans, 2012.

Exum, J. Cheryl. *Art as Biblical Commentary: Visual Commentary from Hagar the Wife of Abraham to Mary the Mother of Jesus*. London: T&T Clark, 2019.

Exum, J. Cheryl. 'The Many Faces of Samson.' Pages 13–31 in *Samson: Hero or Fool?* Edited by Erik Eynikel and Tobias Nicklas. Leiden: Brill, 2014. Reprinted in Pages 283–301 in *Samson and Delilah: Selected Essays*. Sheffield: Sheffield Phoenix Press, 2020.

Fakasiieiki, Ilkani Latu. 'Delilah: A Post-colonial Discourse Reading of Judg 16:4-22.' PhD. Dissertation. Graduate Theological Union, 2015.

Faraone, C. A., B. Garnand and C. López-Ruiz. 'Micah's Mother (Judg. 17:1– 4) and a Curse from Carthage (*KAI* 89): Canaanite Precedents for Greek and Latin Curses against Thieves?' *JNES* 64 (2005): 161–86.

Fernández Marcos, Natalio. 'Kritai/Iudices/Judges.' Pages 155–64 in *Introduction to the Septuagint*. Edited by Siegfried Kreuzer. Translated by David A. Brenner and Peter Altmann. Waco, TX: Baylor University Press, 2019.

Festinger, Leon, Henry W. Riecken and Stanley Schacter. *When Prophecy Fails*. University of Minnesota Press, 1956. Repr. London: Pinter and Martin, 2008.

Fewell, Danna Nolan, and David M. Gunn. 'Controlling Perspectives: Women, Men, and the Authority of Violence in Judges 4 & 5.' *JAAR* 58.3 (1990): 389–411.

Fewell, Danna Nolan. 'Tipping the Balance: Sternberg's Reader and the Rape of Dinah.' *JBL* 110 (1991): 193–211.

Fewell, Danna Nolan, and David M. Gunn. *Gender, Power, and Promise: The Subject of the Bible's First Story*. Nashville: Abingdon Press, 1993.

Fewell, Danna Nolan. 'Deconstructive Criticism: Achsah and the (E)razed City of Writing.' Pages 115–37 in *Judges and Method: New Approaches in Biblical Studies*. Second Edition. Edited by Gale A. Yee. Minneapolis: Fortress, 2007.

Fewell, Danna Nolan. 'The Work of Biblical Narrative.' Pages 3–26 in *The Oxford Handbook of Biblical Narrative*. Edited by Danna Nolan Fewell. Oxford: Oxford University Press, 2016.

Finkel, Irving. *The Ark before Noah: Decoding the Story of the Flood*. London: Hodder & Stoughton, 2014.

Fish, Stanley. *Is There a Text in This Class? The Authority of Interpretive Communities*. Cambridge, MA: Harvard University Press, 1980.

Fish, Stanley. *Doing What Comes Naturally: Change, Rhetoric, and the Practice of Theory in Literary and Legal Studies*, PCI. Durham, NC: Duke University Press, 1989.

Fishbane, Michael. *Biblical Myth and Rabbinic Mythmaking*. Oxford, New York: Oxford University Press, 2003.

Fokkelman, J. P. 'Structural Remarks on Judges 9 and 19.' Pages 33–45 in *Sha'arei Talmon: Studies in the Bible, Qumran, and the Ancient Near East Presented to Shemaryahu Talmon*. Winona Lake, IN: Eisenbrauns, 1992.

Fokkelman, J. P. *Reading Biblical Narrative: An Introductory Guide*. Translated by Ineke Smit. Louisville, KY: Westminster John Knox, 1999.

Foley, John. *Immanent Art: From Structure to Meaning in Traditional Oral Epic*. Bloomington, Indiana: Indiana University Press, 1991.

Freud, Sigmund. 'The Uncanny.' Pages 335–76 in *The Penguin Freud Library. Vol.14: Art and Literature*. Translated by James Strachey. London: Penguin, 1990.

Fritz, Volkmar. 'Abimelech und Sichem in Jdc. IX.' *VT* 32 (1982): 129–44.

Frolov, Serge. 'Fire, Smoke, and Judah in Judges: A Response to Gregory Wong.' *SJOT* 21 (2007): 127–38.

Frolov, Serge, and Mikhail Stetckevich. 'Repentance in Judges: Assessing the Reassessment.' *HS* 60 (2019): 129–39.

Frow, John. 'Character.' Pages 105–19 in *The Cambridge Companion to Narrative Theory*. Edited by Matthew Garrett. Cambridge: Cambridge University Press, 2018.

Frymer-Kensky, Tikva, *Reading the Women of the Bible*. New York: Schocken Books, 2002.

Fuchs, Esther. 'Marginalization, Ambiguity, Silencing: The Story of Jephthah's Daughter.' *JFSR* 5 (1989): 35–45.

Fuchs, Esther. *Sexual Politics in the Biblical Narrative: Reading the Hebrew Bible as a Woman*. JSOTSup 310. Sheffield: Sheffield Academic Press, 2000.

Fuchs, Esther. *Feminist Theory and the Bible: Interrogating the Sources*. Feminist Studies and Sacred Texts Series. Lanham, MD: Lexington Books, 2016.

García-Alfonso, Cristiana. 'Judges: Subaltern Women.' Pages 106–21 in *Postcolonial Commentary and the Old Testament*. Edited by Hemchand Gossai. London: T&T Clark, 2019.

Garcia Bachmann, Mercedes L. *Judges*. Wisdom Commentary Series. Collegeville: Liturgical Press, 2018.

Garsiel, Moshe. *Biblical Names: A Literary Study of Midrashic Derivations and Puns*. Ramat-Gan: Bar-Ilan University Press, 1991.

Garsiel, Moshe. 'Homiletic Name-Derivations as a Literary Device in the Gideon Narrative: Judges VI-VIII.' *VT* 43 (1993): 302–17.

Gerbrandt, Gerald Eddie. *Kingship according to the Deuteronomistic History*. SBLDS 87. Atlanta: Scholars Press, 1986.

Gesenius, W. and E. Kautzsch, *Gesenius' Hebrew Grammar*. 2nd ed. Translated by A. E. Cowley. Oxford: Clarendon Press, 1910.

Gillmayr-Bucher, Susanne. *Erzählte Welten im Richterbuch. Narratologische Aspekte eines polyfonen Diskurses*. BIS 116. Leiden: Brill, 2013.

Gillmayr-Bucher, Susanne. 'Memories Laid to Rest: The Book of Judges in the Persian Period,' Pages 115–32 in *Deuteronomy-Kings as Emerging Authoritative Books: A Conversation*. Atlanta: Society of Biblical Literature, 2014.

Gillmayr-Bucher, Susanne. 'Images of Tranquility in the Book of Judges.' Pages 35–47 in *History, Memory, Hebrew Scriptures. A Festschrift for Ehud Ben Zvi*. Edited by Ian Wilson and Diana Edelman. Winona Lake, IN: Eisenbrauns, 2015.

Gillmayr-Bucher, Susanne. 'Rollenspiel – Deborah und die Richter.' Pages 179–90 in *Ein Herz so weit wie der Sand am Ufer des Meeres, Festschrift für Georg Hentschel*. Erfurter Theologische Studien 90. Würzburg: Echter Verlag, 2006.

Goitein, S. D. 'Women's Literature in the Bible.' Pages 248–82 in *Bible Studies*. Tel Aviv: Yavneh Publishing House, 1967.

Gooding, D.W. 'The Composition of the Book of Judges.' *Eretz-Israel* 16 (1982): 70–79.

Gorospe, Athena E., and Charles Ringma. *Judges*. Asia Bible Commentary. Carlisle: Langham Global Library, 2016.

Grätz, Sebastian. 'Jiftach und seine Tochter.' Pages 119–34 in *Geschichte Israels und deuteronomistische Geschichtsdenken: Festschrift zum 70. Geburtstag von Winfried Thiel*. Edited by Peter Mommer and Andreas Scherer. AOAT 380. Münster: Ugarit Verlag, 2010.

Gray, John. *Joshua, Judges, Ruth*. Grand Rapids, MI: Eerdmans, 1986.

Graybill, Rhiannon. 'No Child Left Behind: Reading Jephthah's Daughter with *The Babylon Complex*', *The Bible and Critical Theory* 11.2 (2015): 36–50.

Graybill, Rhiannon. *Texts after Terror: Rape, Sexual Violence, & the Hebrew Bible*. Oxford: Oxford University Press, 2021.

Greene, Mark. 'Enigma Variations: Aspects of the Samson Story (Judges 13–16).' *Vox Evangelica* 21 (1991): 53–79.
Greenstein, Edward L. 'The Riddle of Samson.' *Prooftexts* 1.3 (1981): 237–60.
Greimas, Algirdas Julien. *Structural Semantics: An Attempt at Method*. Lincoln: University of Nebraska Press, 1983.
Gros Louis, Kenneth R. R. 'The Book of Judges.' Pages 161–62 in *Literary Interpretations of Biblical Narratives*. Edited by Kenneth R. R. Gros Louis, J. S. Ackerman and T. S. Warsaw. Nashville: Abingdon, 1974.
Groß, Walter. *Richter: Übersetzt und ausgelegt*. Herders Theologischer Kommentar Altes Testament. Freiburg im Breisgau: Herder, 2009.
Groß, Walter. 'Michas überfüllte Hauskapelle. Bemerkungen zu Ri 17+18.' Pages 72–88 in *Studien zum Richterbuch und seinen Völkernamen*. Edited by Walter Groß and Erasmus Gaß. Stuttgarter biblische Aufsatzbände Altes Testament 54. Stuttgart: Katholisches Bibelwerk, 2012.
Gudme, Anne Katrine de Hammer. 'Invitation to Murder: Hospitality and Violence in the Hebrew Bible.' *Studia Theologica – Nordic Journal of Theology* 73.1 (2019): 89–108.
Guest, P. Deryn. 'Judges.' Pages 197–207 in *Eerdmans Commentary on the Bible*. Edited by James D. G. Dunn and John W. Rogerson. Grand Rapids, MI: Eerdmans, 2003.
Guest, P. Deryn. 'Judging Yhwh.' Pages 180–91 in *The Oxford Handbook of Biblical Narrative*. Edited by Danna Nolan Fewell. New York: Oxford University Press, 2016.
Guest, P. Deryn. *YHWH and the God of Israel: an Object-Relations Analysis*. Cambridge: Cambridge University Press, 2018.
Gunn, David M. 'Joshua and Judges.' Pages 102–21 in *The Literary Guide to the Bible*. Edited by Robert Alter and Frank Kermode. London: Fontana, 1987.
Gunn, David M. *Narrative in the Hebrew Bible*. Oxford: Oxford University Press, 1993.
Gunn, David M., and Danna Nolan Fewell. *Narrative in the Hebrew Bible*. The Oxford Bible Series. Oxford: Oxford University Press, 1993.
Gunn, David M. *Judges*. Oxford: Blackwell, 2005.
Gutenberg, Andrea. *Mögliche Welten. Plot und Sinnstiftung im englischen Frauenroman*. Heidelberg: Universitätsverlag C. Winter, 2000.
Haak, Robert. 'A Study and New Interpretation of *qsr nps*.' *JBL* 101 (1982): 161–67.
Halpern, Baruch. *The First Historians: The Hebrew Bible and History*. San Francisco: Harper & Row, 1988.
Hamley, Isabelle M. 'Dis(re)membered and Unaccounted For: *Pilegesh* in the Hebrew Bible.' *JSOT* 41 (2018), 415–34.
Hamley, Isabelle M. *Unspeakable Things Unspoken: An Irigirayan Reading of Otherness and Victimization in Judges 19–21*. Eugene, OR: Wipf & Stock, 2019.
Hamon, Philippe. 'Pour un statut sémiologique du personnage.' Pages 41–73 in *Poétique du récit*. Edited by Roland Barthes, Wolfgang Kayser, Wayne Booth, and Philippe Hamon. Paris: Seuil, 1977.
Handy, Lowell K. 'Uneasy Laughter: Ehud and Eglon as Ethnic Humor.' *SJOT* 6.2 (1992): 233–46.
Harding, James. 'Homophobia and Masculine Domination in Judges 19–21.' *BCT* 6 (2018): 41–73.
Herzberg, Bruce. 'Deborah and Moses.' *JSOT* 38 (2013): 15–33.
Hertzberg, H. W. *Die Bücher Josua, Richter, Ruth*. 4th edition. ATD 9. Göttingen: Vandenhoeck & Ruprecht, 1969.
Hillers, Delbert R. 'Micah, Book of.' *ABD* 4:807–10.

Hobsbawm, Eric J. *Primitive Rebels: Studies in Archaic Forms of Social Movement in the 19th and 20th Centuries*. New York: W. W. Norton and Company, 1959.

Hoyt, JoAnna. 'Reassessing Repentance in Judges.' *BibSac* 169 (2012): 143–58.

Hudson, Don M. 'Living in a Land of Epithets: Anonymity in Judges 19–21.' *JSOT* 62 (1994): 49–66.

Hurlbert, Brandon M. 'Cut & Splice: Reading Judges 19 Cinematically.' *BibInt* 30.2 (2022): 125–49.

Ilan, David. 'Storage.' Pages 251–65 in *T&T Clark Handbook of Food in the Hebrew Bible and Ancient Israel*. Edited by Janling Fu, Cynthia Shafer-Elliott and Carol Meyers. London: Bloomsbury, 2022.

Ilan, Tal. 'Gender Difference and the Rabbis: Bat Yiftah as Human Sacrifice.' Pages 175–89 in *Human Sacrifice in Jewish and Christian Tradition*. Edited by Karen Finsterbusch, Armin Lange and K. F. Diethard Römheld. SHR 112. Leiden: Brill, 2007.

Ishida, Tomoo. 'The Leaders of the Tribal Leagues: 'Israel' in the Pre-Monarchic Period.' *RevBib* 80 (1973): 514–30.

Jackson, Melissa A. *Comedy and Feminist Interpretation of the Hebrew Bible: A Subversive Collaboration*. Oxford: Oxford University, 2012.

Jannidis, Fotis. 'Character.' Pages 30–45 in *Handbook of Narratology*. Edited by Peter Hühn, John Pier, Wolf Schmid and Jörg Schönert. Narratology, Vol. 19. Berlin: De Gruyter, 2009.

Jans, Edgar. *Abimelech und sein Königtum: Diachrone und synchrone Untersuchungen zu Ri 9*. ATSAT 66. St. Ottilien: EOS-Verlag, 2001.

Janzen, David. 'Gideon's House as the אטד: A Proposal for Reading Jotham's Fable.' *CBQ* 74.3 (2012): 465–75.

Jeter, Joseph R., Jr, *Preaching Judges*. St Louis, MO: Chalice Press, 2003.

Johansson, Christer. *Mimetiskt syskonskap: En representationsteoretisk undersökning av relationen fiktionsprosa-fiktionsfilm*. Stockholm: Acta Universitatis Stockholmiensis, 2008.

Johnson, Benjamin J. M. 'Character as Interpretive Crux in the Book of Samuel.' Pages 1–13 in *Characters and Characterization in the Book of Samuel*. Edited by Keith Bodner and Benjamin J. M. Johnson. London: Bloomsbury T&T Clark, 2020.

Johnson, Benjamin J. M. 'Making a First Impression: The Characterization of David and his Opening Words in 1 Samuel 17:25–31.' *TynBul* 71 (1) (2020): 75–93.

Johnson, Benjamin J. M. 'An Unapologetic Apology: The David Story as a Complex Response to Monarchy.' Pages 225–42 in *The Book of Samuel and Its Response to Monarchy*. Edited by Sara Kipfer and Jeremy Hutton. Stuttgart: W. Kohlhammer, 2021.

Johnson, Benjamin J. M. 'Humor in the Midst of Tragedy: The Comic Vision of 1 Samuel 4–6.' *JBL* 141.1 (2022): 65–82.

Johnstone, William. *1 and 2 Chronicles. Volume 2. 2 Chronicles 10–36: Guilt and Atonement*. JSOTSup 254. Sheffield: Sheffield Academic Press, 1997.

Jones, Amy Beth W. 'The Stranger Within: Narrative Space and Identity Construction in the Book of Judges.' Ph.D. Dissertation. Drew University, 2014.

Josipovici, Gabriel. *The Book of God: A Response to the Bible*. New Haven, CT: Yale University Press, 1988.

Jost, Renate. 'Der Fluch der Mutter. Feministisch-sozialgeschichtliche Überlegungen zu Ri 17,1–6.' Pages 123–29 in *Feministische Bibelauslegungen. Grundlagen – Forschungsgeschichtliches – Geschlechterstudien*. By Renate Jost. Internationale Forschungen in Feministischer Theologie und Religion. Befreiende Perspektiven 1. Berlin: LIT Verlag, 2014.

Kaiser, Otto. *Isaiah 1–12: A Commentary*. Translated by R.A. Wilson. OTL. London: SCM Press, 1972.

Kalmanofsky, Amy. *Gender-Play in the Hebrew Bible: The Ways the Bible Challenges Its Gender Norms*. Routledge Interdisciplinary Perspectives on Biblical Criticism. New York: Routledge, 2016.

Kaminsky, Joel S. 'Humor and the Theology of Hope in Genesis: Isaac as a Humorous Figure.' *Int* 54.4 (2000): 363–75.

Kaminsky, Joel S. 'Reflections on Associative Word Links in Judges.' *JSOT* 36 (4) (2012): 411–34.

Kaminsky, Joel S. 'Humor and Hope from Passover to Purim.' *Marginalia* (April 12, 2019): https://marginalia.lareviewofbooks.org/humor-hope-passover-purim/.

Kamrada, Dolores G. 'The Sacrifice of Jephthah's Daughter and the Notion of Ḥērem (חרם) (A Problematic Narrative against its Biblical Background).' Pages 57–85 in *With Wisdom as a Robe: Qumran and Other Jewish Studies in Honour of Ida Fröhlich*. Edited by Károly Dániel Dobos and Miklós Kőszeghy. HBM 21. Sheffield: Sheffield Phoenix Press, 2009.

Kawashima, Robert S. '*Homo Faber* in J's Primeval History.' *ZAW* 116 (2004): 483–501.

Keefe, Alice A. 'Rapes of Women/Wars of Men.' *Semeia* 61 (1993): 79–97.

Keil, C. F., and Delitzsch, F. *Biblical Commentary on the Old Testament: Joshua, Judges, Ruth*. Grand Rapids, 1963.

Klein, Lillian. *The Triumph of Irony in the Book of Judges*. JSOTSup 68. Sheffield: Almond Press, 1988.

Klein, Lillian. 'The Book of Judges: Paradigm and Deviation in Images of Women.' Pages 55–71 in *A Feminist Companion to Judges*. Edited by Athalya Brenner. FCB 4. Sheffield: JSOT Press, 1993.

Knohl, Israel. *The Sanctuary of Silence: The Priestly Torah and the Holiness School*. Minneapolis, MN: Fortress Press, 1995.

Kuyper, Abraham. *Women of the Old Testament*. 6th ed. Trans. Henry Zylstra. Grand Rapids, MI: Zondervan, 1934.

Labov, William. *Language in the Inner City: Studies in the Black English Vernacular*. Philadelphia: University of Pennsylvania Press, 1972.

Lacan, Jacques. *Encore: The Seminar of Jacques Lacan Book XX. On Feminine Sexuality, the Limits of Love and Knowledge, 1972–1973*. Edited by Jacques-Alain Miller. Translated by Bruce Fink. New York and London: W. W. Norton, 1999.

Lackowski, Mark. 'Victim, Victor, or Villain? The Unfinalizability of Delilah.' *Journal of the Bible and Its Reception* 6.2 (2019): 197–218.

Landy, Francis. 'Judges 1: The City of Writing, the Sacred, and the Fragmentation of the Body.' Pages 37-50 in *Voyages in Uncharted Waters: Essays On the Theory and Practice of Biblical Interpretation in Honour of David Jobling*. Edited by Wesley J. Bergen and Armin Siedlecki. HBM 13. Sheffield, Sheffield Phoenix Press, 2006.

Landy, Francis. 'Between Centre and Periphery: Space and Gender in the Book of Judges in the Early Second Temple Period.' Pages 133–62 in *Centres and Peripheries in the Early Second Temple Period*. Edited by Ehud Ben Zvi and Christoph Levin. Tübingen: Mohr Siebeck, 2016.

Lee, Sui Hung Albert. *Dialogue on Monarchy in the Gideon-Abimelech Narrative: Ideological Reading in Light of Bakhtin's Dialogism*. BIS 187. Leiden: Brill, 2021.

Létourneau, Anne. 'Campy Murder in Judges 4: Is Yael a Gebèrèt (Heroine)?' Pages 42–86 in *Gender Agenda Matters: Papers of the 'Feminist Section ' of the International Meetings of The Society of Biblical Literature.* Edited by Irmtraud Fischer. Cambridge: Cambridge Scholars Publishing, 2015.

Leuchter, Mark. *The Levites and the Boundaries of Israelite Identity.* Oxford: Oxford University Press, 2017.

Lewis, T. J. 'The Identity and Function of El/Baal Berith.' *JBL* 115 (1996): 401–23.

Lewis, T. J. 'Teraphim.' *DDD* 844–50.

Lilley, J. P. U. 'A Literary Appreciation of the Book of Judges.' *TynBul* 18 (1967): 94–102.

Lindquist, Maria. 'King Og's Iron Bed.' *CBQ* 73 (2011): 477–92.

Loewnstamm, S. E. 'Law, Biblical Law.' Pages 614–37 in *Encyclopaedia Biblica.* Volume 5. Jerusalem: Bialik Institute, 1968 (Hebrew).

Lord, Albert B. *The Singer of Tales.* New York: Atheneum, 1968.

Longman, Tremper III. *How to Read Exodus.* Downers Grove, IL: IVP, 2009.

Maly, Eugene. 'The Jotham Fable – Anti-Monarchical?' *CBQ* 22 (1960): 299–305.

Marais, Jacobus. *Representation in Old Testament Narrative Texts.* Leiden: Brill, 1998.

Marcus, David. 'In Defence of Micah: He Was Not a Thief.' *Shofar* 6 (1988): 72–80.

Margalith, Othniel. 'Samson's Riddle and Samson's Magic Locks.' *VT* 36 (1986): 225–34.

Margulies, Zachary. 'Aesop and Jotham's Parable of the Trees (Judges 9:8–15).' *VT* 69.1 (2019): 81–94.

Marsman, Hennie J. *Women in Ugarit and Israel Their Social and Religious Position in the Context of the Ancient Near East.* Leiden: Brill, 2003.

Martins, Francisco. "'Faut-il que nous soyons gouvernés par un roi?': La fable des arbes (Jg 9,8–15) entre la satire et l'apologie.' *ETR* 93.2 (2018): 209–24.

Matheny, Jennifer M. 'Mute and Mutilated: Understanding Judges 19-21 as a משל of Dialogue.' *BibInt* 25 (2017): 625–46.

Matthews, Victor H. 'Hospitality and Hostility in Judges 4.' *BTB* 21 (1) (1991): 13–21.

Matthews, Victor H., and Don C. Benjamin. *Social World of Ancient Israel: 1250–587 BCE.* Grand Rapids, MI: Baker Academic, 1993.

Matthews, Victor H. *Judges & Ruth.* NCBC. Cambridge, United Kingdom: Cambridge University Press, 2004.

Mayes, Andrew D. H. 'Deuteronomistic Royal Ideology in Judges 17–21.' *BibInt* 9.3 (2001): 241–58.

Mayes, Andrew D. H. *Judges.* Old Testament Guides. Sheffield: JSOT Press, 1985; repr., 1989.

Mazar, Amihai. *Archaeology of the Land of the Bible 10,000–586 B.C.E.* Cambridge: Lutterworth, 1993.

McCann, J. Clinton. *Judges.* Interpretation. Louisville KY: Westminster John Knox Press, 2003.

McCarter, P. Kyle. *1 Samuel.* AB. Garden City, NY: Doubleday, 1980.

McDaniel, Carl. 'Samson's Riddle.' *Didaskalia* 12.2 (2001): 47–57.

Mckenzie, John L. 'The Elders in the Old Testament.' *Biblica* 40 (1959): 522–40.

Merideth, Betsy. 'Desire and Danger: The Drama of Betrayal in Judges and Judith.' Pages 63–78 in *Anti-Covenant: Counter Reading Women's Lives in the Hebrew Bible.* Edited by Mieke Bal. Sheffield: The Almond Press, 1989.

Merling, David. 'Gilead (Place).' Page 504 in *Eerdmans Dictionary of the Bible.* Edited by David Noel Freedman. Grand Rapids: Eerdmans, 2000.

Meyers, Carol. *Rediscovering Eve: Ancient Israelite Women in Context.* Oxford: Oxford University Press, 2013.

Meyers, Jeffrey. 'The Idea of Moral Authority in *The Man Who Would Be King*.' *Studies in English Literature 1500–1900* 8.4 (1968): 711–23.

Miles, Johnny. "'Who are you calling 'Stupid'?": Ethnocentric Humour and Identity Construct in the Colonial Discourse of Judges' 3:12–30.' *The Bible and Critical Theory* 4.1 (2008): 1–16.
Miller, Geoffrey D. 'Canonicity and Gender Roles: Tobit and Judith as Test Cases.' *Bib* 97.2 (2016): 199–221.
Milstein, Sara J. *Tracking the Master Scribe: Revision through Introduction in Biblical and Mesopotamian Literature*. Oxford: Oxford University Press, 2016.
Mobley, Gregory. *The Empty Men: The Heroic Tradition of Ancient Israel*. ABRL. New York: Doubleday, 2005.
Mobley, Gregory. *Samson and the Liminal Hero in the Ancient Nera East*. New York: T&T Clark, 2006.
Monroe, Lauren A. S. 'Disembodied Women: Sacrificial Language and the Deaths of Bat-Jephthah, Cozbi, and the Bethlehemite Concubine.' *CBQ* 75 (2013): 32–52.
Moore, Barrington, Jr., *Injustice: The Social Bases of Obedience and Revolt*. White Plains, NY: M.E. Sharpe, 1978.
Moore, G. F. *Critical and Exegetical Commentary on Judges*. ICC. Edinburgh: T. & T. Clark, 1966.
Moster, David Z. 'The Levite of Judges 17–18.' *JBL* 133 (2014): 729–37.
Mueller, E. Aydeet. *The Micah Story: A Morality Tale in the Book of Judges*. SBL 34. New York: Lang, 2001.
Murphy, Kelly J. 'Judges in Recent Research.' *CBR* 15.2 (2017): 179–213.
Musa, Aysha Winstanley. 'Jael's Gender Ambiguity in Judges 4 and 5.' PhD Thesis, University of Sheffield, 2020.
Na'aman, Nadav. 'The Danite Campaign Northward (Judges XVII–XVIII) and the Migration of the Phocaeans Massalia (Strabo VI 1,4).' *VT* 55 (2005): 47–60.
Nel, Philip. 'The Riddle of Samson (Judg 14,14.18).' *Bib* 66 (1985): 534–45.
Nelson, Richard D. *Judges: A Critical and Rhetorical Commentary*. London: Bloomsbury T&T Clark, 2017.
Niditch, Susan. *The Symbolic Vision in Biblical Tradition*. HSM 30. Chico, CA: Scholars Press, 1980.
Niditch, Susan. 'The 'Sodomite' Theme in Judges 19–21: Family, Community, and Social Disintegration.' *CBQ* 44 (1982): 365–78.
Niditch, Susan. 'Samson as Culture Hero, Trickster, and Bandit: The Empowerment of the Weak.' *CBQ* 52 (1990): 608–24.
Niditch, Susan. *War in the Hebrew Bible: A Study in the Ethics of Violence*. Oxford: Oxford University Press, 1993.
Niditch, Susan. *Judges: A Commentary*. OTL. Louisville: Westminster John Knox, 2008.
Niemann, Herrmann. *Die Daniten. Studien zur Geschichte eines altisraelitischen Stammes*. Forschungen zur Religion und Literatur des Alten und Neuen Testaments 135. Göttingen: Vandenhoeck & Ruprecht, 1985.
Noble, Paul. 'A "Balanced" Reading of the Rape of Dinah: Some Exegetical and Methodological Observations.' *BibInt* 4 (1996): 173–203.
Noegel, Scott B. 'Evil Looms: Delilah: Weaver of Wicked Wiles.' *CBQ* 79 (2017):187–204.
Noth, Martin. *The Deuteronomistic History*. JSOTSup 15. Sheffield: JSOT Press, 1981.
Nünning, Ansgar, and Vera Nünning. 'Multiperspektivität aus narratologischer Sicht. Erzähltheoretische Grundlagen und Kategorien zur Analyse der Perspektivenstruktur narrativer Texte.' Pages 39–77 in *Multiperspektivisches Erzählen. Zur Theorie und Geschichte der Perspektivenstruktur im englischen Roman des 18. bis 20. Jahrhunderts*. Edited by Ansgar Nünning and Vera Nünning. Trier: Wissenschaftlicher Verlag Trier, 2000.

Nussbaum, Martha. *Love's Knowledge: Essays of Philosophy and Literature*. New York: Oxford University Press, 1990.
Obeyeskere, Gananath. *Medusa's Hair: An Essay on Personal Symbols and Religious Experience*. Chicago: University of Chicago, 1981.
O'Brien, Mark A. 'Judges and the Deuteronomistic History.' Pages 235–59 in *The History of Israel's Traditions: The Heritage of Martin Noth*. Edited by S. L. McKenzie and M. P. Graham. JSOTSup 182. Sheffield: Sheffield Academic Press, 1994.
O'Connell, Robert. *The Rhetoric of the Book of Judges*. VTSup 63. Leiden: Brill, 1996.
Oeste, Gordon K. *Legitimacy, Illegitimacy, and the Right to Rule: Window's on Abimelech's Rise and Demise in Judges 9*. LHBOTS 546. London: T&T Clark, 2011.
Ogden, Thomas H. *Reclaiming Unlived Life: Experiences in Psychoanalysis*. London: Taylor and Francis, 2016.
Olson, Dennis T. 'The Book of Judges.' Pages 731–888 in *The New Interpreter's Bible*. Volume Two. Nashville: Abingdon Press, 1994.
Olson, Dennis T. 'Buber, Kingship, and the Book of Judges: A Study of Judges 6–9 and 17–21.' Pages 199–218 in *David and Zion: Biblical Studies in Honor of J.J.M. Roberts*. Edited by Bernard F. Batto and Kathryn L. Roberts. Winona Lake, IN: Eisenbrauns, 2004.
Pace, Leann. 'Tools and Utensils.' Pages 185–96 in *T&T Clark Handbook of Food in the Hebrew Bible and Ancient Israel*. Edited by Janling Fu, Cynthia Shafer-Elliott, and Carol Meyers. London: Bloomsbury, 2022.
Paynter, Helen. *Telling Terror in Judges 19*. London and New York: Routledge, 2020.
Pitt-Rivers, Julian A. 'The Law of Hospitality.' Pages 163–84 in *From Hospitality to Grace: A Julian Pitt-Rivers Omnibus.*' Ed. Giovanni da Col and Andrew Shryock. Chicago: Hau Books, 2017.
Polzin, Robert. *Moses and the Deuteronomist: Deuteronomy, Joshua, Judges*. Bloomington, IN: Indiana University Press, 1993.
Pressler, Carolyn. 'Jephthah's Daughter.' Page 685 in *Eerdmans Dictionary of the Bible* ed. David Noel Freedman. Grand Rapids: Eerdmans, 2000.
Prince, Gerald. *A Dictionary of Narratology: Revised Edition*. Lincoln: University of Nebraska Press, 2003.
Radday, Yehuda T. 'On Missing the Humour in the Bible: An Introduction.' Pages 21–38 in *On Humour and the Comic in The Hebrew Bible*. Edited by Yehuda T. Radday and Athalya Brenner. JSOTSUp 92. Sheffield: Almond Press, 1990.
Radday, Yehuda T., and Athalya Brenner, eds. *On Humour and the Comic in the Hebrew Bible*. JSOTSup 92. Sheffield: Almond Press, 1990.
Reinhartz, Adele. 'Samson's Mother: An Unnamed Protagonist.' *JSOT* 55 (1992): 25–37.
Reinhartz, Adele. *'Why Ask My Name?' Anonymity and Identity in Biblical Narrative*. Oxford: Oxford University Press, 1998.
Reis, Pamela Tamarkin. 'Spoiled Child: A Fresh Look at Jephthah's Daughter.' *Prooftexts* 17 (1997): 279–98.
Reis, Pamela Tamarkin. 'Uncovering Jael and Sisera: A New Reading.' *SJOT* 19.1 (2005): 24–47.
Reis, Pamela Tamarkin. 'The Levite's Concubine: New Light on a Dark Story.' *SJOT* 20 (2006): 125–46.
Rendsburg, Gary. *Diglossia in Ancient Hebrew*. American Oriental Series. Vol. 72. New Haven: CN: American Oriental Society, 1990.
Reviv, H., *The Elders in Ancient Israel: A Study of a Biblical Institution*. Jerusalem, The Magnes Press, The Hebrew University, 1983 (Hebrew).

Riba, Lucía. 'Memoriales de Mujeres: La Sororidad como Experiencia de Empoderamiento para Resistir a la Violencia Patriarchal.' *Franciscum* 58.165 (2016): 225-62.

Rooke, Deborah W. 'Sacrifice and Death, or, the Death of Sex: Three Versions of Jephthah's Daughter (Judges 11:29-40).' Pages 249-71 in *Biblical Traditions in Transmission: Essays in Honour of Michael A. Knibb*. Edited by Charlotte Hempel and Judith M. Lieu. JSJSup 111. Leiden: Brill, 2006.

Rorty, Richard. *Consequences of Pragmatism (Essays: 1972-1980)*. Minneapolis, MN: University of Minnesota Press, 1982.

Rose, Martin. 'Names of God in the Old Testament.' *ABD* 4:1001-11.

Roth, Martha T. 'Marriage, Divorce, and the Prostitute in Ancient Mesopotamia.' Pages 21-39 in *Prostitutes and Courtesans in the Ancient World*. Edited by Christopher A. Faraone and Laura K. McClure. Madison, WI: University of Wisconsin Press, 2006.

Rowley, H. H. *Worship in Ancient Israel: Its Forms and Meaning*. London: SPCK, 1967.

Russaw, Kimberly D. *Daughters in the Hebrew Bible*. Lanham, MD: Lexington Books, 2018.

Ryan, R. J. *Judges*. Readings: A New Biblical Commentary. Sheffield: Sheffield Phoenix Press, 2007.

Sabo, Peter J. and Rhiannon Graybill. 'Arcane Energy: An Afterword on the Bible and *The Testaments*.' Pages 409-21 in *'"Who Knows What We'd Make of It, If We Ever Got Our Hands on it?': Margaret Atwood and the Bible*. Edited by Rhiannon Graybill and Peter J. Sabo. Tübingen: Mohr Siebeck, 2020.

Sasson, Jack M. 'Ethically Cultured Interpretations: The Case of Eglon's Murder (Judges 3).' Pages 571-95 in *Homeland and Exile: Biblical and Ancient Near Eastern Studies in Honour of Bustanay Oded*. Edited by Gershon Galil et al. Leiden: Brill, 2009.

Sasson, Jack M. *Judges 1-12: A New Translation with Introduction and Commentary*. AB. New Haven & London: Yale University Press, 2014.

Sawyer, Deborah F. *God, Gender and the Bible*. Biblical Limits. London: Routledge, 2002.

Schipper, Jeremy. 'Narrative Obscurity of Samson's חידה in Judges 14.14 and 18.' *JSOT* 27.3 (2003): 339-53.

Schneider, Tammi J. *Judges*. BO. Collegeville, MN: Liturgical Press, 1999.

Schneider, Tammi J. *Mothers of Promise: Women in the Book of Genesis*. Grand Rapids: Baker Academic, 2008.

Schöpflin, Karin. 'Jotham's Speech and Fable as Prophetic Comment on Abimelech's Story: The Genesis of Judges 9.' *SJOT* 18.1 (2004): 3-22.

Seeligmann, Isaac L. 'On the Problems of Prophecy in Israel, its History and Nature.' Pages 170-88 in *Studies in Biblical Literature*. Edited by A. Hurvitz et al. Jerusalem, The Magnes Press, The Hebrew University, 1992 (Hebrew).

Shalom-Guy, Hava. 'The Call Narratives of Gideon and Moses. Literary Convention or More?' *JHS* 11, Article 11 (2011) 1-19.

Sharon, Diane M. 'The Gideon Cycle and the Deuteronomist's Critique of Hereditary Monarchy: An Intertextual Perspective.' Pages 595-609 in *Ve-'Ed Ya'aleh (Gen 2:6): Essays in Biblical and Ancient Near Eastern Studies Presented to Edward L. Greenstein*, Volume 1. Edited by Peter Machinist, Robert A. Harris, Joshua A. Berman, Nili Samet, and Noga Ayali-Darshan. Atlanta: SBL Press, 2021.

Shiran, R. 'Deborah's Literary Character and the Portrayal of Her Leadership In Judges 4-5.' PhD. Thesis, Bar-Ilan University, Ramat-Gan, Israel, 2016 (Hebrew).

Sjöberg, Mikael. *Wrestling with Textual Violence: The Jephthah Narrative in Antiquity and Modernity*. BMW 4. Sheffield: Sheffield Phoenix Press, 2006.

Smith, Carol. 'Delilah: A Suitable Case for (Feminist) Treatment.' Pages 93–116 in *Judges: A Feminist Companion to the Bible Second Series*. Edited by Athalya Brenner. Sheffield: Sheffield Academic Press, 1999.

Smith, Carol. 'Samson and Delilah: A Parable of Power?' *JSOT* 76 (1997): 45–57.

Smith, Mark S. *The Early History of God. Yahweh and Other Deities in Ancient Israel*. Grand Rapids, MI: Eerdmans, 2002.

Smith, Mark S. *Poetic Heroes: Literary Commemorations of Warriors and Warrior Culture in the Early Biblical World*. Grand Rapids, MI: Eerdmans, 2014.

Soggin, J. Alberto. *Judges: A Commentary*. 2nd ed. London: SCM Press, 1987.

Soggin, J. Alberto. *Introduction to the Old Testament: From Its Origins to the Closing of the Alexandrian Canon*. 3rd ed. London: SCM Press, 1989.

Southwood, Katherine. *Marriage by Capture in the Book of Judges*. Cambridge: Cambridge University Press, 2007.

Spronk, Klaas. *Judges*. Historical Commentary on the Old Testament. Leuven: Peeters, 2019.

Stager, Lawrence E. 'Forging an Identity: The Emergence of Ancient Israel.' Pages 90–131 in *Oxford History of the Biblical World*. Edited by Michael D. Coogan. New York: Oxford University Press, 1998.

Stager, Lawrence E. 'The Shechem Temple: Where Abimelech Massacred a Thousand.' *BAR* 29 (2003) 26–35, 66–69.

Stähli, Hans-Peter. *Knabe – Jüngling –Knecht. Untersuchungen zum Begriff* נער *im Alten Testament*. Beiträge zur biblischen Exegese und Theologie 7. Frankfurt a. M.: Peter Lang, 1978.

Stanton, Elizabeth Cady. *The Woman's Bible*. New York: European, 1895.

Sternberg, Meir. *The Poetics of Biblical Narrative: Ideological Literature and the Drama of Reading*. Bloomington, IN: Indiana University Press, 1985.

Sternberg, Meir. 'Biblical Poetics and Sexual Politics: From Reading to Counterreading.' *JBL* 111 (1992): 463–88.

Stiebert, Johanna. *Fathers and Daughters in the Hebrew Bible*. Oxford: Oxford University Press, 2013.

Stol, Marten. *Women in the Ancient Near East*. Boston/Berlin:De Gruyter, 2016.

Stone, Ken. 'Gender Criticism: The Unmanning of Abimelech.' Pages 183–201 in *Judges and Method: New Approaches in Biblical Studies*. Second Ed. Edited by Gale A. Yee. Minneapolis: Fortress, 2007.

Stone, Ken. 'Judges.' Pages 87–96 in *Theological Bible Commentary*. Edited by Gail R. O'Day and David L. Petersen. Louisville: Westminster John Knox Press, 2009.

Stone, Ken. 'Animal Difference, Sexual Difference, and the Daughter of Jephthah.' *BibInt* 24 (2016): 1–16.

Stone, Lawson. 'Eglon's Belly and Ehud's Blade: A Reconsideration.' *JBL* 128.4 (2009): 643–63.

Sweeney, Marvin. 'Davidic Polemic in the Book of Judges.' *VT* 47 (1997): 517–29.

Symington, Joan and Neville. *The Clinical Thinking of Wilfred Bion*. London: Routledge, 1996.

Tanner, J. Paul. 'The Gideon Narrative as the Focal Point of Judges.' *BibSac* 149 (1992): 146–61.

Tatu, Silviu. 'Jotham's Fable and the Crux Interpretum in Judges IX.' *VT* 56.1 (2006): 105–24.

Thareani, Yifat. 'Revenge of the Conquered: Paths of Resistance in the Assyrian City of Dan.' *Semitica* 60 (2018): 473–92.

Thelle, Rannfrid Irene. 'Matrices of Motherhood in Judges 5.' *JSOT* 43 (2019), 436–52.

Tolkien, J. R. R. *The Hobbit*. Revised Edition. New York: Ballantine Books, 1982.
Toorn, Karel van der. *Scribal Culture and the Making of the Hebrew Bible*. Cambridge, MA: Harvard University Press, 2007.
Trible, Phyllis. *Texts of Terror: Literary-Feminist Readings of Biblical Narratives*. OBT. Philadelphia: Fortress Press, 1984.
Ullendorff, Edward. 'The Bawdy Bible.' *BSOAS* 42:3 (1979): 425–56.
Urbach, E. E., 'When did Prophecy Cease?' *Tarbitz* 17 (1946): 1–11 (Hebrew).
Valler, Shulamit. 'Strong Women Confront Helpless Men: Deborah and Jephthah's Daughter in the Midrash.' Page 236–54 in *Words, Ideas, Worlds: Biblical Essays in Honour of Yairah Amit*. Sheffield: Sheffield Phoenix Press, 2012.
Van der Walt, Charlene. '"Is There a Man in Here?": The Iron Fist in the Velvet Glove in Judges 4.' Pages 117–32 in *Feminist Frameworks in the Bible: Power, Ambiguity, and Intersectionality*. Edited by L. Juliana Claassens and Carolyn J. Sharp. London: Bloomsbury, 2017.
Van Wijk-Bos, Johanna W. H. 'Out of the Shadows: Genesis 38; Judges 4:17–22; Ruth 3.' *Semeia* 42 (1988): 37–67.
Vargon, Shmuel. 'Saul's Pursuit of David in the Land of Judah and the Geographical Background.' Pages 559–84 in *Marbeh Hòokmah: Studies in the Bible and the Ancient Near East in Loving Memory of Victor Avigdor Hurowitz*. Edited by S. Yona et al. Winona Lake IN: Eisenbrauns, 2015).
Vermeulen, Note Karolien. 'Hands, Heads, and Feet: Body Parts as Poetic Device in Judges 4–5.' *JBL* 136 (2017): 801–19.
Wallis, G. 'אָהֵב 'āhabh.' *TDOT* 1:101–17.
Waltke, Bruce K. & O'Connor, M.P. *An Introduction to Biblical Hebrew Syntax*. Winona Lake, IN: Eisenbrauns, 1990.
Walton, Kendall L. *Mimesis as Make-Belief: On the Foundations of the Representational Arts*. Cambridge, MA: Harvard University Press, 1990.
Webb, Barry G. *The Book of Judges: An Integrated Reading*. JSOTSup 46. Sheffield: JSOT Press, 1987.
Webb, Barry G. 'A Serious Reading of the Samson Story (Judges 13–16).' *RTR* 54 (1995): 110–20.
Webb, Barry G. *The Book of Judges*. NICOT. Grand Rapids: Eerdmans, 2012.
Weber, Max. *Ancient Judaism*. Translated and edited by H. H. Gerth and D. Martindale, Glencoe, Illinois: The Feree Press, 1952.
Weber, Max. *The Theory of Social and Economic Organization*. Translated by A. M. Henderson and Talcott Parsons. London, Edinburgh, Glasgow: William Hodge and Company, 1947.
Weber, Max. *Economy and Society: An Outline of Interpretive Sociology*. Berkeley: University of California Press, 1978.
Weisman, Ze'ev. 'Did A National Leadership Exist in the Era of the Judges?' Pages 19–31 in *Studies in the History of the Jewish People and the Land of Israel*. Fifth Volume. Haifa: University of Haifa, 1980.
Weisman, Ze'ev. *Political Satire in the Bible*. Semeia Studies. Atlanta: Scholars Press, 1998.
Weisman, Ze'ev. *Saviours and Prophets: Two Aspects of Biblical Charisma*. Tel Aviv: Hakibbutz Hameuchad, Aviv Publishing House, 2003 (Hebrew).
Weitzman, Steven. 'The Samson Story as Border Fiction.' *BibInt* 10 (2002): 158–74.
Wenham, Gordon J. *Story as Torah: Reading Old Testament Ethically*. London: T&T Clark, 2000).

Westbrook, April D. *'And He Will Take Your Daughters. . .' Woman Story and the Ethical Evaluation of Monarchy in the David Narrative*. LHBOTS 610. London: Bloomsbury T&T Clark, 2015.

Wharton, James A. 'The Secret of Yahweh: Story and Affirmation in Judges 13-16.' *Int* 27 (1973): 48–66.

Whedbee, William, and Cheryl Exum. 'Isaac, Samson, and Saul: Reflections on the Comic and Tragic Visions.' *Semeia* 32 (1984): 5–40.

Whedbee, J. William. *The Bible and the Comic Vision*. Cambridge: Cambridge University Press, 1998.

White, Ellen. 'Michal the Misinterpreted.' *JSOT* 31 (4) (2007): 451–64.

Williams, Michael James. *Deception in Genesis: Investigation into the Morality of a Unique Biblical Phenomenon*. Studies in Biblical Literature 32. New York: Peter Lang, 2001.

Williamson, H. G. M., 'Prophetesses in the Hebrew Bible.' Pages 65–80 in *Prophecy and Prophets in Ancient Israel, Proceedings of the Oxford Old Testament Seminar*. Edited by J. Day. New York/London: T&T Clark International, 2010.

Willi-Plein, Ina. *Opfer und Kult im alttestamentlichen Israel*. Stuttgarter Bibelstudien 153. Stuttgart: Katholisches Bibelwerk, 1993.

Wilson, Stephen M. 'Samson the Man-Child: Failing to Come of Age in the Deuteronomistic History.' *JBL* 133 (2014): 43–60.

Wolde, Ellen van. 'Does *'Innâ* Denote Rape? A Semantic Analysis of a Controversial Word.' *VT* 52 (2002): 528–44.

Wong, Gregory T. K. 'Is There a Direct Pro-Judah Polemic in Judges?' *SJOT* 19 (1) (2005): 84–110.

Wong, Gregory T. K. *Compositional Strategy in the Book of Judges: An Inductive, Rhetorical Study*. VTSup 111. Leiden: Brill, 2006.

Wong, Gregory T. K. 'Narratives and Their Contexts: A Critique of Gregor Andersson With Respect to Narrative Autonomy.' *SJOT* 20 (2) (2006): 216–30.

Wong, Gregory T. K. 'Judges.' Pages 212–41 in *The Baker Illustrated Bible Commentary*. Edited by Gary M. Burge and Andrew E. Hill. Grand Rapids: Baker, 2012.

Wong, Gregory T. K. 'Unearthing Text-Critical possibilities through Lexical-Syntactic Analysis: A Case Study from Judg 15:3.' *BZ* 65 (2021): 299–307.

Wood, Leon J., *Distressing Days of the Judges*. Grand Rapids, MI: Zondervan Publishing House, 1975.

Wright, Christopher J.H. *Old Testament Ethics for the People of God*. Leicester: InterVarsity, 2004.

Yadin, Azzan. 'Samson's Hîdâ.' *VT* 52 (3) (2002): 407–10.

Yee, Gale A. 'By the Hand of a Woman: The Metaphor of the Woman Warrior in Judges 4.' *Semeia* 61 (1993): 99–132.

Yee, Gale A. 'Ideological Criticism: Judges 17–21 and the Dismembered Body.' Pages 146–70 in *Judges and Method*. Edited by Gale A. Yee. Minneapolis: Fortress, 1995.

Younger, K. Lawson, Jr. *Judges and Ruth*. NIVAC. Grand Rapids MI: Zondervan, 2002.

Zakovitch, Yair and Avigdor Shinan. *From Gods to God*. Lincoln: University of Nebraska Press, 2012.

Zehnder, Markus. *Umgang mit dem Fremden in Israel und Assyrien. Ein Beitrag zur Anthropologie des Fremden im Licht antiker Quellen*. Beiträge zur Wissenschaft vom Alten und Neuen Testament 168. Stuttgart: Kohlhammer, 2005.

www.ingramcontent.com/pod-product-compliance
Lightning Source LLC
Chambersburg PA
CBHW071242230426
43668CB00011B/1544